# STAPLETON'S
# POWER CRUISING BIBLE

Also by Sidney Stapleton:

*Stapleton's Powerboat Bible*

*Chapman's Nautical Guides:*
*Emergencies at Sea*

# STAPLETON'S

## POWER

# *CRUISING*

## BIBLE

• • •

THE COMPLETE GUIDE TO

COASTAL AND BLUEWATER

CRUISING UNDER POWER

• • •

Sidney Stapleton

HEARST MARINE BOOKS • NEW YORK

It is the policy of William Morrow and Company, Inc., and its imprints and affiliates, recognizing the importance of preserving what has been written, to print the books we publish on acid-free paper, and we exert our best efforts to that end.

Library of Congress Cataloging-in-Publication Data

Stapleton, Sidney.
   [Power cruising bible]
   Stapleton's power cruising bible : the complete guide to coastal and bluewater cruising under power / by Sidney Stapleton.
      p.  cm.
   ISBN 0-688-10165-8
   1. Motorboats.  2. Boats and boating.  I. Title.  II. Title:
Power cruising bible.
GV835.S83   1992
797.1'25—dc20                      91-34444
                                      CIP

Printed in the United States of America

First Edition

1  2  3  4  5  6  7  8  9  10

BOOK DESIGN BY PATRICE FORERO

*For Anne,*

*who shares the dream*

# CONTENTS

• • •

## PART ONE: HANDLING HER RIGHT

The shakedown cruise. Developing speed and fuel-
consumption curves. Planning a daily cruising schedule.
Predeparture checklist. Systems and engine checks. Engine
starting tips. Maneuvering away from the dock. Using
your crew, spring lines, and fenders. Coiling and stowing
dock lines.

Practical application of the Rules of the Road in meeting,
crossing, and overtaking situations. Using aids to navigation. Running ranges. Transiting bridges and locks.
Engine checks underway.

Heading in versus staying at sea in heavy weather.
Running inlets. Heavy weather handling. Night running.
Operating in reduced visibility. Tender towing.

## PART TWO: NAVIGATING
## AND COMMUNICATING

# PART THREE: DEALING WITH EMERGENCIES

## 16 FIGHTING FIRES AFLOAT 339

Proper use of an automatic engine room fire-extinguishing system and portable fire extinguishers. Fighting a fire in the engine room, the galley, in belowdecks accommodations, and on deck. Fighting electrical fires.

## 17 ABANDON-SHIP PROCEDURES 346

The abandon-ship drill. Abandon-ship communications. Launching the life raft. The abandon-ship bag and other necessities. Using visual distress devices in daylight, at night.

# PART FOUR: KEEPING THINGS HUMMING

## 18 LIFE ABOARD 361

Trips ashore. Local provisioning, fuel, and water. Harvesting the sea. Accommodating guests.

## 19 MAINTAINING THE ESSENTIALS 375

Recommended daily, weekly, monthly, semiannual, and annual maintenance schedules. Keeping diesel fuel clean. Exterior, electrical, and electronics maintenance.

# PART FIVE: IN FOREIGN WATERS

## 20 INTERNATIONAL BUOYAGE, LIGHTING, AND CHART SYSTEMS 393

Differences between U.S. and international buoy and navigation lighting systems.

## 21 KEEPING LEGAL 396

International passport, visa, immunization, vessel documentation, driver's license, and crew list requirements. Entry procedures at foreign ports. Declaring firearms. If your vessel is boarded offshore, ordered into port, or impounded. Light regulations. Marine radio-telephone and amateur radio operations. Clearance-to-sail procedures. Returning to the U.S.

Dealing with cruising expenses: in cash, with traveler's checks and credit cards. Converting U.S. dollars to foreign currencies at the best rates. Having funds and mail forwarded to foreign ports. Having spares shipped to foreign ports.

# ACKNOWLEDGMENTS

•  •  •

In researching the topics covered in this book, I received the help of hundreds of people who were kind enough to share their special areas of expertise with me and patiently answer my voluminous questions. Any errors that might be found here should not be charged to the experts I consulted but to my inability to correctly understand or communicate what they told me.

It's impossible to list everyone who contributed to this volume in some measure, but a number of individuals deserve special mention:

Ron Locke, chief demonstrator captain for Hatteras Yachts, offered a number of practical suggestions for the chapters on boat handling.

Paul Newland of AT&T Bell Laboratories and Paul Scott of AT&T's High Seas Service were primary resources for the coverage of high frequency marine radio. Master Chief R. E. Mercurio of the U.S. Coast Guard's Radioman School in Petaluma, California, provided a major service by reviewing and commenting on the material regarding emergency marine radio communications.

Capt. John Weseman and Doug Alsip of the Coast Guard's Radionavigation Branch were extremely helpful in the area of electronic navigation.

On the topics of air-sea rescue and survival at sea, I received much useful information from James T. Bailey of the National Oceanic and Atmospheric Administration; Capt. Dennis Feeser, chief of the Coast Guard's Search and Rescue Branch along with Lt. Comdr. Jonathan Embler and Dan Lemon of that agency; Bob Markle, chief of the Coast Guard's Survival Systems Branch;

Lt. (j.g.) Paul Lange, a helicopter pilot of the Coast Guard's search and rescue base at Elizabeth City, North Carolina; Bob Kuntzel of ACR Electronics, Inc., and Kelsey Burr and Ardith Bonner of Survival Technologies Group, Inc. Vicky Lewis, RN, BSN, was of invaluable help in compiling the material dealing with medical emergencies.

Jack Carlson of Alden Electronics, Inc., was a great help on the subjects of weather facsimile charts and receivers, and Dave Crane of D. F. Crane, Inc., provided much useful information on the use of computers in the nautical environment.

On the subject of maritime law, Mike Morrow of the Department of Transportation's Maritime Administration was helpful in explaining the laws regarding emergency assistance at sea; and Maj. Dennis Grealish, deputy director for boating safety of the Florida Marine Patrol and Lt. Col. Joel Brown, president of the National Association of Boating Law Administrators, helped me understand the laws regarding safe boat operation.

Many of the practical tips on the real world of cruising were gleaned from those cruisers under power who have been kind enough to allow me to accompany them on some of their adventures. I will not name them individually here, but they will recognize both their contributions and my appreciation for their insights. I must, however, single out Capt. Fred Edwards, U.S. Navy, retired, and Frank Glindmeier, who read major portions of the manuscript and offered cogent criticisms and suggestions based on their extensive cruising experience.

Last, but by no means least, I must thank my wife, Anne, for her inexhaustible patience and understanding and for sharing with me the dream of one day knowing all those lands beyond the far horizon.

# INTRODUCTION: THE DREAM IS REAL

• • •

You're really going to do it! For years you've dreamed about that seaworthy power cruiser that would take you and yours to distant ports and romantic anchorages in comfort and safety. Now the dream is real. All those drawings you've sketched out on napkins after dinner, all those voluminous lists of gear you've compiled on the backs of envelopes, all your late-night rummaging through boat brochures and marine catalogs, all your careful planning and preparations have become reality.

After, I hope, reading my earlier book, *Stapleton's Powerboat Bible,* and taking advantage of some of its recommendations on selecting, equipping, and organizing a powerboat for coastal or bluewater cruising, your vessel is at the dock rigged and ready to deal with virtually any situation you're likely to encounter, whether your cruising plans will take you along calm, protected inland waters or across wide seas to foreign ports and the far horizon.

But before you cast off your dock lines and nudge out into the current to begin your voyage of a lifetime, make sure you've prepared yourself as carefully as you've prepared your boat.

I assume that since you've progressed far enough in your boating experience to be getting into extended cruising under power, you're familiar with the basics of boat handling. But the first time you look out from the helm of a vessel large enough for you to live aboard for weeks or months at a time and husky enough to deal with the wide variety of situations you're likely to encounter, you'll find the view is nothing like that from the helm of the 30-footer you've used primarily for weekend cruising close to home. In fact, it can be a little intimidating, particularly if your decision to cast off on a cruise of months—or even years—involves a transition from sail to power, from gasoline to diesel engines, or from a single engine to twins. If you've never gotten caught offshore in heavy weather, or had to run an inlet when the weather was kicking up, or had to put your 40-footer into a 50-foot slot between two other vessels with a strong current and a stiff breeze setting onto the dock—and a choir of observers watching your every maneuver—you may ask yourself: "Can I really handle this thing?" You're likely to do most of your cruising with just you and your mate aboard. Are there some tricks to handling a sizable powerboat that don't require half a dozen pair of hands?

I also assume you know the basics of seamanship. But has your boating experience to date familiarized you with the recent changes in the buoyage system for U.S. waters? You're going to be out there with freighters and tankers and all kinds of tugs. Are you aware how the Rules of the Road are applied—or not applied—in the real world? Do you know how to offset the impact of adverse tides and currents, take advantage of those that are favorable, and figure fuel consumption for a long run where fuel docks are few and far between?

If your boating to date has been limited to familiar waters, you may have become a little nonchalant with your navigating skills. In the unfamiliar waters into which you are about to venture, forgetting to allow for set and drift or not knowing how to "read" the bottom in tropical waters could get you into trouble in a hurry. You may have used Loran before, but as you voyage into the fringes of its coverage area, are there anomalies you should be aware of that might affect the accuracy of its readouts? If your lineup of navigation electronics for the first time includes a Transit or Global Positioning System receiver, do you know how to get the most out of it?

What about communicating? You're probably familiar with the basics of a marine VHF radio, but do you know how to use it to stay in touch with family and friends ashore through the nationwide network of Public Coast Stations? If you're headed beyond VHF range, I assume you've had a good single-sideband radio properly installed aboard your vessel, but do you know how to select the best frequency band based on the time of day and the distance to the coast station with which you want to establish contact? Are you aware of the many uses other than placing and receiving radio-telephone calls to which you can put your SSB receiver? Even if you've used single-sideband in the past, are you aware of the wholesale changes recently made in its public correspondence frequencies and the new frequencies that have been added?

Around home you've been able to get just about any repair assistance you needed with a telephone call. Now your extended cruising adventures may well take you a long way from diesel mechanics and electronics repairmen. If your engine suddenly begins to run rough, smoke heavily, or quits altogether, do you know how to diagnose its problem and clear an air lock or disable an injector until you can get to a qualified mechanic? If your Loran receiver starts blinking uncontrollably or one of your radios goes belly up, can you troubleshoot it with some hope of restoring it to health?

Are you prepared to deal with emergencies? If an engine room fire shuts down one engine aboard your twin-screw cruiser, did you know that leaving the other one running while you check out the damage can be disastrous? If you're far offshore and have a serious medical emergency aboard, can you handle it? If not, do you know how to quickly get in touch with authoritative medical advice?

If you plan to visit other nations but have never before entered a foreign port, is the buoyage system of the countries you plan to visit the same as that in the U.S.? As you enter a foreign port, should you display your quarantine flag on your bow staff or on your cruising mast? If your answer is the mast, does the Q-flag go on the starboard spreader or to port? Should you hoist the host nation's courtesy flag as you enter its waters, or wait until you've cleared its customs and immigration procedures? Once ashore, can you expect to find the same foods you're used to at home? If you'll be buying local produce, do you know how to prepare it so you're sure it's safe to eat? Do you know how, when, and where to convert your U.S. dollars to the local currency at the best rate?

Answering these and the hundreds of other questions you'll encounter in the life of cruising under power are the reasons this book was written.

As a boating writer for the past twenty years and more, I've had an opportunity to cruise extensively under power aboard both my own vessels and those of a wide variety of other power cruisers who have been kind enough to let me accompany them through some of the world's most beautiful cruising grounds. With Bill and Alice Templeman, for instance, I had an opportunity to explore much of New England, Nova Scotia, the Bay of Fundy, the St. Lawrence River, and Georgian Bay, and learn the peculiarities of transiting that magnificent area's locks, how to keep off its rocks, and how to deal with its often massive tides. Nat and Mary Robbins were kind enough to share the lessons they had learned in years of cruising as we powered down the Illinois and Mississippi rivers from Peoria to New Orleans. Neville Green taught me a thing or two about anchoring sixty miles offshore on Australia's Great Barrier Reef for the night, and Fritz Stall shared with me his experience negotiating the fjords of Norway on our voyage from Oslo all the way around that beautiful country's southern tip to Bergen. On cruises from Greece to Alaska, from the islands of the Caribbean to the Galápagos Islands off the coast of Ecuador, I've had a chance to gather the practical lessons it took experienced cruisers months afloat, thousands of miles astern—and often hundreds of costly mistakes—to learn.

As a delivery captain, I've been exposed to the varying handling characteristics of a number of different planing, semidisplacement, and full-displacement vessels and learned a few tricks for making them behave around docks and slips amid screaming winds and crosswise currents.

In addition to that on-the-water experience, as I've researched material for magazine articles, other books on boating, and my monthly seamanship and boat handling columns in *Motor Boating & Sailing* magazine, I've spent hundreds of hours interviewing experts in everything from fighting fires at sea and emergency medical care to air-sea rescue procedures and marine communications.

I've put in these pages everything I've learned from my own experience, from other seasoned cruisers, and from the professionals to give you the information you need to make your cruising life a pleasant adventure rather than an endless succession of frustrating difficulties. Whether your main engine has conked out, your radio has gone on the blink, you go aground, have a fire on board, or face a medical emergency and need help fast, I hope you'll find in these pages the essential help you need quickly and accurately.

# STAPLETON'S
# POWER CRUISING BIBLE

# PART ONE

· · ·

# HANDLING HER RIGHT

· · ·

# CHAPTER 1

# GETTING UNDERWAY

• • •

I mentioned in the Introduction that the first time you look out from the helm of your new power cruiser and realize you're about to venture into a largely unknown world, the view can be a little daunting. With that fact in mind, here are a couple of suggestions:

If you have real questions about your ability to handle your new boat, you might want to hire a professional captain to work with you around home (or even better, accompany you on a short cruise) to get you started right. "When we decided to do some long-distance cruising," says Frank Glindmeier, who with his wife Lee ran their displacement vessel *Summer Wind* a total of 35,000 miles, which included an 18,000-mile voyage from Florida to Alaska and back, "we went from a twenty-three-footer to a fifty-seven-footer and were a little overwhelmed by the difference in her size and handling. We hired a delivery skipper who had a lot of experience in the same kind of boat we had bought to come aboard with us for a week or so. What little he charged was a heck of a lot cheaper than what we'd have spent if we'd seriously damaged the boat. Working with him also saved us a lot of potential embarrassment and assured us we really knew what we were doing rather than just winging it."

Also, start off easy. Instead of heading for the back of beyond on your first voyage, take a shakedown cruise in an area where you can get help if you need it but that offers a wide range of new cruising grounds and challenges. Be sure it includes some offshore running, some night running, and is long enough to give both yourself and your boat a real test.

Before you depart on your shakedown cruise, be sure you have all the necessary safety equipment aboard and it is working properly, have your compasses compensated, know your boat's maximum, fully loaded draft exactly, make certain your depth-sounder is accurately calibrated to read total water depth, and set its alarm to sound when the water's depth is within about five feet of your vessel's draft. (In my earlier book I recommended setting a depth-sounder's "zero depth" as the lowest point of a vessel's hull, but I have since changed my mind on that point. Setting a depth-sounder to read total water depth in some cases has the advantage of allowing you to fix your approximate position by comparing its readout with charted depths without having to allow for your vessel's draft.) You should also carefully measure your vessel's structural height above water in a variety of configurations, which will be critical in figuring bridge clearances. One figure should be your vessel's maximum vertical clearance with its communications and navigation antennas raised; another should be with them lowered. If conditions really get tight, you should also know how low a bridge you can sneak under by lowering your radar mast and bimini top. Also measure the exact height of your eye at both the pilothouse and flying bridge steering station. In Chapter 6: Coastal Piloting and Eyeball Navigation, we'll explain how to use that figure to help determine approximate distance to objects in the water and to the shore.

Before departing on your shakedown cruise, it's also a good idea to have a laboratory do an analysis of your lubricating oil, then have the process repeated at least every 500 operating hours. Any significant changes relative to the benchmarks you've established will help alert you to potential problems inside your engine(s).

During your shakedown cruise, it's a good idea to develop some basic information about your vessel's operation and performance which you will use over and over. Make careful notes, for instance, on how much engine oil, marine gear oil, and cooling water your engines use under normal conditions and write down their operating temperatures and pressures. You might want to mark normal maximums on the gauges themselves with tiny strips of red tape to alert you if they are exceeded.

Two other basic factors you should determine accurately during your shakedown cruise are your vessel's speed over the bottom and her fuel consumption at a number of different rpm settings in calm water. You can then use the figures you establish to determine later how those factors are affected by adverse winds, currents, and heavy seas.

## RPM/Speed Curve

In order to develop an rpm/speed curve for your cruiser you can use a series of runs over any known distance, but it's easiest if you make your runs over one of the measured mile courses you'll find indicated on your charts. If most of your cruising will be in coastal waters (other than the Intracoastal Waterway) or the open ocean, select a measured nautical mile course for your runs and figure your vessel speed in knots, because in working with the charts for those areas you normally will figure distances in nautical miles. (The definition of a knot is one nautical mile per hour. A nautical mile equals one minute of arc of a great circle of the earth which, at the equator, is 6,076.115 feet. For ease of calculation, most cruisers round that number off to 6,080 feet.) If you will do most of your cruising in the Intracoastal Waterway (ICW), the Western Rivers, or the Great Lakes, use a measured statute mile course and figure your speed in statute miles per hour because that is the unit of measurement used in the charts of those areas.

It's best to conduct your speed test with full fuel and water tanks, with your vessel loaded with about the maximum stores you will have on board during a typical cruise, and with its bottom clean. If possible, conduct your test at slack water. In any event, at each throttle setting from about 900 rpm to your engines' maximum revolutions—in about 50-rpm increments—make several runs over the measured mile course in each direction to make

25

sure you offset the effects of any current that might be running. Time your runs with a stopwatch and compute speed with the formula:

$$S = \frac{60\ D}{T}$$

where $D$ equals distance run (1 nautical or statute mile) and $T$ equals time. The formula is easier to work if you convert the seconds in the time part of your equation into tenths of a minute by dividing them by 60.

To determine your vessel's speed over the bottom at a particular rpm setting, average the speed of an equal number of downstream and upstream runs. (Any current running during your test will be equal to one half the difference in speed on the runs in the two directions.)

If your cruiser has twin engines, make pairs of runs with both engines operating at the rpm settings you select, then duplicate the runs with only one engine running at each of those same rpm settings to determine the effect running on one engine will have on your vessel's speed. In the case of a diesel-powered full-displacement vessel or a semidisplacement vessel operated at displacement speeds you may be surprised to find that at virtually any rpm setting you select, operating on one engine will give you about 80 percent of the speed you get running both engines at that same rpm. Operating on only one engine, however, will not cut your fuel consumption in half. The engine operating by itself will use about 10 percent more fuel than it will when running in tandem with the other engine, even though its rpm remains the same. The reason is that its governor rack will deliver more fuel to the engine to offset the increased resistance it is encountering.

Once you have computed your vessel's speed at different rpm settings, create an rpm/speed curve by plotting the information on graph paper with engine rpm in hundreds across the bottom and speed in either knots or statute miles per hour (depending on whether you ran a measured nautical mile or statute mile course) up the left-hand side. Some cruisers find it more convenient to then translate the graph information into chart form.

## Fuel-Consumption Curve

It's best to base your fuel-consumption figures on gallons per hour (GPH) at various rpm settings. You must, of course, have some way to accurately measure fuel flow at each rpm setting. If you install fuel-flow meters on the fuel lines serving your engine(s) and your AC generator, they will measure fuel flow and will give you GPH readouts directly during your rpm/speed tests. Another way to measure fuel consumption is to reroute your fuel supply so that all your diesel machinery runs off a single day tank calibrated in tenths of a gallon. Using that method, it's best to run your vessel in calm water at each of the rpm increments you elect to chart and note fuel consumption over a one-hour period for each setting. However you measure fuel consumption, chart it on graph paper with engine rpm in hundreds across the bottom and fuel consumption in gallons per hour up the left-hand side.

Once you have speed and fuel-consumption curves developed for your vessel, you can use them to compute all manner of essential information, such as your vessel's range at a particular rpm setting and an estimate of the fuel required for a particular leg of a voyage (which we'll discuss in detail later in this chapter). If you get into the habit of noting in your ship's log the length of time you run at various rpm settings during a typical day's cruise, you can also keep up with total fuel consumption and how much fuel is left in your tanks. The figures you develop using that method are likely to be more accurate than relying on your vessel's fuel gauges, most of which give you only a very general idea of how much fuel you actually have on board.

(If you must rely on float-type fuel gauges to keep up with the amount of fuel you have on board, you'll find that the configuration of the tank they serve can make their readings very confusing. You may well find, for instance, that it takes many hours of running for the gauge to go from "full" to "¾" but only an hour or so to go from "¼" to "empty." The reason is that most tanks recessed in a vessel's keel are in the shape of a V, but the gauge reflects only the vertical distance its float travels as fuel is consumed. The float's rate of fall, then, is much slower in the top half of the V, which has greater volume, than it is in the bottom half of the V, which has less volume. Here's a technique that will help offset that inherent problem: With your tanks essentially empty, fill them in about 20-gallon increments and note the gauge reading after each increment. You're likely to find, for example, that when the float gauge on a 200-gallon-capacity tank reads "¼," the tank actually contains only about 25 gallons of fuel, not 50; when the gauge reads "½," the tank contains only about 60 gallons of fuel rather than 100; and at "¾" the tank contains only about 125 gallons of fuel rather than 150 gallons.)

Computing your speed and tracking your fuel consumption on subsequent runs over known distances at consistent rpm settings when you are running against adverse winds and current will tell you how those factors are affecting your vessel's performance. Computing those factors after your vessel's bottom becomes fouled will also show you how they are affected by accumulated growth and convince you of the wisdom and economy of cleaning its hull frequently.

After your shakedown cruise, allow yourself a reasonable length of time back at your home base to fix anything that broke along the way, replace anything that didn't work right, and learn what you found you didn't know. Once you get all those things taken care of, you'll probably be ready to handle whatever comes your way.

## Planning a Daily Cruising Schedule

By this point, you've probably conceived the grand design of your first major cruise. Now comes the nitty-gritty part of planning each day's run to insure it's as pleasant as possible and avoids any adverse factors that might lurk in your path.

An ideal daily cruising schedule might allow you to depart the dock or anchorage about nine o'clock in the morning, run till about an hour before dark, then snug up in a quiet anchorage or tie up in a comfortable marina for the night. There will, of course, be precious few times when conditions will allow you to follow an ideal cruising schedule.

The planning of any day's run begins with the basic charts and publications you have on board which tell you what you are likely to encounter. You'll find a list of publications you might want to consider including in your ship's library in the Appendix. With a good selection of information aboard, you'll be in position to take into account the basic factors you'll need to consider in planning a daily cruise:

### Weather

If the forecast for the weather along your planned route calls for high winds, heavy seas, or fog, you're better off not to depart at all but wait for more auspicious conditions. In Chapter 9 we'll talk a good deal more about interpreting the various sources of weather information available to you and how you can do some forecasting based on your own observations of local conditions.

## Distance Versus Daylight

The local mean time of sunrise and sunset, which you can calculate from Tables 4 and 5 of the *Tide Tables,* will determine the amount of daylight you will have to make a particular day's run. By comparing that figure to your vessel's cruising speed, you can compute the distance you can expect to cover under ideal circumstances. The hours of daylight available, however, may be only part of the story, and your run may have to be considerably shorter. In tropical areas, for instance, where patches of coral heads and unmarked channels are a primary concern, you may have to delay your departure until around 1000 and plan to get into an anchorage by around 1600 as only during those hours is the sun high enough in the sky to allow you to read the bottom clearly.

If the distance you plan to cover between ports or anchorages (especially if an offshore run is involved) requires you to make some of the run at night, the general rule is that you want to arrive in daylight if at all possible so you don't have to work your way to a dock or an anchorage in the dark.

## Tidal Range and Currents

In relatively shallow cruising grounds like the Bahamas, your coast pilots, *Tide Tables,* and cruising guides will warn of areas where tidal range may force you to schedule a run at those times when there is enough water over a shoal or bank to allow you to cross it. In more northerly latitudes, your coast pilots and *Tidal Current Tables* will alert you to heavy tidal or river currents through narrow passages which can run up to ten knots—in some places even more. By using your *Tide Tables,* you can construct a schedule which allows you to ride the ebb or flood going the way you want to go, avoid strong currents running in the opposite direction, or transit difficult areas during periods of slack water.

One of the most dramatic examples I've ever encountered of the impact of tidal current flow on a daily cruising schedule was running the Reversing Falls at St. John in the Canadian province of New Brunswick. At low water the level of the St. John River is some 16 feet above that of the Bay of Fundy into which it flows. At the river's mouth, that difference creates a 1,200-foot-long south-flowing waterfall which is the equal of some of the white water rapids on the Colorado River. At high water the Bay of Fundy is 9 feet higher than the St. John, which creates a somewhat less chaotic waterfall flowing in the opposite direction. About two hours before high water, the level of the two bodies of water is virtually equal, which makes a calm and easily navigable millpond of what a few hours earlier is a raging rapid.

## Bridge Clearances

If your charts show any fixed bridges along your planned route whose vertical clearance is anywhere near your vessel's maximum height above the water with your communications and navigation antennas lowered, check their clearances to determine whether (and when) you will have room to pass beneath them. (If you're not familiar with figuring bridge clearances, you'll find the clearest discussion of the topic in the "Tides and Currents" chapter in *Chapman Piloting*.) In doing your calculations, remember that the bridge clearances printed on nautical charts normally are based on heights above Mean High Water, which is the average of all high water levels. Unusually high spring tides, sustained wind from certain quarters, and upland water runoff can result in Predicted High Water at the bridge actually being higher than Mean High Water, in which case the clearance would be less than is indicated on the chart. Also remember that all times listed in the *Tide Tables* are standard time, and don't forget to allow for daylight saving time if it is in effect at the time you will be passing under the bridge.

As a practical matter, once you approach a bridge about which you are concerned, usually you can call the bridge tender on channel 13 to ask what its clearance is at that particular time, or you can read its clearance gauge to make certain that factors such as sustained wind from a certain quarter or excessive upland water runoff has not reduced the clearance below your acceptable minimum.

## Bridge and Lock Restricted Operating Hours

During certain hours (usually about 0700 to 0900 and 1600 to 1900 on weekdays) many bridges, especially along the Intracoastal Waterway, are closed to waterborne traffic or open only on the hour or half-hour. Locks utilize the gravitational flow of water for their operation and during dry periods in some areas limit the number of lockings each day. In a few instances, waterways pass through military reservations and may be closed for training exercises. One such instance which comes to mind is the stretch of the ICW between Swansboro and Snead's Ferry, North Carolina, which passes through the Marine Corps' Camp Lejeune.

Coast pilots list standard hours of restricted bridge and lock operations and closings due to military exercises, but those times can change fairly often and vary with the seasons. Your best sources of information about such restrictions normally will be cruising guides, other cruisers who have recently passed through an area, and local marina operators. If your day's run includes a bridge or lock with restricted operating hours, you may need to depart a little early or increase your normal cruising speed to arrive at the bridge when it's open or at the lock when it's accepting traffic in the direction you want to go. It's not usually a good idea to stick to your normal cruising routine and figure that if you arrive at the bridge or lock when it is not operating you can just anchor off until it opens. Many bridges and locks with restricted operating hours are located over or in narrow channels which offer little anchoring room, have poor holding ground, and are beset with troublesome currents.

## Fuel Consumption

Double-check to make certain you've got enough fuel on board to travel the distance involved, plus a comfortable reserve. When opportunities to take on fuel are numerous, there are two schools of thought on fueling. Some cruisers—usually the owners of semi- and full-displacement boats—fill their tanks every chance they get on the theories that keeping their tanks full reduces condensation, which leads to less water in their fuel and cuts down on bacterial contamination (both of which are true); that they've always got a more than generous reserve; and that if they get into heavy weather, the added weight will give their vessel increased stability. Some planing-hull owners feel that hauling around the extra weight of more fuel than they need for a particular run reduces their speed and fuel efficiency, so they take on only enough fuel to reach their destination—plus a reserve. I've no quarrel with either approach, so long as there is enough fuel aboard to deal with any conceivable contingency.

The basic figure of how much fuel you'll need for a particular run will come from the distance to be covered taken from your nautical charts compared with the chart of gallons per running hour under different conditions and at different rpm settings you worked out on your shakedown cruise.

In projecting your fuel requirements for a particular run, be sure you are comparing apples to apples. If your vessel speed figures are in knots and you happen across a chart which lists distance in both nautical and statute miles, be sure to use nautical miles in computing distances. If you must start with statute miles, multiply by .87 to convert them to nautical miles. If you need to convert nautical miles to statute miles, multiply by 1.15.

In addition to the miles you plan to cover, don't forget to make a generous allowance for the fuel you'll need to deal with any adverse currents, winds, or seas you're likely to encounter, and leave yourself at least a 20 percent reserve to cover difficulties you are unable to anticipate. If the amount of fuel required for a particular run gets close to the maximum capacity of your vessel's fuel tanks as listed on your vessel's specifications sheet, you should reduce that total capacity figure by about 10 percent before you begin your calculations. That reduction is necessary because the ends of the pickup tubes in a fuel system are normally kept about two inches off the bottom of a tank to avoid sucking up the water and sludge that accumulates there. As a result, you have no way to get about 10 percent of the fuel actually in each of your tanks into your engine(s).

Your vessel's rate of fuel consumption normally won't be a problem in inland cruising where fuel is available every 50 or 60 miles. But in offshore cruising or voyages into the boondocks where fuel pumps may be few and far between, it can be critical.

The experience of the father-son team of Bob and Don Baumgartner, who took the 58-foot full-displacement cruiser *Trenora* across the Atlantic on her own bottom, provides some hard data in regard to fuel consumption figures and vividly demonstrates how they can be affected by vessel speed and sea conditions. *Trenora* was powered by twin, naturally aspirated GM 4–71 diesels with N55 injectors which developed 160 shaft horsepower each at 2,300 rpm, and she had total fuel tankage of 2,300 gallons with about 2,000 gallons useable. In order to make sure they had an adequate fuel reserve for the longest leg of the voyage—the 1,779-mile run from Bermuda to the Azores—the Baumgartners equipped *Trenora* with a 100-gallon day tank graduated in one-gallon increments and did a number of carefully measured runs over a test course in calm seas at different rpm settings. With her 52-foot waterline, the vessel's theoretical maximum efficient hull speed ($1.34 \times \sqrt{LWL}$) would be 9.66 knots. During the test, the boat was fully loaded with fuel, water, and stores, and the fuel consumption figures included the operation of a 15 kW generator. They developed the following numbers:

| RPM | Speed (in Knots) | S/L Ratio | GPH | Nautical Miles/Gal. |
|-----|------------------|-----------|------|---------------------|
| 1,400 | 8.3 | 1.15 | 6.6 | 1.26 |
| 1,500 | 8.5 | 1.18 | 8.5 | 1.00 |
| 1,800 | 10.7 | 1.48 | 12.0 | .89 |

Notice that decreasing the throttle setting from 1,500 to 1,400 rpm cost only a 2 percent decrease in speed but reduced fuel consumption by 22 percent. Conversely, in going from 8.5 knots, well under the boat's theorctical maximum hull speed of 9.66 knots, to well over it at 10.7 knots, they achieved a 26 percent speed increase but at the heavy cost of a 41 percent increase in fuel consumption.

Under the actual conditions *Trenora* experienced during the voyage—which included 20-foot seas off Bermuda and 40-knot winds gusting to 60 on her approach to the Azores—she covered a total of 3,818 nautical miles from Fort Lauderdale, Florida, to Villamora, Portugal, in 460.8 hours running time at an average speed of 8.29 knots (an S/L of 1.149). According to the chart derived from the tests in calm water, she should have consumed a shade under 6.6 GPH for a total of 3,041 gallons of fuel or 1.26 nautical miles per gallon. In the realities of the conditions she encountered at sea, she actually consumed 4,588.7 gallons, an average of 10 gallons per hour or .83 nautical miles per gallon. Adverse winds and currents, then, increased the fuel consumption figures projected by the calm water tests by slightly more than 50 percent and cut her nautical miles per gallon by 34 percent.

## Course Plotting

If your day's run involves only running down clearly marked channels, all you have to do is make certain the charts you'll need along the way are handy to the helm and organized in sequence. If the day's run involves an offshore passage, you should carefully plot your course on your charts before you leave the dock or anchorage, a topic we'll discuss in detail in Chapter 6: Coastal Piloting and Eyeball Navigation.

With your day's run planned and plenty of fuel aboard, you're finally ready to get underway.

## Everything Shipshape?

During your cruising life you're going to be getting your vessel underway thousands of times, so develop a standard routine for doing it right and follow that routine religiously.

First make a quick mental check to be sure you've taken care of everything ashore. Your preparations should have included filing a float plan, which includes your itinerary, with a relative or friend, arrangements for them to send someone looking for you if you fail to check in with them on schedule, and instructions on how to reach you in an emergency. (The procedures for contacting you via VHF or SSB radiotelephone are explained fully in Chapter 8.)

Once all your shoreside preparations are complete, take a walk around the entire perimeter of your vessel to make sure anything on deck is properly secured (particularly your ground tackle), and walk through your boat's interior to make sure anything that could come loose in a significant sea is also secured.

Fire up your radios and navigation electronics to make sure they're working properly and double-check to see that all the charts, plotting instruments, your binoculars, and any reference materials such as cruising guides or coast pilots or *Tide Tables* you'll need for the run are handy to the helm.

Next go through your prestart engine-room check. Check the oil and water levels in your main engines (and in your electrical generator if you have one) and top them off if necessary. Engine oil quantity and pressure are critical to the proper operation of a diesel engine, so always make sure the oil level is right at the "full" level on the dipstick and not more than about a sixteenth of an inch above or below it. Your engines' coolant, however, will expand as it is heated, so leave the water level about two inches below the top of the filler tube. Check the bowl of your water/fuel separator(s) and drain off any water that has accumulated, and make a visual sweep of the entire engine room to look for frayed wiring and fuel or oil leaks.

For the first few days underway, it's a good idea to make a list of all the items you need to include in your prestart check and tick off each one so you don't forget anything important. In time, the procedure will become second nature. After this initial departure check, you'll probably find it more practical to check your engine room at the end of each day's cruising so you will know everything is ready for you to get underway the following morning.

In addition to the above routine which you should go through daily, there are other inspections you conduct every week or so: check all the belts on your engine for cracking, glazing, and proper tension (when pressed halfway between their pulleys they should deflect about half an inch but not more); check your batteries for proper electrolyte levels and make sure their connections are tight and free of corrosion; and check the fluid levels in your marine gears with their engine running. Checking a gear's fluid level with its engine off can give you a false reading.

If you plan to run your generator underway, now's the time to fire it up, shift your ship's service over to it, disconnect your dockside connections such as power, water, telephone, and cable TV lines, and store your cables and hoses properly. (Always disconnect the dockside end of your power cable before you disconnect the end that plugs into the boat; that way you are not dealing with a "hot" connection which could fall off into the water and cause an electrical short or fire.)

Back on deck, take a look around at the wind, the state of the current or tide, and any boats fore and aft of you to see what's going to be involved in undocking and plan your departure accordingly. (We'll talk more about the specifics in a minute.)

## Engine Starting Tips

Don't start your main engines until you are satisfied that everything aboard your vessel and in the engine room is shipshape and you are ready to cast off. In the course of your cruising, you're sure to see a lot of guys crank up their diesel engines and let them barely idle at around 400 rpm for a half-hour or so before they get underway on the theory that they're "warming them up." Aside from being annoying as the devil to everybody else in the marina or the anchorage, running your engines for that long at that low an idle is not good for them. The optimum operating temperature for a diesel is 170 to 185 degrees. At anything below about 600 rpm, its internal temperature won't get over about 100 degrees, which isn't hot enough to get its oil, coolant, or fuel systems flowing properly. Idling for prolonged periods causes incomplete fuel combustion, which can dilute the oil in the engine's crankcase, allow the formation of lacquer or gummy deposits on valves, pistons, and rings, and lead to rapid accumulation of sludge in the crankcase. A five-minute warmup while you check for adequate cooling water discharge from the exhaust and take a last-minute look in your engine room is plenty.

Under the heavy load of starting a diesel engine, the temperature in its starter motor can quickly jump up to several hundred degrees. If you press the starter switch and your diesel doesn't fire within 30 seconds, release the start button and wait about two minutes before trying it again to give the starter motor time to cool down. If the engine fails to start after about four 30-second tries, something is wrong and you need to find out what it is and correct it before casting off. When starting a diesel engine that has thoroughly cooled, a brief burst of white smoke from the exhaust is normal. That's simply condensation burning off. But if you get a heavy cloud of white smoke every time you start your engine and it lasts for more than about 15 seconds, try this: As you press the start button, also hold in the stop button for about ten seconds, then release the stop button and continue to hold the start button down until the engine cranks (but not more than 30 seconds). All you are doing is preheating your engine's cylinders, which allows them to burn off the condensation quicker. If you get a heavy cloud of black smoke when you start your engines and it lasts for more than about 15 seconds, you've got a problem and need to have a qualified mechanic find out what it is and correct it.

Once you crank the engines, go ahead and run them up to about 750 rpm to help them get up to their optimal operating temperature quickly, and check your boat's transom to make sure a normal volume of cooling water is flowing out of your exhausts. After you depart from the dock, run your engines about 10 to 15 minutes at half-throttle before you open them up to your normal cruising speed.

## Leaving the Dock

If you've got plenty of room fore and aft and wind and current are setting away from the dock, all you've got to do is cast off your dock lines, close your safety gates, and let wind and current carry you clear. But it won't always be that simple.

## SPRING LINES

Problem: You're tied up to a dock port side to. The stern of one boat is only five feet off your bow and the bow of another is only five feet off your stern. About a knot of current and 10 to 15 knots of wind are striking your vessel on the stern. If you simply cast off your dock lines and try to pull out of the slip, the wind and/or current will carry you down on the vessel tied up ahead of you. How are you going to maneuver out of that space without damaging your boat or the ones fore and aft of you?

The best way to get out of the space without damaging the vessel ahead is to use a spring line. (Here we are concerned only with spring lines used for maneuvering your boat around a dock. Spring lines are also used for tying your boat up to a dock or in a slip, and we'll discuss that use for them in Chapter 4.) I see few skippers using spring lines to help them maneuver their boats, and most who do use them employ them incorrectly. In case you're not intimately familiar with them, we'll go into a bit of detail.

Spring lines—often just called "springs"—are nothing more than your normal dock lines used in a special way, but the terminology involving them can get a little confusing. They are designated, for instance, first by the direction they lead, then by the point at which they are attached to the vessel. Thus, you can have an after bow spring (which leads aft from a cleat at your vessel's bow) or a forward quarter spring (which leads forward from a cleat at your vessel's stern), and you can use either type on either side of your boat.

## Preparing to Free a Spring

If you use a spring line to help you get away from the dock, it should be rigged before you get underway in such a way that your mate will be able to retrieve it without the assistance of anyone on shore. The best way to do that is to "double" it (Fig. 1.1A): secure its eye (loop) around the appropriate deck cleat on your vessel, run the standing part of the line around a piling or cleat on the dock, lead the tail back on board, and cleat it off on the same deck cleat that is securing the eye. Once you are clear of the dock, your mate can simply uncleat the tail of a doubled spring line (Fig. 1.1B),

**Fig. 1.1:** *(A) A spring line doubled for easy release from aboard. (B) Note that the spring is rigged so it doesn't have to cross over itself to avoid the potential for fouling. Note also that the tail rather than the eye is the "running" end, again to avoid fouling.*

A

then quickly pull the standing part around the piling or cleat to bring the line back on board.

If you are springing off a line secured to a dock cleat, your mate can also cast it off without assistance from shore by hooking its eye over only one of the cleat's horns (Fig. 1.2).

## Spring Lines and Deck Cleats

One of the most common mistakes I see cruisers making in their use of spring lines is not properly securing them around deck cleats. A spring line's tail should always be led first to the horn of the cleat opposite the direction

**B**

*Fig. 1.2:* *A spring hooked around only one horn of a dock cleat can be easily released by a line handler on deck.*

from which the strain will be applied (Fig. 1.3). This ensures that the angle between the axis of the part of the spring under tension and the axis of the cleat will always be 90 degrees or less, which takes greater advantage of the cleat's strength.

## Controlling Tension on a Spring

There will be many situations where you will want your mate to be able to take in or let out a spring line to control your vessel's fore and aft movement as you maneuver in tight quarters. Failure to rig the spring properly to allow the mate to safely handle the force involved can result in serious injury. The

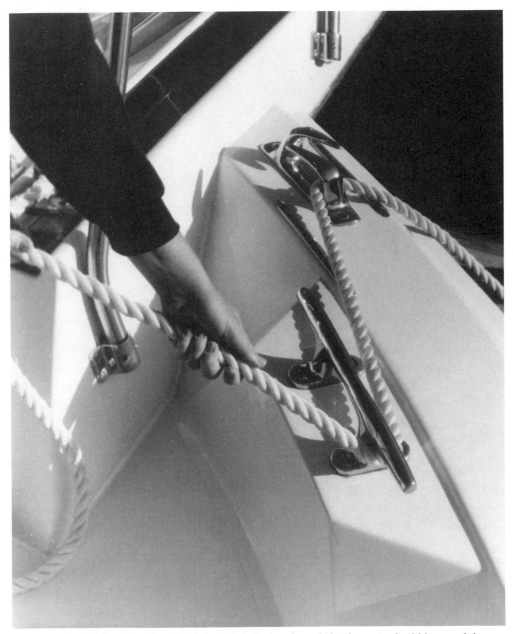

**Fig. 1.3:** *If a spring line is led through a chock or hawsehole, the strain should be regarded as coming from the direction of the chock or hawsehole and the spring should be first led under the horn of the cleat opposite to it.*

basic way of rigging the spring to control tension on it is with a half-turn (Fig. 1.4). A variation some cruisers use which allows the mate to handle even more force is the S-turn (Fig. 1.5). With either a half-turn or an S-turn, even a small mate with limited physical strength can "tail" the spring and hold a boat in position or let out line as the helmsperson directs. Even a strapping mate, however, won't be able to take in on a spring line under heavy tension.

## Springing the Stern Out

In the above example, if the wind and current are setting directly onto the dock or are from astern, the best way to maneuver out of this tight spot is to force your vessel's stern away from the dock by going ahead against a doubled after bow spring (Fig. 1.6). To get ready to do that: double an after bow spring from your port bow cleat counterclockwise around a piling that is about one third to halfway down the length of your vessel from the bow then back to your bow cleat and cleat it off with no slack in it. (To avoid the spring line putting pressure on your lifeline stanchions, rig the spring on the piling below the flare of your bow.)

Springing your stern out involves making your boat pivot around a point which usually will be about a fourth of the way back from the bow. If your vessel has a stout rub rail and it is lying against a piling that is at about the pivot point and is at least a foot above the level of your decks, pivot against that. (Be especially wary of pilings that do not extend at least a foot or so above your boat's deck as your boat's sheer could be lifted over them and cause significant damage to your hull.) If you are lying at a face dock which has no pilings, your vessel's hull will contact the edge of the dock at the pivot point. Protect the hull at that point by rigging a vertical fender on the port side about a quarter of the way back from the bow with the middle of it level with the top of the dock.

Once these preparations are complete, you're ready to spring your stern away from the dock: Man the helm from your vessel's flying bridge and have your mate cast off all dock lines except the doubled after bow spring, then come aboard, shut the boarding gate, and stand by the bow cleat. Check to make certain that as you maneuver away from the dock, you won't interfere with the movement of any other vessels. Turn your helm fully toward the dock. If yours is a single-engine boat, go ahead slowly. With twin engines, slowly go ahead on the starboard engine and in reverse on the port engine.

**Fig. 1.4:** *To prepare to maintain tension on a spring, lead its tail under the horn of the deck cleat opposite the direction from which the strain will be applied, then parallel down the side of the cleat, under the other horn, and back over the top of it.*

**Fig. 1.5:** *A variation some cruisers use which allows the mate to handle even more strain on a spring is the S-turn: the line is led over the top of the cleat and under the opposite horn in the reverse direction.*

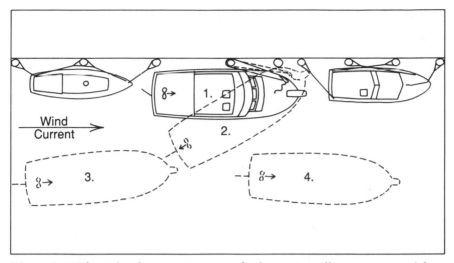

*Fig. 1.6: With wind and current astern, an after bow spring will prevent your vessel from striking the boat tied up ahead of you yet allow you to maneuver your stern clear of the dock.*

The after bow spring will keep your vessel from going forward and striking the vessel tied up in front of you, but you will still need to be careful of your bow pulpit and any anchors mounted on it. The propeller discharge against the rudder(s) will swing your stern away from the dock.

As your stern swings clear of the boat behind you, continue to pivot until your vessel's centerline is at about a 45-degree angle to the dock. Hold that position while your mate quickly uncleats the tail of the spring line from the bow cleat and casts it off, which will leave the line free to be hauled on board. The mate should bring it back aboard quickly to prevent any possibility of its falling into the water and getting fouled in your prop(s). Once the line is cast off, bring your helm amidships, continue to back until you are well clear of the vessels at the dock, then swing your helm slightly to starboard and proceed ahead slowly. Keep your angle of departure in relation to the dock shallow. If you turn your bow too quickly to starboard and try to depart at too sharp an angle, the current could swing your stern around and force it into the vessel that was tied up ahead of you.

## Springing Ahead

If wind and/or current are from dead ahead, you may find you can simply nose your bow away from the dock and the wind and/or current will carry you free. But if wind and/or current are penning you to the dock at an angle, you'll need to swing your bow away from the dock by backing against a forward quarter spring (Fig. 1.7). This technique is neither as easy nor as effective as swinging your stern out with an after bow spring, but it's a technique worth learning and is done this way: Double a forward quarter spring from your vessel's port stern cleat clockwise around a dock cleat or piling that is about a third to halfway down the length of your vessel from the stern. In springing the bow out, your vessel's pivot point is going to be right at its stern. If there is a piling at your stern, you can pivot off of it using your boat's rub rail. If you're at a face dock, rig a horizontal fender at the point of your vessel's port quarter. Have your mate cast off all dock

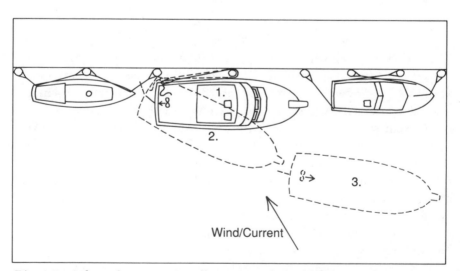

***Fig. 1.7:*** *A forward quarter spring allows you to pivot your bow into wind or current that is setting onto a dock.*

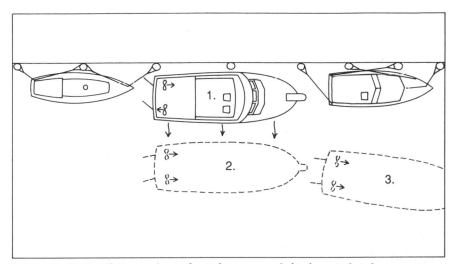

**Fig.** 1.8: To "walk" a vessel out of a tight spot at a dock when wind and current are not a factor, turn your helm fully toward the dock, go forward on the engine toward the dock, and in reverse on the engine away from the dock.

lines except the doubled forward quarter spring, come aboard, close the safety gate, and stand by the stern cleat. Check to make certain that as you maneuver away from the dock, you won't interfere with the movement of any other vessels. Turn your helm fully toward the dock. If yours is a single-engine boat, go in reverse slowly. With twin engines, go ahead slowly on the engine toward the dock and in reverse on the engine away from the dock. The forward quarter spring will keep your vessel from striking the vessel off your stern and the propeller discharge against the rudder(s) will swing your bow away from the dock. Once your bow has swung clear of the boat in front of you and your vessel's centerline is at about a 45-degree angle to the dock, have your mate uncleat the spring line and cast it off, which will leave the line free to be hauled on board smartly to prevent its being fouled in your prop(s). As soon as the spring is cast off, you will be free to bring your helm amidship and clear the dock by going ahead.

A

B

**Fig. 1.9:** *One way of coiling a dock line for stowage: begin at the tail to form coils about two feet in diameter (A); as you near the eye, take three or four wraps around the coils (B); then bring the eye through the loop in the top of the coils (C). You wind up with an eye by which the line can be neatly hung for stowage (D).*

C

D

## "Walking" a Boat Sideways

If no significant wind is blowing, no strong currents are running, and yours is a twin-screw planing-hull boat, another technique you may be able to use to extricate yourself from a tight spot at a face dock is to "walk" it sideways (Fig. 1.8). To walk a twin-engine boat to starboard as in the undocking situation above: put the helm hard over to port, ease the port engine ahead and the starboard engine astern. The port engine going ahead will force water against its rudder to push the stern away from the dock and the bow toward it, while the starboard engine going astern will push the stern toward the dock and the bow away from it. The resulting forces will literally "walk" the boat sideways to starboard while generating only minimal forward movement. Before you try walking your boat around a dock for the first time, it's best to practice a bit in clear water to see exactly how your boat responds. The technique generally works best with planing-hull motor yachts, which don't have a significant keel. The keels of semi- and full-displacement twin-engine boats take such a bite on the water that it's difficult to move them sideways.

## Coiling Dock Lines

As soon as you are clear of the dock or the slip, you or your mate should neatly coil all your dock lines and stow them for the next time you need them. One good way of coiling a dock line so it won't get all tangled up is suggested in Fig. 1.9. By coiling your dock lines this way, you keep them from getting tangled and can handle them easily. The next time you pull up to a dock, you have only to release the wrappings around the coils and shake the coils out to be ready to loop the eye over a piling or dock cleat or toss the eye end of the line to a person on shore waiting to help you tie up. In Chapter 4: Arriving at the Dock, we'll discuss why that's important.

## CHAPTER 2

# ROUTINE OPERATIONS UNDERWAY

• • •

Let's assume that on this particular day's run the weather is going to be glorious, your planned run includes no adverse tides or currents, and you don't have to schedule around bridges or locks with restricted operating hours. On even such an ideal cruising day, you are likely to encounter an incredible variety of situations with which you must be prepared to deal correctly.

## RULES OF THE ROAD

In extended cruising you'll be involved in thousands of situations in restricted waterways where you meet or cross courses with other boats, overtake slower boats, or are yourself overtaken by faster boats. In many of these situations, the encounters will be strictly routine and require you to do nothing more than exercise a bit of common sense. The danger lies in those encounters when an unusual combination of circumstances or the ignorance, ineptitude, or lack of courtesy of the person running the other boat puts your vessel or those aboard it in jeopardy.

The operation of vessels in U.S. inland waters is governed by the 1980 U.S. Inland Navigation Rules (often referred to simply as the Inland Rules). The operation of vessels outside U.S. inland waters is governed by the International Regulations to Prevent Collisions at Sea, 1972 (usually referred to simply as COLREGS). The dividing lines between inland and international waters normally run from headland to headland, are as short and direct as possible, run as perpendicular as possible to vessel traffic flow, are precisely defined by physical objects that are readily visible such as aids to navigation or prominent structures on shore, and are marked on nautical charts by dashed magenta lines sometimes identified as COLREGS DEMARCATION LINE and described in detail in coast pilots and the Inland Rules. In some cases, this demarcation line is much farther inland than you might expect and entire bays, harbors, and inlets are subject to the International Rules rather than the Inland Rules. You must at all times know which navigation rules cover the waters in which you are operating, and you must know what your responsibilities and proper course of action are under the appropriate section of the applicable Rules of the Road.

The discussion that follows is not intended as a comprehensive explanation of the various navigation rules but only as a brief review of how they are normally applied in the real world of cruising. If you are not intimately familiar with the Rules, you should get a copy of the U.S. Coast Guard publication *Navigation Rules—International, Inland*—which is required to be aboard all self-propelled vessels greater than 39.4 feet (12 meters) in length—and study it thoroughly. In this chapter, we'll cover only what you should know about operating under the Inland Rules. We'll cover vessel operation in international waters and the waters of other countries in Chapter 20: International Buoyage, Lighting, and Chart Systems.

## RIGHT-OF-WAY SITUATIONS

The Inland Rules are quite specific on the operation of vessels in meeting, crossing, and overtaking situations when the danger of a collision exists. In such situations, the Rules refer to the boat that has the right-of-way and should maintain its course and speed as the "stand on" vessel, and the boat that does not have the right-of-way and must alter its course or speed if necessary to avoid a collision as the "give way" vessel. In this discussion, we'll use more familiar and customary terminology by describing the former as the "privileged" vessel and the latter as the "burdened" vessel. Note also that in the following discussion the term "passing" can refer to any encounter between vessels covered by the Rules. For clarity's sake, it is not used here, however, to describe a situation in which one vessel overtakes another; such a situation is referred to only by the term "overtaking."

## Whistle Signals

In the Inland Rules you'll find numerous references to the whistle signals that are required in right-of-way situations. These whistle signals consist of short blasts, which last about one second each; and prolonged blasts, which last four to six seconds each. You will find that many—in fact most—skippers of both commercial and recreational vessels don't use whistle signals. One reason they are not used is that technically the right-of-way rules don't come into effect until the possibility of a collision between two vessels exists. A more common reason for their being omitted is simple ignorance, either of the fact that they are required or of the signals that are appropriate in a given situation. I don't recommend that you run up and down the waterways like Steamboat Willy and blast out whistle signals in every instance in which they might be used. I do, however, urge you to familiarize yourself with the signals required in right-of-way situations and be prepared to use them properly any time the possibility of a collision between your vessel and another exists or you receive a whistle signal from another vessel that requires an appropriate response from you.

The Rules allow vessels encountering one another in a right-of-way situation to agree to the manner of meeting, crossing, or overtaking by VHF radiotelephone and omit the sound signals otherwise required. That should be done by one of the vessels calling the other on channel 16. (In a meeting situation, either vessel may initiate the call. In a crossing situation, the vessel that is privileged or believes itself to be privileged normally initiates the call. In an overtaking situation, the overtaking vessel should initiate the call.) Once the vessel being called responds on channel 16, the vessel initiating the call should propose moving to channel 13, which is specifically for bridge-to-bridge communications and on which modern VHF radios automatically reduce their output power to 1 watt. Once the two vessels make contact on channel 13 (using abbreviated operating procedures which omit call signs), the vessel initiating the call should propose the side on which it intends to leave the vessel it is encountering, and the vessel being called should agree, propose another method of passing, or request the calling vessel to take some other action.

Unfortunately, it seldom works that way. In most cases in which VHF is used to communicate during a right-of-way situation, the vessel operator initiating the call will simply state his request or intentions on channel 16 and the operator of the vessel being called will respond on the same channel. There are two things wrong with that. One is that it is an improper use of channel 16, which is strictly for calling, safety, and distress messages. The other is that boat operators who use channel 16 in this fashion almost never reduce their radio's output power to its 1 watt settings, and thus their communication disrupts the proper use of channel 16 for a radius of up to 40 miles around both their vessels. VHF channel 16 is already overloaded and filled with improper traffic. We'd all be better off if everyone would use whistle signals instead of VHF to communicate in right-of-way situations. In many instances, when you sound the proper whistle signal, the skipper with whom you are trying to communicate will fail to respond because he doesn't understand what you're trying to tell him. I grant that's frustrating, but I suggest you try whistle signals first. If you don't get a response, use VHF—but use it properly. I also suggest that if a skipper calls you on channel 16 and proceeds to state his request or intentions on that channel, you respond with the name of his vessel, the name of your vessel, and a polite request that he shift and answer on channel 13.

In right-of-way situations where you are contacted by VHF, you are also likely to hear a kind of shorthand such as "Captain, I'll meet you on one," which means the calling skipper intends to leave you on his port side, or "I'd like to slide by you on two," which means he is asking to overtake you on his starboard (your port) side.

## Meeting Situations

When you meet another power-driven vessel head-on or nearly head-on and your courses, if maintained, may converge and create the possibility of a collision, you are technically in a "meeting situation" (Fig. 2.1) and the following rules apply: (Note that these rules do not apply in situations where two vessels will pass clear of each other if both maintain their speed and heading.)

54

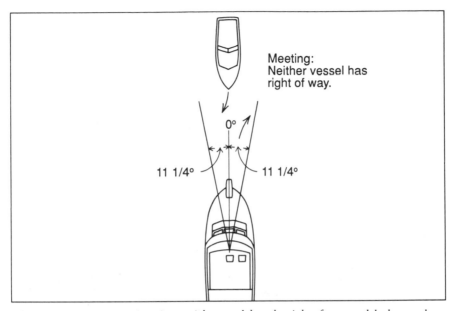

Meeting:
Neither vessel has
right of way.

0°

11 1/4°          11 1/4°

*Fig. 2.1: In a meeting situation, neither vessel has the right-of-way and both must bear off to starboard to avoid a collision unless an alternate method of passing is agreed to by whistle signals or VHF radio communication.*

1. Neither of you has the right-of-way.

2. Unless otherwise agreed, both of you should pass on the port side of the other.

3. Both of you must alter course to starboard, if necessary, to allow clearance for safe passage.

4. When you are within sight of another power-driven vessel and meeting at a distance of a half-mile or less, both of you are required to sound one of three whistle signals: (Both of you are on an equal basis and either can signal first.)

   A. One short blast, which signals: "I intend to leave you on my port side."

    B.   Two short blasts, which signal: "I intend to leave you on my starboard side."

    C.   Three short blasts, which signal: "I am operating astern."

5.    If you hear the one- or two-blast signal from the other vessel you must, if you are in agreement with the method of passing proposed by the signal, give the same signal in return and make any maneuvers required to allow clearance for safe passage. If you consider the proposed method of passing unsafe or are not in agreement, you must sound five or more short blasts, which is the signal for *Danger!*, and make any precautionary maneuvers necessary until a method of safe passing is mutually agreed. You must never answer one short blast with two short blasts or two short blasts with one short blast. These are "cross signals" which are specifically prohibited by the Rules.

6.    If you initiate passing signals and do not receive the same signal in answer, you must immediately make any precautionary maneuvers necessary until a method of safe passing is mutually agreed.

7.    If you initiate passing signals and receive in reply three short blasts meaning "I am operating astern," you must immediately reduce speed to the minimum required to maintain steerage and make no further attempt to pass until a safe method of passing has been agreed by the exchange of appropriate signals.

The Rules do not set mathematical limits within which the meeting situation exists, but court rulings have established it as existing when two vessels approach each other within one point (11¼ degrees) to either side of their respective bows.

In daylight when visibility is good, the easiest way to determine whether you are on a collision course with another vessel is to take a series of compass bearings on the approaching vessel (Fig. 2.2). If the bearing of the other vessel relative to your own does not change appreciably, you may be on a collision course and the appropriate navigation Rule or Rules apply. At night, you know you are in a meeting situation if you can see both an approaching vessel's red and green sidelights or if you see two masthead lights of a vessel in line, one over the other.

In a winding channel, you may first sight an approaching vessel at an oblique angle, but the meeting situation will still apply if you will be head

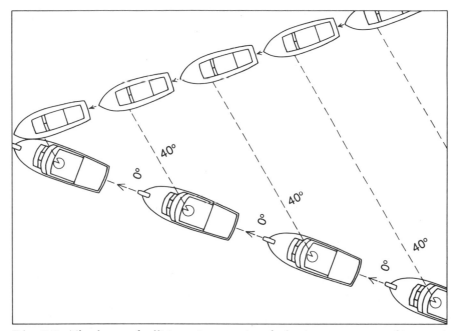

**Fig. 2.2:** *The danger of collision exists any time the bearings on an approaching vessel remain constant.*

on or nearly head on and on convergent courses when you meet. In such a situation, both you and the other vessel must keep to the right of the channel and, if necessary, give way to starboard to allow clearance for safe passage.

There are several exceptions to the meeting rules:

A.  Vessels not under command, vessels restricted in their ability to maneuver (such as large commercial vessels in a restricted waterway), vessels engaged in commercial (but not sport) fishing, and vessels operating under sail alone are all privileged over you as the operator of a power-driven vessel and you must give way. In a meeting situation between yourself and a vessel operating under sail alone, no whistle signals are exchanged.

B.   On the Great Lakes or Western Rivers, a vessel proceeding downbound with the current has the right-of-way over an upbound vessel.
If you are downbound with the current, you would propose the
method of safe passing by initiating the appropriate whistle signals.
If you are upbound, you must hold your course or position as
necessary to permit safe passage.

## Crossing Situations

When you and another vessel approach each other not head on or nearly
head on but on a relative bearing forward of 22½ degrees abaft your respective
beams and the possibility of a collision exists, you are technically in a crossing
situation (Fig. 2.3) and the following Rules apply:

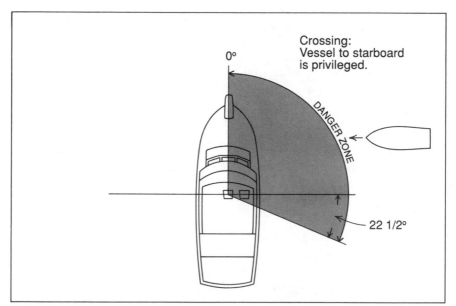

*Fig. 2.3:* A vessel's "danger zone" extends from dead ahead to 22½ degrees abaft its beam
on the starboard side.

1. The vessel that has the other on her starboard side within an arc from dead ahead to 22½ degrees abaft her starboard beam is burdened and must make any maneuvers necessary to provide clearance for safe passage.

2. If the vessels are in sight of each other and will pass within a half-mile of each other, they must sound whistle signals as discussed above for meeting situations. The Rules do not state which vessel should initiate the signals, but it is customary for the vessel that is privileged—or believes itself to be privileged—to signal first.

This Rule leads to the conclusion that a crossing situation exists when two power-driven vessels encounter each another within a half-mile and each bears within 22½ degrees abaft their respective beams to either side. The vessel that has the other vessel within that arc on its starboard side is burdened; the vessel with the other vessel on its port side is privileged. This gives rise to the concept of this arc to starboard as a vessel's "danger zone."

## Overtaking Situations

Under the Rules, you overtake another vessel any time you approach it from astern of a direction 22½ degrees abaft its beam at a speed great enough to close the distance between you (Fig 2.4). As the overtaking vessel, you are burdened and must not interfere with the progress of the vessel you are overtaking, which is privileged. The Rules specifically state that once you are the burdened vessel in an overtaking situation, you remain so until you are past the vessel you are overtaking and clear of it. (This is true even if you pass a vessel on its starboard side and enter its danger zone, in which relationship you otherwise would have the right-of-way.)

Since the Rules require vessels operating in a navigable channel to stay to the right of it and as close to its outer limit as is safe and practical, most passing is done on the port side of the vessel being overtaken. It is, however, legal to overtake in a channel on the starboard side of the vessel being overtaken if the vessel being overtaken agrees to the maneuver.

The Rules require that when you overtake another vessel, you give one of two sound signals: the usual signal would be two short blasts on your horn which signal, "I intend to leave you on my starboard side"; one short blast would signal, "I intend to leave you on my port side."

59

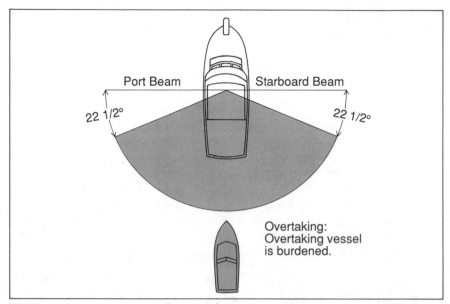

Port Beam      Starboard Beam

22 1/2°              22 1/2°

Overtaking:
Overtaking vessel
is burdened.

*Fig. 2.4: Any time you approach a vessel from a point within an arc between 22½ degrees abaft its beam, you are burdened and must signal your request to pass by whistle or VHF communication.*

If you are being overtaken, the Rules require you to immediately answer the signal of a vessel overtaking you: an answering signal identical to the signal from the overtaking vessel signals, "I agree with your passing on the side you propose." If you do not feel the overtaking vessel can pass safely on the side proposed, you must sound the danger signal of five or more short, rapid blasts. (You should also sound the danger signal if a vessel attempts to overtake you in an unsafe manner without making any signal.) If you are being overtaken, never answer one short blast with two short blasts or two short blasts with one short blast. These are "cross signals," and specifically prohibited by the Rules. Though the Rules don't specifically say so, if the vessel overtaking you proposes by his signal to pass in a manner you consider unsafe but you feel he could pass safely on the other side, you can give the danger signal in response to his initial signal, pause, then give the alternate signal which indicates: "The side on which you propose to overtake is unsafe, but you may overtake safely on the alternate side." If the overtaking vessel agrees and intends to overtake on the side you propose, he should answer your signal with the identical signal.

In addition to the Rules of the Road for overtaking situations, the key to accomplishing the maneuver in narrow channels with a minimum of problems for both of the boats involved is for both of them to slow down (see Fig. 2.5).

Once the appropriate sound signals have been exchanged or the side on which the overtaking vessel will leave the vessel it is overtaking has been properly agreed to via VHF, if you are at the helm of the overtaking vessel, alter course in the direction agreed to and begin to overtake. As your bow comes to within about 100 yards of the stern of the vessel you are overtaking, you should gradually reduce power to your vessel's "no wake" speed. If you are operating a planing hull vessel, by the time your vessel's bow is even with the stern of the vessel you are overtaking, your boat's bow should be fully down and its foredeck should be parallel to the water. If you are going any faster than that, you are throwing too much of a wake. You should continue at a "no wake" speed until your stern is well clear of the bow of the vessel you are overtaking, then swing across its bow to assume your proper position as far to the right of the channel as is safe. Only then should you slowly advance your throttles and resume your normal cruising speed.

If you are at the helm of a vessel being overtaken, as the bow of the overtaking vessel approaches your stern, you should reduce your vessel's speed to the minimum required to maintain steerage and pull over as far as practical to the side of the channel opposite that on which you are being overtaken. As soon as the stern of the overtaking vessel clears your bow, turn sharply into the curl of its wake, take the plunge over it, then swing your bow in line with his stern. Doing that will put you as quickly as possible into the flattened portion at the center of his wake and lead you back into your proper position as far to the right of the channel as is safe, at which point you can resume speed.

So much for what the Rules say. The fact is that in the more congested boating areas of the U.S. such as the Northeast, Florida, and California, the problems associated with high-powered vessels such as planing-hull motor yachts and sportfishermen overtaking lower-powered vessels such as semi-displacement and full-displacement powerboats and sailboats have reached crisis proportions. On one recent cruise down the ICW from Charleston,

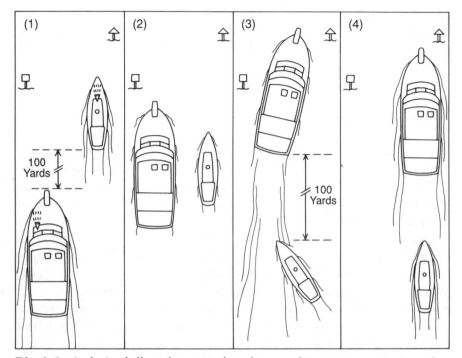

*Fig. 2.5:* A planing-hull vessel can overtake a slower vessel in a narrow waterway with a minimum of delay and disruption if both vessels begin to slow down when the overtaking vessel is about 100 yards off the stern of the vessel being overtaken (1). During the actual passing, the overtaking vessel should be fully off plane (2). Once the overtaking vessel is about 100 yards in front of the overtaken vessel, it can turn to starboard and resume normal speed while the vessel overtaken turns to port to cross its wake (3). Both vessels can then resume their normal position on the starboard side of the channel (4).

South Carolina, to Stuart, Florida, then across the Okeechobee Waterway from Stuart to Fort Myers, Florida, at the helm of a full-displacement vessel that cruised at 8 knots, I was passed by faster vessels several hundred times. I can recall only two skippers of an overtaking vessel communicating their request to pass with whistle signals, and both apparently were professional captains. In about half the overtaking instances, the request to pass was communicated by VHF radio, but in every case it was done incorrectly on channel 16. In the remaining half of the instances in which I was overtaken, the overtaking vessel communicated no request to pass at all.

In about one fourth of the instances, high-powered boats roared by me at full or nearly full-throttle. When their 3- to 4-foot wakes hit my vessel's round-bottomed hull broadside, we took rolls of up to 20 degrees. The operators of a number of express cruisers in the thirty-five- to forty-foot range, and virtually all operators of boats smaller than that, seemed to feel their vessel size somehow exempted them from the Rules of the Road. Thirteen out of a group of 15 express cruisers which were traveling together as a pack whizzed by me at speeds upwards of 30 knots. The operators of some of the planing-hull boats that went by me seemed to think that if they just reduced their throttles to something below full speed, they were passing properly. Running a planing-hull boat at an attitude anywhere between full planing and its "no wake" speed simply digs its stern deeper into the water and causes it to throw an even larger wake. The operators of other planing-hull boats seemed to think that if they passed me in a wide channel and were as much as 100 yards or so off my beam, there was no reason for them to reduce speed. A planing-hull vessel over 40 feet in length with a pair of engines generating on the order of 400 to 500 horsepower each that is operating at planing speed can easily throw a dangerous wake up to 300 yards to either side of its course, and its operator should reduce speed accordingly.

On the other side of the coin, the operators of slower vessels must also bear some responsibility for the cavalier attitude toward passing that now prevails on the water. In several instances on the above cruise, even at my turtle-slow 8 knots I overtook a number of sailboats chugging along on their auxiliary engines at about 6.5 knots. In many of those situations, their operators declined to back off on their throttle at all, which meant the passing took an extremely long time. In at least two instances, oncoming traffic forced me to speed up before I should have in order to get around them.

I'm not simply being an old grouch on this subject. If someone is in the galley of a vessel that is unexpectedly rocked up to 20 degrees by an improper overtaking and has a pot of boiling water on the stove, he or she could easily be scalded. A small child aboard such a vessel could easily be thrown into a bulkhead and seriously injured.

The situation has become so volatile that there are threats of actual violence. In one instance I contacted the operator of a planing-hull vessel that signaled no request to pass and roared by me at full throttle by VHF and strongly criticized his helmsmanship. His reaction was to invite me to stop at the next dock and settle our differences with fisticuffs. In another instance on that cruise, one of the operators I had called down stopped in the same marina where I planned to overnight and actually banged on my boat and invited me to step out on the dock for a fistfight.

The Rules of the Road and most state boating regulations provide penalties for both careless and reckless boat operation. Unfortunately, however, neither the Coast Guard nor most state or local marine patrols will ticket a vessel operator for careless or reckless operation unless their own personnel witness an incident or the improper operation results in personal injury or property damage exceeding $500. If you are the victim of an improper overtaking which does not cause personal injury but does cause property damage under $500, about the only recourse you have against the offender is to swear out a civil complaint with a local magistrate or state's attorney. Even then, you normally will have to have the vessel's state registration number and be able to definitively identify the individual who was at the helm of the vessel at the time the incident occurred. If you succeed in having a warrant issued against the individual, you will have to return to that jurisdiction to testify against him or her in court.

When the problems associated with improper overtaking have reached the level where physical violence is threatened, I suggest it's time for all of us to learn the rules for safe overtaking and obey them. If the maneuver is properly executed, it results in a minimum of delay for the overtaking vessel and a minimum of disruption for the vessel being overtaken.

## No Wake Zones

In waterway cruising through populated areas you'll frequently encounter white rectangular signs with an orange circle which designate No Wake Zones. On the far side of the congested area you'll see similar signs saying "Resume Normal Safe Operation." Areas marked in this fashion are legally designated No Wake Zones by the U.S. Coast Guard or other authority and must be respected. Along the waterways in many communities, the problems of damage from the wakes of passing boats have become so serious that law enforcement agencies are strictly enforcing No Wake restrictions and handing out fines of up to $250 to vessel operators who fail to respect them.

In many other areas along waterways you'll see homemade No Wake signs, which are not legally enforceable. In those cases, your sense of consideration for others will have to determine whether or not you back off your throttles. You should be aware, however, that in any situation where your vessel's wake causes property damage or personal injury, you can be held responsible.

## AIDS TO NAVIGATION

Extended cruising is almost certain to involve runs on some of the waterways, rivers, lakes, and canals that make up America's 30,000 miles of navigable inland waters. In the course of cruising those waters, you may find that some of the aids to navigation you encounter leave you scratching your head in total confusion as to which way you should go. You'll also need to employ some special techniques to keep your vessel off the bottom.

### Basic Buoyage System

In 1989, the U.S. completed the changeover of its basic buoyage from the old lateral system to the International Association of Lighthouse Authorities' System B—Combined Cardinal and Lateral System (red to starboard). This system is now in effect on all navigable waters in the United States that are under federal jurisdiction except the Intracoastal Waterway and "Western Rivers" (the Mississippi River and its tributaries plus other designated rivers). This system is now in effect throughout all of North and South America, the Bahamas, Korea, and Japan. The rest of the world uses System A (red to port), which we'll discuss in Chapter 20.

As its name implies, the new system combines aspects and markings of both lateral and cardinal buoyage systems. In a lateral system, buoys indicate the direction to a danger relative to the course that should be followed (i.e., you avoid obstructions by keeping red to starboard and green to port when entering from seaward). In a cardinal system, buoys indicate the direction to a danger relative to the buoy itself, and a buoy's color directs safe vessel movement in terms of the cardinal points of the compass (i.e., you pass a red-topped white buoy to south or west; you pass a black-topped white buoy to north or east).

If you are familiar with the previous system of aids to navigation, you will find the new system includes two basic changes you have to get used to: green has replaced black as the color normally used to mark the port side of a channel entered from seaward; and flashing white lights, which formerly were used wherever greater light intensity was required (including marking the sides of channels), are now used only on fairway, midchannel, and special-purpose markers.

Aids to navigation in the new system use four basic colors or combinations of colors to indicate their function:

1.  Solid red marks identify the starboard side of a channel "entered from seaward toward the head of navigation," thus the old "red right returning" adage still applies. In shape they may be lighted buoys, nuns, or triangles. They normally do not bear letters but may do so in situations where an interim marker is inserted between two existing markers. Between "16" and "18," for instance, you might encounter "16A." If they bear numbers, the numbers will be even. If lighted, they will have only red lights, which can be fixed or flashing.

2.  Solid green marks identify the port side of a channel entered from seaward. In shape they may be lighted buoys, cans, or rectangles. The only situations in which they bear letters are those in which interim markers are inserted between existing markers. If they bear numbers, the numbers will be odd. If lighted, they will have only green lights, which can be fixed or flashing.

3.  Combination red-and-white vertically striped marks identify safe water or midchannel and may be passed on either side. In shape they may be lighted buoys, spheres, or octagons. They never bear numbers but may be lettered. If lighted, they will have only green lights, which will always be flashing and will flash only the Morse letter "A" (*dit dah*).

4.  Combination red-and-green horizontally striped marks identify a junction or hazard and you can pass them on either side if you are headed upstream. (If you are headed downstream, you must refer to the chart to determine the location of the channel or obstruction relative to the mark.) These marks indicate a preferred channel by the arrangement of their horizontal color bands. If the topmost color is red, the preferred channel is to port of the mark and you should

leave the mark to starboard when you are headed upstream. If the topmost color band is green, the preferred channel is to starboard of the mark and you should leave the mark to port when you are headed upstream. In shape these marks may be lighted buoys, nuns, cans, triangles, or rectangles. They never bear numbers but may bear letters. If lighted, their light will be the same color as the color of their topmost band. Regardless of color, their lights will always be flashing and will flash in the Composite Group (2 + 1) of two *dits,* pause, *dit.*

In addition to these four basic colors or combinations of colors, the new system also uses yellow marks for such special purposes as marking anchorages or the limits of dredging areas. They may appear as lighted buoys, nuns, cans, or diamonds. If lighted, they will have only yellow lights and may flash in any rhythm not in use in the lateral system.

1. Solid yellow buoys mark special anchorage areas.
2. Yellow buoys with green tops are used to mark areas of dredging and survey operations.
3. Yellow-and-black horizontally banded buoys mark fish net areas where fish nets and traps may be placed at or near the surface.
4. Yellow-and-black vertically striped buoys mark areas of seaplane operations.

The new system uses white buoys with international orange marks to present regulatory information such as danger and speed limit zones. They may appear as cans or diamonds and are never lighted.

## Intracoastal Waterway

The Intracoastal Waterway (ICW) has its own marking system which is basically similar to the new system for marking aids to navigation but includes distinctive yellow bands, squares, and triangles. Channel direction on the ICW is not determined by the "entering from seaward" rule. Instead, along the East Coast, channels are assumed to run north to south. Along the Gulf coast, channels are assumed to run first south to north (i.e., along Florida's west coast), then east to west from Apalachicola, Florida, to Brownsville, Texas. The easiest way to remember this when following ICW markings is to assume you are circling the country in a clockwise direction. The basic rule is to leave triangles (think of their shape as resembling nuns) to starboard and squares (think of their shape as resembling cans) to port when running in the direction of the waterway.

Where the ICW crosses other channels, its yellow markings are often displayed on the aids to navigation of other systems. What do you do, then, when you encounter a yellow square (which you should leave to port) on a red nun (which you should leave to starboard)? The answer is that when proceeding along the ICW in the above directions, always keep yellow squares on your port hand; always keep yellow triangles on your starboard hand, regardless of the color of the aid on which they appear.

## Western Rivers

The old lateral system is still in use on "Western Rivers" (the Mississippi and its tributaries plus other designated rivers), but includes some additional shapes and daymarks not found in other areas. In some cases, however, the color green is replacing black. On these rivers, unlighted buoys are not numbered, and the numbers on lighted buoys have no lateral significance. Instead, they indicate the distance upstream from a designated reference point.

## State Waterways

On waterways wholly contained within the borders of a single state, you may encounter aids to navigation identified according to yet a fourth buoyage system—the Uniform State Waterway Marking System. It is essentially a lateral system and is compatible with the basic buoyage system found in waters under federal jurisdiction with several major exceptions:

Buoys that mark the left side of a channel when headed upstream are solid black rather than green. If numbered, their numbers will be odd and increase in the upstream direction; if lighted, their lights will be green. (Buoys that mark the right side of the channel when headed upstream are solid red. If numbered, their numbers will be even and increase in the upstream direction; if lighted, their lights will be red.) If either a solid black or a solid red buoy is lighted, in normal situations the light will be slow-flashing (not more than 30 flashes per minute); at turns, constrictions, or obstructions in the waterway, it will be quick-flashing (not less than 60 flashes per minute). The shape of solid-colored buoys is less important than their color; in some cases red buoys will be of can shape rather than nun.

A red-and-white vertically striped buoy (used in the federal system to indicate safe water or midchannel) indicates that a hazard or obstruction lies between it and the nearest shore. It therefore should be passed outboard. If lighted, its light will be white quick-flashing.

The USWMS uses two aids to navigation not found in the federal system which are cardinal marks rather than lateral marks:

1. A buoy with a red top must be passed to the south or west.

2. A white buoy with a black top must be passed to the north or east.

If either of these buoys is lighted, its lights will be white quick-flashing.

The USWMS also allows the use of mooring buoys, which are white with a horizontal blue band. If lighted, their light will be white and slow-flashing unless they constitute an obstruction, in which case their light will be quick-flashing.

Regulatory and information marks in the USWMS are white with two horizontal bands of international orange, one at the top and one just above the waterline. Between these bands will be a diamond, a circle, or a square or rectangle.

1. A diamond shape warns of danger and may contain a word or words that specify the nature of the danger, such as ROCK, SNAG, FERRY CABLE, etc. A diamond shape with a cross means the area marked is prohibited and may contain explanatory words below it such as SWIM AREA, WATERFALL, RAPIDS, etc.

2. A circle marks a controlled area and normally contains explanatory words such as 5 MPH, NO WAKE, SKIN DIVERS ONLY, etc.

3. A square or rectangle gives information and normally contains place names, distances, or availability of supplies, etc.

## Using Ranges

A range consists of two aids to navigation positioned so that when they are viewed in line, you may be in safe water. The two components of a range are most often vertical rectangular panels painted in vertical stripes of contrasting colors. You will need to check your chart to determine the distance at which a particular range is valid. The extent of a range's limits normally will be delineated by one or more buoys or day beacons. In all cases, the rear marker of a range will be higher than its front marker. At a turn or bend in a channel, a single structure may support the rear marker for two ranges extending in differing directions. Ranges on the ICW are distinguished by a yellow band at the bottom of their front markers. Many ranges are also lighted. If lighted, the front and rear lights normally will be of the same color and may be white, green, or red, but will have differing rhythms. Many ranges now show an equal interval rear light and a quick-flashing front light. In some cases, range lights will be equipped with lenses that allow you to see their full intensity only when you are directly on the range line. If you deviate to either side of the range line, the light's intensity will lessen dramatically.

In running a range remember that if the alignment of the front and rear markers diverges, you must steer your vessel in the direction of the front (lower) marker to bring yourself back on course.

In situations in which it is impractical to install front and rear markers for a conventional range, the midpoint of channels is sometimes marked by a single directional light that shows a white light in a narrow horizontal band visible only if you are centered in the channel it marks. If you enter the channel from seaward and drift to the right of the channel's centerline, you will see a red light; if you drift to the left, you will see a green light.

The compass orientation of a range is sometimes marked on nautical charts, is always given in the description of it in the *Light Lists,* or can be derived from the chart's compass rose. In calm conditions, lining your vessel up precisely on a range line can allow you to check your compass's deviation. But be sure to include the variation and annual rate of increase or decrease given inside the compass rose on the chart of the area.

## BRIDGES

The regulations that govern operations at opening bridges over U.S. waterways are not part of the Inland Rules but are issued by the Coast Guard.

Don't request that a bridge be opened if you can pass under it simply by lowering your communications and navigation antennas. The regulations, in fact, provide penalties for vessel operators who cause unnecessary bridge openings because of "any nonstructural vessel appurtenance which is not essential to navigation or which is easily lowered." Many bridges also have clearance gauges which give the clearance beneath them at the time you arrive.

The basic rule is that as you approach within about half a mile of a bridge you wish to have opened, you must signal your request with one prolonged blast (of four to six seconds' duration) followed within three seconds by one short blast (of about one-second duration).

(While the whistle signal is preferred, the regulations also allow you to signal for the bridge to be opened with a bell, a shout, by any other device that can be heard clearly, or visually by raising and lowering a white flag vertically within clear view of the bridge tender. You may also request a bridge opening by calling the bridge tender on VHF radio, normally on channel 13. If you use channel 13, your radio should automatically reduce its output to 1 watt, and you should use your vessel's name but omit your radio call sign.)

Technically, if a closed bridge will be opened immediately, the tender is supposed to answer your whistle signal with the same signal: one prolonged blast followed by one short blast. (If a visual signal was used to request the openings, the tender may respond with the same visual signal. If several boats are in line and request an opening, the tender normally will respond only to the first signal.)

If a closed bridge will not be opened immediately, the tender is supposed to answer a request for opening by whistle signal with five short blasts. (If the request to open was made by visual means, the tender may respond by horizontally waving a red flag in daylight or a red lantern at night.) Also, when an open bridge is to be closed immediately, the tender is supposed to sound five short blasts which must be acknowledged by any vessel preparing to pass through with the same signal. If the vessel does not acknowledge the signal, the tender is supposed to sound the five short blasts signal until the vessel answers it with the same signal.

You are required to make the request-for-opening signal even though the bridge is already open or is opening for another vessel. If you do not receive an acknowledgment within thirty seconds, you may proceed to pass through.

If a bridge is operating on restricted operating hours, certain privileged craft such as government vessels and tugs with tows may request an opening with five short blasts. I've never been able to learn if, when a bridge on restricted operating hours is opened in such a situation, a recreational vessel may fall in behind the privileged vessel and pass through on the same opening. What I have done in such situations is to position my vessel about a hundred feet astern of the privileged vessel, which declares my intention to pass through, and as I approach the bridge, give the one prolonged, one short blast signal and plan to pass through unless I receive five short blasts in reply. I've always been able to pass through in such situations without incident but was never sure I was legal.

So much for what's supposed to happen. I've passed through literally thousands of bridges and cannot recall a single instance where the prescribed procedures have been followed. What usually happens is that as you approach a bridge you give the prolonged blast/short blast signal, take up station about a hundred yards off the bridge, and wait around to see what happens. Some bridge tenders could not be more considerate of vessel traffic; others seem to delight in seeing if they can get you steamed up. Lack of cooperation (let alone respect for the regulations) by bridge tenders is becoming an increasing problem for inland waterway cruisers, especially in such heavy traffic areas as the Northeast and south Florida. I think we cruisers should protest vehemently if our rights are not respected. I recognize that opening a bridge to let a lone boat through may well inconvenience dozens, even hundreds of motorists. But technically, if a bridge is not operating on published hours of restricted operations, those of us in boats have just as much right to have it opened as motorists have for it to remain closed. I have no problem with a reasonable delay of fifteen minutes or so in opening a bridge during rush hours. What I do object to is tenders who ignore a request-to-open signal simply because they are busy eating dinner or talking to someone on the telephone.

If you request the opening of a bridge not on restricted operating hours and the tender doesn't begin to open it fairly promptly, watch the vehicle traffic going over it. During rush hours, the tender may wait fifteen minutes or so to break the traffic, or he or she may wait until several boats line up to pass through before opening the bridge. If there is no heavy vehicle traffic using the bridge and the tender doesn't open it within about ten minutes, give the request to open signal again. If another ten minutes or so goes by and nothing happens, try to raise the bridge tender on VHF channel 13 or 16 and ask what's going on. If you receive no answer, give the signal a third time. If another ten minutes or so goes by and the bridge still doesn't open, log the date, time, and specifics of the incident and complain to the appropriate Coast Guard District Office.

Once you succeed in getting the bridge opened, pass through at no wake speed, watch the currents, which can be tricky around the base of the bridge's abutments, and watch your antennas. If vessels are passing through a single-opening bridge in both directions, vessels running with the current have the right-of-way.

## LOCKS

Well before you approach a lock that you plan to pass through, check your coast pilot or cruising guide for the appropriate "request to lock through" whistle signal and any restrictions or peculiarities in its operation. The whistle signal at most locks is now the same as for bridges—one prolonged blast followed by one short blast—and should be sounded when you are about half a mile away. Your signal should be answered by the lockmaster with the same signal but probably won't be in this country. Answering signals are commonly used in Canada. Most locks are now marked with red, yellow, and green lights much like street traffic lights. Red or flashing red lights normally mean to stay at least 300 feet away from the lock. Yellow lights normally mean to proceed toward the lock with caution. A green light means you are free to enter the lock at a "no wake" speed. If you have any questions about the proper procedures at a lock, try calling the lockmaster on VHF channel 13. If he doesn't answer, try channel 16, but manually reduce your radio's power output to 1 watt.

Well before you enter a lock, have your crew be prepared to put out stout fenders fore and aft to protect your vessel's topsides. In most locks in the U.S., the lockmaster will hand you bow and stern lines which are affixed to the lock walls. To be on the safe side, however, be sure your crew has your vessel's own dock lines ready at the bow and stern to pass to the lock master if they are not supplied. In most cases, the lockmaster will direct you to tie off to the side of the lock on which its lights are flashing. But there are locks where that is not the case, and other boats may already have filled all the space along the preferred side of the lock. For that reason, any time you approach a lock you should be ready to put out fenders and bow and stern lines on either side of your vessel. In a single-engine boat, if you have a choice, tie off port-side-to so your engine in reverse will walk your stern toward the lock wall rather than away from it.

Locks can be pretty nasty and will quickly soil your lines and fenders. Eventually the dirt, oil, and grease your lines and fenders collect will wind up on your vessel's decks and topsides. If your cruising plans call for you to transit locks frequently, you might want to save your good nylon dock lines by investing in a set of less expensive half-inch manilla lock lines you can afford to replace about once a year. You may also want to protect your fenders with covers you can remove and wash periodically or even cover them with heavy-duty plastic garbage bags.

As you approach the lock, station one line handler at the bow. If you are going to have to use your vessel's dock lines rather than lines affixed to the dock, the line handler should pass the loop end of the line to the lockmaster, then lead the standing part clear of the safety railings and secure it snugly to a bow cleat. If you are fortunate enough to have two line handlers aboard, place the second at the stern on the side of your vessel you plan to lay against the lock wall with a stern line similarly rigged. If only you and your mate are aboard, have your mate prepare the stern line, then rig the bow line as above and stand by it. Enter the lock slowly, pull up to a bollard or ring, and have your mate secure the bow, then go aft to secure the stern line while you hold position if necessary with your engines. Once your vessel is secured fore and aft, if necessary you can leave the helm to man one line while your mate handles the other.

The systems for tying off at locks vary widely.

Most locks with a water level change of six feet or so simply have fixed bollards on the top of their walls. In that case, both lines will have to be tended during the locking process and slack taken in or let out as your vessel is raised or lowered. To tie off in that situation using your own lines, have your crew double bow and stern lines around their respective bollards as we discussed in Chapter 1: With the line's eye secured over the appropriate deck cleat, lead its standing part under the safety railing, flip the standing part over the bollard on shore, and secure it around the same deck cleat that is securing the eye with a half- or S-turn preparatory to taking up or letting out slack. To help keep the line from fouling when it is released, it should be around the bollard "outside to inside," so it doesn't have to cross over itself, i.e.: on the starboard side, run the bow line around its bollard clockwise and the stern line around its bollard counterclockwise; reverse the process on the port side. In locking downstream, it's best not to cleat off a line that is secured around a fixed bollard on the lock wall; the water level could fall quickly and leave your boat dangling from the lock wall.

The locking procedure is far easier at locks that have mooring rings recessed into their walls that rise and fall with the change of water level. In a lock of that type, it's okay to cleat off lock lines since your vessel can't be trapped, but have a crew member standing within reach of them anyway to let them go in case anything unusual happens.

Once the water in the lock has risen or fallen to its new level and the lock doors have begun to open, wait for the lockmaster's signal before releasing your lines and proceeding out of the lock at no-wake speed. In most cases, the "all clear" signal will be communicated by a set of lights at the far end of the lock which will be red during the locking process and will change to green when it's safe for you to proceed.

## ENGINE ROOM CHECKS UNDERWAY

The best way to keep from having irritating or possibly dangerous difficulties with your boat's mechanical systems is to spot potential problems early and correct them before they become serious. The key to doing that is checking your engine room frequently while you are underway and following a consistent routine that ensures you don't overlook anything important. Based on the layout of your particular vessel's engine compartment, make yourself a list of items to check arranged in a logical sequence, post it down there along with a roll of paper towels and a flashlight in their own brackets, and refer to it until your routine becomes automatic.

When you are underway, you should check your engine room every three or four hours. I know it sounds juvenile, but every time I check an engine room underway, a phrase flits through my mind—Love Violets Because THey are Gay—which I developed years ago to remind me of the five things I need to check.

The L stands for leaks and comes first because leaks will alert you to potential problems with your engine(s), marine gear(s), or generator quicker than anything else. Leaks around fuel, oil, and coolant lines or hoses are easiest to spot, of course, if you keep your engine(s), marine gear casing(s), and generator—and the area immediately under them—spotless.

75

The *V* in my bit of doggerel stands for vibration. Again, spotting a bolt or hose clamp that is vibrating loose or an electric wire chafing against metal can allow you to correct a developing problem before it affects your vessel's operation.

The *B* stands for belts. A quick glance at all the engine belts and pulleys assures me all the systems they power are working smoothly or I need to take corrective action.

The *TH* in *TH*ey represents the vessel's through-hull fittings. A quick sweep of a flashlight beam over all through-hulls that are visible in the engine room lets me spot any that might be starting to crack or pull loose.

The *G* reminds me to compare the readings of mechanical pressure and temperature gauges on the engine with the readings I have been seeing on the electrical gauges at the helm and the vacuum gauges in the fuel line to alert me if the filters are clogging up and about to shut off my fuel supply.

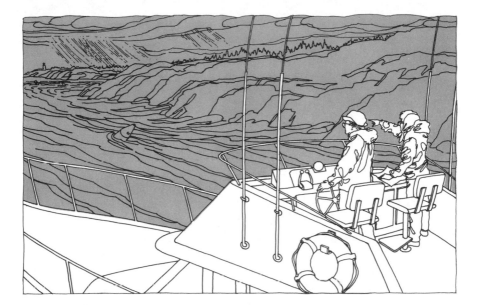

# CHAPTER 3

# SPECIAL RUNNING SITUATIONS

•　•　•

Not all your cruising is going to be between ten in the morning and four in the afternoon across a calm sea with a bright sun shining. Despite your best efforts in cruise planning and weather prognostication, times will come when you get caught in a storm and must negotiate an unfamiliar inlet to reach shelter or take your lumps offshore. At other times you'll probably find you must make an overnight run to reach your next anchorage, or fog will roll in along your course and you'll have to grope your way through the muck.

The keys to handling those special running situations in safety and as much comfort as possible are properly rigging your vessel to deal with any situation you are likely to encounter and making sure you know what you should do as conditions change.

## HEAVY WEATHER HANDLING

If you are in open water and see thunder clouds building along your intended course or weather broadcasts are forecasting severe weather for your vicinity, don't wait for conditions to get serious before you start taking them into account. Most experienced skippers of power cruising boats in the 40- to 60-foot range begin to become concerned about the weather when winds get up to around 30 knots and waves begin to approach 8 feet. Those are conditions that warrant a Small Craft Advisory: winds up to 33 knots (38 mph). If you find conditions approaching that magnitude and weather reports indicate they are likely to worsen, go ahead and prepare your vessel and crew to handle severe weather as safely as possible. Close and dog all hatches and portlights, stow or lash down loose gear, and rig jack lines to enable you and your crew to move fore and aft on deck safely using safety harnesses. If you don't actually put on your life jacket, at least make sure it's handy and order your crew to do likewise. Also make sure your safety harnesses are accessible and allow no crew member to go on deck without wearing one and securing it to the jack lines.

Next, you need to decide fairly quickly whether you are going to try to head for more protected waters or will continue on your course.

If you are in an exposed bay or wide river and are inclined to run for cover, check your chart for the nearest land mass you can put between yourself and the oncoming storm. Unless a well-sheltered cove or harbor lies to leeward and you can reach it easily before the storm's leading edge hits, it's generally wiser to seek protection to windward, which will keep you from having to deal with a lee shore.

If you are offshore on a coastwise passage, you'll probably have to run an inlet to reach protected waters. If that's the case, major factors in your decision will be whether you can run the inlet you intend to use before the storm's leading edge arrives over it and whether the inlet can be run in adverse conditions. If the answer to both those questions is yes, it's usually wise to head inshore. But bear in mind that a front's most violent weather is likely to be on its leading edge, waters are rougher inshore than offshore because shallow water compacts and magnifies wave force, and many inlets are extremely dangerous in adverse conditions, particularly at low tide.

## Inlet Running

Running an unfamiliar inlet with the weather kicking up is quite likely to provide one of the toughest tests of your ability as a competent skipper. Before you get to the inlet itself, gather all the information about it you can to help you plan your entry. This is where you'll be glad you paid that few dollars for a coast pilot. If you don't have the applicable volume aboard, check any cruising guides for the area you do have aboard that might give you valuable information about the inlet's buoyage or lighting system, any ranges that will help you enter on the proper course, tidal currents that can set you off course, and shoals that you'll have to avoid.

If you don't have any of these materials aboard, call the Coast Guard on VHF channel 16 and be prepared to switch to a working channel to ask their advice. If for any reason you can't reach the Coast Guard, try the dockmaster at any marina facility near the inlet or put out a call on VHF channel 16 for "any vessel local to _____ Inlet," then switch to a working channel and ask for their suggestions. If you're lucky, you'll find a knowledgeable local captain planning to run the inlet right in front of you, and you can follow him in. Do not, however, follow just any boat into an inlet you're concerned about. Its skipper may know no more about running it than you do, and you both may wind up on the rocks.

If the information you read or hear indicates that in adverse weather you should run the inlet only with local knowledge, check your charts to see if there is an all-weather inlet further up or down the coast you can enter in greater safety. If you're off the south Florida coast, for instance, and plan to run into either South Lake Worth or Boca Raton Inlet and aren't thoroughly familiar with them, you'd be much better off to divert north to Lake Worth Inlet or south to Port Everglades, both of which are deep, all-weather inlets used by large commercial vessels.

If you must run a dubious inlet in heavy weather, the next step is to pick your time. The best time to run deep-water inlets is on a flood tide; the best time to enter a shallow inlet is at high slack water. The worst time to enter a deep-water inlet is on the ebb when the outflowing tide is opposing incoming wind and waves; the worst time to run a shallow-water inlet is low tide. If necessary, hang offshore a few hours until conditions are the least hazardous.

Let's take a worst-case scenario in which you must run a shallow, shoaling inlet without a written commentary or local knowledge to guide you, only your chart.

First, study your chart carefully to glean every bit of information about the inlet it provides. Make certain you understand the pattern of buoys, lights, or daymarks you are about to encounter and fix their details firmly in your mind. Once you get into the inlet, you will be so busy handling your boat you may not have time to even glance at the chart, much less go over it in detail. Check the chart to see if the entry is marked by a range which will be indicated by a dotted line through a front and rear marker installed either on shore or in the water. Under the stress of running an inlet in adverse conditions, even running a forward range can be confusing. Remember that in order to correct your course, you steer in the direction of the front marker.

While you're studying the chart, lay out a compass course for your entry, but realize you may have to deviate from it if recent storms have caused the inlet's bottom to shift or the Coast Guard to relocate its aids to navigation. If the inlet is not marked by a range, extend your course ashore and see if you can pick out any landmarks you can use to judge your position relative to the channel's centerline.

Once you've gone over your chart carefully, make a couple of circles off the inlet's entrance and study its pattern of waves from your flying bridge to finalize your plan for running in. Breaking waves indicate shoaling, so plan your course to keep your vessel over the calmest water you see, even though it may not be in the exact center of the indicated channel. If waves are breaking across the full width of the channel entrance, it is blocked by a bar. If you must run the entrance anyway, make certain you do so only at high tide to give yourself the best chance of clearing the shallowest water. Also study the waves running into the inlet to note their direction and see if you can discern a pattern. Waves rarely enter an inlet exactly perpendicular to it. If they are running across it at an oblique angle right to left, for example, be aware that you are going to have to steer somewhat to the right of your planned course to keep them from setting you toward the channel's port side.

Once you've decided on your basic strategy for running the inlet, the specific tactics you adopt will depend on the type of vessel you are operating.

In a planing-hull vessel that can run in at a speed at least equal to the speed of the waves, time your dash to coincide with the smallest wave in the series you've divined and run in on its back. Use power to maintain a position about a third of the way back from the wave's crest, increasing power to keep from slipping too far back, which can allow the wave coming up behind you to poop your stern, or reducing power to keep from getting ahead of the wave you are riding, which could drive your bow into the base of the wave ahead and possibly cause you to pitchpole—i.e., turn end for end.

If yours is a displacement-hull vessel or a semidisplacement vessel without enough power to get it up on plane, you probably won't be able to keep up with a single wave and will have to let successive waves pass under your keel while you concentrate on keeping your vessel centered over deep water and her stern squarely before the waves coming up behind you. The one thing you absolutely must avoid is a broach, which can roll you over.

In either type of vessel, the water will be rushing under your keel at a speed greater than your vessel's speed through the water. In that case, you must be aware that your rudder will actually operate opposite to the way it does under normal conditions when water is rushing across it fore-to-aft. You will actually have to turn the wheel in the direction you want your stern to go, not the direction you want your bow to go as you would normally. No amount of textbook learning can teach you how to handle your vessel under those conditions; it can only be learned by experience. My best suggestion is that you be alert to the possibility of this situation developing and "steer by the stern" rather than by the bow.

If you have twin engines, you can best keep your vessel centered over deep water by alternately increasing and decreasing power on your engines. If your bow starts to veer left of your intended course, for instance, increase the power on your port engine to bring the bow back to starboard. In extreme cases where the waves catch your vessel's stern and start to slew it into a broach, you may have to increase power on the windward engine and actually throw the leeward engine in reverse to bring her stern back square to the seas.

In all this maneuvering, don't allow yourself to concentrate so single-mindedly on keeping your vessel's stern square to the approaching waves that you lose sight of your position relative to the channel itself. Keep your eye on the channel buoys, range markers, or other reference points you have picked out ashore to make certain you are not being carried out of the channel.

## Heavy Weather Handling

If you can't reach an inlet leading to safe harbor before the storm's leading edge arrives, or if the inlet is dangerous to run in adverse weather, generally you will be better off to remain in deep water until conditions moderate. The wave action in deep water is likely to be less violent than closer inshore, and you are likely to encounter big rolling waves that stay together rather than more dangerous short, choppy waves with breaking tops.

If you decide to ride the weather out at sea, your next decision is whether to attempt to maintain your course or bear off. In winds of about 30 to 40 knots and waves 8 to 15 feet, your vessel will ride most comfortably downwind. Before running off, make certain you have plenty of room to leeward. Once you've committed to the maneuver, keep your vessel running as squarely as possible before wind and seas, and be constantly alert to the possibility of a broach. In conditions of this magnitude, generally you can keep a twin-screw power cruiser dead before the wind using a combination of the wheel and the throttles. On a single-screw vessel, streaming a long, heavy warp, a drogue, or a storm anchor from the stern will help keep the stern into the wind and the bow pointed directly downwind to help you avoid a broach.

As winds build over about 40 knots and waves pile up over about 15 feet, the tops of the waves will start to break and sea foam will be blown in well-defined streaks. In these conditions, the danger of a broach may make continuing downwind impossible and require you to put your vessel's head to wind. During the turn you must make to accomplish that, her beam will be exposed to the storm's full fury and she will be at her most vulnerable. There are several special techniques you can employ to make that turn as quickly and safely as possible:

First, the longer you wait to make the turn, the worse it will be. As soon as you experience significant difficulty keeping your vessel's bow pointed dead downwind, go ahead and make plans to turn. Postponing the maneuver will only make it more difficult.

Second, keep your cool. Scuba divers have a rule: Plan your dive, and dive your plan. Yachtsmen about to turn head-to-weather in storm conditions should have a similar rule: Plan your turn, and turn your plan. Once you have your turn mapped out, follow your intentions through cleanly and smoothly. An instant's panic or hesitation could be disastrous.

Time your turn carefully. According to some oceanographers, waves tend to travel in a series of seven, with every seventh wave tending to be smaller than the others and the period between it and the wave behind it tending to be longer. That rule is not absolute, but in planning your turn, observe the waves passing under your vessel and see if you can divine which in their series tends to be the smallest and has the longest period between it and the wave following. Plan to make your turn as soon as the crest of that smallest wave has passed under your vessel's keel.

You want to make as much of your turn as possible on the back of that smallest wave so that once you are into the trough behind it, your vessel is properly positioned to meet the next wave rushing toward you. Ideally, to reduce the likelihood of burying your bow into the base of that oncoming wave, it's best to meet it at an angle of about 15 degrees off the bow.

If the period between waves is so short you cannot possibly make the complete turn on the back of a single wave, bear off about 20 degrees as you are lifted on the wave's face, then complete your turn once its crest has passed beneath you.

In a single-engine vessel, about all you can do to get your vessel through the turn as quickly as possible is to put your wheel over hard to windward and increase engine rpm. With a twin-screw vessel, you can use its engines to even greater advantage. In a planing-hull motor yacht, you can normally accomplish the turn quickly by leaving both engines in forward gear, increasing their power slightly, and turning the wheel sharply to windward. With a full-displacement vessel, you may find it necessary to put the windward engine in reverse (while leaving the leeward engine in forward gear), then increase rpms on both engines to swing her bow around quickly (Fig. 3.1).

In any of the three types of vessels, particularly the planing-hull motor yacht, just be sure you don't apply too much power. You could drive your vessel down the back of the wave you are riding so rapidly that you bury her bow in the base of the oncoming wave.

Once you are successful in getting your vessel's head to weather, she probably will ride most comfortably if you continue to take oncoming waves at about 15 degrees off the bow rather than from dead ahead. Just be alert to the danger that an especially large wave could knock her so far off her track that her beam is exposed to the full force of the storm.

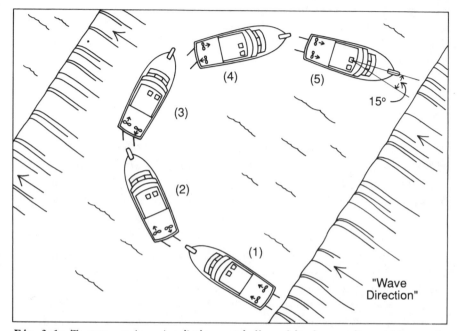

***Fig. 3.1:*** *To turn a twin-engine displacement-hull vessel head-to-weather quickly, put the helm fully over in the direction of the turn and reverse the engine toward the inside of the turn (2, 3, and 4). As the bow approaches the oncoming wave, shift the reversed engine back to forward and straighten the helm (5) to meet the wave at an angle of about 15 degrees.*

In extreme weather (winds over about 50 knots and waves over about 20 feet), don't worry about making forward progress but concentrate on simply maintaining headway. A powerboat caught in extreme weather without headway eventually will lie with her beam to wind and waves. Lying in this position, she will be extremely vulnerable to structural damage because she's likely to present a significant profile against which the wind can exert its capsizing force; she probably lacks a significant keel or ballast to help keep her upright; and she may have vast expanses of salon glass which can be caved in by the force of green water crashing into them.

In the Northern Hemisphere, if the severe weather headed your way is a tropical depression, tropical storm, or hurricane (or, in the North Pacific, a typhoon), its counterclockwise circular motion creates a "dangerous semicircle" in the half of the storm to the right of its forward track in which the storm's forward movement intensifies its winds. You should therefore, if possible, steer your vessel toward the storm's left half where conditions will be at least slightly less severe.

# NIGHT RUNNING

Night running in rivers or inland channels like the Intracoastal Waterway or the Inside Passage to Alaska is not something you want to do if you can avoid it. Navigating at night and reading the nature and intention of other vessels you might encounter from the lights they show is tough enough, but the greatest danger is striking debris in the water, which you may not be able to see regardless of how sharp a lookout you keep.

Nevertheless, in extensive cruising there simply will be times when you will not be able to cover the total distance between ports or anchorages along your planned route in daylight and will have to run at night. The best possible situation is to plan both your departure and your arrival in daylight and confine your night running to open water. If that is not practical, it's best to plan to depart in darkness so you arrive at your destination in daylight. If your destination is a shallow-water anchorage or poorly marked inlet in the tropics, try to plan your arrival no earlier than about ten in the morning and no later than about four in the afternoon, when the sun is high enough in the sky for you to read the bottom.

Ideally your nighttime departure will be down a clearly marked channel and into open water. If you must negotiate a poorly marked inland channel in darkness to reach open water, try to check it out beforehand in daylight and note any obstacles you must avoid.

In preparing for an overnight run, make certain you can keep your helm station dark to protect your night vision and have a red light available by which to read your charts. Get your normal vessel checks out of the way by late afternoon, eat a light dinner, and get to bed early to get as much rest as possible. Before retiring, prepare whatever beverages and food the night watch will require and make sure it is easily accessible to the helm.

Most skippers find they can handle a single night's run of eight to ten hours alone with no problem, assuming they have someone to relieve them at daylight. If you are a cruising couple who normally have only the two of you aboard and your cruising itinerary calls for a run of more than one night in succession, try to invite family or friends along for that leg of the voyage to help out with the helm during daylight hours. Assuming that on the run you will be in open water and your vessel is equipped with a good autopilot, the helmsperson's main responsibility is that of watching for debris in the water or other vessels intersecting your course and monitoring the engine instruments. You should be able to set the vessel up and give even an inexperienced person enough instruction on what to do if he or she has a problem and under what circumstances to call you, to allow him or her to run the vessel for a few hours in daylight while you get a quick nap. If you don't feel comfortable actually going below and stretching out on your bunk, sleeping in the pilothouse or the salon will keep you almost instantly available if anything happens.

## Watch Systems

For more than one overnight run in succession, you'll need to set up a watch system so you always have a rested person at the helm. The ideal length of a watch is four hours during the day and two hours at night. If you have an even number of qualified persons to stand watch, setting up an odd number of watches will ensure that the watches rotate. If you have an odd number of watch standers, rotate the schedule by setting up an even number of watches.

If you have the luxury of four people aboard with whom you are comfortable trusting the helm, your watch system (using the twenty-four-hour clock) might look something like this:

| Watch Hours: | 0800 1200 | 1200 1600 | 1600 2000 | 2000 2200 | 2200 2400 | 2400 0200 | 0200 0400 | 0400 0600 | 0600 0800 |
|---|---|---|---|---|---|---|---|---|---|

Watch
Standers:

| | 0800–1200 | 1200–1600 | 1600–2000 | 2000–2200 | 2200–2400 | 2400–0200 | 0200–0400 | 0400–0600 | 0600–0800 |
|---|---|---|---|---|---|---|---|---|---|
| 1st Night | A | B | C | D | A | B | C | D | A |
| 2nd Night | B | C | D | A | B | C | D | A | B |
| 3rd Night | C | D | A | B | C | D | A | B | C |
| 4th Night | D | A | B | C | D | A | B | C | D |

With three qualified watch standers, you might use this kind of schedule:

86

| Watch Hours: | 0800 1200 | 1200 1600 | 1600 2000 | 2000 2400 | 2400 0200 | 0200 0400 | 0400 0600 | 0600 0800 |
|---|---|---|---|---|---|---|---|---|

Watch
Standers:

| | | | | | | | | |
|---|---|---|---|---|---|---|---|---|
| 1st Night | A | B | C | A | B | C | A | B |
| 2nd Night | C | A | B | C | A | B | C | A |
| 3rd Night | B | C | A | B | C | A | B | C |

Each of the above watch systems will give every crew member at least one eight-hour period in each twenty-four hours for a sound rest.

With only two qualified watch standers aboard, the ideal of four-hour daylight and two-hour nighttime watches is impractical since it does not provide the off watch with a sufficient period of uninterrupted sleep. In that case, it works better to arrange a schedule with six-hour daylight and four-hour night watches which look like this:

| Watch Hours: | 0800 1400 | 1400 2000 | 2000 2400 | 2400 0400 | 0400 0800 |
|---|---|---|---|---|---|

Watch
Standers:

| | | | | | |
|---|---|---|---|---|---|
| 1st Night | A | B | A | B | A |
| 2nd Night | B | A | B | A | B |

If you have only yourself and your mate aboard and prefer to stand the entire night watch yourself, you might construct a schedule (in which you stand watch A) like this:

| Watch Hours: | 1000 1400 | 1400 2000 | 2000 0600 | 0600 1000 |
|---|---|---|---|---|

| Watch Standers: | A | B | A | B |
|---|---|---|---|---|

## Navigation Lights Aboard Your Vessel

Check carefully to see that the navigation lights aboard your cruiser meet the requirements for a vessel of its type and size both underway and at anchor as spelled out in the 1980 U.S. Inland Navigation Rules. You should not simply assume its lights are in compliance—especially if it was built in the U.S. prior to the adoption of the 1980 Rules or was built abroad—because the 1980 act changed certain lighting provisions that had existed up to that time. Showing the proper lights in the manner required by the Rules is not simply a matter of complying with the law. It is even more important that your lights correctly indicate to other vessels you may encounter at night the type of vessel you are and how you are proceeding. Check all your navigation lights for proper operation at least once a month and before embarking on any night runs.

You are required to show your vessel's navigation lights any time you are underway between sunset and sunrise or in conditions of reduced visibility.

## Navigation Lights on Other Vessels

Many cruising skippers pay little or no attention to the lighting regulations for other vessels, with the argument that they are not operating a commercial towing service or engaged in trawling operations and therefore don't need to understand the lighting regulations for vessels engaged in those kinds of activities. They do so at their peril. If you are to conduct your vessel properly during the night runs which eventually become part of extended cruising, the lights aboard other vessels you encounter may well provide your only clue as to their type and intentions and what, if anything, you need to do in respect to them. Therefore it is vital that you to be able to recognize their meaning.

Lighting regulations can be confusing and, unless you make night runs frequently, are easily forgotten. My best advice is to read the section on navigation lights in *Chapman* (which includes illustrations in color) to make certain you understand the basics, then refresh your memory just prior to setting out on any night runs. At night, vessels can have a way of looming up in front of you quickly, and if you don't already have the light rules pretty well in mind, you may not have time to dig out a copy of the regulations in time to figure out whether that pattern of lights approaching you is a vessel operating under sail alone to which you must yield the right of way or is a tug pulling a tow as long as a freight train behind it.

## OPERATING IN REDUCED VISIBILITY

Fog or a heavy downpour of rain can quickly cut your visibility to next to nothing. Any time you can't see at least a half-mile ahead of your vessel's bow, the first thing to do is turn on your vessel's navigation lights. The second thing to do is slow down. Simply pulling back your throttles to about half your normal cruising speed provides an extra margin of safety by increasing the time you have to react if another vessel or an obstacle unexpectedly looms up in your path. If the weather is really thick and your cruiser is not equipped with radar, you may be safer to lay-to (proceed with little or no way on) or anchor in a special anchorage area or outside normal traffic lanes until visibility improves.

The third thing to do is keep an even sharper lookout than you would when visibility is good. If your vessel has both upper and lower helm stations but no radar, in conditions of reduced visibility it's safer to operate from the flying bridge, where you can better see and hear other vessels in your vicinity, rather than from an enclosed wheelhouse or salon, where your vision is likely to be restricted and sounds are likely to be muffled.

When visibility is restricted, your ears can become even more important than your eyes in telling you what is happening around you. That's particularly the case if visibility is limited and you must maneuver your vessel in a crowded waterway. Periodically bring your engines down to idle to quiet them and listen carefully for at least two minutes for any vessels that might be about to cross your course. Also do that just before you make any significant course change. Be especially observant of what may be happening downwind of your position, since even a fairly mild breeze will carry sound away from you.

In reduced visibility it becomes even more important than usual to know exactly where you are and what lies ahead. Make certain your chart of the area you are cruising is within easy reach of the helm and use all the means of electronic navigation at your disposal to keep your running plots of your position accurate and current. Use your Loran receiver, for instance, to maintain a continual update of your position. If you're inshore, set your radar on its quarter- or half-mile scale to keep track of the markers along your route and check each one off on the chart as you go by it. Also keep a sharp eye on its display for any other vessels that might be in your vicinity. The owner of that vessel racing through a downpour toward the inlet entrance at 20 knots might not be as careful as you are and may have no idea you're in his path.

If your vessel's hull is of wood or fiberglass, it presents almost no target to the radar units aboard other vessels in your vicinity. You should have a good radar reflector aboard, and in limited visibility conditions it should be rigged at your vessel's highest point.

## Sound Signals

The best way to meet the sound signaling requirements of the Inland Rules is to equip your vessel with a combined loud hailer/automatic foghorn, which will sound the appropriate signals at the touch of a switch. It will also effectively amplify many sounds within about a hundred yards of your vessel. But bear in mind that its cone-shaped horn is directional. Depending on how you have its horn(s) positioned, it may do little to amplify sounds coming from astern or off your beam to either side.

As in meeting, crossing, and overtaking situations, the basic sound signals for operating in reduced visibility are short and prolonged horn blasts. In conditions of restricted visibility, you are required to make sound signals appropriate to your type and size of vessel and its operational status at intervals not exceeding two minutes. Within that interval:

- If you are making way, you are required to sound one prolonged blast.

- If you are underway but stopped (not at anchor) and making no way through the water, you must sound two prolonged blasts separated by an interval of about two seconds.

- If you are towing another vessel, if your vessel for some reason is not under command, or if you are restricted in your ability to maneuver, you must sound one prolonged blast followed by two short blasts.

- If your vessel is manned and being towed, you must sound one prolonged blast and three short blasts. If possible, this signal should be sounded immediately after the signal of the towing vessel.

90

If you find you must maneuver through a high-traffic area in reduced visibility, one way you can alert other vessels to your presence is to transmit over VHF channel 16: "Security (pronounced SECURI-TAY), Security, Security, channel thirteen," then switch to channel 13 and (at your radio's 1-watt power output), repeat SECURITAY three times, then transmit your position in relation to the area's aids to navigation, your course, and your speed. In extremely crowded conditions such as in a major harbor when visibility is less than about a quarter of a mile, it's advisable to repeat this procedure about every ten to fifteen minutes.

The rules also specify when and how you must use your ship's bell when you are anchored outside the "special anchorage areas" identified on nautical charts, are aground, are towing another vessel, or are being towed. The interval of signals in these instances is not to exceed one minute. Within that interval:

- If your vessel is 39.4 feet to 328.1 feet (100 meters) in length and is anchored outside a special anchorage area, you must ring your bell rapidly for five seconds. If your vessel is less than 39.4 feet in length, you must make "some other efficient sound signal") for five seconds. Either size vessel may also give a three-blast signal to warn of its position and the possibility of collision with an approaching vessel: one short, one prolonged, one short.

- If your vessel is less than 65.6 ft. in length and you are anchored in a special anchorage area, you are not required to make sound signals.

- If you are aground, you must sound the signal of a vessel at anchor and in addition give three separate and distinct strokes on the bell immediately before and after the rapid ringing of the bell.

## TENDER TOWING

There are almost certain to be times in your cruising when the weather is calm, you plan to move your main vessel to a new anchorage only a short distance away, and the move will be executed during daylight hours. You may well decide that under those circumstances you would rather tow your tender than go to the trouble of hoisting it aboard, then have to put it back into the water.

There is nothing wrong with towing a tender if you make proper preparations beforehand and take a few sensible precautions. First, the precautions:

Don't tow your tender at night. If it breaks loose, you'll have the devil of a time trying to find it. By daylight it can be miles away. Even when towing your tender during the day, check it every half-hour or so.

In a displacement vessel, the speed at which you tow your tender shouldn't be a problem. If yours is a planing- or semidisplacement-hull boat, you'll find your tender will tow best if your speed does not exceed 10–12 knots.

A tender under tow is more likely to be flipped over than to be lost altogether. Before you tow your tender, remove loose items such as fishing tackle, snorkeling gear, and the like and stow them aboard your main vessel.

In the unlikely event your tender's outboard is of five horsepower or less, it's best to remove it from the tender and stow it securely in your main vessel's cockpit. With a larger outboard that is too heavy to remove from the tender easily, leave it on the tender but tilt it all the way forward, lock it into that position, and lash it down so it can't slam from side to side.

The distance behind your main vessel at which you tow your tender will depend on whether it has a hard or soft bottom. A hard tender or an inflatable tender with a rigid fiberglass bottom will tow best on the back side of your main vessel's second stern wave. As you approach your destination with this kind of a towing rig, be sure to send someone aft to pull the tender up on short scope and fend it off. If you don't, the tender is almost certain to slam into your main vessel's stern, and its towing line will probably wind up wrapped around your props. Because of its lightness and its lack of a significant keel, the best position in which to tow an inflatable tender with a soft bottom is on the back of the first stern wave your main vessel creates rather than the second. With the tender pulled up that short, it has less room to slew about.

## If You Have an Accident

If you have an accident with your vessel that results in significant damage to property or personal injury that you feel may involve your insurance company, there are several things you should do to make certain you comply with your insurance policy's terms.

One is to protect your vessel from further damage. Most standard yacht policies will pay for towing and assistance if it is necessary to keep the yacht from suffering further damage.

If other people are involved in the incident, be sure to get their full names and addresses. Also try to get the same information on anyone who witnessed the incident.

Contact your insurance agent to inform him or her of the problem as soon as possible. If the incident involves damage to your vessel, try to have your insurer's adjuster authorize any needed repairs before the work is begun. If that proves impossible, try to take pictures of the damage before it is repaired. Again, if possible, get estimates on repairing the damage from two or three reputable boat yards. An even better idea, if possible, is to hire a local marine surveyor to check the damage and give you a complete report. Be certain to get detailed receipts of any expenses you incur.

## CHAPTER 4

# ARRIVING AT THE DOCK

• • •

So far, so good. You've gotten away from your home dock without doing serious damage to your boat or anyone else's, you've run narrow channels without going around, you've done everything by the book in right-of-way situations, correctly identified and read the intentions of other vessels at night from their lights, run a couple of inlets, handled a variety of bridges and locks, a bit of fog, and some heavy weather. Now it's time to put into a marina for fuel or an overnight stop. As you bring your vessel alongside or put her in a slip, you'd like to keep everyone on shore from realizing this is your first time at this sort of thing with this particular boat and convince them you've been handling her in tight quarters for years.

## Dealing with Dock Masters

Dock masters come in two distinct varieties: Some are eminently courteous and can't seem to do enough to help; others are surly ogres who apparently neither need nor want your business and seem to take pride in developing contrariness into an art form. The kind of dock master you wind up dealing with at the end of a long day's run can often be determined by how you initiate the relationship.

A little common courtesy can go a long way toward making the relationship pleasant. If you are planning an overnight stay at a marina, call the dock master on VHF channel 16 about half an hour before your planned arrival time and be prepared to switch to a proper noncommercial working channel. Most marinas will use channel 68 as a working channel; a few will use channels 9, 69, or 71. On this first call, simply give your vessel's length and ask if they can accommodate you overnight. If the answer is yes, most dock masters will ask you to call them back when you are about a mile from their facility. It's appropriate in that initial call to mention fueling or berthing requirements and any special immediate needs you might have, but be aware that he or she is probably busy and don't tie up a lot of time or the working channel asking about such things as restaurants or local transportation in the area. Tend to those matters once you're ashore. If you treat dock masters like human beings rather than servants, they can be fantastically helpful. If you are rude or overly demanding, they can make your cruising experience far more difficult than it needs to be.

On your second call just as you are approaching the marina, ask whether you'll be laying alongside a pier or entering a slip, and ask on which side you should rig your fenders so your mate can prepare them.

Once you're at the marina, if the dock master gives you docking instructions, you're probably better off trying to follow them. He should know a lot more about the effects of wind and current around his docks than you do.

Having said all that, the advice of Fred Edwards, a retired naval captain who with his wife Alice cruised the Mediterranean for five years, is "Don't let dock masters intimidate you. If you don't like the slip offered because of size or exposure, insist on a different one. If the weather starts to turn sour, move. If you are being set down on the pier because the dock master

95

put you on the exposed side, don't assume a siege mentality and just start doubling up lines and adding more fenders. Move! Go to the other side of the pier, to a marina farther up the creek, or anchor out in a more sheltered area."

I heartily agree. Once you are directed to a docking space, look it over carefully to see what's going to be involved in getting your boat into it and what conditions are going to be like in it if the weather turns nasty. If you see that strong currents are running across the space, that you are going to be constantly exposed to the wakes of passing boats, or that you are going to be pinned hard against its pilings with predictable winds from a particular quarter, don't hesitate to voice your concerns and ask what else he has available.

If you make a slip reservation with a marina several days in advance, find out if there is a cutoff time beyond which they will give it to someone else if you haven't arrived. If you find weather or a change in your plans prevents you from keeping a reservation, call and cancel. Nothing makes a dock master see red quicker than holding a slip for you, then having you fail to show up. He's not only lost the revenue from your dockage, he's probably got five potential customers anchored out, staring at the last empty slip in the marina you didn't arrive to take, and cussing him for not giving it to them. Further, dock masters have long memories. If you treat one that way, then turn up the next day or months later expecting him to have a slip waiting for you, don't be surprised if he tells you all his space is taken or sticks you way out on the end of the fuel dock where you'll take a proper bashing from the wakes of passing boats.

## Docking Alongside a Pier

If docking involves nothing more than coming alongside a pier where you have plenty of room and no significant wind or current to worry about, one major factor in determining how best to make your approach will be the torque of your propeller(s).

If you're not familiar with prop torque, think of a propeller as a wheel beneath your boat which actually touches the bottom. Most single-engine powerboats have a right-handed propeller which kicks the vessel's stern to starboard when going ahead and to port when going astern. Since your boat doesn't have brakes, you know you're going to have to shift into reverse to stop it. If yours is a single-screw boat, shifting into reverse will kick your stern to port. Therefore, approach the dock port-side-to whenever possible so that when you shift into reverse your propeller's torque will kick your stern in toward the dock rather than away from it.

If your boat has twin engines, you have a bit more choice. The propellers on most twin-engine boats turn outboard (i.e., their tops turn toward the outside of the vessel). That means the starboard propeller normally will be right-handed and the port propeller will be left-handed. If you want to approach the dock port-side-to, stop your boat by putting your port engine in neutral and shifting only your starboard engine into reverse so the torque of its propeller will pull your stern to port. (If you shift both engines into reverse, the counterforces of the propellers will cancel each other and leave your stern away from the dock.) If you want to approach starboard-side-to, simply reverse the process and the left-handed prop on your port engine in reverse will help pull your stern to starboard.

## Rigging Dock Lines

Before making your approach, alert your mate which side you plan to tie up on so she or he can rig bow and stern lines at their respective cleats on that side of the vessel. A dock line for a cruising powerboat should be of at least ⅝-inch hard-laid nylon, and its eye should be about three feet in diameter. To rig a dock line for instant use, the mate should uncoil it, lay its tail over the safety railings, lead the tail outboard-to-inboard through the chock or hawsepipe and cleat it off, then lay the remaining line on deck with the eye on top of the coils. When the mate picks up the coils and throws the eye over a piling or passes it to someone on shore, the line will not be fouled in the safety lines and will already be in the chock or hawsepipe. Once the eye is secured ashore, the mate can uncleat the tail, take up slack in the line as necessary, then control tension on it or cleat it off.

## Rigging Fenders

If the pier you are approaching has pilings that extend at least a foot above your deck level, it's easiest to simply let your vessel's rub rail come up against them and rig any necessary fenders when you tie up. But if you are approaching a pier that doesn't have pilings, the mate will need to rig vertical fenders at an appropriate height along the hull to protect its topsides. One fender should be rigged at the turn of the vessel's bow and a second about a foot forward of the transom.

## Getting Dock Lines Ashore

Under ideal conditions of no wind and no current, you can simply pull your boat up to the dock and let your mate calmly drop bow and stern lines over an appropriate piling or dock cleat and tie them off on deck. Even under adverse conditions—with a bit of practice—your mate should be able to consistently throw the eye of a dock line over a piling up to about 10 feet away by using the technique described in Fig. 4.1.

You'll avoid a lot of confusion and potential problems if your mate—whenever possible—places the eyes of your dock lines over a dock's pilings or cleats personally rather than passing them to someone on the dock. If someone on the dock offers to take your lines, instruct your mate always to give them the eye end of the line—never the tail—and indicate exactly the piling or the dock cleat around which the eye is to be placed both verbally and by pointing at it. There are a host of reasons for doing that. By passing the eye ashore and controlling the tail on deck, the mate controls the line's length, which can be critical in your docking maneuvers. If the mate puts the eye over a deck cleat on the vessel and passes the tail ashore, the person on the dock controls the line's length and may tie your bow in so tight you don't have room to swing your stern in, or leave so much slack in it your vessel strikes another vessel in front of you. Also, the helpful soul may or may not know how to tie the tail off securely. If he or she doesn't and you put a strain on the line to help you maneuver to the dock, it can pull loose, which can leave you with no line to work against and possibly injure someone on board your boat or on the dock.

## "Walking" to a Dock

If wind and current are not a factor but you need to squeeze into a fairly narrow space at a dock, you can "walk" a twin-screw boat into it sideways the same way we discussed "walking" out of a narrow space in Chapter 1.

Unfortunately the times you can tie up to a dock under the ideal conditions of no wind, no current, and plenty of room are likely to be in the minority, so let's complicate matters a bit.

*Problem:* You need to take on fuel for your 40-foot cruiser but the only space left at the fuel dock is about a 50-foot slot between two other boats, which are already tied up alongside. How are you going to get your boat into that narrow space without a lot of bumping and grinding?

The answer to that question is going to be primarily dependent on the strength and direction of the wind and current around the dock, so before you go charging into this kind of a tight maneuvering situation and create general havoc, lay off about 50 yards and size up the situation.

First, glance around to see if the maneuver you intend is likely to interfere with other vessels already in your vicinity or approaching it.

Next, look around to determine how wind and current are likely to act on your vessel relative to the direction you want it to go. Study the flags or pennants on your own vessel, on nearby vessels, or on shore to determine the wind's direction and approximate velocity. A 10-knot breeze, for instance, will hold a pennant or flag out from its staff, but it will not be taut nor will it snap. If pennants or flags are taut and snapping, the wind is above 15 knots. Water building up on one side of a dock's pilings will tell you the direction in which the current is flowing and its approximate strength. A good rule of thumb is that each knot of current builds up about a half-inch of water on the side of the piling it is striking.

If wind and current are both striking your vessel from the same angle, you must add their effects together to determine their combined effect on its movement. If wind and current are striking your vessel from different angles, you need to mentally compute their relative angles and strengths to figure out their net effect. Your answer to that equation will vary greatly depending on your vessel's draft and windage. Current, for instance, is likely to have greater effect on a deep-keel, full-displacement vessel than will wind, but wind is likely to have a greater effect than current on a planing-hull motor yacht with a great deal of windage, fairly shallow draft, and little if any keel.

Once you have determined the angle and velocity of wind and current, you are in a position to decide how much force you must apply—and in what direction—to counter their effects and dock your vessel with a minimum of fuss.

In planning your maneuver, make whatever combination of wind and current you find yourself facing work for you rather than against you. Since any boat handles far more effectively in forward gear than in reverse,

**Fig. 4.1:** *To prepare to lasso a piling, make sure the dock line's tail is coiled loosely at your feet, extend the eye to its maximum diameter, and lay the standing part of the line along the eye (A); toss the eye toward the piling and allow the standing part to run lightly through your hand (B); once the eye is over the piling, make sure the tail leads underneath the safety railing before wrapping it around a deck cleat to take up tension (C).*

**A**

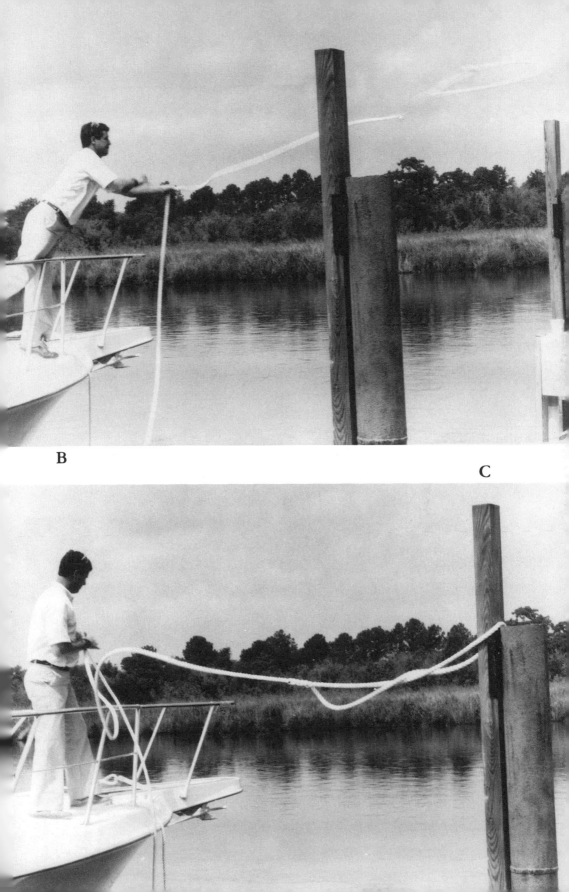

B

C

the best way to do that is to keep wind and current on your bow rather than on your stern whenever possible. That point is easily illustrated by a story: One evening I was placidly tied up to a face dock on a narrow stretch of the ICW at Great Bridge, Virginia, enjoying the children's hour on the fantail when a 40-foot southbound sailboat came boiling down the canal under power with a 4-knot current and about 12 knots of wind on its stern. The skipper decided to tie up in the 45-foot space just off my stern and made his approach bow-on. As the current continued to propel him forward despite a great deal of full-astern racing of his engine and screaming at his lovely young mate to "grab something," he very nearly managed to stick his bow pulpit into my hors d'oeuvres. I fended him off and watched in horror as he made a complete circle for a second try with the same result. With a lot of frantic arm-waving, I suggested he maneuver into the space against the current and wind instead of with them at his back. Once he did so, he was able to gently nose his boat to the dock without mishap.

**A**

*Fig. 4.2: In maneuvering a twin-engine cruiser to a dock with a bow spring, have your mate maintain tension on the spring (A) while you go forward on the engine toward the dock and reverse the engine away from the dock (B). The mate should maintain sufficient tension on the spring to keep you off any vessels tied up ahead, but leave enough slack in the line to allow you to bring the stern to the dock (C).*

If wind and/or current are running parallel to the dock, you don't have much of a problem. Head your bow into them and go forward with just enough way on to offset them until you are opposite the space you want to enter. With your helm, allow your bow to fall off just a bit toward the dock, then bring your wheel back to amidships. The wind and current will straighten you back up so that you are parallel to the dock but a few feet closer to it. Keep repeating this maneuver until you are close enough to the dock for your mate to get a bow line over a piling or cleat and take up the slack. Once it is holding your bow in place, you can use your engine and helm to bring you fully alongside.

## Maneuvering to a Dock with a Bow Line

Let's assume, however, that wind and current are not parallel to the dock but running at an angle to it. Suppose, for example, a 10- to 15-knot offshore breeze is blowing, and a knot or so of current is running out from the dock.

B                                    C

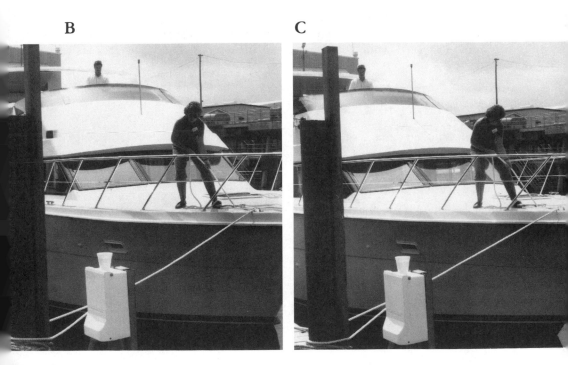

Let's further suppose that the dock has pilings and you want to lie starboard-side-to. With a twin-engine boat, the easiest way to come alongside is by using a simple bow line (Fig. 4.2). Bear in mind that you want, if possible, to keep your boat's bow into wind and current whenever possible. To counter the forces involved, approach the open space bow-on, aiming at the left end of the slip. While you maintain position a few feet off the dock, have your mate go forward to the bow pulpit, throw the eye of a dock line over the piling at the left end of the space you are trying to enter, secure its standing end around the starboard bow cleat with a half-turn or S-turn, and take up tension on its tail. Caution your mate not to pull the bow in too tightly to the dock as doing that will prevent you from swinging the stern in. Turn your wheel sharply to port, shift your starboard engine into neutral, and your port engine into reverse. The port engine in reverse will allow you to back against the bow line and its propeller torque will pull your stern to starboard. If you need a bit of extra push to get your stern over toward the dock, briefly kick your starboard engine in and out of forward gear, but be careful not to get too close to the boat tied up ahead of you. As your stern swings in, instruct your mate to take in slack on the bow line to bring your bow toward the pier.

Once you are tightly alongside, hold the boat in position with its port engine in reverse while your mate cleats off the bow line, then goes aft to rig a stern line.

## Maneuvering to a Dock with Spring Lines

With a single-engine boat, the best way to come alongside a pier in a tight docking situation against offshore wind and/or current is to use an after bow spring. This technique can also be useful with a twin-engine boat if wind and/or current off the dock are especially strong.

To dock port-side-to using an after bow spring (Fig. 4.3), approach the open space bow-on but aim at its center point and have your mate throw the eye of a dock line over a piling as close to the center of the space as possible, secure its standing end around the port bow cleat with a half-turn or S-turn, and take up tension on its tail. Again, caution your mate not to pull the boat in too tightly to the dock as doing that will prevent you from swinging the stern in. The mate should take in only enough slack to make sure your bow doesn't strike the boat tied up ahead of you. Turn your wheel sharply to starboard and go ahead slowly. As you turn, the line off your

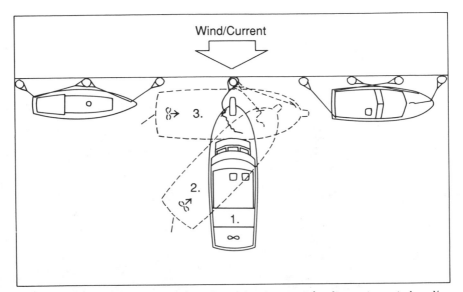

**Fig. 4.3:** *In maneuvering a single-engine cruiser into a tight slip against wind and/or current, approach a piling in the center of the slip bow-on to allow your mate to get a bow spring over it (1); while the mate maintains sufficient tension on the spring to keep you off the vessel tied in the slip ahead, lay your helm fully over in the direction of your turn and go ahead slowly (2) until your stern rests against the dock (3).*

bow becomes an after bow spring. Instruct your mate either to take in slack to keep your bow from striking the vessel ahead or to let out slack to make sure your stern clears the vessel behind you. With your boat's bow held fast by the after bow spring, the discharge current of your propeller will bring your boat's stern to the dock to rest against its rub rail.

Docking with an after bow spring is even easier if your vessel is equipped with forward spring cleats (Fig. 4.4).

Now suppose you're faced with the same fuel dock situation except that the 15-knot breeze is blowing onshore and the current is running toward the dock. In this instance, let's again assume you want to lie starboard-side-

**A**

Fig. 4.4: *Pivoting a vessel alongside a dock is even easier if it is equipped with spring cleats about a third of the way down its length (A) and the eye of the spring is looped over a piling at the stern end of the slip (B).*

**B**

to. If you try to approach the dock bow-on, the wind and current will slam your vessel into the dock and earn you some grimaces from the dock master and your fellow skippers. To solve the problem (Fig. 4.5), have your mate rig a stout fender horizontally right at the point of your starboard quarter. Pull opposite the space you wish to enter and bring your bow into wind and current, which will point your stern toward the dock. Keep your engine(s) in forward gear and ticking over just enough to almost counter the force of the wind and the current. Steer with the helm as you allow your vessel to drift back toward the right side of the open slip until the fender on your starboard quarter touches the dock. As that happens, keep your helm to port and maintain enough throttle to resist most of the force of the wind and tide trying to slam your bow down on the dock. If you have the right touch, your bow will be driven down on the dock with only a modest force and come to rest against a dock piling. The wind and current will keep your boat pinned against the dock while your mate rigs bow, stern, and spring lines.

## Tying Up at a Dock

In a typical docking situation, you'll need four dock lines to hold your vessel securely (Fig. 4.6): a bow line which leads from your bow cleat to a piling or dock cleat forward of the bow; an after bow spring which leads aft from your forward spring cleat to a piling or cleat about two-thirds down your vessel's length; a forward quarter spring which leads forward from the quarter spring cleat to a piling or cleat about a third of the way aft from your vessel's bow; and a stern line which leads aft from your stern cleat to a piling or cleat aft of the stern. Your stern line (Fig. 4.7) will be more effective if you run it from the outboard cleat at your stern rather than from the stern cleat closest to the dock.

Always tie your boat to the dock, not the dock to your boat. That's a way of saying you should always secure the eye of your dock lines to a piling or dock cleat and cleat the tail off to a deck cleat on your vessel—not vice-versa. If you are aboard—as you are likely to be most of the time—and anything happens to require you to move your vessel quickly, you have only to go on deck, cast your lines off, and get your vessel underway. When you cast them off, they will either fall back on the dock or into the water and sink to the bottom; in either case, they won't be a danger to your props. If the bights are secured aboard your vessel and the tails to the dock, you must

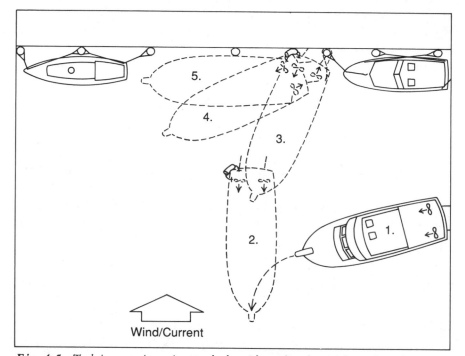

*Fig. 4.5:* To bring a twin-engine vessel alongside starboard-to with wind and/or current setting onto the dock (1), rig a stout fender on the point of your vessel's stern which will lay against the dock (2) and keep just enough way on to allow wind and current to carry you straight back toward the right end of the slip. As your stern contacts the dock (3), turn your helm fully into the current and shift your outboard engine into reverse to help counter the current's tendency to drive you down onto the dock (4 and 5).

108

*Fig. 4.6:* Tying a vessel securely alongside involves a bow line and fore and aft spring lines. Note the fenders hung vertically.

*Fig. 4.7:* In this situation, the stern line led from the side of the transom away from the dock is much more effective than if it were attached on the side of the transom toward the dock.

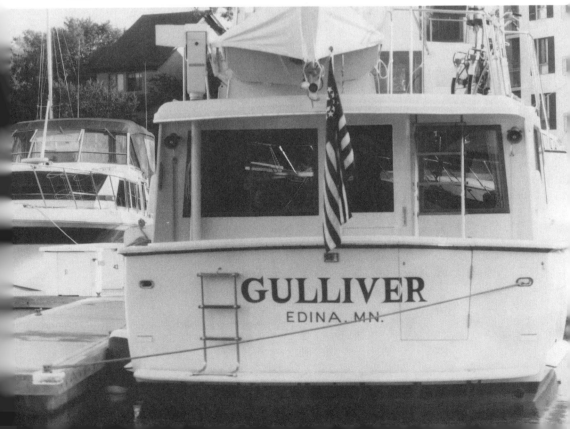

climb down on the dock to release them, then come back aboard and get them out of the water. If you try to pull way from the dock with them trailing in the water, at least one of them is almost certain to get fouled in your prop(s).

Some cruisers don't like to have the tail of a dock line cleated off on deck because they don't want the extra line in their way. Some try to make a neat Flemish coil with the tail, but then stumble over it every time they go on deck. If they stay at a dock or in a slip a few days, the coil traps all manner of dirt underneath it and discolors their deck. A better solution to the problem is simply to coil the excess line and hang it from the railings as detailed in Fig. 4.8.

A few other tricks you might find helpful: If the eye of your dock line is not big enough to go over an especially large-diameter piling, reach through the eye, grab the line's standing part, and pull it through to form a slip knot. If you put the eye of your dock line around a piling above the dock line of another vessel already tied to it, the lower line cannot be released without first removing yours. To eliminate that problem, run the bight of your line up through the bight of the other dock line before looping it over the piling. Then either dock line can be removed without disturbing the other. In areas of extreme tidal range, if the angle of a dock line from your vessel's deck to a piling is downward, a rising tide and the motion of your vessel could pull it loose. To prevent a problem, doubling the bight on itself will hold the bight securely in place.

## Cleating Off Dock Lines

In the course of your cruising life, you'll cleat off lines thousands of times so you want to develop a quick, foolproof technique that you can execute virtually automatically. The method I've found most efficient is presented in Fig. 4.9. Cleating off a line this way has a number of advantages: By standing at the end of the cleat opposite to the direction of the strain, you can quickly run the line under the horn closest to you, across the top of it, and under the horn farthest from you, which puts you in the optimal position to take a strain on the line if necessary. You can also execute the entire maneuver without moving your feet. A line cleated off in this manner will not bind against itself, no matter how much strain is put on it, and will be easy to uncleat.

Unless you're preparing for a storm, there's no need to make more than

*Fig. 4.8:* When tied in a slip, you can stow the tail of a dock line neatly by coiling and wrapping it, leading the tail up through the top of the coil, then securing it around the safety railing with two half-hitches.

two turns of line over a cleat—that will simply take more time to uncleat.

A number of cruising powerboats have hawseholes in the transom or the cockpit covering boards and some—particularly those built in the Far East—have hawseholes in their topsides just above deck level. Throughout the following discussion, any time we discuss securing a dock line to a deck cleat, we will assume that before being cleated off, the eye or the tail of the dock line will first be led outside to inside through the hawsehole if the vessel is equipped with them.

111

**A**

*Fig. 4.9:* To properly cleat off a line, bring it under the horn of the cleat opposite to the direction of the strain (A); take it across the back of the cleat and under the opposite horn in the reverse direction (B); repeat the process in reverse (C); form a loop by flipping the line under itself and drop the loop over the horn in the direction of the strain (D); then give the tail a good pull to set it (E).

**B**

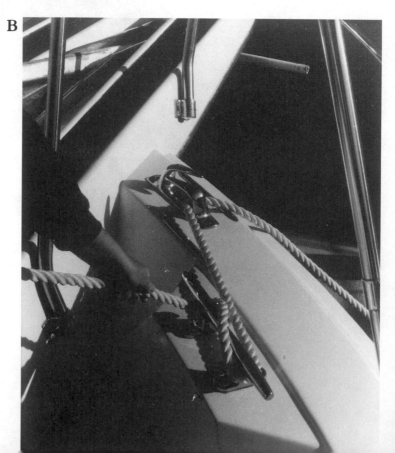

C

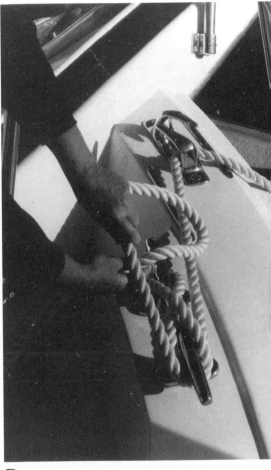

D

E

## Using Fenders and Fenderboards

When lying alongside a face pier that does not have pilings, the most effective protection for your hull is fenders hung vertically from your deck railings (see Fig. 4.10). One should be placed just aft of the turn of your vessel's bow and the other should be two or three feet forward from your stern.

For lying alongside a pier that does have pilings, the best protection is provided by fenderboards between your vessel's hull and one piling just aft of the turn of your vessel's bow and a second two or three feet forward of your stern. If you are tied up to a pier with pilings, you can use cylindrical fenders rigged horizontally to protect your topsides (Fig. 4.10), but they are harder to keep properly positioned than fenderboards.

## Entering a Slip

If an overnight stop at a marina involves putting your boat into a slip, one major factor that will help you decide whether it's best to enter it bow-on or stern-first will be the direction of wind and current. Remember our earlier dictum that your boat will maneuver much better going into wind and current than with either of them on your stern. If the wind and current are from the direction of the slip, you'll find it easier to enter the slip bow-first; if they're setting toward the slip, you'll find it easier to back in.

Another consideration is how you carry your dinghy. If it's carried on deck, it's not a factor. If it's mounted on davits aft, you'll probably want to enter the slip bow-first regardless of the direction of wind and current. If you're towing your dinghy and plan to enter a slip bow-first, secure the dinghy up snugly to your vessel's stern before you start maneuvering into the slip so its painter won't get fouled in your prop(s). If you must enter a slip stern-first, stop off at the fuel dock and tie the dinghy off there before you enter the slip, then walk over and retrieve it.

## Entering Bow-First

Since entering a slip bow-first is a bit less complicated than going in stern-first, we'll cover that first. To keep matters simple at the outset, let's assume that the slip you want to enter faces south and the wind is either nonexistent or coming straight out of the north.

*Fig. 4.10:* *When using a round fender against a piling, tie it just below your vessel's rub rail, tie off the line through its center to widely spaced stanchions so its angle with the fender is shallow rather than perpendicular, and keep your spring lines taut to limit your boat's movement fore-and-aft as much as possible.*

The outboard end of a slip normally is defined by two pilings in the water. As you enter the slip bow-first you need to get the bight of a dock line over each of them to hold your stern. That's not much of a problem if you have two line handlers aboard. Post both of them—each with a dock line in hand—at the bow pulpit, then ease up to the starboard piling and let one crew loop the eye of his or her dock line over it. While that crew member is walking the tail of his or her line along the starboard side-deck to the cockpit (keeping it outside of the railings, of course), ease your bow over to the port piling and let the second crew member loop the eye of his or her line over that piling and walk its tail along the port side-deck to the cockpit. As each crew member reaches the cockpit, he should cross with his line to the opposite corner of the cockpit, take a quick half- or S-turn around the stern cleat, and pull in slack as you slowly motor forward. As the stern pulls even with the pilings, he should let out the stern lines as necessary. Once your bow is about five feet from the dock, have the crew cleat off the stern lines fully. One crew member can then step ashore to receive the bow lines and loop their eyes over dock cleats at the corners of the slip while the other crew member stands by at the bow to cleat their tails off on deck.

This maneuver gets a little more involved if you have only yourself and your mate aboard. In that event, before you attempt to enter the slip (assuming you are entering bow-first), have your mate ready port and starboard bow lines on the foredeck as suggested above, then ready stern lines this way: On the starboard side, loop the eye of a dock line that is at least as long as your vessel over the starboard bow cleat; lead the tail of the dock line outside the safety railing, along the starboard side of the hull, across the cockpit, then cleat it off to the port stern cleat. The line should not be pulled tight but should be cleated off with just about a foot of slack in it. Repeat the process in reverse to rig the port stern line and cleat it off to the starboard stern cleat. (The reason for cleating off the tails of the stern lines to cleats on opposite sides of the cockpit is so that they will be properly crossed once they are deployed.)

With your bow lines ready and your stern lines rigged, post your mate on the bow, ease up to the slip's starboard piling, and have your mate release the eye of the starboard stern line from the bow cleat and loop it over the piling. (That line should then lead from the slip's starboard piling and across your cockpit to your vessel's port stern cleat.) Nudge your bow over to the port piling and repeat the process. Have your mate go to the cockpit and uncleat the tails of both stern lines but keep a grip on them. As you motor slowly into the slip, the mate should take up slack in both lines to keep them out of the props. Once the stern passes the pilings, the mate will need to let both lines out until you call out that the bow is about five feet from the dock. You can then hold the boat in position while the mate cleats off both stern lines. With the stern secure, the mate should go to the bow. If someone is on shore to assist, the mate can simply throw them the eye end of the bow lines and cleat their tails off to the bow cleats. If no one is on the dock to take your bow lines and the mate cannot toss the eye of the bow lines over cleats on the dock, he or she will have to toss the coils ashore, go ashore to place the eyes of the lines over their respective cleats, then come back aboard to cleat them off.

## Backing Down

Since entering a slip stern-first involves operating your boat in reverse, let's talk a bit about that before we get into the specifics of getting into the slip.

Many inexperienced cruising skippers attempt to back their boats just as they would back an automobile—facing forward at the helm and looking over their shoulder to see where the stern is going. Watch an experienced sportfishing charter captain put his vessel in a slip. In almost every case he will face astern and operate the gears and throttles in reverse, which affords him much better visibility.

If you back your vessel facing astern, don't forget that the starboard side of your vessel is still starboard and port is still port.

Backing a twin-screw boat while facing aft can be greatly simplified by repositioning the gear and throttle levers. Most twin-screw boats come out of the factory with both gear levers paired on the starboard side of the helm and both throttles paired on the port side. Many professional captains re-arrange the linkage to put port and starboard gears and throttles on their respective sides of the helm with the throttles inboard and the gears outboard. This allows them to dock a boat facing astern with no confusion as to which levers operate which engine.

If your vessel has a single engine, any time you operate it in reverse, don't forget to take your propeller's torque into account. Since the torque of its right-handed prop going in reverse will pull your stern to port, aim for a point slightly to starboard of where you want the stern to go and let the propeller's torque help you back in a straight line, or offset the torque with a little right rudder. Only experience will tell you how much right rudder you'll need to offset propeller torque on your particular boat. If your stern gets too far to port, you may have to kick the engine into forward gear with a quick in-out motion. Due to your vessel's sternward momentum, you won't actually go forward, but the propeller's right-handed torque going ahead will help swing your stern to starboard.

If your boat has twin engines, think of it as pivoting around a stake running through its center, remember that its engines are off to their respective sides of the vessel's centerline, and think of an engine in reverse as pulling the stern rather than pushing it. These ideas together may help you visualize that when you are at the helm facing aft, the starboard engine in reverse will pull the stern to port both because of its propeller's torque and because it is to starboard of the vessel's centerline. For the same reason, the port engine in reverse will pull the stern to starboard.

Novice skippers of twin-engine boats often find the combination of a helm, two gears, and two throttles a bit intimidating when they are trying to back down. If you are fairly new to maneuvering a twin-screw boat in reverse, you will find backing down easier if you center your helm and set both throttles at about 600 rpm, then back up simply by shifting the throttles between reverse and neutral as required to bring the boat to the dock. If you want the stern to swing to starboard, for instance, leave the starboard engine in neutral and use only the port engine in reverse to bring it around. Conversely, if you want the stern to swing to port, leave the port engine in neutral and shift the starboard engine into reverse to put the boat's transom where you want it.

## Entering a Slip Stern-First

With wind and/or current either minimal or setting directly into the slip, backing into it and handling your dock lines is basically the reverse of the procedures for entering bow-first, with a few minor differences. In rigging the bow lines for deployment, the mate should lead their tails outside the safety lines and cleat them off to their respective bow chocks, then lead their eyes aft and temporarily secure them to a stern cleat on their respective sides of the vessel without crossing them. As you back your stern toward the slip's outboard pilings, the mate should be in the cockpit and place the eye of each bow line over the piling on its side of the slip. If you have a second line handler aboard, he or she can go forward to control tension on the bow lines as you continue to back into the slip. If only you and your mate are aboard, however, the mate need not go back to the bow to control the bow lines as they are well forward and not in danger of getting fouled in your props. As your stern approaches the dock, the mate can either toss the eyes of the stern lines to someone on shore or step onto the dock to place them over a cleat herself, but they should be crossed. Once the stern is secured, you can hold position in the slip with your engine(s) while the mate goes to the foredeck to take up the slack in the bow lines and tie them off to the bow cleats.

118

## Mediterranean Moor

In many parts of the world you'll find the normal way of tying up is stern-first to a quay with an anchor out. Since this "Mediterranean moor" is a hybrid of both anchoring and tying up, and setting the anchor properly is the most critical part, we'll cover it in the next chapter.

# CHAPTER 5

# ANCHORING

• • •

If you cruise very long, you're bound to find yourself swinging serenely on the hook in a lovely cove late one afternoon when a cruising couple will pull in and go through an anchoring routine worthy of the Keystone Kops. Papa will be on the flying bridge waving frantically and yelling orders to his frazzled and frustrated spouse, who will be scurrying wildly around the foredeck. Their anchor will not hold on the first try, and probably not on the second. A few choice expletives will waft across the water. If they finally get an anchor to hold, it probably will be in a position where their vessel's swinging room makes it a danger to yours, and you will have to up anchor and move to a safer location. As the tide rises or the wind gets up in the night, you'll probably hear them repeat the whole routine about two or three o'clock in the morning because they failed to set the anchor properly, were using the wrong kind of anchor or rode, or failed to put out sufficient scope to allow for changing conditions. "I'm amazed," says Brig Pemberton, who with his wife, Louise, has voyaged the length of the Caribbean several times in their power cruiser *Victoire,* "that some people who have cruised for years never learn from their mistakes and go through this completely unnecessary farce every time they try to anchor their vessel."

## Ground Tackle

In *Stapleton's Powerboat Bible,* I deal in detail with the selection of a proper ground tackle setup for extended powerboat cruising. If you haven't read that material and taken at least some of its recommendations into account, I hope you'll do so. In this chapter we'll assume you've equipped your cruiser with the ground tackle she ought to have: a properly sized primary anchor on about 300 feet of all-chain rode; a stout secondary anchor on 300 feet of three-strand hard-twist nylon line and six fathoms of chain; and a heavy-duty electric anchor windlass. At least your primary anchor, and preferably your secondary anchor as well, will be mounted on rollers set into a strong bow pulpit. In the lazaret you'll also have a stern anchor one size smaller than your secondary anchor with its own 150-foot rode of ½-inch or ⅝-inch three-strand twist, hard-laid nylon fitted with about four fathoms of ⁵⁄₁₆-inch chain. In order to set the proper scope, lengths should be marked on both your primary and secondary anchor rodes at about 25-foot intervals. The best system I've found for making a chain rode is to coat individual links with distinctive colors of an industrial grade metal paint: white for 25 feet, blue for 50 feet, and red for 100 feet. Use combinations of those colors to mark the chain in 25-foot increments: white and blue for 75 feet, red and white for 125 feet, etc. For three-strand twist nylon line rode, you can buy kits of yellow plastic markers at 25-foot increments which can be worked into the line's strands.

In addition to this primary ground tackle, you should also have some key anchoring accessories aboard. If you use an all-chain primary rode, for instance, you should have an anchoring bridle to offset the problem of heavy surge causing the chain to grate across the bow roller with a most annoying sound, especially to anyone trying to sleep in the bow stateroom. If you don't use such a bridle, you must install forward of the windlass's wildcat a chain stopper or devil's claw into which you should hook your chain while you are anchored in order to take the strain off the windlass. You might also want to consider rigging a short-scope bridle of the type Frank Glindmeier installed aboard *Summer Wind* for anchoring in congested harbors where limited swinging room might prevent him from putting out as much scope of chain as he would like. He had a boat yard install a stout eye bolt in *Summer Wind*'s stem just above the waterline which looked almost like the trailering eye on a smaller boat. He then eye-spliced a 15-foot length of ¾-inch nylon line into the eye with a thimble and eye-spliced a strong snapshackle to the bitter end. Until this rig was needed, the bitter end was tied off to the bow pulpit. When he was anchored on short scope in a crowded harbor, he would untie the bitter end of the rig from the bow pulpit, attach the snapshackle to the chain, then pay out sufficient chain to let the nylon take the strain. "The roller in *Summer Wind*'s bow pulpit was eight feet off the water," Frank explains. "With this rig we were able to substantially lower the anchor chain's point of attachment to the boat. If we anchored in eight feet of water, the rig cut the amount of scope we needed in half." You might also want to carry along an old but airtight truck tire inner tube and a bicycle pump. Any time you must venture into head seas, cram the inner tube into your chain locker and inflate it to prevent your chain rode from being tossed around inside its locker like spaghetti in a bowl and becoming tangled.

With those assumptions in mind, our objective here will be to help you select a good anchorage and devise a technique to get the right anchor down in the right place on the first try, tie it off securely, then relax for the children's hour and enjoy a chuckle or two as you watch others in the harbor go through their anchoring antics.

## Selecting an Anchorage

In choosing an overnight anchorage, look for the optimum combination of good holding ground, protection form the wind, and water that's shallow enough to let you put out a safe scope of rode with a reasonable amount of chain or line, yet deep enough to leave several feet of water under your keel at low water.

In the tropics, you should start deciding where you will anchor by midafternoon. Except in major harbors, aids to navigation are likely to be few and far between. To get into a suitable anchorage you'll probably have to depend on reading the bottom, as detailed in Chapter 6: Coastal Piloting and Eyeball Navigation, and you want to do that while the sun is still high enough in the sky to give you good visibility. Even in more northerly latitudes, plan to reach your selected anchorage a couple of hours before sunset. If the spot you've selected turns out to have a bottom of solid granite or one with the consistency of oatmeal, you may need an extra hour or so of daylight to select an alternate.

The place to start looking for an anchorage in any waters is your chart, which will tell you of any areas you must avoid such as channels or restricted areas. Your chart will also list any special anchorage areas, which will be marked on the chart with a magenta line and, in some cases, by yellow buoys in the water.

As you consider a possible bay or cove as an anchorage for the night, see what the chart says about the makeup of its bottom. Look for areas of hard sand, a mixture of mud and sand, or mixed mud and clay. Light grass is okay if your anchor's flukes can dig through it down to hard bottom, but stay away from heavy grass. Your anchor may get an initial bite in it and give you a false sense of security; with the first really heavy wind, the grass can pull loose at the roots and leave you adrift. If you have a choice, stay away from areas marked soft mud or rocky. Never anchor over live coral, as your anchor and rode can destroy beauty it took nature thousands of years to develop. If you carry a lead line aboard, soundings with it with a bit of hard wax or grease on the end can tell you a lot about the bottom's consistency and potential holding ability.

Cruising guides can also be a valuable source of information about anchorages in the areas they cover and usually will include sailing directions to enter them along with the location of reefs or shoals to avoid or ranges on shore you can use to make sure you keep your vessel over deep water.

In general you want to put as much land mass between your boat and the prevailing winds as possible, but beware of snugging yourself too far up into a bay or cove without leaving yourself plenty of swinging room and making sure you won't be grounded at low tide. If the land area immediately to windward is high hills or mountains, put out plenty of scope and leave yourself plenty of room to leeward. A saddle between two hills or mountains can funnel wind into an anchorage at twice the speed of the ambient wind. If the wind increases sharply, air pressure can build up on the windward side of hills or mountains and suddenly spill over the top with incredible force. In Alaska these winds, which can reach velocities of 100 miles an hour or more, are called "williwaws." Australians call them by the especially apt name of "bullets."

In figuring the depth of water you'll have under your keel, remember that the water depths on charts list either "mean lower low water" or "mean low water" which are normal averages. At the new and full phases of the moon, spring tides can lower that figure by as much as 20 percent. Also, persistent high winds from certain quarters can drastically lower the mean water figures, so check your tide table for the area carefully and allow yourself all the leeway you can.

Once you've decided on the area in which you plan to anchor, a number of factors will influence exactly where in that general area you drop the hook. Be sure the entire 360-degree circle around your anchor through which your boat can swing as winds or currents shift is clear of obstacles. (That circle's diameter, of course, will be equal to twice the length of rode you plan to put out.) Dropping the anchor in one spot might put your boat in an ideal position as long as the wind stays out of the east, for instance, but make sure that you will still have plenty of room if the wind veers or backs to any other point of the compass.

If other boats are already anchored in the area, don't forget to allow for their swinging room as well. The two circles in which your respective vessels could swing around their anchors should be separated by at least a hundred yards, and two hundred is even better. Don't assume that if the wind or current shifts, all the boats in a particular anchorage will swing the same way. The speed with which different boats react to a shift and the angle at which they lay to wind or current can differ dramatically depending on their draft, the configuration of their bottom, and their windage.

## Anchoring Hand Signals

In anchoring with one person operating the boat's controls at the flying bridge helm and the other on the bow, spoken or shouted communications can become a problem, especially if there's a stiff wind blowing. To avoid confusion, work out a series of simple hand signals with your mate that allow the two of you to communicate clearly. The mate's hand held out horizontally at arm's length with its palm vertical, for instance, should indicate the direction in which the helmsperson is to steer (rather than the direction of an obstruction to avoid). A fist with the thumb pointed downward might be the helmsperson's instruction for the mate to release the anchor. A "thumbs up" might instruct the mate to retrieve the anchor with the windlass. A hand held palm forward like a traffic cop might mean "hold everything," and an "okay" sign from the mate with the thumb and forefinger making a circle might mean the anchor is secured and the helmsperson is clear to proceed.

## Anchoring Technique

When most yachtsmen anchor their vessels they approach the intended point of anchoring from downwind, then cut the power and let the boat drift toward the intended anchoring point until it loses all headway. After the vessel has come to a stop, they drop the anchor and pay out chain or rode as their boat drifts back downwind. Once the anchor digs into the bottom, they finish the job off by backing down to set it firmly.

Frank Glindmeier says he's figured out a better way. Frank and his wife, Lee, should know something about anchoring since they have racked up over 45,000 miles of cruising in a variety of boats. One voyage in their displacement-hull cruiser *Summer Wind,* for example, took them 18,000 miles from Florida to Glacier Bay, Alaska, and back, and another carried them around the entire eastern half of the United States. Given a choice, they prefer to swing on the hook rather than tie up to a dock. As a primary anchor on *Summer Wind,* a Hatteras 48 Long Range Cruiser, Frank mounted a 75-pound plow on the boat's bow pulpit and hooked it to 300 feet of ⅜-inch chain handled by a sturdy windlass.

"When we first started cruising on an earlier boat," Frank says, "we used the standard anchoring technique and found it worked about half the time. The other half of the time the anchor got fouled in the chain or rode and we drug it halfway across the anchorage before we could get it to take hold. I finally realized that when there was little wind to carry the boat astern, we were dropping the anchor, then dumping the chain right down on top of it which virtually guaranteed it a fifty-fifty chance of fouling. I figured there had to be a better way." The technique Frank developed works this way (Fig. 5.1):

Once he picks out an anchoring spot, Lee goes to the bow and prepares the anchor for deployment by removing any tie-downs used to make sure it doesn't break loose in a heavy sea, slacks off the tension on the windlass enough to release about a foot of chain, and kicks the anchor out on its rollers a bit to make sure it will fall free when the tension is fully released.

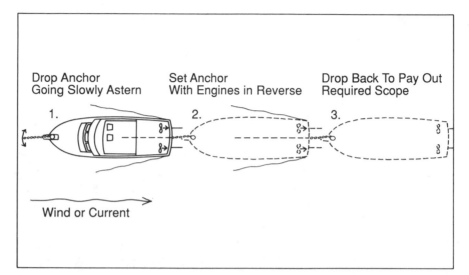

**Fig. 5.1:** *Dropping your anchor while going slowly astern (1) greatly reduces the likelihood of its fouling in its own chain. In setting an anchor with engines reversed (2), the rode should come fully taut and bearings on shoreside objects should indicate no vessel movement astern. In calculating anchoring scope (3), don't forget to include the height of your bow chock above the water's surface and any increase in water depth due to tide.*

Frank slowly approaches his intended anchoring spot in the usual manner from downwind, but deliberately passes over the spot at which he wants to drop the anchor. Once he is about fifty feet upwind of his target, he drops both engines into reverse and backs the boat down toward the spot with its engines just barely ticking over. As the center of the boat is about over the point he wants the anchor to rest, he gives Lee a simple "thumbs down" hand signal and she releases the tension on the windlass to let the anchor and chain run free.

Frank continues to back the boat down slowly as the chain pays out. When all the scope he wants is paid out, he signals Lee to tighten up the tension on the windlass. "Dropping the anchor while you are going slowly astern under power ensures that you string the chain out behind the anchor

126

rather than dumping it on top of the anchor which sharply reduces the chances of getting them tangled up," he says.

Once the windlass tension is down tight, the vessel's slight sternway sets the anchor. "I like to see the anchor chain bow-string-tight," Frank says. "That way I'm certain the anchor is well set and not likely to drag no matter how the wind or current turns the boat."

As you back down to set an anchor, take a bearing on two objects ashore that create a range to make certain you are staying in the same place. Once the catenary (sag) is out of the chain, a well-set anchor should hold your boat steady as a rock. If your bearing on the range ashore indicates you are still moving backward, or if you feel any shuddering, the anchor is still skipping along the bottom and trying to find a purchase. Once you are certain your anchor is well set, periodically check the bearing on the shoreside range you've selected to make certain your anchor isn't dragging.

## Anchoring Scope

Ask a cross section of yachtsmen to define the term "scope" and most will reply, "the ratio of an anchor rode's length to the depth of the water." Close, but no cigar. Under that definition, to achieve a 5:1 scope, the skipper of a 48-foot powerboat anchored in 8 feet of water would put out 40 feet of anchor rode. In fact, even if the water level in the anchorage doesn't rise, that is really a scope of only 2.5:1. If an incoming tide raises the water level in the anchorage, it's even less.

Here's why: The proper definition of scope is "the ratio of an anchor rode's length to the maximum distance from a vessel's bow chocks to the bottom."

That definition takes in two important differences: the tide range, and the height of the vessel's bow chocks above the water. In the example above, the vessel's bow chocks may well be 8 feet above the water which, in an 8-foot water depth, places them at least 16 feet above the bottom. That being the case, a scope of 5:1 would require 80 feet of anchor rode (8 + 8 × 5 = 80) rather than 40 feet. If an incoming tide increases the water's depth 2 feet, the bow chocks would be 18 feet above the bottom which would require 90 feet of rode (8 + 8 + 2 × 5 = 90) to achieve a 5:1 scope.

In computing scope, then, always remember to include the height of your vessel's bow chocks above the water plus the depth of the water at the

127

time you anchor (taken from your depthfinder) and any increase in the water's depth that can be caused by an incoming tide (as indicated by a tide chart for the area).

The minimum scope you should allow for overnight anchoring is a function of your boat's size and type, the strength of wind you're likely to experience, and the type of rode you are using. In even the lightest conditions of wind under 10 knots I'd recommend the skipper of a planing-hull powerboat under 50 feet using an all-chain rode put out a minimum scope of 3:1; for that same vessel using a combination chain-rope rode I'd increase that to 5:1. For a heavier semidisplacement or full-displacement vessel of that length in light winds, and for a planing-hull cruiser in winds to 20 knots, I'd recommend a minimum scope of 5:1 and 7:1 depending on the type of rode they were using. If winds are expected to be over 20 knots I'd increase scope on the planing-hull boat using a chain rode to 7:1 and with a chain-rope rode to 8:1. For a semidisplacement or full-displacement vessel in winds over 20 knots, with all-chain rode I'd increase the scope to 6:1 and with a rope-chain rode to 8:1. Any time the winds are expected to exceed 30 knots, put out all the rode of either type you have or can deploy without the danger of swinging into another vessel.

## Setting Two Bow Anchors

In extended cruising, you're likely to encounter a number of situations where a single anchor really won't hold your vessel securely or exactly where you want it, and you will need to set two anchors off the bow.

In situations where you have adequate swinging room, it's best to set an anchor about 22.5 degrees to either side of your vessel's centerline, which will leave about 45 degrees between them. That would be the case, for instance, any time the winds in the area of your anchorage are predicted to reach over about 30 knots. Setting two anchors in this fashion can also help reduce your boat's tendency (especially if it's a planing-hull motor yacht) to yaw or "skate" from one side of its anchor to the other in fairly high winds.

To create this kind of an anchoring setup (Fig. 5.2), it's best to deploy your secondary anchor first because its rope rode will be easier to handle and make your boat easier to handle while you set your primary anchor on its all-chain rode. Set your secondary anchor as suggested above, but when you drop it, note a pair of objects ashore that, when one is behind the other,

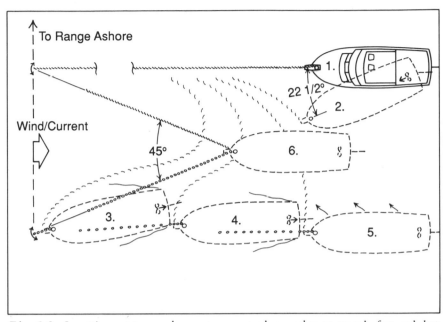

**To Range Ashore**

Wind/Current

22 1/2°

1.

2.

45°

6.

3.

4.

5.

*Fig. 5.2: In setting out two anchors, get your secondary anchor set securely first and drop back to an appropriate scope plus 10 percent (1), then power off at about 22½ degrees (2) until your secondary anchor is abeam, then set your primary anchor going slowly astern (3). Set your primary anchor well with reversed engines (4), fall back to the proper scope on your primary rode plus 10 percent (5), then take up slack on both rodes until the anchors lie off your bow at approximately a 45-degree angle (6).*

establish a line perpendicular to the wind and along which your secondary anchor lies. Fall back until you have paid out about 10 percent more of your secondary rode than is necessary to establish the scope appropriate to the conditions and set your secondary anchor well with your engine(s) in reverse. From that point, have your mate keep the secondary rode out of your props by taking up most of its slack with the windlass's capstan while you power off at 45 degrees to the wind. Go slightly past the line along which your secondary anchor lies, then shift into reverse, go astern slowly until you cross the line, and have the mate drop your primary anchor. Have the mate let out both rodes and fall back until you have paid out about 10 percent more of your primary rode than is necessary to establish the scope appropriate to the conditions. Have the mate leave the secondary rode slack and rig your anchor bridle or engage the devil's claw. Once the strain of the primary rode is off the windlass, set your primary anchor well with your engine(s) in reverse. As you power slowly in the direction of your secondary anchor, have the mate take up slack in the secondary rode with the windlass's capstan until the angle of each rode to your bow is approximately equal and the tension on both rodes is approximately the same. Those relationships will indicate your vessel is lying midway between the two anchors with the proper amount of scope paid out.

This arrangement works well so long as you get both anchors well set with at least a 45-degree angle between them. There is a variation on this theme called a "Bahamian moor," which involves anchors set to port and starboard off your bow at right angles to your vessel's centerline. In theory it is useful when you must anchor in a narrow channel where you are exposed to significant current or tide reversals. The idea is that as the tide reverses you will lie first to one anchor, then the other, with your bow merely pivoting around an essentially fixed position. The idea looks great in the neat boating magazine diagrams, but my experience has been that it seldom works out that way in fact. Even if you get this rig perfectly set, what usually happens is that your boat swings 'round and 'round in small circles until the two anchor rodes are so tightly twisted together it's almost impossible to separate them. If you should get your rodes into this kind of a tangle and have to move your vessel quickly, you'll be in real trouble.

In anything short of an approaching tropical storm or hurricane whose circular motion will create up to a 180-degree wind shift, my advice is to stay away from the Bahamian moor if at all possible. First, don't anchor in a tidal channel without sufficient swinging room if you can avoid it. If anchoring in such a place is unavoidable, bury a single good, heavy plow or Bruce anchor deeply on plenty of chain. In anything less than about 4 knots of current and 20 knots of wind, you will find that the chain dragging on even a bottom of hard-packed sand will take the strain off your vessel as it reverses direction and won't actually put strain on your anchor at all. Even if a heavy plow or Bruce anchor should pull loose as the angle of pull on them is reversed, their design makes it highly likely they will reset themselves as your vessel puts tension on them from the other direction.

## Stern Anchors

You may well encounter a situation, particularly with a planing-hull motor yacht, in which heavy winds cause your vessel to yaw or "skate" first to one side of a single anchor, then to the other. Even semidisplacement or full-displacement vessels can skate around their anchors if wind is pushing them in one direction and a strong tide or current is pushing them in another. As your vessel skates well off to one side, it can be struck nearly broadside by oncoming waves, which is not only quite uncomfortable but can be dangerous since the changing angle of tension on your anchor could pull it loose.

As noted above, setting a secondary anchor off the bow at 45 degrees to your primary anchor can be an antidote to skating, but even that may not provide the stability you need. In such a case, set a stern anchor. If only you and your mate are aboard: Set your primary anchor in the usual way but let out double the scope appropriate to the conditions, wait until your vessel is lying in line with the wind and/or current, and have your mate let a second anchor go over your stern. Power straight toward your primary anchor while you take up the slack in the primary rode with your flying bridge windlass switch and your mate pays out the stern anchor rode, being careful to keep it from becoming fouled in your prop(s). Once the appropriate amount of scope is paid out astern, have your mate cleat off the stern rode and set the stern anchor by going ahead against it with a brief burst of power. With the stern anchor well set, take in most of the slack on your bow anchor rode and lie to it while tension on the stern anchor rode keeps your stern from swinging off the wind.

## Anchor Watches

If you follow the suggestions above, you should have your boat so securely anchored that under normal circumstances you won't need to wake up every few hours to check it. If the weather is turning nasty, you are unavoidably anchored off a lee shore, you are going to have a significant tide change in the middle of the night, or you are concerned about the holding quality of the bottom you're anchored in, you might want to set your alarm clock for the time of the tide change to make sure your anchor holds as your boat swings around.

Even under normal circumstances, just to be on the safe side, you might want to set an electronic anchor watch with your depth-sounder, navigation receiver, or radar or some combination of the three. (But make certain you can hear their alarms in your stateroom and that they are loud enough to wake you from a deep sleep. If not, have an electronics technician rig them to trigger a separate alarm next to your bunk.) To use your depth-sounder as an anchor watch, set its depth alarm at about five feet less than the amount of water you should have under your keel within the circle described by your anchor rode at low tide. If your anchor drags and you drift out of that circle toward shallow water, the alarm should go off. Many modern Loran and GPS receivers allow you to describe a circle around your vessel and sound an alarm if the signals they receive indicate you have drifted out of it.

Both of these systems will alert you if your vessel moves out of the circle described by your anchor rode, but neither will warn you if something intrudes inside that circle. In a crowded anchorage with the wind getting up, you can set your radar's guard zone to cover a circle about a hundred yards in diameter around your vessel and sound an alarm if it receives signals from anything that has intruded into it. If the radar's alarm goes off in the night, a nearby vessel has probably dragged its anchor and is bearing down on you, so you'll want to scurry topside in the hope of fending it off.

## Tropical Storm or Hurricane Anchoring

If you find yourself at anchor under the threat of a tropical storm, remember that as the storm passes over you its motion (counterclockwise in the Northern Hemisphere, clockwise in the Southern) will cause a 90- to 180-degree wind shift depending on whether you are at the edge of the storm or directly in its path. Because of this radical wind shift and the forces involved, about all you can do is put out anchors off your bow at appropriate angles to your vessel's centerline.

For those anchors to be effective, you need to set one in the direction from which the wind will strike your vessel as the storm approaches and the second in the direction from which the wind will strike your vessel as it recedes. Those directions will be determined by your position relative to the storm's track, which you can plot from weather broadcasts.

In the path of an approaching tropical storm or hurricane, you obviously want to pay out the maximum scope possible on both anchors. If you set your secondary anchor by dropping back to the full extent of your primary rode, then taking up on the primary rode until you are lying roughly halfway between your two anchors, you would not get the advantage of maximum scope on your primary rode. In a storm anchoring situation, it's better to set your primary anchor with your vessel, then set your secondary anchor with your dinghy at the appropriate angle from your vessel's bow and at the full extent of your secondary rode. If possible, add a sentinel or kellet to both your primary and secondary anchor rodes. These are simply any kind of weights of 25 pounds or so affixed to your rodes at about their midpoints which increase their catenary and help keep the pull on your anchors horizontal. If you rig an anchoring setup like this, you'll probably have a fine mess of tangled rodes to unscramble after the storm passes, but you may find you've saved your vessel.

In most storm anchoring situations, the greatest danger to your vessel probably won't be from the effects of the storm itself but from other vessels seeking shelter in the anchorage where you have chosen to hole up. About all you can do to prevent damage from other vessels that are driven down on you is to put out all the fenders you have, hope you remembered to pay your boat insurance, and pray. When winds reach over about 30 knots, trying to fend off other vessels becomes an exercise in futility and could well cause you serious injury.

As a tropical storm or hurricane approaches, once you have anchored your vessel as securely as you know how, the next question you face is whether you should stay aboard and try to help her survive or seek shelter ashore and let her fend for herself. If the storm is likely to reach hurricane force by the time it reaches your position (winds of 64 knots or 75 miles an hour), my advice would be to head for shore. I have ridden out winds in excess of 90 miles an hour at anchor and found it a truly frightening experience. Under those conditions, there is really nothing you can do to help your vessel survive and you could well be placing your own life in jeopardy. Journalistic assignments put me in St. Thomas in the U.S. Virgin Islands in the aftermath of Hurricane David, and in Charleston, South Carolina, shortly after Hurricane Hugo struck, and I can testify that the devastation they left in their wakes was unbelievable. Both storms hurled well-constructed vessels of 60 and 70 feet ashore and stacked them one atop the other like cordwood. Anyone foolish enough to have tried to stay aboard them would almost certainly have been seriously injured or killed. In my view, no boat—however expensive and even if it's uninsured—is worth your life.

## Letting Go in an Emergency

If the wind is really howling, your anchor is dragging and refuses to reset, and you are rapidly drifting down on a lee shore, or if another vessel is slamming into yours, you may have to let your anchor go in a hurry in order to allow you to maneuver out of harm's way with your engine. You can cut through the fiber part of a chain-rope rode with a rigging knife. An all-chain rode should be attached to your vessel to prevent losing its bitter end overboard by accident, but you can make provision to sever it quickly in an emergency by rigging a length of ¾-inch nylon line between the chain's bitter end and a stout pad eye in your chain locker. The line must be long enough to reach the deck if all the chain is pulled out, and the connection between it and the chain's bitter end must be small enough to pass readily through your deck pipe. If you have sufficient room, let all the chain run out and cut the nylon line with a rigging knife when it appears on deck. If you don't have enough leeway to let out all your chain and expose the line, about all you can do is maneuver under power as best you can with the chain still out. At least its weight should keep it low enough in the water to keep it out of your props.

## Security at Anchor

Virtually anywhere in North America, you are probably safer at anchor than you would be walking down Main Street after dark in any sizeable town in the U.S. About the only places I can think of where I would have the least concern about anchoring would be in the Bahamas, particularly along the west coast of Andros Island, which is a popular takeoff point for drug smuggling into the U.S., and in a few deserted stretches along the coasts of South and Central America and Mexico. The danger in those latter areas is not so much from professional criminals as it is from local people locked in poverty to whom the glistening yacht of a rich North Americano might provide an irresistible temptation. Even there, the potential danger is not so much personal harm to those aboard as it is the theft of a dinghy or any items of value carelessly left around on deck.

The best protection at anchor is prevention. If you are anchored in an area that concerns you, lock your vessel's exterior doors at bedtime, keep loose items of value stowed out of sight, and secure your dinghy with a stainless steel painter and a stout padlock. If you're really nervous, try to anchor near another cruiser (but not in the vicinity of a rusty old tanker that appears to be offloading large bales of something into a fleet of small, fast speedboats). As mentioned above, you can also set the guard zone on your radar to sound an alarm if it receives signals from another vessel that intrudes into it.

If you should venture far into the boondocks and invite the locals aboard, keep the groups small so you're aware of what's going on, limit beverages to the nonalcoholic variety, and keep small items of value out of sight. Again, it's not so much that your guests deliberately intend to prey on you as it is that they might not be able to resist the temptation of slipping a shiny example of the outside world—like an expensive clock or your navigation computer—beneath their mumu. On the positive side, carry a good stock of colorful ballpoint pens as giveaways (they love the kind that go click-click) and take along a camera that develops its own photos and a liberal supply of film.

## Anchor Retrieval

Setting an anchor can prove to be the easy part. If your anchor is really set deeply or becomes fouled, the hard part begins when you try to retrieve it.

Any time you are bringing your anchor up, bear in mind that it is designed to produce its maximum holding power when the force exerted on it is horizontal in the direction of its flukes, and to begin to break out of the bottom when vertical force is exerted on it at an angle greater than about eight degrees to the horizontal.

For normal anchor retrieval, post your mate on the bow and slowly motor forward while the mate directs you toward the anchor with hand signals and takes in the rode with the anchor windlass. (Never use your windlass alone to pull your boat up to an anchor, as the strain could burn out its electric motor or strip its gears.) Be careful not to go forward faster than your mate can retrieve the rode to avoid scarring your topsides. As your vessel's bow passes over the anchor, forward momentum should break the anchor free. Your mate can then retrieve the remaining rode, bring the anchor up tight to the bow roller, and secure it.

If the anchor doesn't break free immediately, don't force it too much by advancing your throttle(s) because all the strain is being borne by the windlass and you could strip its gears. If a little added force doesn't break the anchor free, it is either extremely well set or it is fouled and you will have to apply successive tactics to break it free. As an initial attempt to break it out, turn your rudder(s) to one side or the other, which will force your vessel to pivot around the anchor. This maneuver alone may change the angle of force on the anchor enough to break it out. If it doesn't, once you are 180 degrees to the course you were on when you originally set the anchor, shift to reverse and back slowly but steadily. If the anchor is simply well dug in, this should change the angle on its shaft enough to pull it out and let you go on your merry way.

If the anchor still refuses to budge, have your mate check to see that your bow is still directly over the anchor and the rode is hanging straight down. If it's not, ease forward until you've gotten all the slack out of the rode, and try backing again slowly but steadily. If this doesn't break the anchor out, it is clearly fouled and you will have to resort to extraordinary measures to retrieve it.

If there is any significant wave action in the anchorage, try to get all possible slack out of the rode by snubbing it tighter every time your boat's bow dips into a wave trough. Once you get virtually all the slack out of the rode, the action of the bow lifting on the waves may be sufficient to pull the anchor free.

If that doesn't help, snorkel or scuba dive down to the anchor if possible, find out what it's hung up on, and see if you can free it by hand or secure a line around its head which you can cleat off to your vessel and use to back the head out of whatever is holding it.

If diving down to the anchor is impractical, assume that one of your problems is that the force you are exerting on the anchor rode is working on the end of the anchor's shaft, which is not the most effective angle for freeing the head. Also assume that if you apply an excessive amount of force to the rode, you're likely to part it or bend the anchor's shaft or break it off all together.

Your best option at this point is to try to get a line around the head of the anchor which will allow you to pull it straight out in the direction opposite to that of its flukes. To do that: Check again to see that your vessel is headed opposite to the direction you were going when you set the anchor; that your vessel's bow is directly over the anchor; and that you've gotten all the slack you can out of the anchor chain. In the line end of your secondary anchor rode or the heaviest, longest line you have aboard, use a bowline knot to tie a bight about two feet across which runs around your anchor chain (i.e., your anchor chain should be inside the bight). Lower this bight down around the anchor chain with a gentle shaking motion. What you're trying to do is work the bight down over the shaft of the anchor and have it settle around the anchor's head like the loop of a lasso. Once the bight has reached the bottom, keep a little tension on its line but slack off the tension on your anchor chain. This should allow the anchor's shaft to fall into a nearly horizontal position and help hold the bight in position around the head of the anchor. While your mate pays out both the anchor chain and the line with the bight in it, slowly back your vessel until you are about 50 feet away from the anchor and lying opposite to the direction of the point of its flukes. Have the mate leave the anchor chain fully slack, but take up tension on the line with the bight and cleat it off. Once that is done, back your vessel slowly. If you've been successful in looping the bight around the head of the anchor, this should put enough tension on the anchor at the optimum angle opposite to the point of its flukes to pull it out.

If this maneuver doesn't work, about all you can do is disconnect the anchor chain from your vessel, tie a marker buoy to the end of it, and come back later with diving gear to try to retrieve your anchor and rode.

The best way to avoid getting into a mess like this in the first place is to outfit your anchor with a trip line any time you anchor in an area where it is likely to be severely fouled. To be effective, the trip line must be stout enough to stand the force you may have to exert on it, and it must be attached to the anchor's head with a stout shackle. The Bruce anchor and most plow-type anchors have a fitting at their head to attach a trip line. On a Danforth-type anchor, don't try to tie the trip line around the head or the stock as it could interfere with the anchor's holding ability. Instead, drill a hole in one of the anchor's crown plates and attach the trip line with a shackle.

Any time you set a trip line, buoy it so that it is well marked and as short as possible to prevent it fouling the propeller of a passing boat. An empty plastic milk jug does fine for a trip line buoy, but mark it with your vessel's name and something like "ANCHOR, DO NOT DISTURB." If you don't do that, some local youngster in a skiff may well come by and pull the trip line to see what's on the other end—and bring your anchor up in the process.

## Anchor Signals

Vessels more than 23.0 feet (7 meters) in length but less than 65.6 feet (20 meters) at anchor outside special anchorage areas from sunset to sunrise must show an all-around white light wherever it can best be seen.

Such vessels at anchor outside special anchorage areas during the day must display a ball-shaped daymark at least 2 feet (0.6 meter) in diameter forward where it can best be seen. (I've never actually seen a recreational vessel display such a daymark, but thought you ought to know it's required.)

## Mediterranean Moor

In many parts of the world the normal way of tying up is stern-first to a quay with an anchor out. This "Mediterranean moor," then, is a hybrid of both anchoring and tying up, but since the most critical part of the maneuver is properly placing your anchor and setting it well, we'll cover the topic here (Fig. 5.3).

Prepare for the maneuver by figuring how much anchor rode you need to pay out based on a scope of about 5:1. Also have your mate put out vertical fenders port and starboard, lay out two stern lines for deployment in the cockpit, and get the anchor ready to fall freely.

Stand out a little further from the quay than the length of rode you need to pay out to get the 5:1 scope and line your vessel up in front of the spot you intend to occupy. As soon as your vessel gathers sternway, have your mate release the anchor. After you've gone astern about half the distance to the quay (and while your stern is still well clear of the bows of any boats already tied to the quay), go through your anchor setting routine: have your mate fully tighten the tension on the windlass; then back down with your engines. With the anchor set, have your mate go to the cockpit and prepare to fend off other vessels already moored if necessary and rig the stern lines.

At this point, your job at the helm becomes a little like patting your head while rubbing your tummy because you must do two things simultaneously: Use the flying bridge switch for your windlass to let out scope on your anchor rode (but keep the rode taut to keep your bow from falling off); and work your gear(s) to back toward the space you're aiming for. With a single-engine boat, don't forget that in reverse your right-handed propeller will tend to set your stern to port. Aim your stern a bit to starboard of where you want it to go or offset the prop's torque with a bit of right rudder. If a significant crosswind is blowing, your bow is likely to be set down more than your stern. If your stern gets too far to port, you may have to kick the engine ahead briefly, which will use the propeller's torque to help swing your stern to starboard.

While you're backing down, your mate at the stern should fend off the

138

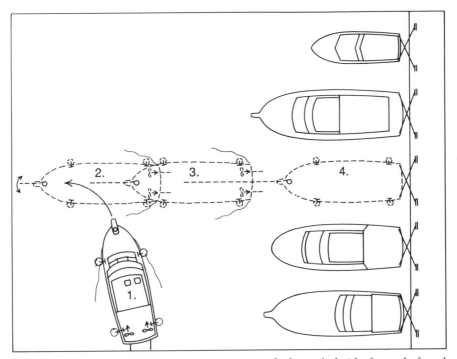

**Fig. 5.3:** *To execute a Mediterranean moor, put out fenders on both sides fore and aft and line your stern up with the space you intend to occupy (1); drop your primary anchor while going astern (2); then pay out rode as you continue powering astern (3) until your mate can tie off to the quay with crossed stern lines (4).*

vessels to either side if necessary. Once you are about five feet from the dock, kick your engine(s) into neutral. If you've kept the tension on your anchor rode properly taut, it will check your sternway and hold the boat in position while your mate either passes the eye end of your stern lines to someone ashore or steps ashore to secure them. The stern lines should be crossed to help reduce the sideways motion of your stern.

Once you're safely tied up, take up the appropriate tension on your anchor rode to hold your bow in place, and set your anchor bridle.

You'll also need to rig a gangway for going ashore over the stern. If your cruising itinerary calls for you to spend much time in areas where Mediterranean mooring is the norm (English Harbour, Antigua, and Acapulco in North America, many harbors in the Pacific, and just about anywhere in the Mediterranean), you should include in your ship's inventory a collapsible stern gangway with a swivel fitting at the transom, rollers for the end that rests on the quay, side-rails, and some kind of topping lift arrangement that allows you to raise it clear of the quay when a heavy surge is running.

• • • •

# PART TWO

# NAVIGATING
# AND
# COMMUNICATING

• • • •

# CHAPTER 6

# COASTAL PILOTING AND EYEBALL NAVIGATION

•  •  •

Unless you're planning to strike off across an ocean, you'll find that 80 or 90 percent of your cruising will be done within sight of land. For the vast majority of this inshore cruising you'll plan your vessel's course on a nautical chart, then keep a check on its progress and position by visual references to aids to navigation such as channel markers and buoys or to shoreside landmarks. In crossing open bodies of water such as large bays or inlets you'll employ dead reckoning to determine your approximate position, then make any necessary course corrections as soon as you are within sight of one or more aids to navigation or shoreside landmarks. This whole realm of seamanship is referred to as piloting, and you need to develop the skills it requires regardless of how elaborately your vessel is equipped with navigation electronics. Loran and satellite receivers are modern marvels, but—being electrical—they are always subject to malfunction and you may well find that your skill as a pilot is the only thing that is going to get your vessel and all aboard her to safe harbor. Even if all your electronic navigation instruments are working perfectly, you should still maintain a course plot on a chart to make certain the positions and courses they are giving you are accurate.

The essential tools for piloting are a full complement of up-to-date charts covering the area you plan to cruise, the instruments necessary to plot your course and determine your position accurately, and a basic knowledge of piloting procedures. Beyond these essentials, there are a number of other tools such as the *Tidal Current Tables, Coast Pilots, Light Lists,* and cruising guides that can help you anticipate potentially adverse conditions before they arise and help keep you out of trouble.

## NAUTICAL CHARTS

Your nautical charts are among the most valuable and essential tools you'll have aboard your vessel. I can't stress enough the importance of having a full complement of charts of the area you plan to cruise. Without them you are "flying blind" and have no idea of the hazards that may lie in wait for you. In the Appendix you'll find a complete listing of the types of charts that are available for different parts of the world along with the sources from which they can be obtained. Charts are expensive and you may be tempted to cut corners by buying one small-scale chart covering a large area rather than investing in several large-scale charts that cover the area in greater detail. Don't do it; if conditions turn sour you'll need all the detail you can get—and lack of it can be disastrous. Also make certain any chart you carry aboard is either the latest edition or has been completely updated from all the Notices to Mariners for the area it covers that have been issued since its publication. A chart even a year or two old that has not been updated can provide all manner of erroneous information. In the ensuing years, storms and erosion may have shifted channels and the entrances to inlets, the Coast Guard may have removed or relocated buoys, and development may have demolished some shoreside structures and erected new ones where none existed before. The result can be a significant difference between what the

144

chart pictures and what is really there. In a tight navigation situation, particularly under adverse weather or sea conditions, that difference can be extremely dangerous.

Some cruisers try to save money by purchasing used charts, which are available from chart stores or from cruisers who have traversed a route and no longer need the charts they accumulated for the journey. I would buy a used chart only if I was fully comfortable that it had been completely updated from Notices to Mariners by someone who really knew what he was doing. One sign that you're probably safe to trust a used chart is if the seller includes with it a complete file of the Notices to Mariners from which it has been kept current. One of the best ways to locate used charts is to spend $22 a year to join the Seven Seas Cruising Association (521 S. Andrews Ave., Suite 10, Fort Lauderdale, FL 33301) as an associate member in order receive its monthly *Commodores' Bulletin*. Though the SSCA is composed primarily of people who cruise under sail, its active members tend to be well-qualified, knowledgeable skippers. If one of them offers a set of used charts of an area through the *Bulletin,* their updating has probably been rigorously maintained. If you use an older chart that has been updated, be especially careful to note the annual increase or decrease in magnetic variation listed inside the chart's compass rose, note its cumulative effect from the year the chart was printed to the year you are using it, and remember to apply that cumulative effect to any magnetic bearings you plot.

Even using the most recently published chart for an area or one that has been conscientiously updated by a qualified mariner doesn't necessarily guarantee its accuracy, especially if the area has been raked by severe weather. I made a run along the coast of South Carolina in the wake of Hurricane Hugo and found many inlets, channels, and markers either no longer existed or were a long way from where even the most recent chart of the area said they were. In addition to charts covering every inch of the route you plan to follow, it's also a good idea to include in your inventory charts of any inlets and/or harbors along the way you don't plan to enter but might have to duck into in an emergency.

Having a complete inventory of up-to-date charts on board doesn't do much good if you can't quickly lay your hands on the one you need and it's not been properly taken care of. Develop an inventory system that tells you what charts you have aboard and where they are stowed. Hopefully your wheelhouse will include several large, shallow drawers where you can store your charts and a large area where you can work with them without having to fold them. If your wheelhouse doesn't have adequate chart stowage, the best place to stow large charts until they are needed is beneath a bunk mattress—but make sure the area is not subject to dampness. If you must fold charts, vary the manner in which you fold them each time you store or use them to avoid developing deep creases along which they will be likely to tear and information will be obscured. Any time you take a chart to the flying bridge, encase it in a vinyl chart protector to prevent moisture damage.

## Piloting Instruments

There are all manner of chart-plotting instruments available, from basic dividers and parallel rules to course plotters and protractors. Which one will work best for you is largely a matter of personal preference. I personally find the traditional parallel rules and dividers work best. I do suggest, however, that you carry two sets of dividers aboard. For precise plotting work where you have plenty of time, one pair should have an adjustable screw-type crossarm which will firmly hold a separation and prevent accidental changes in the setting. For situations where you need to work quickly and can afford to be a bit less precise, the second should be of the "one hand" variety which you can open by squeezing the top and close by squeezing the bottom. I've found that the simplest dividers, which have only a single pivot point, soon become so loose that they can't be relied on.

A No. 2 lead pencil is the best device to lightly draw course lines and enter information on your charts because its markings are easily visible and can be erased without damaging the chart. Also, its relatively soft lead won't cut deeply into the chart surface. Keep your plotting pencils well sharpened so they describe a fine line, and even then hold your parallel rules or course plotter slightly off the line you are describing to allow for the thickness of the pencil lead. For erasing marks, art gum will do far less damage to the chart surface than a rubber eraser.

Another critical piloting instrument you'll need is a good pair of binoculars. If your binoculars don't have an integral magnetic bearing compass, you'll also need a good hand-bearing compass.

## Choosing Binoculars

Good binoculars are expensive (in the $500 to $800 range through nautical catalogs), but don't cut corners. The first time you're in a nasty sea beneath gray skies and have to depend on your binoculars to spot a tiny entrance marker to reach safety, you'll be glad you invested in the best pair of binoculars you can afford. Go over the specifications of any binoculars you consider purchasing very carefully. My suggestion would be that you select a pair of 7 × 50 binoculars with a relative light efficiency above 80, individual rather than center focusing, waterproof, armored, and reasonably light-weight. Whether you select a pair with an integral bearing compass is largely a matter of whether you are willing to pay a substantial weight penalty for the added accuracy and convenience. To go through those recommended specifications in more detail:

The first number in the 7 × 50 designation represents the lenses' magnification power. A 7 × glass makes an object appear seven times larger than when viewed with the naked eye and is about the highest magnification the average person can hold steady on a pitching deck. The second number is the diameter in millimeters of the objective lens (the lens farthest from your eye). The diameter of the objective lens divided by the lens's magnification power equals the binoculars' exit pupil—the diameter of the sphere of light you see if you hold the binoculars at arm's length. That figure is important because the average diameter of the pupil of a human eye in bright sunlight is about 4 to 4½ mm, but in reduced light expands to about 7 mm. A 50-mm objective lens with a 7 × magnification has an exit pupil of 7.14, which takes maximum advantage of the eye's expanded pupil diameter in reduced visibility. Binoculars with magnification power above 7 × and objective lenses smaller than 50 mm have exit pupils as small as 5 to 6 mm, which makes them almost useless in low-light conditions.

Relative light efficiency (RLE) measures the percentage of available light that a lens is able to gather and transmit through the binocular to your eye and is a function of the lens's optical quality. The higher that percentage the more expensive the binocular, but the better you'll be able to see a small marker on a gray sea under a gray sky. For use at sea, I consider an REL of 75 an absolute minimum and feel it is well worth the extra money to buy a pair of binoculars with an RLE of at least 80.

Binoculars with center focusing must be set for the distance to an object; binoculars with individual focusing on each eyepiece are set once for your eyes and do not have to be set for distance. While individual-focusing binoculars are more expensive than the center-focus type, they are easier and quicker to use. Their construction makes it far more difficult for moisture to get inside the barrels, which means they are more resistant to fogging.

147

In the marine environment fogging is a major problem and can render a pair of binoculars unusable, so binoculars that have been tested not to admit moisture even when immersed in water are worth their extra cost.

At some point or another, binoculars on a boat are almost certain to be dropped or knocked about. Armoring is important because it helps absorb shocks and prevent the binoculars' delicate lens arrangement from being knocked out of alignment. As further protection from shock, equip your flying bridge and wheelhouse steering stations with binocular holders and make certain you put them back in their holder every time you use them so you or a guest won't accidentally tip them over or knock them to the sole. It's also a good idea to fit your binoculars with a strap and get into the habit of flipping it over your neck every time you use them.

I find I pick up my binoculars anywhere from 50 to 100 times during the course of a typical day's inshore cruising. Lifting a pair of binoculars to your eyes that often makes weight (which in top quality binoculars ranges from just over 2 pounds to about 3.5 pounds) important. The matter of weight influences whether you select binoculars with an integral-bearing compass or use a separate hand-bearing compass. There can be little argument that taking bearings with an integral compass in your binoculars allows you to get a more precise bearing (under ideal conditions, within a degree) simply because you can see the object more distinctly. The problem is that an integral compass significantly increases weight and you probably won't use it more than 2 or 3 percent of the time you pick up the binoculars to get a better look at a distant object. I personally prefer to forgo an integral compass to keep my binoculars as light as possible.

## Choosing a Hand-Bearing Compass

If you elect to use a separate hand-bearing compass, your choice comes down to the degree of accuracy you are willing to settle for and the amount of money you want to spend. The simplest and least expensive types, such as those offered by Davis and Silva, utilize a standard magnetic compass card, yield readings accurate to about 5 degrees, and sell for around $30 to $80 respectively. The "hockey puck" types such as the Mini 2000 yield accuracies to within about 2 degrees and sell for around $100. In taking bearings with any of these compasses, you have to wait a few seconds for the card to settle down. The Autohelm electronic hand-bearing compass is also accurate to within about 2 degrees and sells for around $125 but has the added advantage of a timer and will remember the degrees and times of up to nine bearings. The KVH Datascope, which sells for just under $400, utilizes a fluxgate electronic sensor which is gimbaled up to 20 degrees, is accurate to about 2 degrees, has a timer and 5 × magnification, can remember the times and degrees of up to nine bearings, and also includes a range finder.

Because the readings of hand-bearing compasses normally are accurate only to within 2 to 5 degrees and because they are normally used away from the major sources of magnetic interference aboard a vessel, their deviation is not normally taken into account when computing bearings. You would be wise, however, to take readings with your hand-bearing compass at a number of locations around your vessel to find a convenient place where its readings conform most closely to the steering compasses in your pilothouse and on your flying bridge, then take hand bearings only from that location.

## Plotting Techniques

If you are running a well-defined inshore channel such as a stretch of the Intracoastal Waterway where markers are closely spaced and easily visible, it's not really necessary to keep a running plot of your position and course. Your course will be determined by the bearing to the next mark, and all you have to do to keep up with your position is to check off each marker as you pass it. You do, of course, have to keep an eye out ahead (both on the water and on the chart) to anticipate any problems that might lie in your path. But any time you venture out of clear sight of land, it is essential that you carefully and correctly plot your progress on the appropriate chart. Knowing how to plot your vessel's position and course and constantly maintaining a plot on the chart are necessary regardless of the number and sophistication of the electronic navigation instruments you have on board. As we mentioned above, electronic navigation instruments are wonderful things, but they can be wiped out by an electrical short or power failure, their information can be garbled by outside interference, or their readings can turn out to be inaccurate because they were improperly programmed. If your Loran C or satellite receiver goes on the fritz, that old-fashioned penciled plot on a paper chart will be worth its weight in gold for figuring out where you are and which way you need to go to reach your destination.

If you are not well versed in the skills and techniques of piloting, I strongly suggest you take a good course in the subject such as the one offered by the U.S. Power Squadron. Some of the information you will learn in such a course will in time slip from your memory, so it's a good idea occasionally to review the coverage of piloting techniques in a basic boating book like *Chapman Piloting, Seamanship & Small Boat Handling.* Here we will discuss only the basic position and course-plotting techniques which as a cruiser under power you are likely to use most frequently.

In plotting a position or course, it's important to employ a standardized system to avoid confusion. The basic question you have to answer is whether you are going to plot positions and courses in true or magnetic degrees. Assuming your steering compasses are magnetic rather than the newer electronic compasses, which employ a flux-gate sensor and can be programmed to read out in true degrees, the traditional method of position or course plotting dictates that you start off with true degrees, then apply magnetic variation (including any annual increase or decrease) and compass deviation to arrive at a course to steer. A number of experienced cruisers disregard true degrees altogether, rely on the inner magnetic readings on their charts' compass rose, and plot courses in magnetic degrees. I don't have strong feelings about which method you choose to use except to suggest that you choose one method and stick to it to avoid confusion, that you make sure you have your magnetic compasses swung periodically, and that you always remember to apply compass deviation to any magnetic bearings you work with. A number of skippers are not aware of it, but the amount of variation to be applied to a course or position can differ from one area to another of the same chart. In some areas where local magnetic attraction is especially strong, that change in variation can be dramatic as 45 degrees within the same chart. Therefore, in plotting a position or course in magnetic degrees, always be sure to use the compass rose nearest to your position on the chart. In shooting a nasty reef entrance, an error of even a degree that results from improperly applying magnetic variation and compass deviation can be the difference between entering harbor safely or winding up on the rocks.

A dead reckoning (DR) track is the line you intend your vessel to follow. In plotting a DR track (see Fig. 6.1), always begin at a known position, label its direction above the line with the letter *C* followed by the course in degrees as a three-digit numeral (94 degrees would be expressed as 094; 2 degrees would be expressed as 002), and identify its course with the suffix *T* if it is a true course or *M* if it is a magnetic course. The degree symbol is omitted. If you are plotting a DR track for planning purposes prior to departure, indicate below the line (normally right beneath the course information above the line) the distance in nautical or statute miles you will

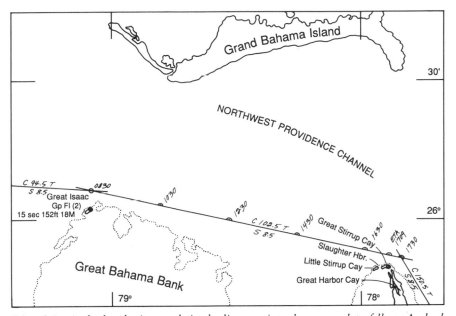

*Fig. 6.1:* A dead reckoning track is the line you intend your vessel to follow. A dead reckoning position—indicated on the chart by a dot on the course line enclosed by a half circle above the line, and labeled with the time it is plotted expressed by the twenty-four-hour clock written at an angle to the course line—is determined solely by the elapsed time you have traveled along a DR track at a specific speed without reference to aids to navigation or shoreside landmarks and with no allowance for the effects of current.

travel on that course preceded by the letter *D*. Once you are underway, replace the distance designation with your vessel's speed through the water in knots or statute miles per hour preceded by the letter *S*.

A fix is a location where you determine your vessel's position precisely by reference to aids to navigation, shoreside landmarks, sextant sights, or electronic navigation instruments. A fix along a straight course line is indicated by a dot enclosed by a complete circle; if a change of course occurs at the time the fix is taken and charted, the fix is indicated by enclosing the intersection of the old and new course lines with a complete circle. A

151

fix is labeled by the time it was taken in the twenty-four-hour clock written horizontally.

In coastal cruising, you'll most often determine a fix by taking magnetic bearings from your vessel to marks such as aids to navigation or shoreside landmarks with a hand-bearing compass, adding or subtracting the deviation of the steering compass for the boat's heading at the time the fix is taken, then taking the reciprocals of the corrected bearings to plot the magnetic bearings from the marks to your vessel on a chart. If a magnetic bearing from your vessel to the mark (after compensating for the deviation of the steering compass) is less than 180 degrees, get its reciprocal by adding 180 degrees to it; if the bearing from your vessel to the mark (after allowing for the steering compass's deviation) is more than 180 degrees, subtract 180 degrees. In plotting that reciprocal as magnetic degrees, use the compass rose's inner ring. If you wish to plot a reciprocal on your chart as true degrees, you must correct the boat's heading at the time the bearing is taken for both magnetic variation and deviation before taking the reciprocal, then use the outer ring of the compass rose on your chart.

A dead reckoning position is determined solely by the elapsed time you have traveled along a DR track at a specific speed without reference to aids to navigation or shoreside landmarks and with no allowance for the effects of current. A DR position is indicated on the chart by a dot on the course line enclosed by a half circle above the line, and is labeled with the time it is plotted expressed by the twenty-four-hour clock written at an angle to the course line. A DR position not involving a change in speed or course normally is entered on a chart at hourly intervals. A DR position is plotted and labeled with the time at any change in course or speed. If you are proceeding along a DR track and arrive at a place where you can fix your vessel's position (say you pass within a mile of a buoy), plot a DR position based solely on elapsed time and course steered and label it with the time, then proceed to the vicinity of the buoy, plot your position as a fix and begin a new DR track. As we'll discuss a bit further along, you can use the difference between the DR position and the fix to calculate the effect current is having on your vessel and determine what you need to do to offset it.

An estimated position (see Fig. 6.2) is a dead reckoning position that has been modified to allow for the effects of a known or estimated current. It is plotted as a dot inside a small square which is joined by a line to the DR position from which it was modified. An estimated position is not labeled but takes its time from the time of the DR position from which it was modified.

152

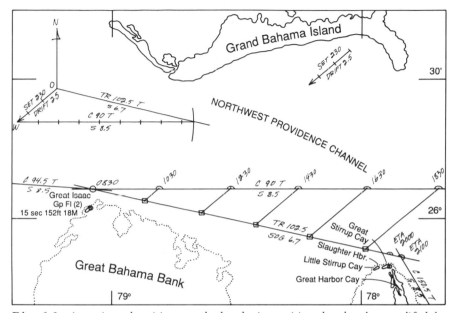

*Fig. 6.2:* An estimated position—a dead reckoning position that has been modified by constructing a current diagram to allow for the effects of a known or estimated current—is plotted as a dot inside a small square which is joined by a line to the DR position from which it was modified. An estimated position is not labeled but takes its time from the time of the DR position from which it was modified.

## CURRENT AFFAIRS

Here's a typical cruising situation: You're motoring along, keeping a marker in the distance squarely on your bow or adhering strictly to the compass course you've charted, and are therefore certain you are in safe water when suddenly you feel the sickening thud of your hull bouncing along the bottom. If you're lucky, you quickly correct your course in the proper direction and maneuver your vessel back into deep water. If you're not so lucky, you find yourself hard aground on a falling tide. In either case—once you recover

153

from the surprise—your first question becomes: "If I was proceeding straight toward my objective or was right on a course that should have kept me in safe water, what happened to put me onto the rocks or the sandbar?"

The most likely explanation is that you failed to realize that an adverse current was deflecting your vessel far enough off your intended course to get you into trouble. If that's what happened, you're not the first skipper who's ever encountered the problem and you certainly won't be the last. Failing to recognize the presence of a deflecting current and to properly correct course to offset its effects probably puts more skippers on the beach than any other single navigating factor.

Even though you keep a distant marker exactly on your bow, a deflecting current can sweep you to one side or the other of the line you think you are following and carry you into shoal water. You can firmly fix this idea in your mind by thinking of your vessel as something like a tetherball with its bow attached to the mark by a string, then imagining that the deflecting current is moving your vessel sideways. That sideways force theoretically can carry your vessel through an arc of 360 degrees around the mark, yet the mark will not budge an inch from being directly off your bow. If there is shoal water anywhere inside that 360-degree arc, you can wind up aground.

A deflecting current can also put you aground even though you adhere exactly to a predetermined compass course that should keep you over deep water. Imagine your compass course as a straight rod that runs directly through your vessel's centerline toward the mark. Now envision the deflecting current setting your vessel sideways. You can remain exactly on that course, but the deflecting current will carry you wide of the mark. If there is shoal water on the side of your course toward which the current is setting you, you can wind up on the rocks.

The best way to avoid problems with deflecting current is to know in advance that it will be running, calculate its set (the direction it will be running) and its drift (its speed) from the appropriate volume of *Tidal Current Tables* (see Appendix), then construct a current diagram to figure out how much and in what direction you must alter your intended course to reach your destination.

## Current Diagram: Known Set and Drift

To walk through the construction of a current diagram where the set and drift of a current are known, let's consider a hypothetical voyage down

Northwest Providence Channel in the Bahamas from Great Isaac Light to Great Stirrup Cay Light (Fig. 6.2). Begin by drawing a vertical line of indeterminate length either on the chart itself or on a plain piece of paper; label its upper end N to represent true north, and label its lower end O to represent the origin point of your calculation. On the chart, you have previously plotted course 102 degrees true as the DR track from Great Isaac to Great Stirrup. With a protractor, draw a line of indeterminate length from point O in the direction 102 degrees relative to the line O–N. The *Tidal Current Tables* give the set of the current in Northwest Providence Channel at the time you will be making this run as 230 degrees true and its drift as 2.5 knots. Plot the set as a line in the direction 230 degrees relative to line N–O. Adopt a convenient scale of units, indicate a point along that line 2.5 units from point O, and label it as point W. Set the spread of a pair of dividers at the number of units equal to your vessel's typical speed through the water—in this case 8.5 knots. Place the left point of the dividers at point W and swing a circle with a radius of 8.5 units across the line that represents your DR track of 102 degrees. Label the intersection of these two lines as point P. With your protractor, measure the angle of line W–P relative to line N–O which comes out to 90 degrees true. This will be your course to steer and should be plotted on the chart. Bear in mind that you must apply variation and deviation to this course to arrive at a compass course to steer. The distance from point O to point P divided by the unit scale you have adopted will yield your vessel's speed over ground which in this case comes out to 6.7 knots.

Once you are underway from your 0830 fix at Great Isaac, plot DR positions on the course line of 90 degrees true based on elapsed time and your vessel's 8.5-knot speed through the water. The current's 230-degree set is 140 degrees relative to your course of 90 degrees (230 − 90 = 140). Extend a line from each DR position in the direction 140 degrees relative to your course of 90 degrees until it crosses your TR line of 102 degrees. Put a dot on the TR line where the extended line touches it and enclose the dot with a small square. After taking the current's effect into account, this will be your vessel's actual position at the time the DR position was plotted. By 1830 you will be well within sight of the lighthouse on Great Stirrup Cay, and its position should confirm your estimated position at that time and allow you to safely proceed to the point beyond Great Stirrup Cay where you can plot a fix on its lighthouse and take up your new course.

## Current Diagram: Observed Set and Drift

You can also use current diagrams to determine the set and drift from your observation of its effects on your vessel and to determine what you must do to allow for them.

Assume you wish to proceed eastward across North Carolina's Pamlico Sound from the Neuse River Entrance Light to Royal Shoal Light. Along the way you will pass between Brant Island Shoal Light and a marker identified on the chart as WR2 which is .82 nm to the southeast of it. You lay out a course from Neuse River Entrance Light to Brant Island Shoal Light of 83 degrees true and from Brant Island Shoal Light to Royal Shoal Light of 77 degrees true. You plan to run your vessel at its normal 8.5 knot cruising speed through the water. You run toward Brant Island Shoal Light on the 83 degrees true course, but when you arrive in its vicinity you realize that your course made good has actually brought you south of both it and WR2. It's obvious you have been deflected from your intended track by current. The problem is to compute the current's set and drift and make allowance for it as you proceed toward Royal Shoal Light.

By taking bearings on both Brant Island Shoal Light and WR2 you fix your position, which reveals you have actually made good a course-over-ground of 88 degrees true and a speed-over-ground of 7.25 knots. By measuring the angle between Brant Island Shoal Light and the fix you just took, you determine that the set of the current is 206 degrees true. By measuring the distance from Brant Island Shoal to your fix, you determine that the current's set is .9 knots. Since you have now determined the current's set and drift, you can construct the same sort of current diagram you used to determine your course to steer from Great Isaac Light to Great Stirrup Cay in the Bahamas. That diagram will tell you that to reach Royal Shoal Light you must steer a course of 73 degrees true and your vessel's speed-over-ground will be 7.9 knots.

## Rule-of-Thumb Navigation

When you're out of sight of land, navigating by current diagrams is indispensable if you don't have navigation electronics aboard, but in inshore waters there are some less formal but effective ways of recognizing when a deflecting current is carrying you off course and some rule-of-thumb methods

156

for figuring out how much you need to correct your course to offset its effects.

The easiest way to detect the presence of a deflecting current is to constantly compare the course you have plotted to the course you must steer to reach a mark along that course. Suppose, for instance, you plot a course of 50 degrees true, allow for magnetic variation and compass deviation, and arrive at a compass course to steer of 52 degrees. Once underway, however, you find you must steer a compass course of 57 degrees to keep the mark on your bow. Don't assume that your course plot is in error or there's something wrong with your compass and simply compensate enough to keep heading toward the mark. If you must take up a different course to reach the mark, recognize that you are not approaching the mark along the line you think you are but along another line, which runs at an angle to it. If there is shoal water anywhere along that line between where you are and the mark, you will run right into it and realize you have been carried off course only when you feel your keel kissing the bottom. If a quick recheck of your plot indicates no error, you're safe to assume that a current is deflecting you 5 degrees off your course. You must determine exactly where you are, if necessary work your way back to the course line you plotted, then add 5 degrees to your plotted course to arrive at your proper course to steer.

Another way to check for the presence of a deflecting current is to take frequent bearings to make certain you are where you think you are. If you are within sight of shore, take frequent cross bearings on shoreside landmarks to make sure the position they indicate is close to where you think you are on the chart. If you're running a straight marked channel in open water and can see a marker both fore and aft of you at the same time, draw an imaginary line between them. If you aren't pretty close to that line, you are being affected by a deflecting current and must take steps to counter it.

But how can you detect the presence of current if the markers you are running are spaced so far apart or visibility is so limited that you can see no shoreside landmarks and only one marker at a time? In that case (assuming, of course, that the markers are in a straight line), pass as close to a marker as is safe, hold carefully to your plotted course, and once you are a couple of hundred yards past the marker take a relative aft bearing on it by standing on your vessel's centerline facing aft and sighting toward the retreating mark over a fixed point on your vessel's centerline such as its ensign staff. If the mark is behind—or very nearly behind—the staff and stays there, you don't have enough current to worry about. If the mark is significantly to one side of the staff, current is carrying you in the opposite direction.

157

You can't determine how much you need to correct your course until you figure out the angle at which you are being set off of it. The best way to do that is to use your hand-bearing compass to determine the aft magnetic bearing of your vessel's centerline, then determine the aft magnetic bearing of the mark and compute the difference. That difference, compensated by any deviation in your hand bearing and your steering compass, will be the amount of the current's deflection. In order to make good the course you plotted, you will need to get back on your original course line, then alter your course by that number of degrees in the direction of the mark.

Detecting the presence of a deflecting current and determining its set is fine, assuming you can return to your original course line. From that point, altering your plotted course by that number of degrees in the direction of the mark should keep you on track.

But what if you're running a line of widely spaced markers in an open body of water where a deflecting current is carrying you off course and you must figure out how to return to your original course before you can make the appropriate compensation? Assume your vessel cruises at 10 knots and you are running a compass course of 60 degrees attempting to navigate a line of markers placed five nautical miles apart. You depart the first marker and pay close attention to maintaining your course. After running for half an hour, by which time you should have reached the second marker, it is nowhere in sight, which is your first signal that you are being set off your course by current. You make a large circle, locate the second marker, and find you were carried well to the east of it. To get back on track, pass close by the second mark and, as you depart it, hold to your 30-degree course as closely as possible for a specific interval of time—say ten minutes. Take an aft bearing on the mark relative to your vessel's centerline and compute the number of degrees by which the current is deflecting you from your course. Assume it's 20 degrees toward the southeast. To get back to your original course line, double the 20 degrees by which you have determined the current is deflecting you and subtract that number (40 degrees) from your 60-degree compass course to get a new compass course of 20 degrees. Turn to that compass course and proceed on it for the same length of time by which you ran away from the mark before you took the aft bearing. What you are doing is describing an equilateral triangle, in which two sides and the angles opposite them are equal, which will put you back on your original course. Once you are back on your original course line, take up a heading of 40 degrees (60 − 20 = 40), which will offset the 20-degree set of the deflecting current and allow you to hit the next marker pretty closely on the nose.

## FIGURING DISTANCE OFF

In Chapter 1 I suggested that one of the things you should do during your shakedown cruise is accurately measure the height of your eye at both the flying bridge and the pilothouse helm stations. You can use that figure to determine the distance to the horizon from either station by plugging it into the formula

$$D^b = 1.17 \sqrt{H}$$

in which $D^b$ (distance to the horizon in nautical miles) equals 1.17 times the square root of $H$ (the height of the observer's eye above sea level). Once you have calculated that distance, you can use it to estimate the distance to any object in the water that you can see (Fig. 6.3). Suppose, for instance, that you work the formula out based on an eye height of 9 feet at the pilothouse helm station and 16 feet at the flying bridge helm station and find that the distance to the horizon from the two stations will be 3.51 and 4.68 nautical miles respectively. If you're at the flying bridge helm station and see a marker approximately halfway between your position and the horizon, you know immediately that it is about 2.3 miles away.

You can also extend the formula to get a rough idea of how far you are off an object which itself has height such as a light tower. Suppose, for instance, that you see a light just at the horizon and a check of your chart of the area indicates that its source is most likely a light tower that is 25 feet high. You have already determined that the distance to the horizon from your flying bridge is just a touch under 4.7 nautical miles. Applying the $D_h = 1.17 \sqrt{H}$ formula to the light tower indicates the distance to the horizon from the top of it would be 5.85 nautical miles. Add the two together and you can deduce that your position is approximately 10.55 nautical miles from the light tower. Since you can actually see the light rather than just the top of it, you are actually a bit closer than that, say 10 nautical miles.

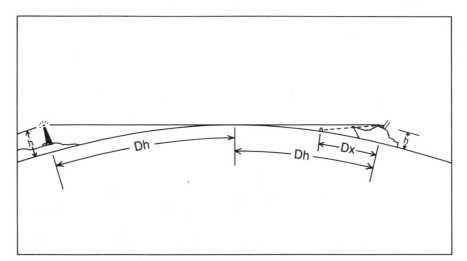

***Fig. 6.3:*** *If you know the height of your eye aboard your vessel you can apply the "height of eye formula": to quickly estimate the approximate distance to the horizon, to objects in the water, to the show, and to objects whose height above the water can be determined from a chart.*

## READING THE BOTTOM

If your cruising takes you into tropical waters, you are likely to encounter situations where storms and currents have shifted a sandy bottom so much that aids to navigation are useless or missing altogether. In that situation your chart—and thus your Loran or satellite receiver—is not reliable. Since your depth-sounder reads only water depths beneath your keel and not in front of you, you'll find that you have to visually read the bottom to work your way into an entry channel or an anchorage.

Reading the bottom visually requires at least three things: good light, a good vantage point, and a bit of experience to know whether that dark spot just off your bow is a grassy patch, a rock, or a coral head. It's also helpful if you are studying the water through a pair of sunglasses that polarize the reflection of the sun's rays off the water's surface.

Good light, preferably sunlight that is high and behind you, is essential to spotting any dangers the water in front of your vessel might hold. If at all possible, avoid trying to maneuver your vessel through shoal waters before about 8:00 A.M. or after about 4:00 P.M. when the sun's rays are slanting into the water at an oblique angle. It won't always be possible, but also try to avoid picking your way through rocks and coral heads when the sky is overcast.

The best vantage point from which to read the water ahead is a flying bridge. If your vessel doesn't have one, position a lookout right on the bow. For communications, give your lookout the hand-held VHF and reduce your installed unit to its one-watt output setting, or agree on a set of clear, simple hand signals and instruct your lookout to point in the direction in which it is safe to proceed, not toward obstructions.

As for interpreting what the various colors you see in the water indicate, a few simple rhymes may help. "Blue go through" reminds you that when the water is a rich, dark blue, it's likely to be deep enough to provide safe passage to the typical recreational powerboat with a draft of less than six feet.

"Green may be lean" reminds you that water that is deep green in color is probably eight to twelve feet deep, but a light green color indicates shallows.

"Brown go around" is a handy reminder that water appearing either brown or brownish yellow in color could well conceal a bar, a rock, or a coral outcropping. The difference between the appearance of rocks and coral heads is that a coral head will often be ringed with a circle of white sand. Black or extremely dark brown spots normally indicate grassy patches.

Reading the bottom visually takes a bit of time and some practice, but it can pay big dividends in keeping your vessel off the hard stuff and over deep water where it belongs.

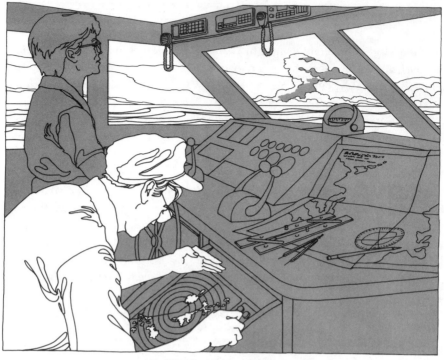

<br />

## CHAPTER 7

# ELECTRONIC NAVIGATION

•　•　•

Any time I hear a boat operator extolling the accuracy and dependability of the expansive array of electronic navigation equipment aboard his yacht, one vivid image invariably leaps into my mind: that of a beautiful 58-foot motor yacht sitting high and dry on the rock jetty at Port Bolivar along the Texas coast. A delivery skipper was running the boat back to its home port in Galveston Bay from Cozumel, Mexico. After clearing the Yucatán Channel he programmed the latitude/longitude coordinates of the entry to Bolivar Roads into the vessel's Loran receiver, engaged the autopilot interface, and both he and the mate settled down for a nice long snooze (assisted, I suspect, by a large bottle of Old Bilgewater). The Loran's margin of error was just

<br />

162

enough to let them hit the end of the jetty at high water and full tilt. The tide ran out and there they sat.

Modern electronic navigation devices are wonders of the age which, if properly used, can make the cruising yachtsman's primary job of knowing where he is and where he's going a great deal easier, simpler, and safer. The key phrase in that sentence, however, is "if properly used." The great danger in relying on electronic navigation devices lies in trusting them too much. I've known more than one skipper who got himself into a great deal of trouble by failing to recognize that his navigational electronics are mechanical gadgets that are vulnerable to a loss of power, that they all contain a degree of inaccuracy that must be allowed for, that they can be wrong either because they simply malfunctioned or we fed them bad data, and that we can interpret accurate information they provide us incorrectly.

The age-old adage that the prudent mariner will never rely on a single source of information to determine his position or course applies in spades to the use of electronic navigation devices. All those pretty lights reading out degrees to tenths of a minute and distances to a tenth of a nautical mile are great, but realize that inaccuracies not only occur but are inherent in their systems, constantly compare what one instrument is telling you with what another is telling you to make sure they are in reasonable agreement, keep up your dead reckoning plots to alert you when something is going haywire, and at every opportunity confirm your position with visual observations and fixes.

Aside from always being a bit skeptical about the information your electronic navigation instruments are giving you, another key to using them successfully is to really master the full range of their functions. Don't content yourself with the quick run-through the electronics salesman may give you. Pore over the owner's manual word by word. If you don't completely understand a function and how to perform it, go over it again and again until you do. If the owner's manual doesn't tell you all you need to know on a specific topic, supplement your knowledge with research into books and magazine articles on the subject by knowledgeable experts. In the process of really getting to know your gear, get in plenty of hands-on practice, preferably in your home waters or on a shakedown cruise when conditions are favorable and a mistake is not likely to be too costly.

This chapter is not intended as a basic primer on using your radar, Loran C, or satellite receiver since each of these topics is well discussed at book length elsewhere. The intention here is to provide a few hints that might help you get the most out of this equipment and avoid some of the most common mistakes in their use.

## NAVIGATING BY RADAR

Radar is not only an invaluable navigating tool at night or when visibility is poor but can be equally useful in daylight when the weather is bright and sunny. Even if your boat is loaded with other electronic navigation equipment, learning to use your radar to maximum advantage can help you keep a check on the accuracy of your Loran and satellite navigation receiver and could provide a valuable backup if any of your primary navigation devices goes on the blink.

One principal value of radar as a navigation instrument is that it can see farther—and in some cases better—than you can. As we discussed in the preceding chapter, the distance to the horizon at sea in nautical miles is 1.17 times the square root of the height of the observer's eye in feet above sea level. Since your radar's antenna normally will be mounted higher than your eye level, its distance to the horizon will be greater. Also, because the radio waves it emits bend slightly, its view extends about 7 percent beyond the horizon. Assume your eye height on the flying bridge of your vessel is 12 feet above sea level. The distance to the horizon will then be 3.9 nautical miles. If your radar's antenna is mounted 16 feet above sea level and the bending of its radio waves allows it to see 7 percent past your visual horizon, it will be able to detect objects at about 4.9 nautical miles farther away than you can, a difference of 1 nautical mile or just over 25 percent. Your radar can often see a number of aids to navigation better than you can because they incorporate radar-reflecting panels which the radar can "see" electronically better and more accurately than you can visually. In coastal cruising or crossing large bodies of open water where markers are out of your visual range but can be detected by your radar, its greater visual range and accuracy can be extremely useful for determining your position and the proper course to steer.

Radar can be used to determine bearings from your vessel to aids to navigation or shoreside landmarks within its range. By using this feature to determine the bearings of at least two—preferably three—marks, then converting those bearings to bearings from the objects to your vessel and plotting them on a chart, you can create a triangle of position within which you are located. The more accurate your bearings, the smaller that triangle—and thus the more accurate your fix. The type of bearings your radar provides and the way you use this feature depend on the level of your radar's sophistication.

A basic radar has a "course up" display which indicates the boat's heading as zero degrees, and an outer 360-degree ring. By simply lining up the center of the display's screen representing your vessel's position and any identifiable object on the display with a straight edge, you can read the bearing from your vessel to the object off the display's outer ring. But bear in mind that a bearing to an object determined in this manner is relative to your boat's heading at the time you take the bearing. It is not a magnetic or a true bearing, and before you can use it to plot your position on a chart you must convert it to one or the other. To convert a relative bearing to a magnetic bearing, you must first add or subtract compass deviation for the vessel's heading at the time the bearing is taken, then add the relative bearing to it. If the sum of those two figures is more than 360 degrees, subtract 360 from it. The result will be the corrected magnetic bearing from your vessel to the object, and its reciprocal will be the magnetic bearing from the object to the vessel. If you plan to do your plotting in true degrees, you must correct your vessel's heading at the time the bearing was taken by compensating for both magnetic variation and the deviation of your steering compass, which will yield your vessel's true heading at the time the bearing was taken. Add the relative bearing to this course. If the sum is greater than 360 degrees, subtract 360 degrees. The reciprocal of that figure will be the bearing from the object to your vessel in true degrees.

Some newer radars have one or more Electronic Bearing Lines (EBLs), which will read out the bearing from your vessel to a mark either in relative or magnetic degrees. If the readout is in relative degrees, you will have to go through one of the processes described above to convert that relative bearing to magnetic or true degrees before you can plot it on a chart. If the readout is in magnetic degrees, you need only correct your vessel's heading for compass deviation, then take the reciprocal to get the magnetic bearing from the mark to your vessel, which you can plot on a chart. Newer type radars with raster scanning have the added ability to momentarily "freeze" the display electronically to determine relative or magnetic bearings even more precisely.

You can also fix your vessel's position by using your radar's range scale to compute your distance from two or more objects that are on your chart.

All radar displays have concentric rings from which the distance from the vessel to an object can be roughly estimated, and newer units have variable range markers, which will calculate distance down to tenths or hundredths of a nautical. Once you have used your radar to determine your vessel's distance from two—preferably three—objects, describe the distance from each object on the chart with a pair of dividers. Where the lines cross will be your vessel's approximate position, with the accuracy of the fix dependent on the accuracy with which you measured and plotted the distances.

A third way you can fix your vessel's position with radar is to convert a relative bearing from your vessel to a single object into a true or magnetic bearing from the object to your vessel, which allows you to plot a line of position, then use the radar's range-finding ability to determine your position along that line.

Once you've mastered these position-fixing techniques, you can use your radar to determine your vessel's speed over ground. First use your radar to determine your vessel's position at one point and note the time. After a convenient interval of time such as 15, 30, or 60 minutes, use your radar to again determine your vessel's position, measure the distance between the two points in nautical miles, and note the length of time it took you to travel between them. Multiplying the distance by 60, then dividing the result by the time in minutes will give you your speed in knots. The speed calculation is even easier if the chart you are using has a logarithmic speed scale in the margin: Put one point of a pair of dividers on distance run and the other on minutes run. Without changing the divider's spread, place its right point on 60. The left point will indicate your vessel's speed in units per hour.

You can also use your radar to detect the presence of any current that is deflecting your vessel from its course and compensate for it. That process is most simple if you are running a course between markers that are in a straight line (Fig. 7.1). Lining up your vessel's heading on the radar's display screen with a pair of markers and keeping it there will give you the course to steer. Any difference between that course and the course you plotted for the run between the two markers alerts you to the deflecting current's presence and, if you wish, you can take the added step of constructing a current diagram as discussed in the previous chapter to determine its set and drift. You can also use your radar to take aft bearings on a single mark relative to your vessel's centerline and use that information as discussed in the previous chapter to detect the presence of a deflecting current and determine its set.

166

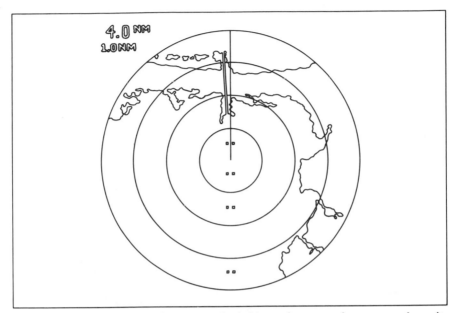

*Fig. 7.1: By lining your radar up on a fixed object such as a marker, you can detect the presence of any offsetting current and construct a current diagram to determine the direction it is setting you and its strength.*

Your radar can also alert you to adverse weather you cannot see but are about to encounter. If a thunderstorm beyond your visual range shows up on your radar, you can track its progress relative to your course and decide if you need to batten down the hatches to prepare for it or take evasive action to get out of its way. We'll discuss this use of radar in more detail in Chapter 9: Predicting the Weather.

Still another valuable use of radar is to alert you to the course and speed of other vessels in your vicinity that might pose a danger. By noting the position of a vessel within your radar's range at a series of time intervals, you can determine its speed and whether or not its course will cross your own. With that information (which some more sophisticated radars will even track for you), you can decide on any evasive action you need to take.

167

## NAVIGATING WITH LORAN C

The reasonable (under $1,000) cost of a basic receiver makes Loran C the electronic navigation instrument of choice for the yachtsman who limits his cruising to the system's primary coverage area, which extends out to 50 nautical miles from the east, west, and Gulf coastlines of the U.S. or to the 100-fathom curve, whichever is greater. If you use the equipment to its maximum advantage and confirm its output by other means, Loran can also be a useful navigation aid in its secondary coverage area, which takes in such popular cruising grounds as the Bahamas, the northern coast of South America, and the western coast of Central America and Mexico.

One key to navigating by Loran effectively lies in fully understanding its limitations.

On the matter of Loran's accuracy, think of it as a navigation system that under ideal conditions will help you find your way across a state, a city, into the right neighborhood, and even put you in the front yard of a particular house, but it won't lead you up to the front door. While the margin of error in Loran C's absolute accuracy (the first time it acquires a fix on a position) is typically as little as 100 feet (and under ideal conditions can be even less), it can easily be as much as a quarter of a mile and in some cases up to two miles. Its repeatable accuracy (reacquiring a fix on a location it has fixed earlier) can be as little as 50 feet or can be up to several hundred feet. In open water where there are no obstacles to a vessel's passage, margins of error of those magnitudes are not likely to be critical. But any time you are relying on your Loran—especially on its absolute accuracy—for inshore navigation where an error of even 50 feet or less can be disastrous, be extremely alert to the system's potential error factor and use at least one other electronic system, such as your radar, or visual sightings to make certain you are where you think you are.

Navigating by Loran is most accurate when the receiver is used in conjunction with charts printed with Loran time delay (TD) overlays and plotting is based on TDs rather than on the receiver's latitude/longitude conversions. A Loran receiver's lat./long. readouts are mathematical conversions from time differences (TDs), and the conversion process itself induces an additional margin of error.

Most skippers, however, are far more comfortable basing their navigation by Loran on latitude and longitude coordinates. Fig. 7.2 is a typical plot of a planned Loran-navigated voyage from Oriental to Ocracoke, North Carolina, using the lat./long. positions of primary markers as waypoints along the route. If you use a Loran's lat./long. conversions as your primary navigational references, you should double-check them frequently by comparing them to known lat./long. positions you can confirm by laying your vessel alongside a charted aid to navigation. If there is a significant difference in the two, be sure to allow for it. Some more sophisticated Loran receivers allow you to program in lat./long. bias, but if you use this feature, remember that the bias you input is valid only for a specific geographic area and will be wiped out of the receiver's programming if you turn the unit off.

In using magnetic bearing readouts from your Loran, be aware that your receiver determines them from a computer program that can allow for magnetic variation but does not allow for local magnetic disturbances, which in some areas can induce errors of up to several miles. If you rely on this feature

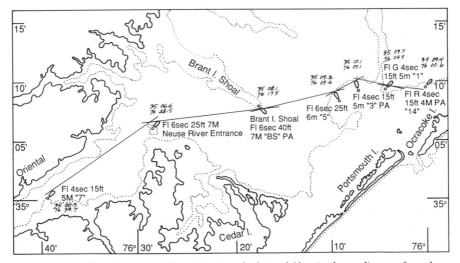

*Fig. 7.2: A plot of an intended track using the latitude/longitude coordinates of markers along the route as Loran waypoints. Positions based on a Loran receiver's lat./long. conversions should be checked at each marker and allowances made for any differences noted.*

of your Loran, also be sure that it has been programmed with the current year and periodically compare the variation it is using with the variation shown on a current chart of the area you are cruising.

If you use the speed-over-ground, course-over-ground, or steering indication functions of your Loran, be aware that they are not instantaneous but are computed from a series of positions over time. In areas of weak Loran signal reception, you'll find that increasing the interval of time over which your receiver averages positions to compute these readouts will make them more accurate.

Although it gets pretty technical, you'll never get the maximum use out of Loran until you understand the characteristics of its signal pulse, the importance of its tracking point, the concept of "cycle slip," and the uses of "cycle stepping." If your owner's manual doesn't cover these topics fully, I suggest you carefully read the treatment of them in Bonnie Dahl's *The Loran C User's Guide* (Richardson's Marine Publishing, Inc.; P.O. Box 23, Streamwood, IL 60103). Suffice it to say here that the optimum tracking point to which all Loran receivers are set at the factory is 35 microseconds into the pulse, which places it at the zero crossing point of the pulse's third cycle. This point is far enough into the pulse to avoid interference from noise, but not so far into the pulse that it will be contaminated by erroneous sky-wave transmissions which first begin to arrive thirty-five microseconds after the ground-wave pulse. In areas where Loran signals are weak, your receiver can experience "cycle slip," in which the point at which it tracks the signal from either a master or a secondary Loran transmitter—or both— slips one or more cycles farther into the pulse or closer to its beginning. Most Loran receivers flash some kind of warning when cycle slipping occurs. But since each cycle has a duration of 10 microseconds, cycle slipping results in a distinctive plus-or-minus 10-microsecond error in TD readouts. You can therefore detect and identify cycle slipping yourself: If you accurately fix your position by some means other than Loran on a chart with Loran overlay lines and find that fix varies from the position your Loran indicates, compare the two. If your position is along the line-of-position (LOP) described by the master transmitter in the chain you are using but is a multiple of 10 microseconds off the LOP described by the secondary transmitter LOP, your receiver is experiencing cycle slip in the signal from the secondary transmitter. If your position is along the LOP described by the secondary transmitter but is a multiple of 10 microseconds off the LOP described by the master transmitter, you're experiencing cycle slip in the signal from the master. If your position is a multiple of 10 microseconds off the LOP described by both the master and the secondary transmitters, you're experiencing cycle slip in the signals from both.

Some Loran receivers provide a "lock" or "track" mode which allows you to manually restore the tracking point or points to their correct position. If you cannot get the receiver to hold the nominal tracking point but it will hold a consistent tracking point, you can often continue to use the signal by allowing for the 10-, 20-, or 30-microsecond error. If you use manual tracking to do this, particularly if you are allowing for error in the signal from both a master and a secondary transmitter, it's critical that you frequently confirm the positions your Loran is giving you by other navigational means.

Some Loran receivers allow you to manually force them to read a tracking point farther into a pulse where signal strength is greater. Using "manual cycle stepping" is a bit tricky, but if you know how to do it properly you can get reliable readouts from your Loran receiver in areas far outside its primary coverage area. In using manual cycle stepping, be sure you understand that stepping up the tracking point of a signal from a secondary transmitter by 10, 20, or 30 microseconds causes the TD of that signal to read that number of microseconds higher and you must allow for the increase in plotting your position. Stepping up the tracking point of a signal from a master transmitter by 10, 20, or 30 microseconds causes the TDs of the signal from both the master and the secondary transmitter to read that number of microseconds lower, and you must allow for the decreases in plotting your position. Stepping up the tracking point of a signal from all the transmitters the Loran is tracking by 10, 20, or 30 microseconds does not cause any TDs to change.

If you use cycle stepping to increase the range at which you can navigate by Loran, it's critical that you remember to allow for any error you have deliberately induced and frequently confirm the positions your Loran is giving you by other navigational means.

## SATELLITE NAVIGATION

Although the Global Positioning System is not scheduled to be declared fully operational in three dimensions (latitude, longitude, and altitude) until the first quarter of 1993, when all twenty-one operating and three spare satellites are expected to be in orbit and functioning properly, the system is now operational twenty-four hours per day worldwide in the two dimensions of latitude and longitude required for marine applications.

As marvelous and accurate a navigation system as GPS provides, there are a few things you need to know about its operation.

The major consideration regarding its use is whether the Department of Defense will stick to its announced policy of downgrading the system's Standard Positioning Service (SPS) available to nonmilitary users, which is technically capable of accuracies to 30 meters (just under 100 feet). Once the system is fully operational, the DOD intends to deliberately downgrade that accuracy to 100 meters (just under 500 feet) by activating "selective availability." A number of commercial and safety organizations are lobbying Congress in an attempt to get that policy reversed, but as of this writing they have not met with success.

The propagation of GPS signals can be affected by the atmosphere, and thus its accuracy levels can vary, which makes the present system unsuitable for precise inshore navigation. The Coast Guard is now working on a differential GPS system covering major harbors and harbor approaches along America's east, west, and Gulf coasts, Alaska, and Hawaii, which will monitor the system's signals, compute the atmospheric effects on their propagation in real time, then transmit correction factors to GPS receivers in the area. Assuming Congress appropriates the necessary funds, the installation of differential GPS stations should begin in 1994 and be completed by early 1996.

GPS signals are not subject to the additional secondary factors that affect Loran C signals and thus there is no essential difference in its absolute and repeatable accuracy. GPS signals are not subject to cycle slip and thus there is no reason for you to have to get involved in cycle stepping.

A GPS receiver displays position only as latitude and longitude, which it derives from a computer conversion of the solution it calculates from satellite signals. Since the system provides you with no data comparable to Loran TDs, you need no special charts with overlays of the type you use with Loran.

Most GPS receivers can display course and bearings in either true or magnetic degrees. If you use magnetic readouts from your GPS receiver, bear in mind that they are computer conversions of true data and are averaged over a fairly wide (50–100 miles) geographic area. They may not conform exactly to your magnetic compass, and they will not take into account strong local magnetic disturbances.

Speed-over-ground and course-over-ground readouts from a GPS receiver, like those from a Loran receiver, are averages. But because a typical GPS receiver updates its position about once a second, changes in SOG or COG readouts are virtually instantaneous.

Satellite navigation can be highly accurate. Fig. 7.3 shows an actual plot

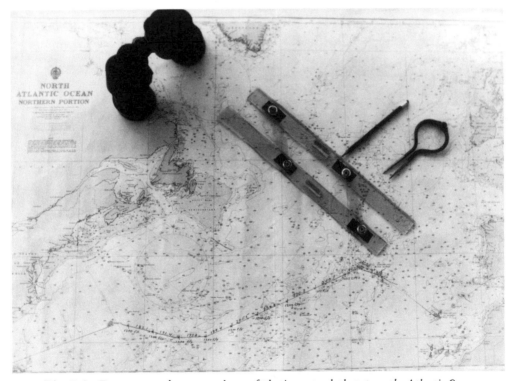

**Fig. 7.3:** *Few power yachtsmen can boast of plotting a track that spans the Atlantic Ocean from Ft. Lauderdale, Florida, to Villamora, Portugal. This plot of the transatlantic voyage of the 58-foot displacement-hull cruiser* Trenora *shows a deep southward deviation from the Great Circle route between Bermuda and the Azores, which was necessary to avoid a major storm sweeping down off the Grand Banks.*

of the motor vessel *Trenora's* track across the Atlantic Ocean from Fort Lauderdale, Florida, to Bermuda; the Azores and Madeira to Villamora, Portugal. During the voyage, her position was maintained by the older Transit satellite navigation system which, though less accurate than today's GPS, guided her to her destinations with errors of only a few feet.

## NAVIGATING BY AUTOPILOT

If you plot an intended track on a chart, then crank that course into an autopilot that has no external sensors and expect it to carry you to your destination, don't be surprised if you wind up on the rocks. As we mentioned in our discussion of running compass courses in the previous chapter, your autopilot can keep you precisely on the course you fed it but deflecting current can carry you wide of the mark and straight into trouble.

If you interface your autopilot to a Loran C or GPS receiver then it will indeed proceed to the next waypoint you specified, offset the effects of deflecting current, and even sound an alarm when it arrives. With the more sophisticated navigation receivers, once you reach an initial waypoint your autopilot will automatically make course changes and carry you to a subsequent waypoint.

The only caveats I will mention in all this are that both your autopilot and your navigation receiver are mechanical devices and subject to error, and they are only as good as the data you feed into them. If you fail to notice shoal water along the course you instructed your electronics to follow, they will faithfully put you right on top of it. If a log happens to be floating across that course, your electronics will carry you into it with unfailing accuracy. No matter how sophisticated your navigation setup, there is no substitute for keeping a good lookout.

## NAVIGATING BY DEPTH-SOUNDER

In feeling your way down an unmarked channel or into a secluded anchorage, your depth-sounder will be worth all your radars, your Loran C receivers, and your GPS receivers put together. Just bear in mind that it only reads water depth directly under its transducer, not in front of your vessel, behind it, or to the side. In navigating with your depth-sounder, the main thing you are looking for is trends in the slope of the bottom. If you took the suggestion in my earlier book, *Stapleton's Powerboat Bible,* and outfitted your vessel with dual depth-sounders with separate transducers spaced as widely as possible in your hull, you can ping your way along and figure out where deep water lies.

In an emergency where you have lost all your other navigation electronics, you can use your depth-sounder to reach safety by correlating its readings to the bottom contours on a chart to help you figure out where you are, then follow a given contour in the direction you must go to reach safe harbor.

## NAVIGATING BY KNOT METER/DISTANCE LOG

Should you lose all your other electronic navigation equipment, it's possible to do at least rudimentary navigation by proceeding in a certain compass direction for a certain length of time at a given speed as measured by your knot meter or for a certain distance as measured by your distance log. If you should be reduced to navigating in this manner, bear in mind that a common knot meter/distance log with a paddle-wheel-type impeller measures only speed through the water based on the speed at which its impeller turns and measures only distance through the water by the number of revolutions of its impeller at a given speed. In the presence of current, your actual speed and distance over ground can be significantly different from what your knot meter/distance log is telling you and you will have to take that current's effects into account in your calculations.

**CHAPTER 8**

# CRUISING COMMUNICATIONS

• • •

The marine radios aboard your vessel are your primary links with other vessels and the world ashore, are indispensable to the operation of your vessel in such situations as passing through bridges and locks, can be critical in an emergency to your vessel's safety, and are your primary source of weather information which can materially affect your cruising plans. You need to know how to use them properly (which the vast majority of recreational boat owners don't), how to get the most out of them, and how to fix at least minor problems if they go on the blink.

In my earlier book, *Stapleton's Powerboat Bible,* I discuss at length how marine radios work, recommend criteria for equipment selection, and cover proper installation. In this chapter we'll assume you have good equipment properly installed on your vessel and put our emphasis on the routine use of your VHF set, which you'll use for communicating with other vessels and coast stations within roughly 40 miles of your position, and the SSB unit you'll need for long-range communications if you head farther than about 40 miles offshore or into foreign waters. (We'll cover the use of marine radios in emergency situations in Chapter 10.)

## USING YOUR VHF MARINE RADIO

Because VHF radio waves have no significant ground wave and are of such high frequency that they are not reflected back to earth by the ionized layers in the earth's atmosphere, they are useful only along a clear "line of sight" between the antenna of the transmitting station and that of the receiving station (Fig. 8.1). Due to the curvature of the earth, the reliable range of VHF radio wave ship-to-ship transmissions is normally limited to around 10 to 15 miles because the vessels' antennas are so close to the earth's surface. Reliable VHF transmissions in ship-to-shore communications can range up to about 40 miles because the shore-based antenna normally is several hundred feet high. Note the term "reliable transmissions." Under certain atmospheric conditions, VHF radio waves can transmit considerably in excess of these approximate ranges, but you shouldn't depend on those anomalies to provide consistent communications.

### Selecting an Appropriate Channel

The Federal Communications Commission places very strict regulations on how VHF marine radios may be used. Its first requirement is that certain channels are to be used only for certain purposes.

As the operator of a noncommercial vessel, you normally will use only about nine simplex channels (which send and receive on the same frequency) plus the four "receive only" channels WX 1 through WX 4, which carry NOAA weather information.

- Channel 16 may be used only for calling other vessels and for communicating safety and distress messages both ship-to-ship and ship-to-shore.

177

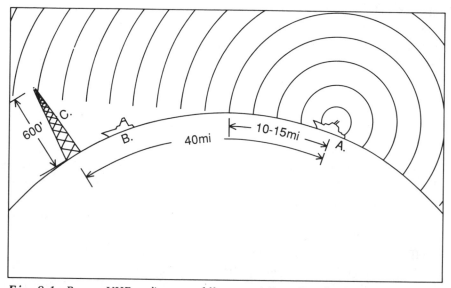

**Fig. 8.1:** *Because VHF radio waves follow essentially a line-of-sight path, vessel* A *is unlikely to be able to communicate with vessel* B, *even though it can communicate with land-based tower* C *which is further away.*

- Channel 6 may be used only for communicating safety messages ship-to-ship and is the primary channel for communicating with Search And Rescue (SAR) vessels and aircraft of the U.S. Coast Guard.

- Channels 9, 68, 69, 71, 72, and 78A are the primary working channels for nonrecreational vessels. All but channel 78A may be used either ship-to-ship or ship-to-coast. Channel 78A may be used only ship-to-ship.

- Channel 13 is the primary channel for communicating with bridge tenders and lockmasters and may be used for communicating navigational information with other vessels.

- Channel 22A is the primary working channel for talking with the Coast Guard (after first establishing contact on channel 16) and is the primary channel over which the Coast Guard broadcasts messages regarding navigational safety and weather alerts. (The suffix "A"

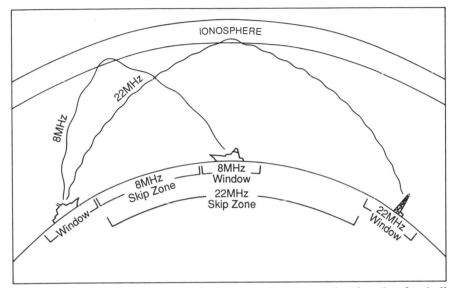

*Fig. 8.2: Propagation—the ability of radio waves of certain wavelengths to be reflected off layers in the ionosphere—is the key to worldwide communications by single-sideband marine radios.*

following a channel number indicates its use and/or frequency in the U.S. are different from those in other countries. In the U.S., all marine VHF channels except for the Public Correspondence channels 24–28 and 84–88 send and receive on a single frequency. In most other countries of the world, channels with the suffix "A" send on one frequency and receive on a different frequency.)

Except in certain special instances, operations on VHF channels 13, 17, and 67 must be conducted at your VHF radio's minimum one-watt power output setting rather than at its normal maximum power output of twenty-five watts. VHF marine radios manufactured after January 21, 1987 must automatically shift to this one-watt setting when those channels are dialed up and must have a manual override to allow maximum power in emergencies.

In addition to these calling, safety, working, and weather channels, you may also use Public Correspondence channels 24, 25, 26, 27, and 28 for placing and receiving marine radiotelephone calls through marine operators, which we'll cover in detail later in this chapter.

In high-traffic areas such as major ports and busy commercial sea lanes, you may also find it helpful to monitor channels 12, 14, 20, 65A, 66A, 73, and 74 to determine the intentions of other vessels. There is also the possibility you might use channel 17 to communicate with state-controlled vessels, such as dredges, and law enforcement officials. The remaining channels are strictly for commercial or U.S. government use and there should be no reason for you to transmit over them with the single exception that in an emergency you may use any VHF channel to attract help and summon assistance.

## Proper Use of VHF Channel 16

The improper use of VHF channel 16 for extended conversations has reached epidemic proportions, and I hope as a responsible vessel operator you'll do all you can not to condone this misuse or contribute to it. Channel 16 is designated solely for calling, safety, and distress messages, and the format for using it has been carefully designed to ensure that it is kept clear as much as possible for the transmission of distress messages. Any time it is tied up with casual conversation, it cannot be used for the purposes for which it was intended and could put someone's life and/or property in jeopardy.

Under normal circumstances, you should transmit on channel 16 only to establish contact with other vessels or the Coast Guard. If you use channel 16 to try to contact another vessel within about a half-mile of your position, manually reduce your radio's output to 1 watt, which will mean your transmission will occupy the channel for only about a mile radius around your vessel rather than 15 to 20 miles. If you are trying to reach a shore station other than the Coast Guard, you should first try to contact them on an appropriate working channel. If you are trying to reach a marina, call them on channel 9. If you are trying to reach a marine operator, try them on one of the Public Correspondence channels, which in most areas are channels 24–28.

The correct way to call another vessel or the Coast Guard is to first scan the appropriate working channels (for communicating with other noncommercial vessels those will be primarily 9, 68, 69, 71, 72, and 78A; for communicating with the Coast Guard it will be channel 22A) to find one that is not in use. Once you have found a clear working channel, shift your radio back to channel 16, wait for a break in any traffic that might be already in progress on it, then transmit the name of the vessel you wish to contact. Unless atmospheric conditions are causing problems in communicating over VHF, you should transmit that vessel's name only once, and for goodness sake don't add such tag lines as "Come in" or "Bob, do you read me?"

Following the name of the vessel you are calling, say "This is" and transmit the name of your own vessel and your vessel's radio call sign. If you have had previous contact with the vessel you are calling, giving the name of your vessel once should be sufficient. If you are calling a vessel for the first time, you might want to say your vessel's name twice to make sure the person on the other end knows who to respond to. (Technically you should end the call with the word "over," which means "I have finished my transmission and a reply from you is required and expected," but it normally is omitted in the interest of brevity.)

If the vessel you are calling answers, simply say "Reply Channel ____" and give the number of the working channel you have selected. Shift your radio to the working channel and say the name of your vessel once. It is not necessary to give your vessel's radio call sign on a working channel until you conclude your conversation. Once the vessel you are calling shifts to the working channel and replies with its own name, you have confirmed the contact and are free to proceed with your message.

When you have concluded your conversation on the working channel, give the name of your vessel and its radio call sign once and say "out," which frees the channel for others to use.

If you initiate a call on channel 16 or a working channel and receive no response, you should wait at least two minutes before repeating the call. If you initiate a call to the same vessel or a shore station three times at two-minute intervals and receive no response, wait at least fifteen minutes before transmitting the call again.

If yours is the vessel called on Channel 16, your proper response is to give the name of the vessel calling, say "This is," and give your vessel's name and its radio call sign. Once the individual calling you has suggested a working channel, you should confirm that you are shifting to that channel by saying its number. If for some reason you are unable to respond on that channel, you should propose an alternate working channel. If the alternate is agreeable to the individual calling, he or she should indicate agreement by repeating the number of the working channel you have proposed. Once

181

you have completed your conversation on a working channel and the individual who initiated the call has cleared the channel with his vessel's name, its radio call sign, and the word "out," you should give your vessel's name and its radio call sign and say "out," which clears the channel for others to use. Don't make the mistake of saying "Over and out," which in the world of marine radio are contradictory terms. "Over" means "This is the end of my transmission and a reply from you is required and expected." "Out" means "This is the end of my transmission to you and no response from you is required or expected."

If you contact another vessel frequently, you can use an abbreviated form for establishing contact. To initiate such a call you would transmit on channel 16 the name of the vessel you are calling, give your vessel's name and radio call sign, and say "Reply _____" to indicate an appropriate working channel. The operator of the responding vessel would shift to the working channel and reply with his or her vessel's name and radio call sign. You then respond with your vessel's name, continue the conversation, then end it and clear the working channel as above.

Any time you are transmitting over marine radio, of course, you should speak slowly and distinctly. In poor atmospheric conditions, you may need to use procedure words or spell words phonetically in order to be sure you communicate clearly and concisely. You'll find a list of procedure words and their meanings in Fig. 8.3 and the phonetic alphabet in Fig. 8.4 at the end of this chapter.

FCC regulations require that if you are aboard your vessel and its VHF radio is turned on, you should monitor channel 16 at all times when you are not actually using your radio to transmit or receive on a working frequency. There is so much garbage on channel 16 these days that monitoring it can be both frustrating and irritating, but you need to listen in anyway. If you were in trouble and trying to use channel 16, you'd want everyone with a VHF radio to be listening, and you owe that effort to your fellow mariners.

## Digital Selective Calling

The relatively new technology of Digital Selective Calling (DSC) allows you to receive an alerting message that another vessel or a shore station wants to talk to you without using VHF channel 16.

The DSC system is part of the Global Maritime Distress and Safety

# RADIO PROCEDURE WORDS

**AFFIRMATIVE**    You are correct, or what you have transmitted is correct.

**BREAK**    I separate the text from other portions of the message; or one message from another message which follows immediately.

**FIGURES**    Figures or numbers follow. Used when numbers occur in a message such as: "Ladye Anne is four eight, repeat four eight feet, in length."

**I SPELL**    I shall spell the next word phonetically. (See Fig. 8.4—Phonetic Spelling Alphabet)

**MAYDAY**    The international distress signal indicating that a vessel or person is threatened by grave and imminent danger. Spoken three times. (MAYDAY is the accepted English pronunciation of the French word "m'aider"—"help me.") The MAYDAY distress call and message have priority over all other transmissions.

**NEGATIVE**    You are not correct, or what you have transmitted is not correct.

**OUT**    This is the end of my transmission to you and no reply from you is required or expected.

**OVER**    This is the end of the current portion of my transmission to you and your response is necessary and expected.

**PAN PAN**    The international urgency signal indicating a vessel or person is in jeopardy but the danger is not life-threatening. The phrase is spoken three times. Properly pronounced: "PAHN PAHN." The PAN PAN urgency signal has priority over all transmissions except the MAYDAY distress signal.

**ROGER**    I have received your last transmission satisfactorily and understand your message.

**SECURITY**    When used as the international safety signal, is spoken three times and properly pronounced Say-curiTAY. The SECURITY safety signal has priority over all other transmissions except the MAYDAY distress signal and the PAN PAN urgency signal.

**THIS IS**    This transmission is from the station whose name and/or call sign immediately follows.

**SILENCE**    When used to order the cessation of interfering transmissions over a channel or frequency being used for emergency communications, SILENCE is correctly pronounced "SEE-LONCE" and spoken three times.

**SILENCE FINI**    Used to signal the resumption of normal working on a channel or frequency previously used for distress communications. Pronounced: SEE-LONCE FEE-NEE.

**WAIT**    I must pause for a few minutes. Stand by for further transmission.

*Fig. 8.3*

# PHONETIC SPELLING ALPHABET

| Letter | Identifying Word | Spoken As |
| --- | --- | --- |
| A | Alfa | AL fah |
| B | Bravo | BRAH vo |
| C | Charlie | CHAR lee |
| D | Delta | DEL tah |
| E | Echo | ECK oh |
| F | Foxtrot | FOKS trot |
| G | Golf | GOLF |
| H | Hotel | Hoh TELL |
| I | India | IN dee ah |
| J | Juliett | JEW lee ETT |
| K | Kilo | KEE low |
| L | Lima | LEE mah |
| M | Mike | MIKE |
| N | November | No VEM ber |
| O | Oscar | OSS ker |
| P | Papa | PAH pah |
| Q | Quebec | Keh BECK |
| R | Romeo | ROW me oh |
| S | Sierra | See AIR rah |
| T | Tango | TANG go |
| U | Uniform | YOU nee form |
| V | Victor | VIK ter |
| W | Whiskey | WISS kee |
| X | X-ray | ECKS ray |
| Z | Zulu | ZOO loo |

*Fig. 8.4*

System (GMDSS), which will allow governmental authorities to communicate critical weather and safety information to vessels at sea. It works this way: In the U.S., the Federal Communications Commission (and its counterpart agencies in other countries) assigns vessels which must or wish to utilize DSC a unique nine-digit "sel-call" number. Member nations of the International Radio Consultative Committee (CCIR) have set aside VHF channel 70 exclusively for the transmission of DSC "alerting messages." When a vessel's DSC number is transmitted over channel 70 as a series of electronic tones, those tones activate a receiver on board the vessel.

Even though DSC was not developed primarily to facilitate communications between recreational vessels or between recreational vessels and shoreside stations, we can take advantage of it. To receive a DSC "alerting message" that someone is trying to reach, you must apply to the Federal Communications Commission for a nine-digit DSC number which will be unique to your vessel, and you must install a VHF radio or an accessory to your present VHF radio that is capable of decoding DSC alerting messages. As of this writing, the only VHF marine radio on the market that is equipped to decode DSC signals is the DSC 500 produced by Ross Engineering (12505 Starkey Road, Largo, FL 34643. Telephone: (813) 536–1226). When the DSC 500 is installed aboard a vessel, it is programmed to decode that vessel's sel-call number. When it detects that number, it electronically displays the DSC number of the calling party, in some cases the name of the vessel or shoreside station trying to reach you, and a brief message such as one requesting you to reply on a working VHF channel.

Existing VHF radios equipped with channel 70 can be upgraded to detect DSC alerting messages with the addition of the Auto-Kall 10 decoder produced by MoTron Electronics (310 Garfield St., Eugene, OR 97402. Telephone: (800) 338–9058). The MoTron unit does not have the capability to display information about the calling party, but can only flash a light to indicate that the sel-call number with which it has been programmed has been detected.

In order to call another vessel or shoreside station using DSC, you must know that vessel or station's sel-call number, and your VHF radio must be equipped with a touch-tone pad capable of transmitting that number as a series of electronic tones.

As required by FCC regulations, you should monitor VHF channel 16 any time you are on board your vessel and have your radio turned on. A means of decoding DSC alerting messages, however, could prove valuable

185

in those times when you are ashore or aboard your vessel with the radio turned off.

## Placing and Receiving VHF Marine Operator Radiotelephone Calls

In addition to contacting other vessels and shoreside installations, you can also use your VHF marine radio to contact marine telephone operators who can connect you to the worldwide land-based telephone system.

The Atlantic, Pacific, and Gulf coasts of the U.S. mainland, the Great Lakes, principal inland river systems, Hawaii, Puerto Rico, and the Virgin Islands are covered by a network of over 200 of these operators which are known formally as Public Coast Stations. These are private companies, some of which are divisions of major telephone companies such as the regional Bell Telephone companies or GTE, while others are independent operations. The ownership and names of companies that provide marine operator service change frequently. The most complete and up-to-date listing of marine operators and the channels they use I've seen is included in the *Marine Radiotelephone Users Handbook,* which is published by The Radio Technical Commission for Maritime Services. It can be ordered from RTCM, Post Office Box 19087, Washington, DC 20036, and costs $7.95.

If you want to place a VHF radiotelephone call from your vessel and have a listing of marine operators and the channels they use, call the one nearest you on its working frequency. If you don't have a listing, simply transmit a call to "Marine Operator" on channel 16. They will answer and ask you to switch to their working frequency.

The rates for marine operator services vary from company to company but generally run around $2.50 to $3.00 for the first three minutes and about a dollar for each additional minute. In addition, you will be charged the applicable long distance rate from the marine operator's location to the number you are calling. You can place calls either station-to-station or person-to-person.

The billing procedures for VHF marine calls can be a bit of a hassle. The VHF marine operators owned by companies like the Baby Bells and GTE that also provide regular land-based telephone service issue Marine Identification Numbers (MIN) which allow you to charge calls to your vessel. Contact the business office of the VHF marine operator nearest you and they will either send you an application or tell you where to get one. Some—

186

but not all—privately owned VHF marine operating companies will also honor MIN numbers. Some companies that don't honor MIN numbers will allow you to charge a call to a regular telephone company credit card, your home phone, or a third number. Others won't allow charges to home or third numbers unless they can call and verify the billing information. In billing calls any of those ways, you are broadcasting information which anyone listening on the working channel could use to charge calls without your authorization. The best way for handling billing, providing the party you call agrees to accept the charges, is to call collect.

If you expect family, friends, or business associates to contact you from shore via VHF, it will be a great help if you give them your vessel's name, your call sign, and at least a rough itinerary of where you will be and when. Also give them a listing of VHF marine operators in the area you will be cruising. To reach you, they simply dial 0 and ask for the VHF marine operator in the town closest to where you are expected to be at that point in your cruise.

One way to find out if someone is trying to reach you via VHF is to monitor channel 16. If you are expecting a call and don't hear your call sign on 16, call the VHF marine operator in the area you are cruising on their appropriate working channel and ask if they are holding traffic for you. The companies don't charge for traffic inquiry calls, but some of their operators get a bit testy if you bug them too often.

As discussed above, a VHF radio or decoder capable of detecting your vessel's sel-call number could be used to alert you to the fact that a marine operator has a call waiting for you. As of this writing, the companies that provide VHF marine operator services are taking a "wait and see" attitude before making the investment required to use DSC, but it appears to be a system that in time they will have to adopt.

## Using Your Hand-Held VHF Radio

Technically your installed VHF radio is your vessel's "ship station." If you use a hand-held VHF radio in your cruising, it is an "associated ship unit" and the call sign you should use any time you transmit from it in your dinghy would be your vessel's radio call sign followed by the designation "Unit 1." The proper procedure for calling your main vessel from your dinghy, then, would be "WX 1234—THIS IS WX 1234 UNIT 1—OVER." (In transmitting from their dinghy over a hand-held VHF, many cruisers use as a call sign the name of the main vessel plus the designation "Mobile 1," but this is technically incorrect. That designation would be correct only if the hand-held VHF were being used on board the main vessel.)

Legally (except in an emergency) you may use your hand-held VHF only to communicate with your main vessel, you may not operate it from shore, and you may transmit only at 1 watt output power. Every cruiser I know blithely ignores all the foregoing.

## USING SINGLE-SIDEBAND MARINE RADIO

### SSB Band Selection

The whole theory of single-sideband operation is based on the fact that high-frequency radio waves are reflected off the layers of ionized gases in the ionosphere. Because ionization of the ionosphere is affected daily by the rising and setting of the sun, the range of the various HF SSB bands (i.e., the "windows" in which communication on a particular band is possible) and the "skip zone" over which signals in a particular band pass and communication is impossible (see Fig. 8.2) vary greatly by time of day. Therefore, one of the most important factors in achieving optimum SSB communications is selecting a band that will allow you to communicate over a given distance at a given time of day.

One of the best ways to learn which band to use to communicate over a given distance at a given time of day is to listen to your SSB and make notes in a logbook. In a loose-leaf notebook, assemble separate pages for distance groupings of under 500 miles, 500–1,000 miles, 1,000–2,000 miles, and over 2,000 miles. Down the left side of each sheet, space out the hours of the twenty-four-hour clock. At their scheduled times, listen to the traffic list broadcasts of the High Seas coast stations and the U.S. Coast Guard's Notices to Mariners broadcasts. Try each of the channels on which each broadcast is made. When you hear a station clearly, identify its location and compute its distance from you. On the sheet in your listening log for that distance, make a note of the station received and the channel under the appropriate hour heading.

Once you have twenty or thirty entries in your log and are ready to make a call, compute the distance over which you wish to communicate.

(If you are trying to place a radiotelephone call through a High Seas coast station, the critical distance is from your vessel to the High Seas coast station's antenna, not the distance to your call's ultimate destination.) On your log sheet for that distance, alongside the hour you wish to make the call will be the channels over which you are most likely to make contact over that distance at that time of day. After a month or so of this kind of practice, you'll find it becomes almost automatic to make the calculations in your head. Where your log indicates you have a choice between two or more bands, try the higher one first as it is more likely to provide the greatest signal strength and the lowest atmospheric noise.

After you've worked with your SSB for a while, you'll find the following characteristics of the various SSB bands tend to be generally accurate:

The reliable range of frequencies in the 2–3-MHz bands is about 200 miles during the day, around 500 miles at night. The band is susceptible to static from thunderstorms but since it is ground wave, it has no significant skip zone.

Channels in the 4-MHz band can be virtually useless from sunrise to late afternoon. In early evening, range increases to around 600 miles. At night, its skip zone makes contact difficult within 100 to 200 miles, but maximum range stretches up to 2,000 miles or more.

Channels in the 6-MHz band have a range of about 500 miles in daylight hours and stretch out to about 2,000 miles at night. However, because the 6-MHz band is subject to a number of anomalies, it is the least used of the HF SSB bands. A few 6-MHz channels are used by the Coast Guard and High Seas station WHA operates over two, but they are not used by the AT&T High Seas stations nor by WLO.

Channels in the 8-MHz band have a reliable range of around 700 miles all day with minimal skip zone. At night, skip zone is about 500 miles but beyond that, range can be 3,000 miles or more.

The 12-MHz band is inactive or weak until midmorning. Around noon skip zone begins to stretch out to around 500 miles and range to 2,000 to 3,500 miles. After sunset, skip zone gradually widens to about 1,000 miles and range to about 4,000 miles.

The 16- and 18-MHz bands are inactive or weak until late morning. Around noon skip zone widens to around 750 to 850 miles and range gradually increases to 4,000 to 6,000 miles. Both bands fade sharply two to three hours after local sunset.

The 22- and 25-MHz bands are inactive or weak until around noon, then strengthen with skip zone widening to 1,500 to 2,000 miles and range extending to 7,000 to 8,000 miles. Both bands fade shortly after sunset.

Bear in mind that these are averages. Any of the SSB bands can be rendered temporarily unusable by atmospheric conditions or ionospheric disturbances for periods ranging from a few hours to several days.

If basing your selection of an SSB band on logbook entries seems a bit primitive to you, you might want to investigate the new Automatic Link Establishment (ALE) option recently introduced by Harris Corporation (1680 University Avenue, Rochester, NY 14610. Telephone (717) 244-5830). This plug-in option for the company's RF 3200 SSB radio selects the best band automatically.

## SSB Frequency Changes

Because of significant advances in radio technology and the advent of the Global Maritime Distress and Safety System scheduled to be implemented in 1992, sweeping changes have been made recently in the allocation of frequencies used for high-frequency radiotelephone transmission in the 4,000 to 27,500-kHz range. The changes that most directly affect recreational mariners who use single-sideband marine radio became effective at 0001 Universal Coordinated Time on July 1, 1991. The most significant of those changes was to shift the paired frequencies of all the HF channels, which meant that the ship's transmit and ship's receive frequency of every channel of every SSB radio had to be reprogrammed. Unless you can manually dial in transmit and receive frequencies, you cannot communicate over ITU channels with an SSB radio that has not been reprogrammed with the new frequencies.

It's important to note that the changes affected only channels in the 4-MHz band and above. Thus, channel 2.182 MHz (normally referred to by its kilohertz designation simply as "twenty-one-eighty-two"), which is reserved internationally as a calling and distress frequency, was not affected. The changes did, however, add the frequencies 4125 kHz and 6215.5 kHz as supplementary distress frequencies to 2182 kHz.

## Using SSB Modes

All the marine SSB radios on the market have a "mode" switch which allows you to select one of several modes for signal emission, but none of their manufacturers bothers to explain very much about how they differ nor how they are used. The FCC has recently helped to confuse the matter even further by assigning new designations to many of the emission modes. Here's a rundown:

- The bulk of SSB operation in pleasure cruising is conducted in the J3E mode on the Upper Sideband (USB). (On older SSB radios, this mode is referred to by its previous designation—A3J). In addition to marine SSB, this signal emission mode is also used by amateur radio operators on their 15- and 20-meter bands. Many of the newer marine SSB radios allow you also to operate in the J3E mode on the Lower Sideband (LSB), which puts you into the 40- and 80-meter ham radio bands. You can listen to transmission on the ham bands, but transmitting over them is illegal unless you hold a valid and appropriate ham radio license. We'll say more about LSB operation when we cover the use of ham radio in cruising later in this chapter.

- Some SSBs now on the market also operate in the R3E mode, which is used primarily for accessing marine telephone operators in parts of Europe and Canada, though transmission in this mode can also be handled by the AT&T High Seas stations. (This mode used to be called A3A, and its carrier signal had to be reduced to 40 percent of Peak Envelope Power. Under the new FCC regulations, its carrier signal now must be reduced to 25 percent of PEP—i.e., to 37.5 watts on a marine SSB radio with 150 watts PEP.)

- The H3E mode (formerly designated A3H) is the old double-sideband (DSB) mode, which has been largely displaced by USB operation but is still used in some parts of the Caribbean and South America. On the mode selection switch of some marine SSB radios it is identified as the AM or AME mode. It is full carrier with amplitude voice modulation on the Upper Sideband.

- The CW mode stands for Continuous Wave and is used for sending or receiving Morse code. Communication via Morse code is used

191

primarily by commercial vessels with professional radio operators aboard and is gradually being phased out of use in the marine service.

- FSK stands for Frequency Shift Keying, which is important only to those who use shipboard telex.

## International Radiotelephone Alarm

Your SSB radio may have an internal international radiotelephone alarm which in an emergency can be used to alert receiving locations such as U.S. Coast Guard and High Seas coast stations that you are about to transmit an emergency message. We'll discuss its use fully in Chapter 10: Emergency Use of Marine Radios.

## Placing and Receiving SSB Marine Operator Radiotelephone Calls

There are two types of marine radiotelephone services that handle SSB calls from and to your vessel—the Coastal Harbor Service and the High Seas Service. Coastal Harbor Service stations handle SSB calls only on the MF 2–3-MHz band and are used primarily by marine interests on the nation's inland waterway system. Most yachtsmen who cruise offshore place ship-to-shore calls and receive shore-to-ship calls through coast stations in the High Seas Service which handle calls on both the MF 2–3-MHz band and all the HF bands allocated for marine use.

There are four High Seas stations in the continental U.S. and one in the U.S. Virgin Islands. AT&T operates what experienced cruisers call the "big three"—WOM in Fort Lauderdale, Florida; WOO in Manahawkin, New Jersey; and KMI in Point Reyes, California. Mobile Marine Radio, Inc., operates WLO in Mobile, Alabama. Global Communications Corporation operates WAH in St. Thomas, U.S. Virgin Islands.

*Placing High Seas Radiotelephone Calls:* While any High Seas coast station can handle calls to and from vessels anywhere in the world, each does tend to concentrate its high-gain directional antennas toward particular parts of the world. If you are in the Pacific, it makes sense to try KMI first; if in the Caribbean or Gulf of Mexico, WOM should be your first choice; if in the North Atlantic, try WOO first. The proximity of your vessel to a

192

particular High Seas station, however, is less important than propagation factors. After placing a few High Seas calls, you'll get a feel for which stations you can reach most easily at different times of day and which is most likely to have an open channel.

Each station broadcasts "traffic lists"—the names of vessels for which they are holding calls—on specific channels at specific times. In general, you will be able to communicate with any High Seas station whose traffic list you can hear clearly. One way to place a call through a High Seas station is to listen to its scheduled traffic list broadcasts and try to make contact as soon as the traffic list is over on the channel through which you are receiving the traffic list most clearly. The only problem with that is that the minute the traffic list ends, a dozen or more vessels usually try to get the High Seas station at the same time, so you may have to wait an hour or more to get through.

To relieve congestion, the High Seas stations urge customers also to place calls at times other than following the traffic list broadcasts. To do that, figure the approximate distance from your vessel to the High Seas station you want to use. From the listening log we suggested earlier that you create, select the highest band that is likely to provide communications at the time you want to place the call and over that distance. Tune your radio to one of the channels in that band listed for the High Seas station you want to call and listen to it for about three minutes. Remember that you are listening only to the channel's station transmit frequency. If someone on another vessel is talking to the High Seas station, he'll be on the channel's ship transmit frequency and you won't be able to hear him. If after about three minutes you don't hear any traffic on the channel, go ahead and make your call. A typical call to WOM might sound like this: "Whiskey, Oscar, Mike . . . Whiskey, Oscar, Mike . . . Whiskey, Oscar, Mike. This is the motor yacht *Mad Hatter,* Whiskey, X-ray, Yankee 1234, calling from offshore St. Lucia on channel eight thirty-one." Giving the channel number you are using in your initial call helps the technician at the High Seas station select it from among the twenty or more channels he or she is monitoring to respond to your call. Giving your vessel's position in your initial call helps the technician know where to point the station's high-gain directional antennas for the best connection. After making your initial call, wait about a minute before trying it again. If your call was heard, it probably will take the technician that long to select and tune the station's equipment. You may get a recording telling you all technicians are busy and to stand by. Stay on that channel and the technician will get to you.

If the first channel you try is busy or after three or four calls you can't raise a technician, shift your radio to another channel in the band listed for that High Seas station and listen there. Chances are after two or three tries you'll find a channel that is not in use. If all channels in that band listed for that station are busy, go to a channel in that band listed for the next logical High Seas station based on antenna coverage.

Once you get a technician, you will be connected to a telephone operator who will take the calling details and billing information and connect you with your party. If you want time and charges on the call, tell the telephone operator (not the High Seas technician) before she makes the connection. Telephone operators will not honor time-and-charge requests after the call is completed. All High Seas calls are handled as person-to-person calls, even if you agree to speak with anyone who answers, and charges do not begin until the individual you call answers. Once you get your party on the line, if he or she is not familiar with radiotelephone calls, briefly explain that you both need to say "over" after you have finished a segment of the conversation and the listener should not speak until he hears the speaker say "over." If you don't, you'll probably find you have to repeat a lot of missed conversation. If you encounter difficulties during a marine radiotelephone call, have the person you are talking to momentarily depress the switchhook on his or her telephone. This will stop billing time on the call and signal the operator. The telephone operator can then retry the call or bring in the High Seas technician if necessary to try another frequency.

When your land party hangs up, stay on the channel until the telephone operator comes back on the line. If you have other calls, go ahead and give her the information and she will try to place them. When you are through with your last call, again wait until the telephone operator comes on the line, have her reconnect you with the High Seas technician, and sign off the channel with the High Seas station.

As far as the AT&T High Seas stations (WOM, WOO, and KMI) and WLO are concerned, so long as the final destination of your call is in the United States (including Alaska and Hawaii), Canada, Mexico, Puerto Rico, or the U.S. Virgin Islands, the charges will be a flat rate no matter which of the coast stations you place the call through or the position of your vessel. (At this writing, the rate is $14.93 for the first three minutes and $4.98

194

for each additional minute.) If you are calling a country other than those listed, you will also be charged the person-to-person rate from the High Seas coast station to the call's destination.

You can place calls through the High Seas stations collect or have them billed to your home or office phone. But you will save yourself a lot of time and hassle passing billing information if you preregister your vessel with the High Seas stations before you leave on your cruise. You can preregister your vessel for calls to all three AT&T High Seas stations with a single toll-free call to 1-800-SEA-CALL, but you will have to preregister separately with the owners of WLO and WAH. Once your vessel is preregistered, all you have to do is instruct the operator to "bill the vessel calling," and you won't have to give her a string of numbers which might become garbled in transmission. You also won't be giving out information such as your telephone credit card number which someone else might overhear and use to charge calls without your authorization.

*Receiving High Seas Radiotelephone Calls:* If you want your family, friends, or business associates to be able to reach you on board your vessel and you plan to use the AT&T High Seas coast stations as your primary radiotelephone link with shore, give them your itinerary, your vessel's name, its radio call sign, and its Digital Selective Calling number if you have asked the FCC to issue one (we'll talk more about DSC further along in this chapter) and instruct them to call 1-800-SEA-CALL which will connect them with AT&T's central High Seas operator 11362 in Pittsburgh, Pennsylvania, where traffic lists for all three of the company's High Seas coast stations are compiled. All three AT&T stations broadcast the same traffic list, and you may return a call to the station of your choice. If you will be using High Seas Coast Station WLO as your primary radio telecommunications link, instruct them to call 1-800-633-1634 and ask for the High Seas operator. Your vessel will be listed on the coast stations' next traffic list and will stay on the list until you answer or the shore party cancels their call. In cases where the call is not answered and the coast station cannot contact the calling party for instructions, the vessel normally will be removed from the traffic list after twenty-four hours.

One way to find out if someone is trying to reach you via SSB radiotelephone is to periodically listen to the scheduled traffic list broadcast over any of the High Seas stations to see if your vessel's name is listed. Another is to call a High Seas station to see if they are holding traffic for you. There is no charge for such an inquiry, but it's best to limit calls to other than the peak traffic hours during the midmorning, late morning, and early evening.

If you use the AT&T coast stations as your radiotelephone link, the easiest way to know if someone is trying to reach you via SSB is to add peripheral equipment to your SSB that will alert you when an AT&T's High Seas coast station is holding traffic for you. AT&T's coast stations WOO in New Jersey and KMI in California now broadcast traffic lists as virtually continuous data signals which can trigger a decoder connected to your SSB. Once activated, the decoder rings a bell and flashes a light to alert you that you have a call waiting. These signals can carry two types of information: your vessel's radio call sign, which it transmits as SITOR in the Forward Error Correcting (FEC) mode; and/or your vessel's Digital Selective Calling (DSC) number.

MoTron Electronics Co. (310 Garfield St., Eugene, OR 97402) sells a device called an Auto-Kall AK-100 which will decode either signal and sound a bell and flash a light when it recognizes your vessel's call sign or its DSC number. The light continues to flash until you turn it off so you will know that the High Seas coast station tried to reach you even if you were not on board when the call was attempted. The AK-100 also has an RS-232C output port through which it can be connected to an on-board personal computer to receive, decode, and print out distress messages, urgent safety messages, and weather reports. (The SITOR portion of WOO's broadcast includes NOAA High Seas weather forecasts every two hours at twenty minutes past even UTC hours.) It lists for $479.

WOO transmits these data signals on 8051.5 kHz, and KMI transmits them on 8087.0. To receive them, you would tune your SSB radio when it's not in use to either 8049.8 kHz (to monitor WOO) or 8085.3 kHz (to monitor KMI).

## For Further Information

On the subject of High Seas radiotelephone calls, AT&T offers a very useful *Fingertip Guide* which gives the frequencies, traffic list, and weather broadcast schedules for all their stations. You can get one by calling 1-800-SEA-CALL. Both the call and the guide are free. WLO offers a guide to its marine communications services which is available by writing to

Mobile Marine Radio, Inc., 7700 Rinla Avenue, Mobile, Alabama 36619-5110.

## TROUBLESHOOTING GUIDE TO MARINE RADIOS

In an emergency, a VHF or SSB marine radio doesn't do you any good if you can't transmit, and hopefully receive, over it. If you need your radio for emergency communications and it doesn't seem to be working properly, here are some things to quickly check:

1. Is your ship's service battery system working properly?
    A. If none of the equipment aboard your vessel that is powered by your ship's service battery is working, the problem is probably with the battery itself. Check to see that it is filled with water and that the cables connected to it are tightly affixed and not corroded. If necessary, refill the battery with water and/or remove, clean, and reattach the battery cables securely.
    B. If some, but not all of the equipment aboard your vessel powered by your ship's service battery is working, the problem is probably in your vessel's electrical distribution panel. Trace your radio's power cable to its connection at the distribution panel. Check the fuse or circuit breaker serving the terminal to which the radio's power cable is connected. If your distribution panel uses fuses, check the fuse in the circuit serving your radio. It normally will be a small, clear glass tube with metal caps on either end, each of which snaps into a small pair of prongs. A thin wire or small strip of metal will run through the glass tube lengthwise. If either of the metal caps at the ends of the fuse shows signs of a chalky green or white substance, it is corroded. Remove the fuse from the prongs into which it snaps and scrape both the cap and the prongs down to bright, shiny metal. (Be careful not to allow any metal such as a knife blade or screwdriver to contact the sets of prongs which hold the two ends of the fuse at the same time. You

197

could get an electrical shock.) Hold the fuse up to a light and shake it gently. If the wire or metal strip is broken or loose, replace the fuse with another of the same type and size.

If your distribution panel uses circuit breakers, check to make certain the breaker is not tripped and, if necessary, reset it.

If after either of these steps you still have doubts that the terminal is delivering power to your radio, disconnect the radio's power cable and attach it to another circuit serving equipment powered by your ship's service battery that is working, such as a Loran receiver or a knot meter.

If your radio seems to be the only piece of equipment aboard your vessel powered by your ship's service battery that isn't working, the problem is probably with the radio's electrical power supply, its antenna system, or the radio itself.

2.  Is the radio turned on?

Make certain the radio's "power" switch is in the "on" position. If the power switch is on and the radio is working, the lights on its front panel should be glowing. The fact that the lights are glowing indicates the radio is getting some electrical power, but the fact that they aren't glowing doesn't necessarily mean the radio isn't transmitting or receiving properly. If the lights aren't glowing but you can receive any noise over the radio, even just static, the light bulbs or the circuit board to which they are connected could be burned out, loose, disconnected, or their contacts corroded. If the lights aren't glowing and you can't receive even static over the radio, turn the power switch on and off several times. It may be shorted out or corroded. If so, you will have to disconnect the radio and remove it from its case to clean, tighten, or replace the switch.

3.  Is the radio connected to an adequate source of power?

If the radio's front panel lights aren't glowing and you can't receive even static over it, check its fuse. The fuse can either be in the back of the radio case behind a small knob marked "fuse" or housed in a cylindrical fitting in the radio's power cable. If so, the fitting usually will be about an inch long and half an inch in diameter and will be black. Once you've located the fuse, unscrew the knob or the fitting, remove the fuse, and check it and its contacts as suggested above for a fuse in the distribution panel. If one or both of the metal caps on the ends of the fuse are corroded, clean them and their contacts inside the fuse housing. If the wire or metal strip inside the fuse is loose or broken, replace the fuse.

4. Is the radio properly connected to a functioning antenna?

    A. A marine radio will not transmit or receive adequately if it is not properly connected to a functioning antenna. Check the lead from your radio to the base of its antenna to make certain the connections at both ends are securely tightened and are not corroded. If necessary remove, clean, and resecure them. Check along the length of the antenna lead to make certain it is not broken.

    B. Check the antenna itself to make certain it has not been damaged or swept away. In either case, connect the radio's antenna lead to an emergency replacement antenna or construct a jury rig. In the case of a VHF radio, a random length of wire will function as a jury-rig antenna. It preferably will be about 6 feet long, and must be oriented vertically and installed as high on your vessel as possible.

    You can also jury-rig an antenna for your marine single-sideband radio provided you have an automatic antenna tuner installed between the jury rig and the radio. Construct the jury-rigged antenna from a length of wire about 25 feet long, insulate it at both ends, and connect it to your vessel's RF grounding system. Before connecting the lead from the antenna tuner to it, make certain the radio is turned off as the jury rig will carry a significant amount of electrical current. Once you have made the connection, warn your crew to stay well clear of the jury rig, or they could receive a nasty electrical shock. Before you attempt to transmit with such a jury-rigged antenna, turn off all other electronic equipment aboard your vessel as the SSB's RF signals could burn them out.

5. Is the radio transmitting?

    A. If the radio appears to be receiving adequate power from your ship's service battery and to be properly connected to an undamaged or jury-rigged antenna, you may find you can receive over it but cannot transmit. When you depress the microphone's transmit button, a light on the radio's front panel marked "transmit" should glow. The fact that the "transmit" light does glow indicates you are transmitting, but the fact that it doesn't glow doesn't necessarily mean you aren't transmitting. The bulb may simply be loose, its base could be corroded, or it could be burned out. Push on the bulb and wiggle it to see if you can establish contact. If not, you will have to disconnect and disassemble the radio to clean the bulb's contacts or replace it. The best indication that you are not transmitting is that you are able to receive on a channel but when you transmit on it you receive no acknowledgment.

B.   Activate the microphone's transmit button several times to see if the "transmit" light comes on. The switch itself may be loose or corroded. If so, you will have to disassemble the microphone to clean, tighten, or replace it.

C.   Check any external connection between the microphone and the radio itself. Some microphones are attached to their radios by a connector which could be loose or corroded. If your microphone has such a connector, make certain it is not corroded and is securely tightened. If necessary, clean and retighten it.

If none of the above steps convinces you that your radio is working properly, about your only recourse is to disconnect the radio, remove it from its case, and check inside for any signs of corrosion on any of its terminals, or for loose or disconnected wires.

# CHAPTER 9

# PREDICTING THE WEATHER

• • •

As a cruising yachtsman there are few topics of more critical concern to you than the weather, and there are few skills you can develop that will be of more practical value than being able to predict with reasonable accuracy the weather conditions you are likely to encounter. Developing that ability involves learning something about the forces that create basic weather systems; learning how to gather information from your own observations or broadcast weather data concerning the current status and likely movement of those basic systems; and interpreting that information in terms of your own cruising plans.

## Understanding Basic Weather Systems

You can't really make maximum use of the wealth of weather information available to you until you understand the fundamental processes that determine basic weather systems. Stated in their simplest terms, those processes begin (Fig. 9.1) with the sun's rays striking the earth and heating its surface. Heat reflected from the earth's land masses heats the air above them, causing that air to rise. As the air rises, it leaves a center of low pressure beneath it. As the heated air rises, it flows toward cooler air, becomes cooled itself and sinks back toward earth. This downward flow of air creates a center of high pressure. The difference in pressure between the high and low thus formed creates a "pressure gradient" which causes masses of air in the high-pressure area to flow toward the area of lower pressure, thus creating surface winds.

Since the earth is round, the sun's rays strike the earth most directly at the equator. As the earth at the equator is heated and in turn heats the air above it, that air rises. The upward rush of that heated air leaves in its wake a band of low pressure girdling the earth that meteorologists call the Intertropical Convergence Zone (ITCZ) (Fig 9.2). As this heated air rises to a height of about 12 miles, it gradually cools and becomes more dense (heavier) and a major portion of it sinks back to earth around 30 degrees north and south latitude. This air pressing down on the earth forms what meteorologists refer to as the subtropical high-pressure zones. (To put the area of the subtropical high in the Northern Hemisphere in perspective: in North America, the line of 30 degrees north latitude runs across northern Mexico, just north of San Antonio and Houston, Texas, virtually through New Orleans, Louisiana, and just to the south of Jacksonville, Florida.) The pressure gradient created by the difference in pressure between the subtropical high and low atmospheric pressure of the ITCZ causes masses of air in the subtropical high-pressure zones to flow toward the lower-pressure area of the ITCZ.

If the earth did not rotate on its axis, the high-pressure air masses from the subtropical high-pressure zone around 30 degrees north would flow directly southward toward the equator, and the air masses in the subtropical high-pressure zone around 30 degrees south would flow directly northward toward the equator. But because the earth is rotating on its axis from west to east

202

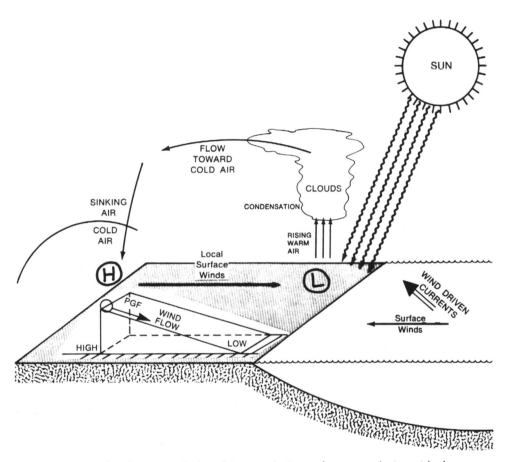

**Fig. 9.1:** *The "heat engine" that drives our basic weather systems begins with the sun striking the earth and heating the air above it, causing that air to rise. (Courtesy Alden Electronics, Inc.)*

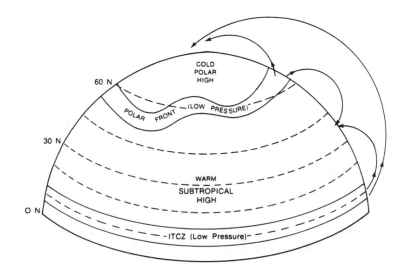

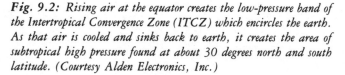

*Fig. 9.2:* Rising air at the equator creates the low-pressure band of the Intertropical Convergence Zone (ITCZ) which encircles the earth. As that air is cooled and sinks back to earth, it creates the area of subtropical high pressure found at about 30 degrees north and south latitude. (Courtesy Alden Electronics, Inc.)

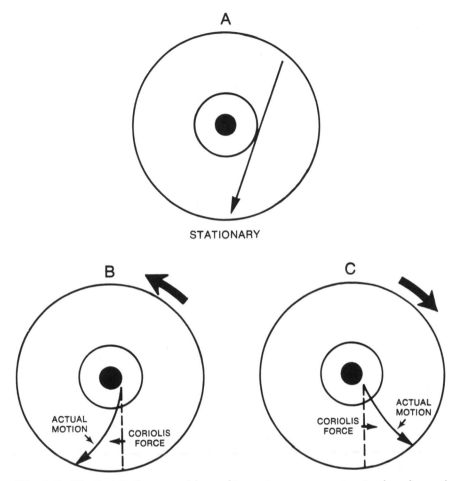

**Fig. 9.3:** *The Coriolis force created by earth's rotation causes us to perceive descending cool air as wind whose prevailing direction in the Northern Hemisphere is from the east toward the west. (Courtesy Alden Electronics, Inc.)*

it creates what is known as the Coriolis force (Fig. 9.3), which deflects this air flow toward the west and causes us to perceive it as coming from the east. In the Western Hemisphere we refer to these basic air flows (Fig. 9.4) as the northeast trade winds, which sweep roughly across northern Africa, then southwesterly across the North Atlantic toward the Caribbean Sea; and the

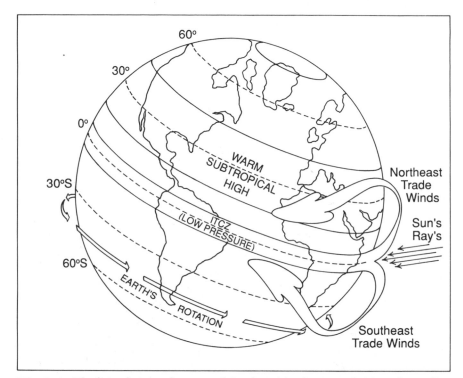

***Fig. 9.4:*** *The force of air at the equator being heated by the sun and rising, then cooling and sinking back to earth in the subtropical high, combined with the Coriolis force created by the earth's rotation, gives rise to the northeast trade winds in the Northern Hemisphere and southeast trade winds in the Southern Hemisphere. (Courtesy Alden Electronics, Inc.)*

southeast trade winds, which sweep roughly across southern Africa, then northwesterly across the South Atlantic toward Brazil.

In the Northern Hemisphere, as warm air rises and leaves an area of low pressure in its wake, surrounding air is drawn into the void (what meteorologists call convergence). The Coriolis effect, combined with centrifugal force, causes the air around this area of low atmospheric pressure to circulate counterclockwise (Fig. 9.5). As cooled air sinks back to earth creating an area of high pressure, it is forced outward (what the meteorologists call

TOP
VIEW

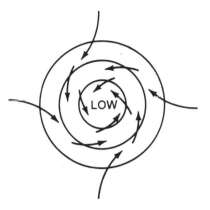

SIDE
VIEW

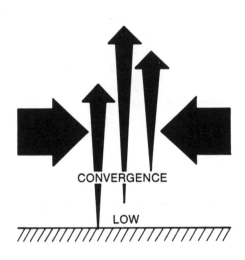

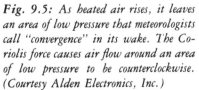

*Fig. 9.5:* As heated air rises, it leaves an area of low pressure that meteorologists call "convergence" in its wake. The Coriolis force causes air flow around an area of low pressure to be counterclockwise. (Courtesy Alden Electronics, Inc.)

divergence) and the Coriolis effect, combined with centrifugal force, causes the air around the high to circulate clockwise (Fig. 9.6). In the Southern Hemisphere both directions are reversed.

Within this basic system, of course, are subsystems that create other wind patterns with which mariners are familiar (Fig. 9.7). Some of the air heated at the equator, for example, flows all the way to the poles before it sinks to earth, creating high-pressure zones around both the North and South poles and a band of low-pressure polar fronts between the polar highs and the subtropical highs at about 60 degrees north and south latitude. In the Northern Hemisphere, air masses flowing down the pressure gradient from the polar high zone toward the lower pressure of the polar front with a clockwise rotation imparted by the Coriolis effect and centrifugal force create polar easterly winds. Pressure gradients also cause some high-pressure air masses in the subtropical high-pressure zone to flow northward toward the lower-pressure area of the polar front. Their clockwise rotation imparted by the Coriolis effect and centrifugal force creates midlatitude westerlies.

These factors are also primarily responsible for the basic patterns of upper air level movement which provide the steering currents for much of the surface winds with which we as mariners must deal. The same fundamental forces that create the northeast trade winds, for instance, steer hurricanes born off the west coast of Africa across the North Atlantic to landfall somewhere between the Lower Antilles and the southeast coast of the United States (Fig. 9.8).

The basic wind patterns created by the heating/cooling process, the Coriolis effect, and centrifugal force are in turn responsible for the basic ocean currents (Fig. 9.9). A persistent area of high pressure over the North Atlantic (often referred to as the Bermuda High), for example (Fig. 9.10), normally is centered roughly at about 30 degrees north latitude and creates a basically clockwise ocean current pattern in the North Atlantic. When that flow piles up against the continental shelf along the east coast of North America, it is concentrated and creates the northeasterly-flowing Gulf Stream.

All these basic weather systems are affected by the fact that the earth's axis of rotation is inclined about 23½ degrees to the plane of its orbit around the sun, which means that in the summer the Northern Hemisphere is closest to the sun and thus warmer while the reverse is true in winter. This not only accounts for the reversal of seasons in the two hemispheres but creates winter/summer shifts in basic weather patterns. During the summer months, for instance, the Bermuda High tends to migrate to the northwest, bringing high pressures and associated fair weather to most of the East Coast of the U.S. Dur-

TOP
VIEW

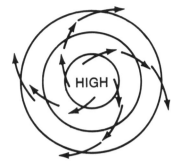

SIDE
VIEW

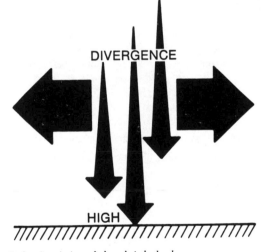

*Fig. 9.6:* As air is cooled and sinks back
to earth, it creates an area of high pressure
meterologists refer to as "divergence." The
Coriolis force causes air flow around an area
of high pressure to be clockwise. (Courtesy
Alden Electronics, Inc.)

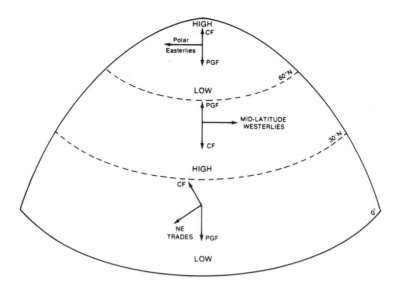

**Fig. 9.7:** *The combination of heated air rising, cooling air falling, and the Coriolis force created by the earth's rotation makes up the basic forces behind the Northern Hemisphere's northeasterly trade winds, the midlatitude westerlies, and polar easterlies. (Courtesy Alden Electronics, Inc.)*

ing winter, that system tends to migrate southwesterly, leaving the East Coast shrouded in the rain and fog typical of an area of low pressure.

## UNDERSTANDING BASIC WEATHER PATTERNS

Once you understand basic weather *systems* you are in a position to predict the basic weather *patterns* they create in a given cruising area at a particular time of year, take advantage of favorable conditions, and avoid weather patterns you know will be adverse.

## HIGH-PRESSURE SYSTEMS AND FRONTS

The downward flow of dense, cold air which produces the subtropical and polar high-pressure zones we have discussed creates four distinct types of

210

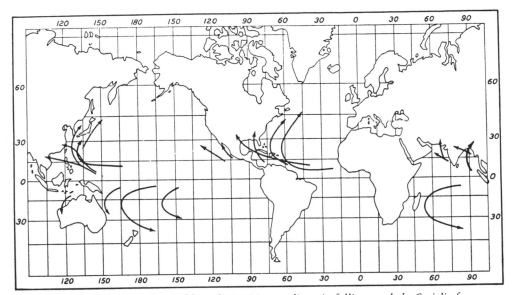

*Fig. 9.8: The basic forces of heated air rising, cooling air falling, and the Coriolis force give rise to the earth's prevailing wind patterns and strongly influence the paths of tropical storms. (Courtesy Alden Electronics, Inc.)*

high-pressure air masses, which are classified by the region over which they are created and by whether they are formed over land or water. While in the Northern Hemisphere all four have the characteristic clockwise air flow imparted by the Coriolis effect and centrifugal force, these high-pressure air masses vary widely in their temperature and moisture content:

1. *Maritime tropical* air masses are formed over ocean areas in the sub-tropical high region and tend to be warm and moist. In the northern half of the Western Hemisphere, the Bermuda High is a typical example.

2. *Continental tropical* air masses are formed over land areas in the subtropical high region and tend to be warm and dry. In the northern half of the Western Hemisphere, the fairly persistent area of high

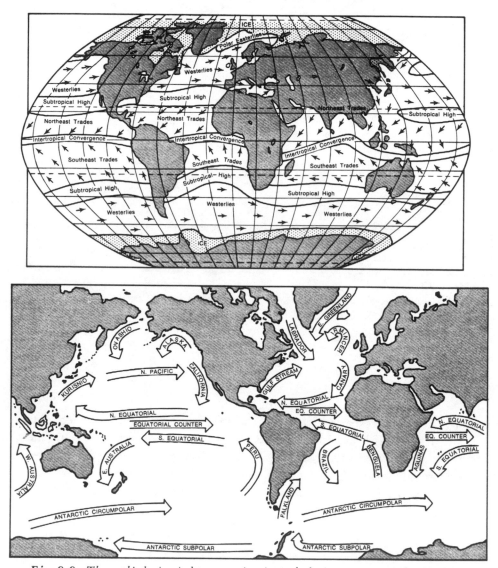

**Fig. 9.9:** *The earth's basic wind patterns give rise to the basic ocean currents that mariners encounter around the world. (Courtesy Alden Electronics, Inc.)*

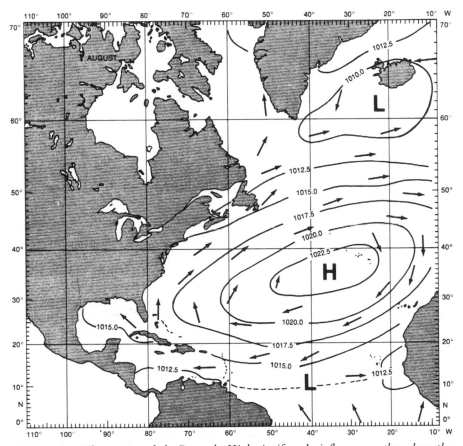

*Fig. 9.10:* The position of the Bermuda High significantly influences weather along the Eastern Seaboard of the United States and is a primary factor in determining ocean currents in the North Atlantic. (Courtesy Alden Electronics, Inc.)

pressure centered over the desert areas of the southwest portion of the United States is a typical example.

3. *Maritime polar* air masses are formed over ocean areas in the polar high region and tend to be cold and wet. A typical example in the North Atlantic is generally found off the northeastern coast of Canada.

213

4.  *Continental polar* air masses are formed over land in the polar high region and tend to be cold and dry. An example is the area of persistent high pressure found generally over northwestern Canada.

As these air masses form, they are carried along by prevailing winds and atmospheric pressure gradients. The effects of unequal global warming during winter and summer cause their center in the Northern Hemisphere to move generally toward the equator during the winter months and poleward during the summer months. The combination of these two factors causes these high-pressure air masses to move in a more or less consistent—and therefore reasonably predictable—pattern. In North America, their pattern of movement can tell you a great deal about the basic winter and summer weather across the United States and its coastal waters.

The first of these is the series of maritime tropical air masses that are spawned in the subtropical high-pressure zone off the coast of California and Mexico and flow northward toward the lower pressure of the polar front with a clockwise rotation which carries them with their heavy moisture content up into the Gulf of Alaska. From there they sweep down into North America as midlatitude westerlies and are steered eastwardly by the jet stream at a typical rate of about 400 statute miles a day. If the jet stream is running well to the north, they come ashore about British Columbia, sweep over Canada's southern provinces and America's northern tier of states and the Great Lakes, then exit into the North Atlantic roughly between Nova Scotia and Newfoundland. If the jet stream is running approximately over the U.S.–Canadian border, these air masses tend to come ashore somewhere from Oregon to northern California, sweep eastward across the Great Plains, and cross the East Coast between roughly Washington and Boston. If the jet stream dips well southward into the central part of the U.S., these air masses are driven more southeasterly across the U.S. and tend to exit into the North Atlantic somewhere between about Washington and the South Carolina–Georgia border.

A second primary air mass pattern that strongly influences weather conditions in North America in winter is a strong southward shift of the subtropical high-pressure zone which leaves lower pressure in its wake and allows continental polar air masses spawned in the polar high region of western Canada to sweep down the pressure gradient and carry their icy blasts down into the continental U.S. The extent of the southward migration of the subtropical high combined with the location of the jet stream largely determines whether subfreezing temperatures will extend only to the midportion of the country or all the way down to the Gulf Coast. In rare instances, an extreme southern flow of the jet stream can force freezing temperatures all the way down into southern Florida and Texas.

Other primary air mass patterns that influence weather patterns in the eastern half of the U.S. are the maritime tropical highs that form off the west coast of Africa just above the equator, then sweep across the Atlantic and up through the eastern Caribbean at a typical rate of advance of about 250 miles a day. A weak Bermuda High over the North Atlantic tends to allow these fronts to sweep up the East Coast. A strong Bermuda High in the North Atlantic tends to force these air masses into the Gulf of Mexico. Once in the Gulf, depending on the strength and location of the jet stream, which provides their primary steering currents, they usually head in one of four general directions. A jet stream running over northern Canada allows them to curve to the north and cross the Gulf Coast of the U.S. through about Mississippi and Louisiana, where they often recurve and sweep inland just to the west of the Appalachian Mountains. A jet stream running about over the U.S.–Canadian border steers them toward the Texas–Mexican border. A jet stream running even farther south forces them across the Yucatán Peninsula or into Central America.

While changing conditions can alter the speed and direction of these air masses, you can watch their ebb and flow across the U.S. on any daily weather map and use this kind of basic information to make some fairly reliable predictions regarding likely boating conditions along your planned route and thus determine your schedule.

## Fronts

A front is simply the leading edge of one of the four types of air masses we have described and is the area along which significant weather changes are likely to take place as two—and in some cases three—air masses with differing relative temperatures encounter each other. While the basic air mass behind a front consists of high pressure, a front itself is an area of low pressure called a trough and is a transition zone that is likely to involve rapid change in temperature, pressure, wind, and moisture. While fronts are basically classified as cold and warm, the basic importance of those terms is not the absolute temperature of a front itself but its degree of coldness or warmth in relation to that of other air masses it encounters. The greater the tem-

215

perature differential between two colliding air masses, the greater the likelihood that their collision will result in severe weather.

## Cold Fronts

In the Northern Hemisphere, cold fronts such as those at the leading edge of a maritime or continental polar air mass tend to move roughly northwest to east or southeast at about 20 knots. As their leading edge encounters warmer air, the two air masses do not mix. Instead, the warm air is forced upward where it cools and condenses into clouds and the moisture it contains often precipitates out as rain (Fig. 9.11). Because the blunt edge of an advancing cold front forces the warmer air upward at a fairly sharp angle, rain along its leading edge is likely to develop quickly and be intense but is often limited in area and clears quickly. As a cold front passes through a location, wind direction will shift from the southwesterly flow of the warm air mass in front of it to northwest, then to north and possibly even into the northeast and the temperature and humidity will drop. The atmospheric pressure will drop as the leading edge of the cold front passes, then increase as the cold air mass advances.

## Warm Fronts

In the Northern Hemisphere warm fronts such as those at the leading edge of a maritime or continental tropical air mass may travel in a variety of directions and even change directions but normally proceed at a somewhat slower pace than cold fronts—typically at about 15 knots. As a warm front passes a location, the wind will shift from approximately southwest to approximately west and the temperature and relative humidity will generally increase. Atmospheric pressure will decrease as the front passes, then increase as the warm air mass comes in behind it. As warm air rides up over the colder air in front of it, it will be forced upward where it will cool and condense into clouds and possibly rain (Fig. 9.12). Because the vertical slope of a warm air front normally is not as steep as that of a cold front, adverse weather where a warm front rides over colder air is likely to develop slowly; high cirrus clouds can precede the arrival of the front itself by a day or more. Adverse weather created by the arrival of a warm front is not likely to be particularly intense but is likely to cover a wide area and last for several days.

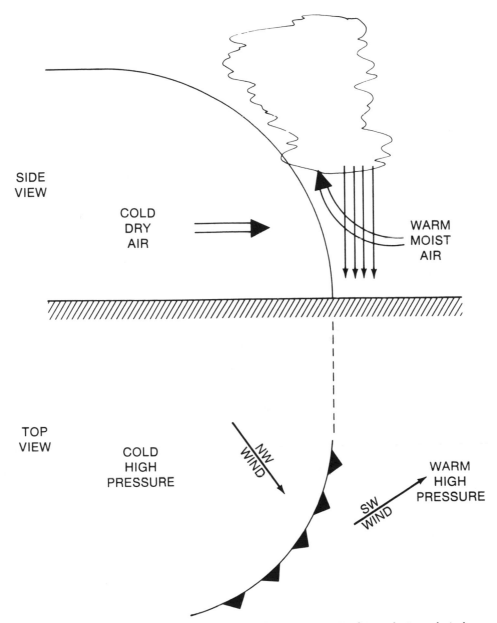

**SIDE VIEW**

COLD DRY AIR

WARM MOIST AIR

**TOP VIEW**

COLD HIGH PRESSURE

NW WIND

WARM HIGH PRESSURE

SW WIND

*Fig. 9.11: A cold front pushing its way beneath warm, moist air often results in a relatively narrow band of showers, which can be intense but are likely to be of only brief duration. (Courtesy Alden Electronics, Inc.)*

217

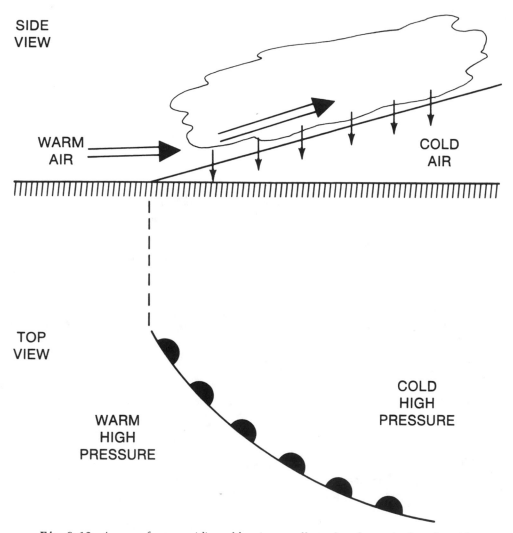

SIDE
VIEW

WARM
AIR

COLD
AIR

TOP
VIEW

WARM
HIGH
PRESSURE

COLD
HIGH
PRESSURE

*Fig. 9.12: A warm front overriding colder air normally produces heavy clouds and a wide band of usually light rain. (Courtesy Alden Electronics, Inc.)*

## Occluded Fronts

An occluded front involves not simply cold air and warm air but air that is warm, cold, and colder. It develops this way:

Because cold fronts tend to travel faster than warm fronts, they overtake warm fronts fairly frequently. Remember that by definition, the air on the front side of a warm front is cooler than the air behind it. When a cold front overrides this situation, one of two conditions occurs: if the air behind the advancing cold front is colder than the air in front of the warm front, the colder air forces the warm air upward; if the air behind the advancing cold front is not as cold as the air in front of the warm front, the advancing cold front rides up over the warm air.

## LOW-PRESSURE SYSTEMS AND CYCLONES

While high-pressure systems are formed by fundamental weather processes, tend to be more or less permanent, and cover vast areas, with a few exceptions, such as the more or less permanent low-pressure system in the North Atlantic over Iceland, low-pressure systems are more transitory in nature, cover smaller areas, and tend to be formed by the collision of air masses of different temperature. The Coriolis effect, convergence, and centrifugal force combine to cause air flow around them in the Northern Hemisphere to be counterclockwise.

### Extratropical Cyclones

The condition of a cold front overtaking a warm front which results in an occluded front often creates an extratropical cyclone that has the counterclockwise air movement around a center of low-pressure characteristic of a tropical cyclone (called a hurricane in the North Atlantic). While the two systems are similar, they also have important differences. Extratropical cyclones can occur over either land or water, where tropical cyclones normally are born only over water; they occur in the midlatitudes north or south of the ITCZ; they generally cover a larger area (500–1,000 miles compared to 400–500 miles for a tropical cyclone); their internal wind speeds are only about half those of a tropical cyclone; and in the Northern Hemisphere they tend to move from west to east where tropical cyclones tend to move from east to west.

Both systems, however, are created in the same manner (Fig. 9.13):

Because the air mass behind both a cold front and a warm front is high pressure, in the Northern Hemisphere the air flow along both fronts is clockwise, which means that where the two fronts meet, their air movement is

219

SIDE
VIEW

TOP
VIEW

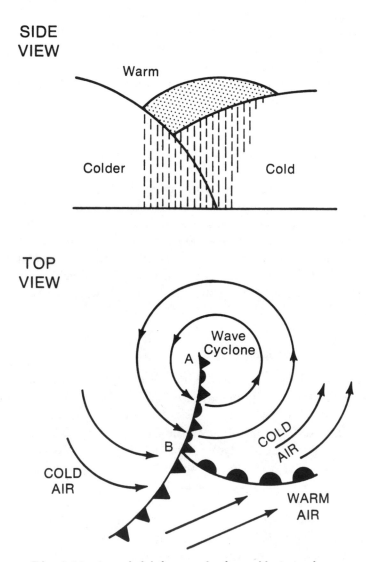

**Fig. 9.13:** *An occluded front results from cold air in the upper atmosphere overriding warmer air nearer the earth. The counter rotation of the two bodies of air can produce a wave cyclone of intense low pressure around the point where they intersect. (Courtesy Alden Electronics, Inc.)*

opposed. (You may not have trouble grasping the concept that two clockwise air flows can be opposed, but I did and figured it out this way: Think of two gears side by side, both turning in a clockwise direction. If they are forced together, the right half of the gear on the left will be turning downward while the left half of the gear on the right will be turning upward; thus their movement will be opposed.)

As the cold front pushes under the warm front, the warmer air rises. The upward rush of this warm air creates a center of low pressure, around which air—because of the Coriolis effect and centrifugal force—in the Northern Hemisphere begins to circulate counterclockwise. If the temperature differential between the warm front and the overtaking cold front is not extreme, then the only result of the overtaking is to create an area of bad weather which can extend outward from the center of the low pressure for several hundred miles. These are the "low pressure" systems which we see on the daily weather map, marching in a more or less regular rhythm across the continental U.S. at intervals of roughly four to ten days, spreading wind and rain along their leading edge, which can extend for several hundred miles. If temperatures along the leading edge of these low-pressure systems are cold enough, the precipitation the system generates will fall as freezing rain, sleet, or snow.

If the temperature differential between the cold front and the warm front is extreme, however, the circulation around this center of low pressure can become extreme and create the kind of storm conditions we normally associate with the word "cyclone."

## SOURCES OF BASIC WEATHER PATTERN INFORMATION

The best sources of basic long-range weather pattern information for U.S. waters are the various volumes of the NOS coast pilots, which provide information on general weather patterns in the areas they cover and meteorological tables that list by month prevailing wind directions and percentages of observations in which winds exceed gale force (34 knots) and sea heights exceed 10 feet. Similar information for foreign waters is found in the various volumes of *Sailing Directions* published by the Defense Mapping Agency.

## SOURCES OF BROADCAST WEATHER INFORMATION

### Voice Weather Broadcasts

The best source of information on English language voice marine weather broadcasts is *Selected Worldwide Weather Broadcasts,* which is published by the National Weather Service and is available through the Government Printing Office. Ask for NOAA—S/T 81-184.

This publication lists the location, call signs, and frequencies of all VHF radio stations broadcasting continuous marine weather information in the U.S., Canada, and Puerto Rico.

It also lists the location and call signs of radio stations worldwide that broadcast marine weather information over single-sideband radiotelephone. The listings include the times, frequencies, and contents of broadcasts along with the areas they cover.

### Radiofacsimile Weather Broadcasts

*Selected Worldwide Weather Broadcasts* also lists the location and call signs of radio stations worldwide that broadcast radiofacsimile marine weather charts. The listings include the times, frequencies, and contents of transmissions along with the areas they cover, which makes it indispensable for programming an automated weatherfax receiver.

The Naval Eastern Oceanography Center in Norfolk, Virginia, which broadcasts a wide variety of radiofacsimile weather charts over its high-frequency station NAM, issues a *Facsimile Products Guide* which lists its schedules and provides a valuable summary of the information transmitted in each type of broadcast. The publication is distributed by Alden Electronics, 40 Washington Street, Westboro, MA 01581.

## INTERPRETING WEATHER INFORMATION

Having access to accurate, up-to-date, and comprehensive weather information does you little good if you don't know how to interpret it and apply it to both your long-range and your immediate cruising plans. Here are a few suggestions regarding what to look for.

## Interpreting Basic Weather Pattern Information

Information regarding basic weather patterns is helpful primarily in long-range cruise planning.

As an example: Some friends called recently asking my comments on a nine-month cruise they were planning which would commence in Key West, Florida, in January, take them westward across the Gulf of Mexico, through the Yucatán Channel between Cuba and Mexico, down the east coast of Belize and Central America, then along the northern coast of South America, and return them to the U.S. via the Windward and Leeward Islands. My response was that I didn't think much of their program. I suggested that if they would study the available information on basic weather patterns along their planned route at the time of year they planned to be in each area, they would discover a couple of discouraging facts: that the run eastward along the northern coast of South America was certain to be a windward slog into the teeth of 15- to 20-knot easterly trade winds; and that their schedule would take them through the eastern Caribbean in August and September, which is the height of that area's hurricane season (Fig. 9.14). I suggested they consider altering their schedule to depart Florida in late October, after the worst of the hurricane threat has passed, and reverse their route, which would turn their journey along the northern coast of South America into a downhill sleigh ride rather than an uphill battle against wind and current.

As a second example: I am currently planning an extended voyage from the southeast coast of the U.S. through the Bahamas and the eastern Caribbean, thence across the northern coast of South America, through the Panama Canal, up the west coast of Central America, Mexico, and the U.S., then up the Inside Passage to Glacier Bay, Alaska. A study of basic weather patterns in the areas I plan to cruise reveals the following: I don't want to depart Florida until October, after the worst of the hurricane threat has passed; I will have a beam reach across the northwest trade winds as I proceed south down the chain of islands of the eastern Caribbean; I will have basically a downwind run along the northern coast of South America; I need to depart San Diego no earlier or later than early May in order to take advantage of moderate summer weather conditions for the long slog up and down the west coast of the U.S.; I need to depart Glacier Bay by August 1 in order

223

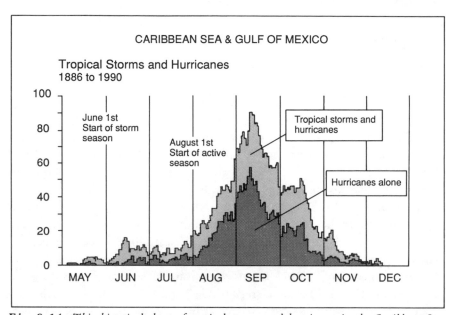

*Fig. 9.14: This historical chart of tropical storms and hurricanes in the Caribbean Sea and the Gulf of Mexico provides ample justification for postponing the departure of a cruise to either area until late October, after the threat of storms has largely passed.*

to get well south of San Francisco before consistent bad weather begins to close in along the northwestern coast of the U.S.; I don't want to return by way of the northern coast of South America because I would have to run into the teeth of the easterly trades, therefore I will come back by way of the Yucatán Channel and the Gulf coast of the U.S.

## Interpreting Voice Broadcast Weather Information

Voice broadcast marine weather information is helpful principally for planning your cruising itinerary from one day to about a week into the future. As a typical example, suppose you are in south Florida aboard your 8-knot displacement boat planning to cross the Gulf Stream for a cruise through the Bahamas. The weather reports you are receiving over VHF indicate that winds currently are out of the southeast at 10 knots and seas are two to three feet. The five-day forecast predicts that a low-pressure system off the New England coast is drifting southward and is expected to arrive off south Florida in about three days. That information tells you that current conditions for crossing the Stream are close to ideal, with the winds light to moderate and out of the south, which puts them in line with the current of the Gulf Stream. It also tells you that two to three days from now, the winds will build in advance of the low-pressure system coming down from New England and will shift into the north. That will put them in opposition to the Gulf Stream current and seas are likely to be six to eight feet. You had better either cast off and get the Stream crossing behind you while conditions are favorable or plan to wait at least a week to depart while the low-pressure system drifting down from New England passes through south Florida and the winds—hopefully—moderate and return to flow out of the south.

## Interpreting Radiofacsimile Weather Charts

Radiofacsimile weather charts are useful primarily for planning your cruising itinerary from one to two weeks into the future. As an example of how this information can be used in the real world of cruising, suppose you are in English Harbor, Antigua, planning a ten-day run down through the islands to Grenada. Your preferred schedule is to depart tomorrow morning and run the first day to Guadeloupe, then run the second day to Martinique, where you will pick up friends who are flying in for a week's stay aboard. The third day will be spent touring Martinique, the fourth and fifth days visiting St. Lucia, the sixth through eighth days exploring the Tobago Keys, and the tenth day getting to Grenada, from which your friends are scheduled to fly back to the States. Is that a workable plan?

You begin to answer that question by consulting your copy of *Selected Worldwide Marine Weather Broadcasts* and the *Facsimile Products Guide* for radio station NAM and arranging to receive the following weather charts for the eastern Caribbean and/or the North Atlantic Ocean:

1. A surface weather analysis chart, which will show current weather patterns.

2. Three surface weather prognosis charts, which will indicate predicted

weather conditions over the coming twenty-four, thirty-six, and forty-eight hours.

3. Several extended surface weather prognosis charts, which will indicate predicted weather conditions over the coming two to five days.

4. A wave analysis chart, which will depict current wave heights and directions.

5. A wave prognosis chart, which will forecast wave heights and directions for the coming twenty-four hours.

6. A satellite weather photo, which will show cloud cover and indicate positions of disturbances and tropical cyclones.

7. A radar chart, which will show areas of storm development including local thunderstorms.

In order to take maximum advantage of these charts, you must first understand the symbols they employ (Fig. 9.15) and what they represent. The meanings of most of these symbols, such as *H* for the center of an area of high pressure and *L* for the center of an area of low pressure, are self-explanatory. The symbols used to represent cold, warm, occluded, and stationary fronts are a bit more difficult to keep straight but are extremely important since it is along these fronts that most significant weather occurs. (I find it helps me remember which symbol depicts which type of front by thinking of the triangles which represent a cold front as icicles and the semicircles which represent a warm front as small suns.)

Among the most valuable symbols on the charts:

—Wind arrows whose shafts show the direction of winds and whose feathers and pennants show the strength of winds (a half feather indicates 5 knots, a full feather 10 knots, and a solid triangular pennant 50 knots).

—Wave symbols which indicate dominant wave direction, dominant wave period, and dominant wave height.

Once you have received the charts you have selected, you find the surface weather analysis and wave analysis charts for the eastern Caribbean indicate current conditions for your planned voyage are close to ideal: winds are 15 to 20 knots out of the ENE, the wave period is 14 seconds, and the dominant

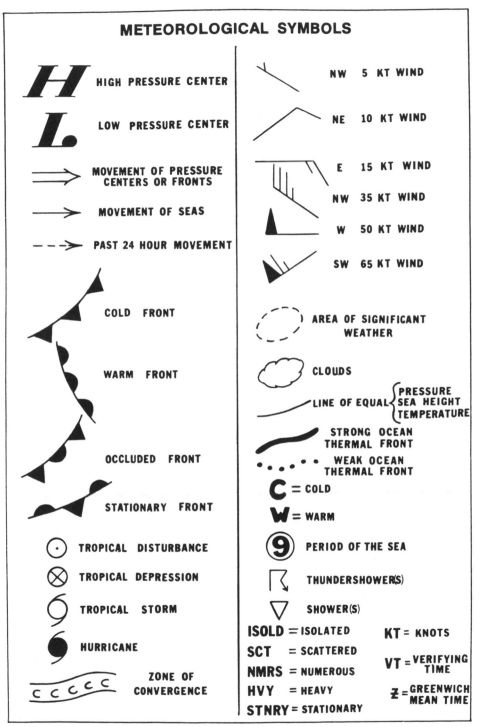

Fig. 9.15: *The standard meteorological symbols printed on weather facsimile charts provide the key to understanding what the charts tell you about the weather you are likely to encounter on a forthcoming leg of a cruise. (Courtesy Alden Electronics, Inc.)*

wave height is six feet. The surface weather prognosis and wave prognosis charts indicate these conditions are likely to remain unchanged for the next twelve, twenty-four, and thirty-six hours. The radar chart shows no significant area of storm development in the eastern Caribbean.

The extended surface weather prognosis chart, however, indicates that trouble may be on the way. It shows that on the fourth day of your trip, wind velocities in the eastern Caribbean are predicted to increase to 30 knots, the wave period will decrease to nine seconds, and dominant wave heights will increase to 14 feet. On the fifth day, winds are expected to build to 40 knots, the wave period will further decrease to six seconds, and dominant wave heights will build to 20 feet.

A check of the satellite weather photo for the North Atlantic identifies the source of your difficulties: a significant system of low pressure that is building off the western coast of North Africa and over the next ten days will drift inexorably toward the eastern Caribbean.

On the basis of the information you have drawn from your radiofacsimile weather charts, you will probably be able to meet your friends in Martinique with no problem. Your planned crossing of the St. Lucia Channel on day four in 30-knot winds and 14-foot seas, however, would be a bit adventurous. You might be well advised to step up your schedule and make that crossing on day three before conditions build. It's obvious your cruise through the Tobago Keys will have to be postponed as that low-lying area is no place to be in predicted 40-knot winds and 20-foot seas. You decide to call your friends and tell them to plan to reschedule their departure from the international airport at Vieux Fort, St. Lucia, as it is unlikely the coming weather will allow you to get them to Grenada in time for their scheduled departure.

For further information on interpreting radiofacsimile weather charts, I suggest you obtain a copy of *A Mariner's Guide to Radiofacsimile Weather Charts,* written by Dr. Joseph Bishop and published by Alden Electronics, Inc. You will find it in a number of marine electronic dealers, marine bookstores, and catalogs, or it is available directly from Alden at the address above. Its list price is $19.95.

## READING LOCAL WEATHER SIGNS

One late summer evening early in my boating career I was at anchor with my family in the Intracoastal Waterway just north of Belhaven, North

Carolina, when one of my daughters pointed skyward and asked, "What does that pretty halo around the moon mean, Daddy?" "Oh," I replied sagely, "that means we're going to have beautiful weather tomorrow."

The hurricane struck about four o'clock the following afternoon.

Since that rather humbling experience, I have developed a more than casual interest in being able to read the signs of coming weather that Mother Nature offers us in abundance if we will but take the time to read and understand them. If you will do likewise and devote a little time to observing such factors as changing patterns of cloud formation, changing wind directions, and halos around the sun and moon, you will find you can develop the ability to predict weather approaching your vicinity with an amazing degree of accuracy.

If I were asked that question about the halo around the moon today, for instance, I would quote the rhyme of the ancient mariners: "When a halo rings the moon or sun, the rain will come upon the run." Since that night north of Belhaven I've learned that the rhyme's accuracy is based not on mystic superstition but on scientific fact. A halo around the sun or moon is caused by light passing through ice crystals in the high, thin layer of cirrostratus clouds that form well in advance of the low-pressure systems that bring wet weather.

Close observation of halos around the sun or moon will even tell you something about the severity of the approaching weather and the quarter from which it will come. The halo will begin to form on the side of the sun or moon from which the low pressure is approaching. A light, broken halo indicates only scattered cirrostratus in advance of a weak low-pressure system whose effects will not be severe. A bright, well-defined halo and even double and triple halos indicate the thick cirrostratus associated with deep low-pressure systems and their accompanying heavy rain and high winds. As the storm approaches, the dark altostratus clouds on its leading edge will obscure a portion of the halo and the wet weather will come from the obscured quarter. Observations by the National Weather Service have established that a halo around the sun accurately predicts wet weather about 75 percent of the time and that a halo around the moon accurately predicts wet weather about 65 percent of the time.

The formation of rainbows can also tell you whether the coming weather is likely to be fair or foul. If a rainbow forms to windward of your position, you can expect the curtain of moisture in which it forms to be headed in your direction. If a rainbow is to leeward of you, the moisture with which it is associated is receding away from you. If you see a rainbow in the morning, it is likely to be in the west and you probably are in for a wet day. If you see a rainbow in the late afternoon or early evening, it is likely to be toward the east. The storm has probably passed your position and the sky behind it will be clearing.

One of the best ways to detect the approach of foul weather is to observe cloud formations in your vicinity. Thin, wispy cirrus clouds, often called "mare's tails," normally portend fair weather. But if they lower and thicken into the cirrocumulus clouds of a "mackerel sky," wet weather is probably on the way. The mackerel sky is likely to broaden into cirrostratus clouds, which form their characteristic halo around the sun or moon, then thicken to an almost uniform layer of altostratus, then to dark nimbostratus clouds which will bring heavy rain.

By the same token, white, puffy cumulus clouds normally mean fair weather. But on hot summer afternoons if they build up and rise high into the sky and their tops begin to be sheared off by the jet stream, they are transformed into cumulonimbus—with their characteristic flat anvil top and dark, boiling layer of nimbostratus underneath—which spawn violent thunderstorms. The direction in which the horn of their anvil shape points will be the direction in which they are being carried by winds aloft.

Because the prevailing wind currents across the United States tend to be northwest to southeast, if you note the development of these thunderstorm clouds to the west or northwest of you, they are likely to come in your direction. They normally set off bright flashes of lightning and deep rolls of thunder. Because the lightning travels to you at the speed of light and the sound of the thunder reaches you at the slower speed of sound, you can estimate the thunderstorm's proximity by timing the interval between lightning and thunder in seconds and dividing by five. The result will be the storm's approximate distance from you in statute miles. If you sense a distinct drop in air temperature, the storm has probably approached to within about three miles of you and will be on top of you shortly.

If cumulonimbus clouds form to the south or southeast of you, the rain and high winds they contain are likely to be carried away from you by the prevailing winds.

Still another interesting way you can detect the onset of wet weather is by listening. In fair weather, sound tends to be dissipated quickly. If sounds become unusually bright and clear and seem to carry a longer way than normal, the reason is that sound waves are being held close to the earth by a lowering, thickening atmosphere. A low-pressure center with its characteristic rain is likely to be on the way.

## Interpreting Barometer Readings

If you carry a barometer aboard your vessel, you can combine its readings with observations of wind direction to determine the direction from which the approaching bad weather will come and how winds will shift in the storm's wake. If the barometer begins to fall and the wind is from points between south and southeast, the storm is approaching from west of northwest and will pass near you or to your north within twelve to twenty-four hours. As it passes, winds will veer (swing clockwise) into the northwest. If the wind is from points between east and northeast, the storm is approaching from the south or southwest and will pass near or to the south of you within twelve to twenty-four hours. As it passes, winds will back (swing counterclockwise) into the northwest. You can determine approximately how rapidly the low-pressure system is approaching and its likely severity by the speed with which the barometer is falling. A rate of fall of .02 to .03 inches of mercury per hour indicates a weak, slow-moving storm; a rate of fall of .05 to .06 inches per hour indicates the low-pressure system is a deep one and it is approaching rapidly.

## The Law of Storms

If an approaching storm is an extratropical cyclone with its characteristic counterclockwise wind pattern, you can determine its approximate position relative to your own by the law of storms. As you face the wind, the storm's center will be in the direction of your outstretched right hand. If you take a series of bearings on the storm's center in this fashion over a period of hours, you can predict its course. If the position of your right hand moves clockwise or counterclockwise, the storm's center will pass you to the appropriate side. If the position of your right hand does not change appreciably, the storm's center is headed right toward you. If you are at sea in such a situation, you should remember that in the right half of an extratropical storm, relative to its centerline, winds and seas are highest because they are augmented by the storm's forward movement. You would therefore want to set your vessel's course to carry it toward the storm's left or navigable semicircle.

231

Employing the techniques recommended here to make certain you have access to comprehensive weather information, interpret it correctly, and observe the signs of weather all around you won't guarantee that you'll never have to deal with howling winds and angry seas, but it can help you be aware of any adverse weather coming your way and help you prepare to deal with it.

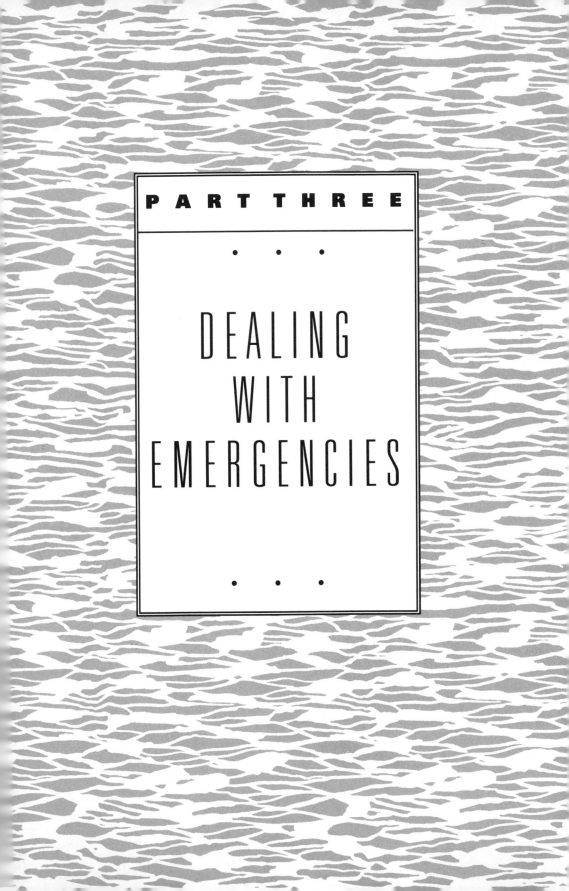

PART THREE

. . .

DEALING
WITH
EMERGENCIES

. . .

## CHAPTER 10

# EMERGENCY RADIO USE

• • •

In any emergency on the water, your VHF and/or single-sideband marine radios are likely to be your primary means of summoning help. If you find it necessary to use them in an emergency, whether to deal with a problem aboard your own boat or aboard another vessel you are trying to assist, it's important to know how to use them properly. The procedures presented here are not simply the way the Federal Communications Commission's rules and international treaties require you to handle emergency radio traffic, nor are they arcane formats left over from the blue-blazer-and-white-bucks school of yachting etiquette. Their primary value is that they are internationally agreed-on ways of handling distress radio traffic that compress essential

235

information into practical and efficient formats that clearly communicate critical information in the shortest possible time.

## Keep Calm

Emergencies on the water seldom seem to happen at midday in calm seas when communication conditions are ideal. Under Murphy's Law that whatever can go wrong will—and at the worst possible moment—marine emergencies seem to be far more likely to occur in the dead of night when the wind is howling, the sea is heaving, rain is pouring in buckets, your engine has quit, you're off a lee shore, and every channel you try is either jammed with traffic you can't break through or crackling with static. Any time you're involved in distress radio traffic, the last thing you want to do is confuse the situation with inaccurate, incomplete, or incomprehensible transmissions. Remain calm and take extra care to speak slowly, clearly, and distinctly. Use radio transmission procedure words properly and be careful to pronounce them correctly. If you feel there is any doubt that you will be understood, use phonetic spelling.

## International Radiotelephone Alarm Signal

Some VHF and SSB marine radios are equipped with an automatic international radiotelephone alarm generator which is activated by pressing a clearly marked button on the front of the radio's panel. If your radio is so equipped, you should activate the alarm signal before every transmission of the Mayday distress call and message. The signal consists of two audio frequency tones transmitted alternately for a duration of one quarter of a second each. One tone has a frequency of 2,200 Hertz and the other a frequency of 1,300 Hertz. Transmitted together, they sound something like the wail of an ambulance siren. The signal alerts radio officers on watch at coast stations and aboard a number of commercial vessels that a Mayday distress call and message is about to be transmitted and activates automatic equipment to record it. Once you punch the button on your set, it will generate the alarm for the required interval of at least thirty but not more than sixty seconds. Your radio will generate the alarm over any transmit frequency to which your radio is tuned.

With one exception, the radiotelephone alarm may be transmitted from a vessel only to announce that a Mayday distress call and message will follow. The single exception to that rule is that it also may be used to precede a Pan Pan urgency call and message involving a man overboard where assistance is required which cannot be satisfactorily obtained by the use of the urgency call and message without preceding it with the radiotelephone alarm signal.

## Make an Urgency or Distress Call Immediately

If you get into a life-threatening situation at sea, the first thing you must do is get off a Pan Pan urgency or a Mayday distress call and its associated message.

The importance of getting off an urgency or distress call and message the instant a serious emergency strikes is best illustrated by the experience of my friend Sumner Pingree when a turbocharger fire erupted aboard his 53-foot sportfisherman *Roulette* off the coast of Puerto Rico. "By the time my son was halfway up the flying bridge ladder to tell me about the fire, smoke was everywhere," he told me later. "I immediately got off a Mayday call to the Coast Guard. I said I was not declaring an emergency but asked them to stand by. We opened the engine-room door, and the fire reignited with a whoosh. I raced back up to the flying bridge to call the Coast Guard again, but the fire had already burned through the battery cables and the radio was dead. Ten minutes after we first realized we had a fire aboard, we were swimming. I was amazed how quickly she burned."

As you will see, Sumner technically should have transmitted a Pan Pan urgency call rather than a Mayday distress call, but the point is that had he waited to transmit a call and message until he assessed the damage the fire had caused, he would have found his radio had already been knocked out of commission.

## Mayday Distress Call and Message

The Mayday distress call and message has absolute priority over all other radio traffic.

Transmit a Mayday using the format given in Fig. 10.1. Don't omit any items or use any other format. The first distress call and message you transmit may be the only one you are able to transmit, and the format provides the essential information potential rescuers will need quickly, clearly, and concisely.

237

# Format for Transmitting
## MAYDAY Distress Call and Message

Fill out for your vessel and keep near your radiotelephone.

Speak SLOWLY - CLEARLY - CALMLY

1) Activate international radiotelephone alarm signal

2) "MAYDAY—MAYDAY—MAYDAY"

3) "THIS IS: _____, _____, _____"
   (your boat name)   (your boat name)   (your boat name)

   _____"
   (your call sign)

4) "MAYDAY: _____"
   (your boat name)

5) "POSITION IS: _____"
   (your vessel's position in degrees and minutes of latitude
   NORTH or SOUTH and longitude EAST or WEST; or as
   distance and bearing [magnetic or true] to well-known navigation landmark)

6) "WE _____"
   (state nature of your emergency)

7) "WE REQUIRE _____"
   (state type of assistance required)

8) "ABOARD ARE _____"
   (give number of adults and children on board and conditions
   of any injured)

9) "_____ IS A _____-FOOT
   (your boat name)   (your boat's length in feet)

   _____ WITH A _____ HULL
   (type, sloop, motor yacht, etc.)   (hull color)

   AND _____ TRIM."
   (color of trim)

10) "I WILL BE LISTENING ON CHANNEL 16/2182"
    (cross out channel or frequency that does not apply)

11) "THIS IS: _____ _____"
    (your boat name)   (and call sign)

12) "OVER"

*Fig. 10.1: This standard format for transmitting a Mayday distress call and message communicates vital information quickly, accurately, and concisely.*

Technically, the Mayday distress call and message procedure consists of three elements:

1. The international radiotelephone alarm signal

2. The distress call, consisting of:
   A. The distress signal MAYDAY, spoken three times
   B. The words THIS IS:
   C. The name of the vessel in distress, spoken three times
   D. The radio call sign of the vessel in distress spoken once

3. The distress message, consisting of:
   A. The distress signal MAYDAY, spoken once
   B. The name of the vessel in distress, spoken once
   C. The position of the vessel in distress expressed:
      —as degrees and minutes of latitude north or south and longitude east or west, or
      —by bearing (specify whether true or magnetic) and distance to a well-known reference point such as an aid to navigation or shoreside landmark.
   D. The nature of the distress
   E. The type of assistance required
   F. Any other information that might facilitate rescue such as:
      —The length of the vessel
      —The type of vessel
      —The color of the vessel's hull, superstructure, and trim
      —The number of adults and children on board
      —The injuries suffered by anyone on board and the medical assistance they require

The word OVER indicates the end of your Mayday transmission and requests a response.

If your Mayday is acknowledged and you are uncertain of the extent of your emergency, ask the vessel or station you have contacted to stand by. If, as in Sumner's case, the emergency escalates rapidly and knocks out your radio, you will at least know that someone is aware you are in trouble and knows your position, the nature of your distress, and the number of souls on board, and has a description of your vessel. Even if you do not receive an acknowledgment, you have the hope that someone heard your message but was unable to acknowledge it before you lost the ability to receive.

The Mayday distress call and message should never be transmitted in any but extreme emergencies that pose genuine and serious dangers to your vessel or threaten the lives of your crew. Such situations as being lost, having someone aboard suffer a serious but not life-threatening illness or injury, having mechanical difficulties, or running out of fuel are not sufficient justification for transmitting a Mayday unless those factors place your vessel or crew in grave and immediate danger.

Anyone foolish enough to transmit a Mayday for frivolous or nonexistent reasons is subject to significant criminal and civil penalties. Using your radiotelephone to transmit a false Mayday can subject you to a fine of up to $10,000 and/or up to a year in jail and can result in the loss of your FCC radiotelephone operator license for life. In addition, the Coast Guard has prosecuted individuals who transmitted false Maydays and has gotten judgments against them to recover the costs of search and rescue efforts resulting from them which ran into the thousands of dollars.

Don't transmit the Mayday distress call and message in a man-overboard situation, even if you require the assistance of other vessels. Instead, transmit the Pan Pan urgency call and message, the proper procedure for which is briefly recounted below and in detail in Chapter 14.

## VHF DISTRESS CALLS

In an emergency serious enough to require you to transmit the Mayday distress call and message, you may use any VHF channel to attract attention. Your first choice, however, should be channel 16 (156.8 MHz), which is the International Distress, Safety, and Calling channel both ship-to-coast and intership and is continuously monitored by the Coast Guard.

Since VHF radio waves travel only in a line of sight, 20 miles is about the maximum distance over which you can reliably expect to communicate with your installed VHF radiotelephone. (Its range may be considerably greater if you are within line of sight of a tall receiving antenna on shore. If your VHF antenna is ten to fifteen feet off the water, for instance, and is in line of sight of a 2,000-foot-high receiving antenna on shore, your radio's range under optimum conditions could be as much as 75 miles, but you don't want to bet your life on it.)

If you encounter a serious emergency well offshore and do not have a marine single-sideband radio aboard, you should of course transmit your Mayday distress call and message on your VHF radiotelephone as there is always the possibility that your transmission could be received by another vessel within a 20-mile radius of your position. But again, you don't want to trust your vessel or your life to that kind of a gamble.

After transmitting the distress call and message on VHF channel 16, wait thirty seconds for any vessel receiving it to respond. If no answer is received, retransmit the distress call and message a second time over that same channel. If no answer is received following that transmission, try channel 6 (156.3 MHz), the intership safety channel. If you still receive no response, retransmit the distress call and message on any VHF channel frequently used in the area. One technique is to scan the VHF channels until you hear traffic, then break into the traffic with your Mayday distress call and message. If you do not hear traffic on any VHF channel, try transmitting your Mayday on channel 22A (157.1 MHz), the primary Coast Guard liaison channel, or channel 72 (156.625 MHz), which at sea is used as an international ship-to-ship channel. If you still receive no acknowledgment and have time, try one or more of the Public Correspondence channels. The Public Correspondence channels vary from area to area, but the primary ones are channel 26 (ship's transmit, 157.3 MHz; ship's receive, 161.9 MHz) and channel 28 (ship's transmit, 157.4 MHz; ship's receive, 162.0 MHz).

## SSB DISTRESS CALLS

In an emergency serious enough to require you to transmit the Mayday distress call and message, you may use any SSB channel or frequency to attract attention. Your first choice, however, should be frequency 2182 kHz, which is the SSB International Distress, Safety, and Calling frequency both ship-to-coast and intership and is continuously monitored by the Coast Guard.

After transmitting the distress call and message on 2182 kHz, wait thirty seconds for any vessel receiving it to respond. If no answer is received, retransmit the distress call and message a second time over that same frequency. If no answer is received following that transmission, retransmit the distress call and message on any SSB frequency used in the area. Good second choices would be 2670 kHz, a primary Coast Guard working channel, or one of the following ITU channels which (effective at 0001 UTC July 1, 1991) have been designated for radiotelephone safety and distress traffic as part of the Global Maritime Distress and Safety System (GMDSS):

## EMERGENCY CARRIER FREQUENCIES

| ITU Channel | Ship Transmit (kHz) | Ship Receive (kHz) |
|---|---|---|
| 421 | 4125.0 | 4417.0 |
| 606 | 6215.0 | 6516.0 |
| 821 | 8255.0 | 8779.0 |
| 1221 | 12290.0 | 13137.0 |
| 1621 | 16420.0 | 17302.0 |
| 1806 | 18795.0 | 19770.0 |
| 2221 | 22060.0 | 22756.0 |
| 2510 | 25097.0 | 26172.0 |

If you still receive no acknowledgment, scan the ITU channels used by the High Seas stations and break into any traffic you hear with your Mayday. You will have a better chance of being heard if you break in when you think the person on land is speaking. If you hear no traffic, you can try transmitting your Mayday over one or more of the channels used by the High Seas stations, but to have a reasonable chance of being heard you will have to select an appropriate megahertz band based on your distance from the station and the time of day.

## Canceling a Mayday

If, after you transmit a Mayday, you find you are able to handle the emergency in such a way that you do not require assistance and you have not delegated control of the distress traffic to another vessel or coast station, you must cancel your distress call and message whether or not it was acknowledged. If your Mayday was acknowledged by the Coast Guard or other appropriate authority, contact them in the normal, nonemergency way, and inform them of the cancellation. They will then normally transmit a "notification of resumption of normal working." If your Mayday was not acknowledged by the Coast Guard or other appropriate authority, or you cannot contact the authority that acknowledged your Mayday, you are required to cancel it using the format described in Fig. 10.2.

## Pan Pan Urgency Signal and Message

The Pan Pan urgency signal and the message that follows it have priority over all other transmissions except the Mayday distress call and message. The urgency signal may be transmitted to a specific vessel or to "all stations." The proper format for transmitting the Pan Pan urgency signal and message will be found in Fig. 10.3.

A typical situation in which you would transmit the Pan Pan urgency signal "to all stations" would be one in which a person fell overboard from your own vessel and you required the assistance of other vessels to retrieve him or her. That is the only emergency in which the Pan Pan urgency call and message may be preceded by the radiotelephone alarm, and even then, the alarm should be used only if you feel you cannot satisfactorily obtain the assistance you require through the urgency signal alone without the use of the radiotelephone alarm.

A typical situation in which you would address the Pan Pan urgency signal to a specific vessel would be one in which you observed a person fall overboard from that vessel and no one aboard that vessel appeared to be aware of the accident.

Other examples of the proper use of the urgency call and message would be a situation in which you have a serious but not life-threatening medical emergency on board or your vessel has struck a submerged object and is taking on water but is not in imminent danger of sinking. If you feel the situation might become serious enough to require assistance, transmit the Pan Pan urgency call and message to alert rescue services or other vessels in your vicinity that you may need their help. Still another example would be a situation in which your vessel has lost power or steering in a busy traffic area and could pose a hazard to other vessels.

If you transmit the Pan Pan urgency signal addressed "to all ships," you must cancel it once the emergency is over by transmitting the cancellation on that same frequency using the format in Fig. 10.4. If you addressed the urgency signal to a specific vessel, its cancellation is not required.

# Format for
## Cancelling a
## MAYDAY Distress Call and Message
## by a Vessel

To cancel a MAYDAY distress call and message you, as the vessel in distress, previously transmitted when the cancellation cannot be accomplished through a coast station:

1) "MAYDAY"

2) "HELLO ALL STATIONS, HELLO ALL STATIONS, HELLO ALL STATIONS"

3) "THIS IS: _____, _____"
          (your boat name)   (your call sign)

4) "THE TIME IS: _____"
          (state time of this transmission by the 24-hour clock)

5 "_____, _____"
   (your boat name)   (your call sign)

6) "SEELONCE FEENEE"

7) "_____, _____"
   (your boat name)   (your call sign)

8) "OUT"

To cancel a MAYDAY distress call and message you previously transmitted on behalf of a vessel in distress, though you were not in distress yourself:

1) "MAYDAY"

2) "HELLO ALL STATIONS, HELLO ALL STATIONS, HELLO ALL STATIONS"

3) "THIS IS: _____, _____"
          (your boat name)   (your call sign)

4) "THE TIME IS: _____"
          (state time of this transmission by the 24-hour clock)

5) "_____, _____"
   (the name of the vessel and call sign of the vessel in distress)

6) "SEELONCE FEENEE"

7) "_____, _____"
   (your boat name)   (your call sign)

8) "OUT"

*Fig. 10.2: You are required to cancel a Mayday distress call and message as soon as the threat that caused it to be broadcast has passed.*

## Format for Transmitting
## PAN PAN
### Urgency Call and Message

1) "PAN PAN—PAN PAN—PAN PAN" (Properly pronounced PAHN PAHN)

2) "ALL STATIONS" (or the name of a particular vessel)

3) "THIS IS: _____, _____"
        (your boat name)     (your call sign)

4) "_____"
    (state nature of urgent situation)

5) "_____"
    (state assistance required or give other useful information such as your po-
    sition, a description of your vessel, or the number of people on board)

6) "THIS IS: _____, _____"
        (your boat name)     (your call sign)

7) "OVER"


*Fig. 10.3: The Pan Pan urgency call and message is used when a person or vessel is in jeopardy but the danger is not life-threatening.*


## Security Safety Signal

The Security safety signal and message are transmitted to alert others to information concerning the safety of navigation or important meteorological warnings. They are most often transmitted by coast stations to warn of hazards to navigation or severe weather systems. However, they may also be transmitted by vessels. The safety signal is transmitted on a distress channel and includes instructions for receiving stations to switch to a working channel. The safety message is then transmitted over the working channel specified in the safety signal.

A typical example of situations in which you might transmit a safety signal and message would be one in which you spot a large submerged object that could pose a serious danger to other vessels. You should first attempt to contact the Coast Guard to alert them to the danger, and they would

## Format for
## Cancelling a
## PAN PAN Urgency Call & Message
## By a Vessel

To cancel a PAN PAN urgency call and message you previously transmitted "to all stations"

1) "PAN PAN—PAN PAN—PAN PAN"

2) "HELLO ALL STATIONS, HELLO ALL STATIONS, HELLO ALL STATIONS"

3) "THIS IS: _____, _____"
        (your boat name)  (your call sign)

4) "THE TIME IS: _____"
        (state time of this transmission by the 24-hour clock)

5) "_____, _____"
    (your boat name)  (your call sign)

6) "SEELONCE FEENEE"

7) "_____, _____"
    (your boat name)  (your call sign)

8) "OUT"

*Fig. 10.4:* *A Pan Pan urgency call and message addressed "to all stations" must be canceled once the emergency has passed.*

then probably transmit a Security signal on VHF channel 16 instructing vessels to switch to VHF channel 22A to receive the message concerning it. If you are unable to reach the Coast Guard and feel the object poses sufficient danger to require notifying other vessels in the area, find a working channel that is not in use. Good working channels on VHF would be channels 6, 68, or 72; on SSB channels 2635 kHz and 2638 kHz (and in U.S. waters, 2738 kHz). Then transmit a Security signal over a distress channel (inshore you normally would transmit on VHF channel 16; offshore on SSB 2182 kHz) and instruct receiving stations to switch to the working channel you have selected to receive the message. Switch to the working channel you specified in the Security signal and transmit the safety message, which includes a description of the object, its location, its approximate depth below the surface, and the direction it is drifting, if any. The proper format for transmitting the Security safety signal and message is given in Fig. 10.5.

## If You Receive a Mayday Distress Call and Message

Under federal law,* as the individual in charge of a vessel in waters subject to U.S. jurisdiction or of an American-flag vessel operating on the high seas, you are legally required to render assistance to any individual found at sea "in danger of being lost" so far as you can do so without serious danger to your own vessel or crew. If you fail to render such assistance, you are liable to a fine of up to $1,000 or two years imprisonment, or both.

### Acknowledging Mayday Distress Calls

The FCC rules state that if you receive a Mayday distress call and message from a vessel that beyond any possible doubt is in your vicinity, you must immediately acknowledge it. The lone exception to the rule is that if you are in an area where reliable communication between the vessel in distress and a coast station is "practicable," you may defer your acknowledgment for a "short interval" so that a coast station may acknowledge receipt. The regulations adopted by the World Administrative Radio Conference governing radio communications in the GMDSS contain similar wording, but neither precisely defines the length of a "short interval."

The language of the regulations can put a responsible cruising skipper who receives a distress call and message in a bit of a quandary. On the one hand, he would want to respond as quickly as possible to let the vessel in distress know someone had heard the signal. On the other, he would not want to interfere with communication between the vessel in distress and a coast station that had also received the call. Given the sophistication of maritime radio services today, there's really nowhere in the world in which reliable communication between a vessel in distress (assuming it has a functioning SSB radio) and a coast station is not "practicable." (The exception,

*Public Law 98–89, Duty to Provide Assistance at Sea, enacted by Congress, August 26, 1983 (46 U.S. Code 2301–2304).

## Format for Transmitting
## SECURITY Safety Signal and Message

To transmit the SECURITY safety signal:

Transmit on VHF Channel 16 or SSB frequency 2182 kHz:

1. "Say-curiTAY—Say-curiTAY—Say-curiTAY—ALL STATIONS"

2. "THIS IS: _____, _____"
            (your boat name)   (your call sign)

3. "LISTEN: _____"
            (state working VHF channel or SSB frequency)

4. "_____ OUT"
   (your call sign)

To transmit the SECURITY safety message:

Transmit on working VHF channel or SSB frequency designated above:

1. "Say-curiTAY—Say-curiTAY—Say-curiTAY—ALL STATIONS"

2. "THIS IS: _____, _____"
            (your boat name)   (your call sign)

3. "_____"
   (state SECURITY message)

4. "_____ OUT"
   (your call sign)

*Fig. 10.5:* A Security safety signal is transmitted over a distress frequency. Its accompanying message is transmitted over an appropriate working frequency.

I suppose, would be a situation in which you were more than about fifty miles offshore and received a distress signal on VHF that might indicate the vessel in distress either didn't have SSB or its SSB wasn't working.) The conventional wisdom on this topic says that if you receive a Mayday, you should do nothing, just listen. I have written elsewhere that I strongly disagree and said that if I were in an area where there was the least doubt about the ability of a vessel in distress to reach a coast station and I received a Mayday call from a vessel anywhere near me, I would acknowledge it as quickly as the distress message was concluded and I could get to my radio's microphone. After discussing the matter with the experts at the Radio Technical Commission for Maritime Services, I have modified my position. The RTC staffers point out that after receiving a distress signal, it may take land stations up to a minute to swing their antennas around to the direction from which the distress signal was received in order to respond effectively. Their primary concern is that a number of vessels don't jump onto the frequency immediately and make it impossible for them to get through. On that basis, then, if I heard a distress signal I would wait about a minute before acknowledging to give land stations time to respond. But if no land station responded within about a minute, I would acknowledge the call so the hapless soul in deep enough trouble to be transmitting the Mayday would know someone had heard him.

If you are called on to acknowledge a Mayday distress call and message, do so using the format found in Fig. 10.6.

If you acknowledge receipt of a Mayday distress call and message and a legitimate authority such as the Coast Guard later comes on the channel, you should state your vessel's name and call sign and ask if they wish you to continue to attempt to provide assistance to the vessel in distress

## Format for Acknowledging
## MAYDAY Distress Call and Message

On channel or frequency over which you received the MAYDAY:

1. "_____, _____, _____"
   (name of vessel in distress, spoken three times)

2. "THIS IS: _____, _____, _____, _____"
   (your boat name, spoken three times)        (your call sign)

3. "RECEIVED MAYDAY"

4. "OVER"

*Fig. 10.6: You are required by law to immediately acknowledge a Mayday distress call and message from a vessel in your vicinity.*

or simply stand by on that frequency in case your assistance is required.

If you receive a Mayday distress call and message from a vessel that beyond any possible doubt is not in your vicinity, the FCC rules say you must allow a "short interval of time" to elapse before acknowledging receipt of the call and message to allow stations nearer the vessel in distress to acknowledge them without interference. Again, the FCC doesn't define "short interval." The World Administrative Radio Conference regulations governing radio communications under the GMDSS specifically state that a ship receiving a distress alert on the HF radiotelephone frequencies shall not acknowledge it at all but, if it is not acknowledged within three minutes, relay it to a coast station. The bureaucrats can make all the rules they want to, but if I heard a Mayday from a vessel I knew was far away from me and no one else acknowledged it within about a minute, I would let the poor fellow know someone heard him and was relaying his message.

## Cease Transmitting and Listen

The FCC rules state that anyone who hears a Mayday must immediately cease any transmission capable of interfering with the distress traffic and continue to listen on the frequency over which it was transmitted. The FCC rules prohibit any vessel not involved in the distress from transmitting on the frequency being used until the station controlling the traffic broadcasts a "resumption of normal working" with the words "SEELONCE FEENEE" or "PRU-DONCE." If the vessel in distress was in my vicinity, if its distress call had been acknowledged by a coast station, and if I apparently was the vessel best positioned to render possible assistance, I would alter my course in the direction of the vessel in distress and attempt to contact the controlling coast station through normal, nonemergency means. If I was able to contact the coast station, I would inform the personnel there of my position, ask if I could help, and follow their instructions. If I was unable to contact the controlling authority by nonemergency means, I would get back on the frequency carrying the distress traffic, wait for a break, quickly inform the controlling authority of my position and ask if my assistance was required, then follow their instructions. If another vessel apparently in a better position to assist was involved in the distress, my actions would be determined by the situation. If I felt there was any reasonable chance my assistance might be required, I'd steam toward the vessel in distress and inform the controlling authority of my availability to assist if needed. If there appeared to be little likelihood my assistance would be required, I'd continue on my course but monitor the frequency until I heard the message announcing resumption of normal working. If I clearly was not in a position to assist, I'd probably continue to monitor the distress traffic as a matter of personal interest and make certain I did nothing to interfere with it, but otherwise go about my normal business.

The FCC rules do state that if you hear a Pan Pan urgency signal you must continue to listen on the frequency over which it was broadcast for three minutes. If no message follows the urgency signal, you should relay to the nearest coast station that you heard an urgency signal but no message followed it. If a message follows the urgency signal but is not addressed "to all ships," after three minutes you may resume normal working. Beyond that, the FCC rules get a little murky. They say if the urgency message was addressed "to all ships," the vessel that transmitted it must cancel it as soon as it knows action is no longer required. The rules are silent, however, on what those who have heard the urgency signal and message are supposed to do. If the emergency was in my vicinity, I'd monitor the channel over which the urgency message was transmitted until I heard the cancellation or was pretty certain no action on my part was required. If the emergency was clearly well away from me, I'd probably go back to normal working.

## Offer of Assistance

Once you acknowledge receipt of a Mayday distress call and message, you are not only required by federal law to respond but are also required by FCC rules to transmit an offer-of-assistance message to the vessel in distress as soon as possible. (Wait long enough to allow coast stations or other vessels to respond to the Mayday and work out your own position relative to the vessel in distress and formulate your intentions.) The format for your offer-of-assistance message is found in Fig. 10.7.

If, after you transmit your offer of assistance and are underway to provide assistance, a legitimate authority such as the Coast Guard enters the search and/or rescue effort, state your vessel's name and call sign and ask the authority whether they wish you to proceed or simply stand by to render assistance if it should be required.

251

## Format for
## Offer of Assistance Message
## in Response to a
## MAYDAY Distress Call and Message

On the channel or frequency over which you acknowledged receipt of the MAYDAY distress call and message:

1. "_____"
    (the name of the vessel in distress, spoken once)

2. "THIS IS: _____"
            (your boat name)

3. "OVER"

On hearing the word "OVER" from the vessel in distress, continue:

4. "I AM _____"
        (state your intentions: i.e., "PROCEEDING TOWARD YOU FROM
        TEN MILES. EXPECT TO ARRIVE IN ONE HOUR")

5. "_____"
    (state other useful information: i.e., "COAST GUARD HAS BEEN NOTI-
    FIED, INCLUDING YOUR NEED FOR DOCTOR")

6. "_____, _____"
    (your boat name)    (your call sign)

7. "OVER"

*Fig. 10.7: If you acknowledge a Mayday distress call and message from a vessel in your vicinity, you are required by FCC rules to transmit an offer-of-assistance message to the vessel in distress as soon as possible.*

## Relay of Mayday Distress Messages

Under certain circumstances, if you learn a vessel is in distress, you must relay a Mayday distress call and message, even if you are not in a position to assist. Under FCC rules, you must relay a Mayday distress call and message in the following circumstances:

1.   If the vessel in distress cannot transmit the distress call and message.

2.   If you believe that further assistance is required.

3.   When you hear a distress message that has not been acknowledged, even if you are not in a position to assist. In this case, you must also attempt to notify a proper authority, such as the Coast Guard, of the distress message you have received.

The proper format for relaying a Mayday distress call and message is given in Fig. 10.8. Note that it should be preceded, if possible, by the radio telephone alarm.

## Control of Distress Radio Traffic

If you transmit a Mayday and it is acknowledged by the Coast Guard or other appropriate authority, that authority normally will assume control of any radio traffic related to the distress. If your Mayday is not acknowledged by the Coast Guard or other appropriate authority, you are the controller of the distress traffic. You may retain that control yourself or you may delegate it to another vessel.

Being the controller of distress traffic imposes on you certain responsibilities.

The station controlling the distress traffic has the authority to impose silence on the frequency being used for distress traffic on all vessels or coast stations that interfere with the distress traffic. Such imposition of silence on the frequency being used for the distress traffic may be addressed "to all stations" or to an individual vessel or coast station, followed by the words SEELONCE MAYDAY. No further instructions or identification of the controlling station is required, and the SEELONCE MAYDAY order must be respected.

If essential, any other vessel in the vicinity of the vessel in distress—even though it has not been delegated as the station controlling the distress traffic—may also impose radio silence on the frequency with the words

## Format for Relaying
## MAYDAY Distress Call and Message

1. Activate radiotelephone alarm signal.

2. "MAYDAY RELAY—MAYDAY RELAY—MAYDAY RELAY"

3. "THIS IS: _____, _____, _____, _____"
                  (your boat name, spoken three times)          (your call sign)

4. "_____"
      (state the distress message: i.e., the name of the vessel in distress, its position, the nature of the distress, the nature of assistance required and any other useful information such as a description of the vessel, the number of people on board and any injuries they have sustained.)

5. "I WILL BE LISTENING ON CHANNEL 16/2182"
   (cross out channel or frequency that does not apply)

6. "_____, _____"
    (your boat name)   (your call sign)

7. "OVER"

*Fig. 10.8: You must relay any Mayday distress call and message you receive, even if you are not in a position to assist.*

SEELONCE DISTRESS followed by that vessel's own call sign and/or vessel name.

## EMERGENCY MEDICAL COMMUNICATIONS

If you encounter a medical emergency at sea that you do not feel qualified to handle without professional advice, you can usually make contact with a doctor through the Coast Guard on VHF channel 16 or SSB frequency 2182 kHz. The Coast Guard has access to military and U.S. Public Health physicians and, through its AMVER system, keeps track of ships at sea that have medical staff aboard.

    If you can't contact the Coast Guard in a serious medical emergency on board, you can call Medical Advisory Systems, Inc. (MAS). This private company operates a Medical Telecommunications Response Center in Owings, Maryland, which is staffed around the clock by its own physicians. It serves primarily commercial marine vessels and remote industry locations that subscribe to its services, but it will provide assistance to nonsubscribers in a serious emergency.

If you are within range of a VHF marine operator, you can call MAS at (301) 257-9504. Offshore you can call them direct on SSB marine radio using their call sign: WHD-576. The company continuously monitors SSB frequency 12356.0 kHz and scans 2182.0 kHz, 4983.0 kHz, 6227.0 kHz, 7952.0 kHz, 8294.0 kHz, 16531.0 kHz, and 22165.0 kHz. You can also call them at the above telephone number through a High Seas marine operator.

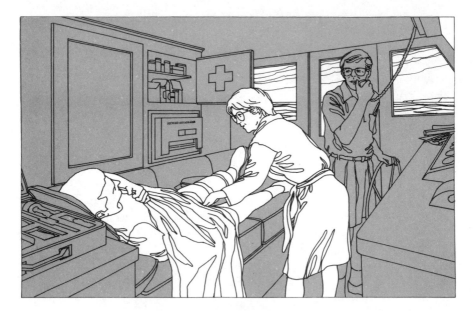

# CHAPTER 11

# MEDICAL EMERGENCIES

• • •

We in the United States suffer from what might be called the 911 syn-drome—the belief that emergency medical assistance is always just a tele-phone call away, and if trouble strikes a fully equipped ambulance staffed by at least two well-trained emergency medical personnel will come screaming around the corner in minutes. Not so in the cruising life. Even in coastal cruising in U.S. waters, you can easily find yourself hours away from doctors and hospital emergency rooms. If you venture into the boon-docks and foreign waters, you could find that help is days away. Emer-gency personnel call the first sixty minutes following a medical trauma the Golden Hour, and know that treatment administered during that brief time—or the lack of it—can be literally a matter of life or death. As a skipper responsible for the well-being of your crew and guests, you have at least a moral (and in our litigious society a potentially legal) obligation to prepare and equip yourself to deal with virtually any medical emergency that might arise aboard your vessel until you can reach professional assistance.

In *Stapleton's Powerboat Bible* I discuss at some length the things you should do prior to departing on a cruise to prepare for handling medical emergencies aboard, such as attending a Red Cross Standard or Advanced First Aid Course (and having at least one crew member attend as well in case you are the victim), assembling the medical supplies and equipment appropriate to your type of cruising, and making sure you and your crew and guests have thorough medical and dental checkups and appropriate immunizations. In the previous chapter we discussed using your marine radios to contact professional medical assistance for advice. Our emphasis in this chapter will be the immediate steps you should take if a medical emergency strikes a member of your crew or a guest aboard your boat when qualified medical assistance is not immediately available.

## Victim Assessment

If someone suffers an accident or becomes ill aboard your boat, your first step should be to conduct a rapid assessment of the individual's condition to identify the primary medical emergency and determine if your intervention is required. The injury or difficulty you notice first is not necessarily the victim's most serious or the one with which you should attempt to deal first. For example: A crewman slips on your vessel's foredeck. You rush to him and note an obvious broken arm and a severe gash on his forearm. Before you attempt to treat the broken arm or the wound, check to make certain he does not have a far more serious difficulty such as an injury to his spinal column. In this situation, hasty action on your part before you determine his primary medical emergency could result in an even more serious injury or possibly even death.

If the victim is conscious, ask "Are you okay?" As detailed below, his response or the lack of a response will tell you much about his condition. Ask next: "What happened?" Again, his response will help direct your attention toward the primary emergency.

If the victim does not respond to your questions or is unconscious:

*Check respiration:* Within seconds after being deprived of oxygen, the heart begins to develop dangerous irregular beats. If the brain is deprived of oxygen for as little as four to six minutes, irreversible damage is highly likely; after ten minutes it is virtually certain unless the victim's core body temperature has been drastically reduced. For those reasons, checking the victim for adequate respiration is your first responsibility.

If the victim is not obviously inhaling and exhaling on his own, put your ear to his lips to listen for the passage of air into and out of his lungs. Try to feel his breath on your cheek. Look for chest movement. If he is heavily clothed in a sweater or foul weather suit, rest your hand lightly on his upper abdomen to feel for movement. A conscious victim grabbing his throat or struggling for breath or a wheezing noise in the breathing of an unconscious victim indicates an obstruction in his *airway.* The absence of breathing may indicate an *airway obstruction, respiratory failure,* or *heart attack.* A conscious victim who complains of severe chest pain may be suffering *angina* or be in the early stage of a *heart attack.*

*Check circulation:* Feel for the presence of a pulse, preferably at one of the carotid arteries in the victim's neck, where the pulse is more pronounced than in the wrist. To locate a carotid artery, place an index and middle finger on the victim's Adam's apple, then slide them to one side into the groove between the Adam's apple and the neck muscle. Check for the presence of a pulse in only one carotid artery at a time, and exert only light pressure; heavy pressure could restrict the flow of blood to the victim's brain.

In checking the victim's circulation, you are primarily concerned with the presence or absence of a pulse. Count the pulse for 15 seconds by your watch. In a normal, healthy adult, you should count between 15 and 20 beats. Fewer than 12 beats in 15 seconds could indicate the victim is going into *shock.* The absence of a pulse indicates the victim has already gone into serious *shock* or *cardiac arrest.*

*Check skin temperature and moisture:* Cool, clammy skin indicates such conditions as *shock, heat exhaustion,* and *insulin shock.* Hot, dry skin indicates such conditions as *heat stroke* and *diabetic coma.* Flushed skin, swollen welts over large areas of the body, and swelling of the face and lips indicate *anaphylaxis.*

*Check skin color:* Reddened skin indicates *heat stroke.* Pale, white skin indicates such conditions as *shock* or *insulin shock.* Bluish skin indicates an *airway obstruction, respiratory failure,* or *cardiac arrest.*

*Check eye pupils:* Significant differences in the size of the two pupils can indicate *head injury.* Significant dilation of both pupils indicates *cardiac arrest.*

*Check mental alertness:* Significant disorientation indicates a *head injury.* A victim who is knocked unconscious in an accident, rouses to near normal alertness, then later lapses into unconsciousness again could be suffering from *internal bleeding* in the head.

*Check mobility:* In a conscious victim, total inability to move indicates a *spinal injury* in the vicinity of the neck. The ability of a conscious victim to move his arms but not his legs indicates a *spinal injury* below the neck.

## Deciding When to Provide Assistance

After you have determined the victim's primary medical emergency but before you do anything, make certain your intervention is truly necessary and warranted. The human body is a remarkable mechanism which often has the capacity to care for itself if simply left alone. Deciding whether and when to intervene is one of the toughest areas of providing emergency medical assistance, especially when professional medical care is a long way off.

Your *immediate intervention* is appropriate in three medical emergencies: the victim is *not breathing* at all; the victim has *no pulse;* the victim is *bleeding profusely* from an open wound.

*No immediate action* on your part other than preventing further injury is appropriate if you suspect that: the victim has suffered a *spinal injury;* a conscious victim is choking on a foreign body in his throat (he may well expel it through his own exertions); or the victim is suffering a *convulsion* or *seizure.*

*Wait and see* is the appropriate attitude if: a victim is conscious but breathing weakly or gasping for breath; the victim has a weak or racing pulse; the victim is unconscious but breathing on his own and has a pulse. In these situations, avoid the "hero syndrome" of rushing to provide assistance, which may not be necessary and could actually do more harm than good. Instead, watch the victim carefully and see if a condition develops that warrants your intervention.

## The ABCs of Emergency Medical Care

Attend to the ABCs of emergency medical care first: *A*irway, *B*reathing, and *C*irculation.

### Airway

The victim's airway can be blocked by a foreign object or, especially if he is unconscious and lying on his back, by the soft tissues of his own throat and tongue.

## Foreign Object Obstruction

If a conscious victim is choking and you suspect his airway is blocked by a foreign object, do not immediately attempt to assist him if he is passing any air in and out of his lungs. Give him time to dislodge the obstruction on his own. Only if he ceases to pass any air in and out of his lungs should you attempt to help him expel the obstruction by employing the *Heimlich maneuver:*

If the victim is standing, get behind him and wrap your arms around his torso just above his waist (Fig. 11.1). Grasp one fist with the other hand and place the thumb side of your fist halfway between the victim's belly button and the arch of his ribs where they divide at the lower end of the breastbone. Thrust your fist into his abdomen with a sharp, decisive upward squeeze. If the maneuver does not immediately dislodge the object, repeat it until the object is expelled or the victim loses consciousness.

Choking often causes the muscles in the victim's throat to spasm, thereby trapping the object and preventing the passage of air in and out of the lungs. Once the victim loses consciousness, the spasm often ceases, the object is released, and the victim resumes breathing normally. If a choking victim lapses into unconsciousness, assist him gently to the sole or deck, lay him flat on his back, and *clear his airway*. Never attempt to clear a victim's airway

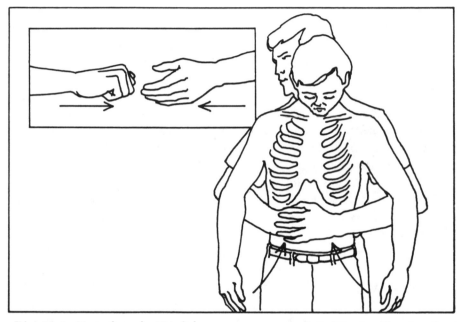

**Fig.** *11.1:* *To perform the Heimlich maneuver on a standing victim, position your fist halfway between his belly button and the arch of his ribs and sharply thrust your fist into his abdomen with a decisive upward motion.* *(Reprinted from* Chapman's Nautical Guides: Emergencies at Sea, *Hearst Marine Books)*

by lifting up on his neck. If he has suffered a spinal injury in the vicinity of the neck, exerting pressure in that area could inflict severe damage or death. Instead, use the *chin-lift/head-tilt* method (Fig. 11.2):

Place one hand on the victim's forehead. Place two fingers of the other hand under the front edge of the victim's jaw. Simultaneously tilt the victim's head backward by pressing on his forehead with one hand while you lift the jaw upward with the fingers of the other. This maneuver will bring the tongue forward and clear it from the airway. *Check* the victim's *respiration*. Often simply clearing the victim's airway will allow him to pass air in and out of his lungs and expel the foreign object.

If the victim is still not breathing and his mouth is not already open, open it using the *cross-finger* technique: cross your index finger over your thumb. Place the tip of your thumb on the bottom of the victim's upper teeth and the tip of your index finger on the top of his lower teeth, then force them apart. Holding the mouth open in this fashion, use the forefinger of the other hand to sweep the inside of the victim's mouth and attempt to locate the foreign body and remove it.

If you are unable to locate the foreign body, straddle the victim's hips (Fig. 11.3). Place the heel of one hand against his abdomen halfway between his belly button and the arch of his ribs where they divide at the lower end of the breastbone. Point the fingers of that hand toward the victim's head. Place your other hand on top of the first. Thrust inward and upward toward the victim's head with a sharp, decisive motion. If the maneuver does not immediately dislodge the object, repeat it six to ten times. Employing the Heimlich maneuver on an unconscious victim who is lying on his back may dislodge the foreign body from his airway but not expel it from his mouth. If the object is not expelled from the mouth, it may fall to the back of the victim's throat and continue to obstruct his breathing. Open his airway as described above, then see if you can locate the obstruction with a finger sweep and remove it.

## BREATHING

If an unconscious victim is not breathing after opening his airway, administer artificial ventilation using *mouth-to-mouth ventilation* (Fig. 11.4):

Use the *head-tilt/chin-lift* method to clear the victim's airway. Keep his head tilted back by continuing to exert pressure on his forehead with the

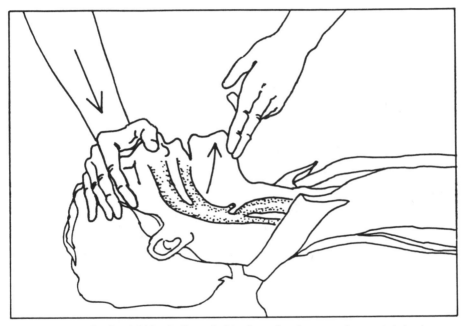

**Fig.** *11.2: The chin-lift/head-tilt method is the preferred way to clear a victim's airway. (Reprinted from* Chapman's Nautical Guides: Emergencies at Sea, *Hearst Marine Books)*

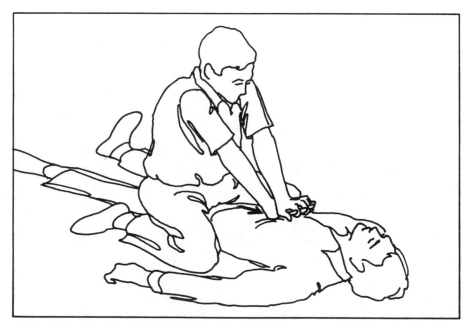

*Fig. 11.3: The Heimlich maneuver can be executed in a prone position by straddling the victim's hips, placing the heel of one hand against his abdomen halfway between his belly button and the arch of his ribs, then thrusting forward with a sharp, decisive motion. (Reprinted from* Chapman's Nautical Guides: Emergencies at Sea, *Hearst Marine Books)*

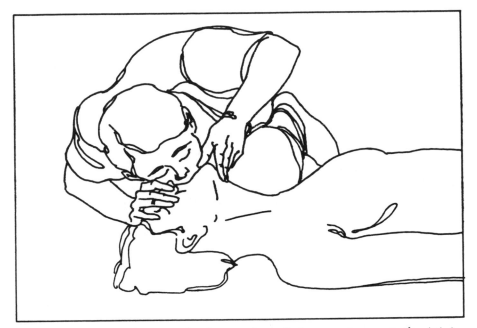

*Fig.* 11.4: *To properly execute mouth-to-mouth ventilation, exert pressure on the victim's forehead with the heel of one hand to tilt his head backward, and use the thumb and forefinger of that same hand to pinch the fleshy tips of his nostrils together. (Reprinted from* Chapman's Nautical Guides: Emergencies at Sea, *Hearst Marine Books)*

heel of one hand. Use the thumb and forefinger of that same hand to pinch the fleshy tips of his nostrils together. Use the thumb of the other hand to pull down on the victim's chin to keep his mouth open. Open your mouth wide as if you were preparing to take a big bite out of an apple. Take a deep breath, place your mouth completely over the victim's mouth, and exhale deeply. Out of the corner of your eye, if you exhale hard enough, you should be able to see the victim's chest rise. After exhaling, remove your mouth to allow the chest to fall. Keep your ear near the victim's mouth to listen for his breathing, try to feel his breath on your cheek, and watch his chest for signs of movement. If necessary, release the hand holding his chin and place it on his upper abdomen to feel for movement. If the victim is not breathing on his own, put your mouth completely over his and exhale into it a second time hard enough to make his chest expand. You should complete these two breaths in three to five seconds.

If the victim is not breathing on his own after your second exhalation, release the hand holding his chin and use it to check the pulse in his carotid artery as discussed above under *Check circulation*. If you detect a pulse, continue mouth-to-mouth ventilation at the rate of one exhalation about every five seconds with each exhalation lasting approximately 1.5 seconds until the victim is breathing on his own.

## CIRCULATION

If you do not detect a pulse in the carotid artery, the victim may be suffering *cardiac arrest* and you must immediately begin to administer *chest compressions*.

If the victim is not already lying on his back on a hard, flat surface, move him to such a position as quickly as possible.

Kneel next to his chest with your knees slightly apart. One of the most important phases of administering chest compressions is placing your hands in the proper position. Improper hand placement can result in ineffective compressions, broken ribs, or damage to the victim's internal organs. To locate the proper hand position (Fig. 11.5): Place the middle finger of your hand that is nearest the victim's feet as high as possible into the arch where his ribs divide at his breastbone. Lay the forefinger of that hand immediately adjacent to the middle finger. Place the heel of your other hand on the victim's breastbone immediately adjacent to your forefinger. Release your hand nearest the victim's feet, place it exactly on top of your other hand,

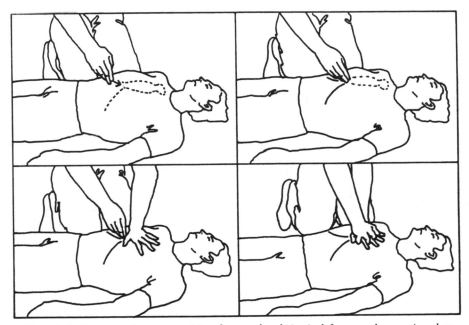

**Fig. 11.5:** *Locating the proper position for your hands is vital for correctly executing chest compressions. (Reprinted from* Chapman's Nautical Guides: Emergencies at Sea, *Hearst Marine Books)*

interlock your fingers, and raise them slightly so that your are exerting pressure on the victim's breastbone with the heel of your lower hand only.

To execute *chest compressions* (Fig. 11.6), lock your elbows and lean forward, rising slightly so your shoulders are directly over the victim's chest and you are exerting pressure directly downward. After depressing the victim's chest 1½ to 2 inches, release your pressure on the victim's chest just enough to allow it to return to its original position. Your hands should not bounce off the victim's chest. Repeat this process until you have delivered 15 chest compressions evenly and rhythmically. The process should take about 10 seconds.

After 15 chest compressions, quickly shift back to the mouth-to-mouth ventilation position described above and check the victim's breathing. If he is not breathing on his own, deliver two full exhalations into the victim's lungs with each lasting approximately 1.5 seconds. Allow the victim's chest to fall between breaths.

After two exhalations, return to your chest compression position, place your hands properly as described above, and deliver another 15 chest compressions evenly and rhythmically over the next 10 to 11 seconds. This combination of mouth-to-mouth ventilation and chest compressions is generally referred to as *cardiopulmonary resuscitation* or *CPR*. You should always begin and end CPR with mouth-to-mouth ventilation. Maintain this ratio of 15 chest compressions to two mouth-to-mouth ventilations until the victim is breathing on his own, you are relieved by professional medical assistance or another rescuer, or you are exhausted.

If, in addition to administering CPR, you are the only person aboard your vessel who can call for help, the best time to do so is after you have performed four cycles of 15 compressions and two mouth-to-mouth ventilations each. By that time, you should have forced enough air into the victim's lungs and circulated enough oxygenated blood through his vital organs with chest compressions to give you a minute and a half to two minutes to try to summon help. Broadcast a Mayday call on VHF channel 16 or single-sideband frequency 2182. If you do not get an immediate response, return to the victim and resume CPR, beginning with two exhalations of mouth-to-mouth ventilation.

CPR conducted by two rescuers with one performing the mouth-to-mouth ventilation and the other performing the chest compressions requires precise coordination and should not be attempted unless both rescuers are well trained in the procedure. If you have initiated CPR and another indi-

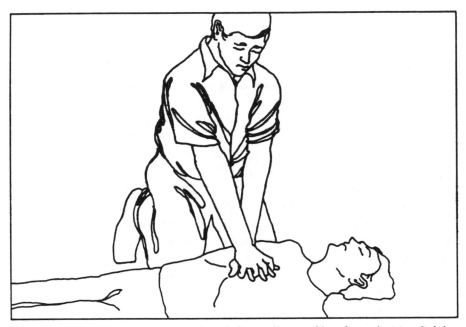

*Fig.* 11.6: *In executing chest compressions, lock your elbows and lean forward, rising slightly so your shoulders are directly over the victim's chest and you are exerting pressure directly downward. (Reprinted from* Chapman's Nautical Guides: Emergencies at Sea, *Hearst Marine Books)*

vidual offers to help, continue CPR by yourself and send the other person to summon help.

Once the victim's *Airway, Breathing,* and *Circulation* are stable, attend to other medical emergencies as recommended below.

# SEVERE BLEEDING

## External Bleeding

Apply direct pressure to an open wound by putting your hand over it and pressing steadily. As soon as possible, put a sterile dressing between your hand and the wound. Once the bleeding stops or slows significantly, apply a compression bandage to the wound: Leave the sterile dressing in place and position the center of a long strip of cloth over it. Maintain a steady pull on the cloth strip as you wrap both ends of it around the extremity, then tie a knot directly over the sterile dressing.

If possible, elevate the wound above the level of the victim's heart to further retard the flow of blood.

If the wound continues to bleed profusely, restrict the blood flow at the primary artery serving the affected area by pressing the artery against a bone at a pressure point (Fig. 11.7).

Apply a tourniquet only in extreme cases. If applied, a tourniquet should not be so tight that it completely cuts off the blood supply from the remainder of the extremity. If the remainder of the extremity beyond the wound begins to turn blue, the tourniquet is too tight. Ease its pressure slowly and gradually. Once you have a tourniquet properly applied, do not loosen or remove it. The sudden loss of blood from the heart could throw the victim into severe *shock*.

Where blood loss is substantial, treat the victim for *shock* as detailed below under *shock*.

## Internal Bleeding

An individual who suffers a major blow to the abdomen that injures the spleen or one to the head that ruptures an artery, a victim who suffers a simple fracture of the ribs or a large bone, or a person who suffers from the eruption of a bleeding ulcer can lose a life-threatening amount of blood with

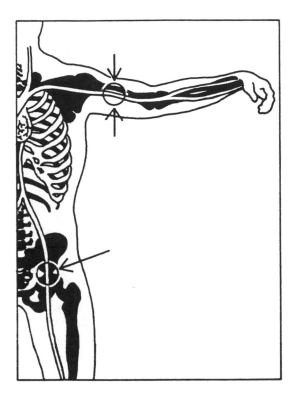

*Fig.* 11.7: *The primary pressure points for controlling severe bleeding in an arm or leg are located on the inside of the upper arm and on the inside of the groin. (Reprinted from* Chapman's Nautical Guides: Emergencies at Sea, *Hearst Marine Books)*

little or no external signs of the bleeding being observable.

Bleeding, however slight, from the rectum, nonmenstrual bleeding from the vagina, blood in the victim's urine or stool, or the coughing or spitting up of blood should lead you to suspect serious internal bleeding. Bleeding from the nose, mouth, or ears can also indicate internal bleeding, especially if it is not obviously the result of a cut inside the mouth or recent scuba diving activity.

If the victim is suffering from severe internal bleeding, these signs will often be accompanied by other indications such as a weak, rapid pulse; cold, moist skin; dull eyes with pupils that are slow to respond to light; excessive thirst; nausea; vomiting; anxiousness; and a marked feeling of depression. The stomach of a person suffering from a lacerated spleen will become tender and swollen.

If the internal bleeding is the result of a large broken bone in the arm or leg, applying a splint will help slow the bleeding. Aside from applying a splint and treating the victim for *shock,* there is virtually nothing you can do to treat severe internal bleeding without advanced medical training and sophisticated equipment. The victim's condition may well be life-threatening. You should call for help and, if you cannot transport the victim to professional medical assistance within half an hour, request helicopter evacuation.

## SHOCK

*Shock* is a collapse of the cardiovascular system in which the flow of blood which carries oxygenated blood to the body's vital organs slows and eventually ceases. After even a few minutes without an adequate flow of oxygenated blood, the cells of certain organs, primarily the brain and the heart, die and cannot be regenerated.

Shock can be brought on by a number of causes such as severe blood or fluid loss due to a large open wound or burn or internal bleeding; damage to the spinal cord that disrupts its control of the nervous system; the dilation of blood vessels in reaction to excessive heat; panic reactions; and failure of the heart to pump effectively. *Respiratory shock* is caused by a failure of the respiratory system.

The signs of shock include cold, clammy skin; profuse sweating; a pale skin color and, in the advanced stages of shock, a bluish color to the lips; shallow, labored, gasping, or rapid breathing; a weak, rapid pulse; extreme thirst; nausea or vomiting.

To treat for shock, clear and maintain the victim's *airway.* Lay him on his back and keep him warm with blankets or clothing, but do not employ artificial sources of heat such as heating pads, electric blankets, or hot water bottles, and do not allow him to become overheated. If available, administer oxygen. If he exhibits no signs of head, neck, or back injury; is not experiencing convulsions, seizures, or respiratory distress; and is not bleeding severely, elevate his feet eight to twelve inches higher than his head. Elevating the feet places the weight of the internal organs on the diaphragm, which could cause breathing problems, so watch the victim carefully for signs of labored breathing and lower his feet if it occurs.

A victim of shock is likely to complain of intense thirst. If medical help

272

is less than two hours away, do not give him fluids but allow him to suck on a piece of moistened gauze or cloth. If medical assistance is more than two hours away, give him fluids only if he is conscious and shows no signs of brain, abdominal, or respiratory injury and is not convulsing. The best fluid to administer is a mixture of 1 level teaspoon of salt and ½ level teaspoon of baking soda dissolved in a quart of tepid water. For adults, give not more than one ounce every fifteen minutes in small sips; for children one to twelve years of age, give half that amount; for infants to one year old, give one quarter that amount. Never give a victim of shock any type of alcohol.

*Anaphylaxis,* a type of shock that can be caused by severe allergic reaction to certain types of ingested poisons and by stings from insects and hazardous marine life, is discussed below under *Poisoning.*

## OPEN WOUNDS

If a wound is bleeding severely, attempt to staunch the flow of blood as discussed above under *Severe Bleeding,* then treat the victim for *shock.* If a severe wound is in one of the victim's extremities, apply a splint which will help control the bleeding, help prevent bleeding from resuming if the victim must be moved or transported, and help relieve the victim's pain.

If an open wound involves a flap of skin that has been torn from the body, attempt to maintain blood circulation in the flap by realigning it to its original position, making certain the portion that remains attached is not twisted or kinked. Apply a saline-dampened sterile dressing and a compression bandage. If the injury involves a flap of skin or a portion of an extremity that has been entirely torn from the victim's body, wrap it in saline-dampened sterile gauze, place it in a plastic bag and keep it in a cool place until you can transport it and the victim to professional medical assistance. Do not allow the flap or portion of the extremity to freeze.

An open wound that exposes internal organs in the abdomen must be kept moist. Cover or wrap the wound with a moistened sterile dressing, cover the dressing with material that is impermeable to air such as plastic food wrap or aluminum foil, then secure the impermeable material in place with a bandage.

In the case of a sucking chest wound where air is escaping from the victim's lung, cover the wound with a sterile dressing, shut off the escaping air by wrapping the victim's chest with plastic kitchen wrap or other air-

273

impervious dressing, then secure the impermeable material in place with tape on three sides only.

If an open wound is not bleeding profusely, remove foreign particles with gauze, cleanse the wound with soap and water, and blot it dry. If professional medical attention will be available within six hours, apply a dry, sterile dressing and a bandage. If medical attention will not be available within six hours, saturate the wound with an antiseptic solution before applying the sterile bandage. One exception to this rule is cuts from coral, which should be cleaned as above but not covered, and instead left open to the air. Open cuts should not be reimmersed in salt water until they are well healed.

## Puncture Wounds

Do not remove an object protruding from a puncture wound if its removal is likely to induce severe bleeding. Leave the object in place, saturate the entry and, if necessary, the exit wound with antiseptic solution, cover the wound(s) with a dry, sterile dressing, and bandage the object securely in place. If the injury is severe, treat the victim for *shock*.

If you remove the object: cleanse the entry and, if necessary, the exit wound with soap and water, saturate the wound(s) with antiseptic solution, then apply a dry dressing and bandage. If the injury is severe, treat the victim for *shock*.

A fishhook that has penetrated the skin far enough to bury its barb is best left in place if medical assistance will be available within approximately eight hours. If it will be much longer than eight hours before the victim can reach medical assistance, the possibility of a serious infection in the bloodstream dictates that the hook should be removed. First determine how far the barb has penetrated below the skin surface. If it is less than a quarter of an inch, clean the area around the hook's entry into the skin, saturate it with antiseptic solution, and make a small incision with a razor blade or sharp knife which has been sterilized by dipping in alcohol or holding over a flame then allowed to cool. Make a small incision behind the barb to expose its tip, grasp the shank of the hook with a pair of needle-nose pliers, and back the hook out. If the barb has penetrated much more than a quarter of an inch beneath the surface of the skin, the best course is to force the point of the hook on through the flesh until the barb emerges, clip it off with wire cutters, then grasp the shank of the hook with a pair of needle-nose pliers and back the remainder of the hook out. In either case, soak the area liberally with antiseptic solution and massage the area to encourage the solution to penetrate into the wound as deeply as possible. Blot the wound dry and cover it with a sterile dressing and bandage. If available, administer a general antibiotic such as penicillin. As soon as possible, consult a doctor regarding the advisability of the victim's receiving a tetanus booster shot.

## FRACTURES AND DISLOCATIONS

Do not attempt to set a fracture or force a dislocated bone back into its socket. Immobilize the affected area with a splint constructed of any material that is close to hand such as a dinghy oar, a rolled newspaper or magazine, or even a pillow. If the skin in the vicinity of the fracture is broken, treat it as an *open wound,* control any *severe bleeding,* and treat the victim for *shock.*

If you suspect a *spinal injury,* do not move the victim. Immobilize him, especially his head and neck, using at-hand materials such as pillows, settee cushions, or boat cushions placed on each side of his head. Call for professional medical assistance immediately.

## CHEST PAIN

A victim who complains of a tightness or a severe pain in his chest may be suffering from a lack of oxygen to his heart muscle. If the tightness or pain follows a period of exertion, emotional stress, or even a big meal, it may be *angina,* which is due to a constriction of the vessels that deliver blood to the heart. The pain of angina most commonly begins beneath the breastbone and may spread to the left arm, the jaw, and the upper region of the abdomen. An attack of angina in itself is not life-threatening and does not result in permanent damage to the heart. If it is the result of exertion or stress, it is often relieved simply by allowing the victim to rest in a cool, calm location, during which the supply of oxygen gradually equals the heart muscle's oxygen requirement. Many individuals who suffer occasional attacks of angina carry with them a small bottle of nitroglycerin tablets, which rapidly dilate blood vessels, thus dramatically increasing the flow of oxygenated blood. If nitroglycerin is available, place one tablet beneath the victim's tongue and allow it to dissolve. If the pain persists, administer additional nitroglycerin tablets

275

at the rate of about one every three to five minutes. If the pain is indeed angina, it should subside within six to eight minutes. Due to nitroglycerin's rapid dilation of blood vessels, the victim may be left with a mild or even a severe headache, which should ease after a half-hour or so of quiet rest.

If an individual experiences tightness or severe pain in his chest that does not follow a period of exertion or stress, is not relieved by nitroglycerin, or lasts more than ten to fifteen minutes, it may be the result of a far more serious situation—a blood clot blocking the main artery which delivers blood to the heart muscle. If the blockage is complete, the heart can immediately develop an irregular beat or cease to beat at all and death can be virtually instantaneous. If the blockage is not complete but is substantial, death or serious damage to the heart muscle may result within four minutes of the onset of the attack.

If an individual aboard your vessel complains of tightness in his chest or severe chest pain that answers the above description, your response can be literally the difference between his life and his death:

First, remain calm and deal with him in a reassuring manner. Agitating or alarming him can cause the situation to deteriorate quickly.

Allow the victim to sit in a cool, quiet location and observe him to see if the pain passes. Make certain he is breathing easily and regularly. If nitroglycerin is available, place one tablet under his tongue about every three to five minutes. If the pain increases rather than decreases and persists for more than about fifteen minutes, call for help. If you will not be able to transport the victim to professional medical assistance within thirty minutes, request emergency helicopter evacuation.

If the victim experiences difficulty in breathing, breaks out in a profuse sweat, his skin pales and his eyes lose their focus or roll back in his head, he may well be experiencing serious and life-threatening *cardiac arrest.*

As quickly as possible, lay him on his back on a hard surface, make certain his *airway* is clear, assist his *breathing* with two slow, full *mouth-to-mouth ventilations,* and check his pulse. If you do not detect a pulse, assist his *circulation* with *chest compressions* as detailed above. Call for help as soon as possible and request emergency evacuation.

## DROWNING ACCIDENTS

Enter the water to rescue a drowning victim only as a last resort, as you risk becoming a drowning victim yourself. The rule is, "THROW, TOW,

ROW, and only then, GO." First, *throw* the victim a floating object such as a life jacket, a life ring, or a buoyant cushion. If that is impractical, throw or push an object such as a rope or dinghy oar out to the victim and *tow* him to safety. If the distance is too great, attempt to *row* out to the victim in a dinghy or even on a surfboard, a Windsurfer, or any other object that will float. Only if all these methods are impractical should you *go* into the water and attempt a rescue yourself. Even then, be alert to the probability that the person will be panicky and may well attempt to grab hold of you and could pull you down with him. If at all possible, approach him from behind and try to get him to calm down, then wrap your arm over his shoulder and grab him with your hand below his armpit to tow him to safety on his back.

Remove the victim from the water and immediately *check* his *airway.* In a drowning incident, the victim's larynx often involuntarily constricts in a spasm in an attempt to keep water from entering the lungs. The spasm normally will relax as soon as the victim is removed from the water. Attempt to restore the victim's *breathing* by administering two slow, full exhalations of *mouth-to-mouth ventilation.* Check his *circulation* by taking his pulse at the carotid artery. If no pulse is felt, execute *chest compressions.* Alternate fifteen chest compressions with two mouth-to-mouth ventilations until the victim is breathing on his own, you are relieved by trained medical assistance or another rescuer, or you are exhausted.

## SCUBA DIVING ACCIDENTS

The most serious scuba diving accidents are those related to ascending from a dive to the surface too rapidly or failing to breathe normally during an ascent.

As a scuba diver descends into the water, the pressure on his body, and thus on the air in his lungs and on the oxygen and nitrogen dissolved in his bloodstream, is greatly increased. If, following a dive, he ascends to the surface slowly, the differing pressures inside and outside his body are gradually equalized without injury. If he breathes normally during such an assent, the nitrogen dissolved in his bloodstream is also released gradually and is expelled by the normal action of his lungs.

If, however, a scuba diver ascends to the surface too rapidly, the air pressure in his lungs remains at a high level while the external pressure on his body decreases rapidly. As a result, the air in his lungs expands rapidly and ruptures tiny vessels in his lungs. The air thus released can enter the space in his chest that contains his lungs, the space in his chest that contains his heart, or it can enter his bloodstream and create a plug which blocks the normal flow of blood to his brain, his heart, and other vital organs. An air bubble trapped in the bloodstream will often lodge in a joint where blood vessels are smallest. Because of the differences in air pressure involved, air bubbles in the bloodstream can occur in dives as shallow as six feet.

A scuba diver suffering the effects of ascending too rapidly will experience difficulty in breathing or pain in his chest, pain in his joints or abdomen, dizziness, nausea or vomiting, and may have a mottled coloration to his skin and exude a pink or bloody froth from his mouth and nose. Normally he will experience these difficulties immediately upon returning to the surface.

If a scuba diver fails to breathe normally during an ascent from a single dive or repetitive dives to a depth exceeding 60 feet for a total bottom time greater than 60 minutes, the nitrogen dissolved in his bloodstream is not expelled by the normal action of his lungs and can create bubbles in his bloodstream which also block the normal flow of blood to his brain, his heart, and other vital organs. A diver suffering from nitrogen bubbles in his bloodstream will exhibit the same signs as the diver suffering the effects of an air bubble, with two important differences: First, pain in his abdomen and joints will be so severe that he will actually double over, which gives this condition its name: *the bends*. Second, he may not suffer difficulties until several hours after he has returned to the surface.

The emergency treatment for both types of scuba diving injuries is the same:

If necessary, clear and maintain the victim's *airway*, restore his *breathing* with *mouth-to-mouth ventilation*, and restore his *circulation* with *chest compressions*. Once the victim's ABCs are restored, lay him on his left side to help keep the air or nitrogen bubbles in his bloodstream from migrating to his heart, elevate his feet eight to twelve inches to help keep the bubbles from migrating to his brain, keep him warm and, if possible, give him pure oxygen. Call for help immediately and arrange to evacuate him to the nearest recompression chamber. You can normally obtain information on the nearest recompression chamber's location and arrange evacuation through the Coast Guard. An excellent resource for advice and assistance in handling any diving accident victim is the Diver's Alert Network, a nonprofit organization which is staffed twenty-four hours a day. You can reach them through a VHF or High Seas marine radiotelephone operator at (919) 684-8111. If evacuation is to be by air, make certain the pilot understands you suspect the victim has air or gas bubbles in his bloodstream. The air pressure inside the aircraft should not exceed that experienced at 500 feet above sea level.

# BURNS

## Heat Burns

If the victim's skin is red but not blistered or weeping, the injury is a first-degree burn which has injured only the top one or two layers of the skin. Immerse the affected area in cold (not ice) water or cover it with a cloth soaked in cold water. Apply an anesthetic spray or ointment to relieve the pain. If necessary, apply a dry dressing, cover it with a bandage, and administer an oral pain medication such as aspirin.

If the victim's skin is blistered or weeping, he has a second-degree burn. Immerse the affected area in cold (not ice) water or cover it with a cloth soaked in cold water. Do not break any blisters that are present; do not attempt to remove burned tissue; and do not apply any kind of antiseptic sprays, ointments, or grease. Apply only a dry dressing and a bandage. If possible, keep the affected areas above the level of the victim's heart. If the affected area is extensive, treat the victim for *shock*.

If the victim's skin exhibits a whitish charring, he is suffering from a third-degree burn. Do not attempt to remove any burned tissue or adhered clothing. If the affected area is extensive, do not immerse the victim in cold water or apply cold compresses, as cold could intensify his reaction to *shock*, which invariably accompanies a sizeable third-degree burn. If the affected area is limited, cold compresses can be applied. Do not apply any sprays or ointments. Apply only a dry, sterile dressing and a bandage. If the affected area is the victim's head or an extremity, elevate it above the level of his heart. Administer oral pain medication. If the burned area is large or deep, treat the victim for *shock*. Administer fluids as recommended above under *shock* only if the victim is conscious and not vomiting and medical help is more than an hour away.

279

## Chemical Burns

If necessary, remove the victim's clothing from the area of the burn and flush the affected area with water for five minutes. Depending on the severity of the burn, treat the affected area as above under *Heat burns*.

# POISONING

## Poisoning by Mouth

If the victim is conscious, give him water or milk to dilute the poison. If medicinal charcoal is available, give him that. Attempt to determine the source of the poisoning. If its container indicates a specific antidote, give it to the victim if it is available.

Do not attempt to administer fluids if the victim is unconscious.

If the source of the poisoning is unknown but an acid, alkali, or petroleum product is possible, do not induce vomiting.

If a substance other than acid, alkali, or a petroleum product is known to be the source of poisoning, induce vomiting by administering an emetic solution or poking your finger down the victim's throat.

## Seafood Poisoning

One of the joys of the cruising life is the opportunity to harvest the bounty of the sea, but there are dangers of which you should be aware.

*Ciguatera:* Larger specimens of carnivorous reef feeders such as grouper, snapper, jack, and barracuda can become infected with ciguatera toxin, which can be extremely poisonous and, in extreme cases, fatal.

Individual reactions to ciguatera vary widely. Where two individuals eat the same amount of a contaminated fish at the same time, one may experience no or very mild effects while the other may become extremely ill. Symptoms normally appear within about six hours. A distinctive symptom of ciguatera poisoning is the victim's reversed reactions to hot and cold. Other telltale signs include numbness and/or a tingling sensation, especially around the mouth; severe stomach cramps; often violent vomiting; diarrhea; excessive sweating; and a pale complexion. Some victims may become disoriented or hallucinate, and some may exhibit varying degrees of paralysis. A suspected victim of severe ciguatera poisoning must be transported to professional medical assistance as quickly as possible.

Many physicians are not familiar with treating ciguatera poisoning. If you encounter such a situation, you might inform the physician of the procedures suggested by Dr. Richard J. Lewis of Santa Monica, California, an avid cruiser who has extensively researched treatment of ciguatera poisoning. His recommendations, as published in the *Commodore's Bulletin* of the Seven Seas Cruising Association, are as follows: For severe cases, establish a 30 ml/hour flow of intravenous saline or Ringer's solution, then piggyback 20 percent mannitol at 500 ml/hour until symptoms disappear or to a maximum dosage of 5 ml per kilogram of the victim's body weight. The infusion of mannitol should be interrupted if blood pressure drops more than 15 mmHg. Symptoms usually respond to this treatment within 10 minutes. For mild cases of ciguatera poisoning, Dr. Lewis recommends prescribing one 25 mg tablet of amitriptyline twice daily for two to three weeks.

*Paralytic Shellfish Poisoning:* Bivalves such as oysters, scallops, clams, and mussels can become infected with a toxin associated with so-called "red tides" that is very similar to that responsible for ciguatera. It can cause paralysis and, in extreme cases, can be fatal. It is not destroyed by cooking or steaming.

Incidents of paralytic shellfish poisoning most often occur during the summer months and are most common along the coasts of New England and the Pacific Northwest.

Symptoms normally occur within thirty minutes. Victims may experience a tingling or numbness of the facial muscles, especially around the mouth; labored breathing; headache; nausea; vomiting; diarrhea; abdominal cramps; a floating sensation; muscle weakness; increased salivation; increased thirst; and difficulty in speaking which may indicate the onset of muscular paralysis.

A suspected victim of paralytic shellfish poisoning should be transported to professional medical assistance as rapidly as possible. Antihistamines such as epinephrine can help relieve respiratory distress if it is present.

*Neurotoxic Shellfish Poisoning:* Bivalves harvested along the coasts of Florida during the summer months can become infected with a poisonous waterborne organism related to—but not the same as—the organism that causes paralytic shellfish poisoning. This neurotoxic shellfish poisoning is not fatal and the symptoms normally will disappear within a few days.

Signs of paralytic and neurotoxic shellfish poisoning are similar, except victims of neurotoxic poisoning do not exhibit respiratory distress or muscular paralysis.

*Tetrodotoxin:* This toxin, a chemical relative to the toxin that causes paralytic shellfish poisoning, is principally associated with the puffer fish—the Japanese delicacy *fugu*—but is also found in porcupine fish, ocean sunfish, and blue-ringed octopus.

It concentrates primarily in the liver, intestines, gonads, and skin of the fish and can be eliminated only by cutting away the toxic parts, a task that in Japan can be performed only by a licensed chef who has received special training.

Fugu devotees consider a mild toxic reaction from eating the dish—a tingling of the lips and tongue, flushing of the skin, and mood elevation—as part of its appeal. Of the 3,000 cases of fugu poisoning reported in Japan over a 20-year period, 51 percent were fatal.

*Scombroid Poisoning:* Fish with dark meat such as tuna, wahoo, bluefish, amberjack, bonito, mackerel, skipjack, and mahimahi are susceptible to scombroid poisoning, which is most often caused by inadequate refrigeration of the fish after it is caught. Lack of prompt refrigeration can cause bacteria on the surface of the fish to penetrate the flesh and contaminate it. This bacteria is not eliminated by cooking. It may, but does not often, impart a sharp or peppery taste to the meat.

Symptoms of scombroid poisoning may appear within minutes after contaminated fish is eaten or up to several hours later. They can include labored respiration, dizziness, nausea, vomiting, diarrhea, and a flushed or burning sensation. The victim's skin may become reddened to the point that it appears to be sunburned. Fortunately, scombroid poisoning is not fatal and symptoms normally will disappear within twelve to twenty-four hours. Antihistamines such as epinephrine can help relieve respiratory distress if it is present.

## Insect Poisoning

For reactions to poisoning from insect bites or stings such as severe swelling, apply a mildly constricting band between the site of the bite and the heart and keep the affected area below the level of the victim's heart. Apply ice or cold cloths to the infection site and administer a mild pain reliever such as aspirin.

In the case of a sting from a wasp or hornet and bees other than the honeybee, scrub the site of the bite with soap and water, then attempt to remove the stinger and venom sac with tweezers sterilized by immersion in alcohol or being heated over a flame and allowed to cool.

The barbed stinger of a honeybee can continue to inject poison into the victim for up to twenty minutes after the initial attack. Do not use tweezers to remove the stinger as their squeezing action can inject more poison. Instead, remove the stinger by scraping it from the skin.

## Poisoning by Marine Life

*Tentacle stings:* Contact with jellyfish, Portuguese man-of-war, anemones, and certain types of coral can deposit toxic cells on the victim's skin which can cause significant skin irritation, pain, nausea, vomiting, and muscle cramps.

First flood the affected area with rubbing alcohol, ammonia, or household vinegar, which will help to neutralize the toxin. If available, cover the affected area with meat tenderizer. It contains an enzyme that will destroy the toxin. Lastly, if available, cover the affected area with talcum powder, which will dry the skin and cause the toxic cells to stick together so you can scrape them from the skin.

*Puncture wounds:* Puncture wounds from such marine life as stingrays, sea urchins, cone shells, catfish, stonefish, toadfish, weevers, oysterfish, scorpion fish, zebra fish, and surgeonfish contain a toxin that is susceptible to heat. Immerse the affected area in water as hot as the victim can stand for thirty to sixty minutes, but be careful not to scald him as his reaction to the toxin may temporarily negate his normal reaction to the pain of excess heat.

Once the pain has subsided, flood the puncture wound with rubbing alcohol, ammonia, or household vinegar to deactivate the toxin. If medical help is more than six hours away, wrap the extremity between the wound and the heart with a mildly constrictive elastic bandage (not a tourniquet) to retard the flow of the toxin to the victim's vital organs.

Appropriate treatments for poisoning by marine life are summarized in Fig. 11.8.

## Poisoning by Plants

Remove any of the victim's clothing that may have become contaminated by the plant's poisonous oils. Generously flush the affected area with water, then wash it with soap and water. If possible, follow this scrubbing with

### Emergency Treatment of Marine Animal Injuries

| Type of Injury | Marine Animal Involved | Emergency Treatment | Possible Complications |
|---|---|---|---|
| Bite or Laceration | Major wounds by<br>  Shark<br>  Barracuda<br>  Alligator gar | Control Bleeding<br>Treat for shock<br>Administer CPR<br>Splint injury | Shock<br>Infections |
| | Minor wounds by<br>  Moral eel<br>  Turtle<br>  Corals | Cleanse wound<br>Splint injury | |
| Sting | Jellyfish<br>Portuguese man-of-war<br>Anemones<br>Corals<br>Hydra | Inactivate the toxin with<br>  alcohol, meat<br>  tenderizer<br>Apply talcum powder<br>  and scrape<br>  nematocysts from skin | Allergic reactions<br>Respiratory arrest |
| Puncture | Urchins<br>Cone shells<br>Stingrays<br>Spiny fish | Soak in hot water | Allergic reactions<br>Collapse<br>Infections<br>Tetanus |
| Poisoning | Puffer fish<br>Scrumboids (tuna<br>  species)<br>Ciguatera (large colored<br>  fish)<br>Shellfish | Induce vomiting<br>Dilute with water or<br>  milk<br>Administer CPR<br>Prevent self-injury from<br>  convulsions | Allergic reactions<br>Asthmatic reactions<br>Numbness<br>Temperature reversal<br>Respiratory and<br>  circulatory collapse |

*Fig. 11.8*

284

rubbing alcohol, ammonia, or household bleach diluted 50 percent with water. If the skin rash is mild, apply calamine or aloe lotion.

## Poisoning by Venomous Snake

Encourage the victim to sit or lie down and calm him to slow the spread of the toxin through his system. If the affected area is an arm or leg, wrap constricting bands (not a tourniquet) both above and below the bite to contain as much as possible of the toxin in the bite area. A pulse should still be detectable beyond the band farthest from the heart. Immobilize the arm or leg with a splint. Do not give the victim any fluids.

If possible, have your crew kill or capture the snake. Knowing what kind of snake caused the bite will be important to professional medical personnel in determining which antivenin to administer.

If the victim can be transported to professional medical personnel within thirty minutes, keep him lying down and calm and transport him as quickly as possible. If possible, contact professional medical assistance and let them know you are on the way and what kind of snake was involved. In many locations, snake antivenin must be ordered from central supplies and your call will help speed the process.

If professional medical assistance is more than thirty minutes away, attempt to assess whether the snake actually injected a significant quantity of venom into the victim. If the bite area exhibits two distinct puncture wounds about an inch apart, it is likely from a pit viper such as a rattlesnake, a copperhead, or a cottonmouth. If within five to ten minutes of the attack the victim does not experience a burning sensation at the site of the bite, it is unlikely a significant quantity of venom was injected. Keep the victim calm and transport him to professional medical assistance as quickly as possible.

If the bite area exhibits two distinct punctures and the victim experiences a burning sensation at the site of the bite, a significant quantity of venom has probably been injected, which could be life-threatening. If medical assistance is more than thirty minutes away, you will have to suction as much of the venom out of the wound as possible. With a razor blade or sharp knife which has been sterilized in alcohol or by being heated over a flame and allowed to cool, make a one-half-inch incision a quarter of an inch deep over each puncture wound. The cut should run along the long axis of the victim's arm or leg to avoid cutting across muscle tissue. If a snake bite kit is available, use its suction cup to suction out the venom. If no snake bite kit is available and you have no open cuts or sores in your mouth, suck and spit out as much of the venom as possible. Snake venom works through the bloodstream and is not harmful in the digestive tract. Transport the victim to professional medical assistance as rapidly as possible.

## Anaphylaxis

Many victims of certain types of ingested poisons and of stings and bites from insects and hazardous marine life suffer a severe allergic reaction called *anaphylaxis,* which is a type of *shock.*

Anaphylaxis is often marked by a flushing, itching, or burning of the victim's skin, especially in the face and upper chest; swollen welts spreading over the body; swelling of the face, tongue, and lips; and a bluish coloring to the lips. The victim may also experience a tightness or constriction in his chest; wheezing and/or coughing; and difficulty in exhaling.

Many individuals who are subject to such severe allergic reactions carry with them a small kit containing injectable epinephrine and an oral antihistamine. If such a kit is available, inject the epinephrine into a muscle in the victim's upper arm or hip. If the victim is conscious, administer the kit's oral antihistamine. Watch the victim closely. The injection of epinephrine may relieve his symptoms momentarily, but they may reoccur and he may require additional injections of epinephrine or oral administrations of antihistamines.

If epinephrine and antihistamines are not available, the victim of anaphylaxis may well experience severe difficulties in breathing and may experience cardiac arrest. If the victim stops breathing, open and maintain his *airway* and administer *mouth-to-mouth ventilation.* If he does not have a pulse, execute *chest compressions.*

## INSULIN SHOCK/DIABETIC COMA

Glucose (sugar) is as vital to the functioning of the brain as oxygen. Brain cells deprived of glucose can suffer severe and permanent damage. Glucose enters the body in the foods we eat, but it cannot enter the body's cells without the presence of insulin, a natural hormone normally produced by the body itself.

Diabetics are individuals whose bodies produce no or insufficient levels of insulin. Diabetics whose bodies produce no natural insulin must inject insulin daily. Diabetics whose bodies produce insufficient levels of insulin often can control their condition by balancing their intake of glucose in the foods they eat.

Diabetics can suffer medical emergencies from either of two situations: *insulin shock,* in which the level of glucose in their blood is too low; or *diabetic coma,* in which the level of glucose in their blood is too high.

The signs of both conditions (Fig. 11.9) are similar and make distinguishing between and treating them appropriately very difficult. The primary difference which will be readily apparent is that the symptoms of insulin shock often appear in a matter of minutes while the symptoms of diabetic coma normally appear over several hours. Diabetics normally are quite familiar with their disease and, if they are conscious, can tell you which condition they are suffering from and what you should do to help them.

## Insulin Shock

Of the two conditions, *insulin shock* is by far the more serious. If it is not treated promptly, severe brain damage can result. Insulin shock can be brought on by the victim's taking too much insulin; taking a regular dose of insulin but not eating enough food, or exercising excessively and using up his body's available store of glucose. The victim of insulin shock will usually have pale, moist skin, sweat profusely, experience dizziness and/or headache, and may appear to be "drunk" before suffering a *convulsion* or *seizure* and/or lapsing into unconsciousness.

The appropriate treatment for insulin shock is to give the victim sugar. Fortunately, administering sugar to the victim of insulin shock is likely to correct his condition in a few minutes and prevent serious brain damage or death but does not create long-term harmful effects in the victim of *diabetic coma.*

For that reason, if you suspect either insulin shock or diabetic coma and the victim is conscious, *give the victim sugar.* The best way to administer sugar is in fruit juice, if possible sweetened with additional sugar, a candy bar, or even cake-decorating gel.

If the victim is not conscious, check and maintain his *airway.* If he suffers

287

## Signs of Diabetic Shock/Diabetic Coma

| Observation | Diabetic Shock | Diabetic Coma |
|---|---|---|
| Skin | Pale and moist | Warm and dry |
| Pulse | Normal, or rapid and full | Rapid and weak |
| Breathing | Normal, or rapid | Gasping |
| Breath odor | Normal | Sweet or fruity |
| Thirst | Absent | Intense |
| Hunger | Intense | Absent |
| Vomiting | Unlikely | Likely |
| Headache | Present | Absent |
| Mood | Irritable | Restless |
| Food intake | Insufficient | Excessive |
| Insulin dosage | Excessive | Insufficient |
| Possible complications | Seizure or coma | Coma |
| Response to treatment | Immediate after sugar administered | Gradual within six to eight hours following medication |

*Fig. 11.9*

a convulsion or seizure, treat him as detailed below under *Convulsions and Seizures.* Attempting to administer sugar in a liquid form such as fruit juice to an unconscious victim of insulin shock creates the danger of choking him. However, if it will be more than thirty minutes before you can get the victim to professional medical assistance, you must get sugar in some form into his bloodstream. Place a glucose-laden substance such as refined sugar, syrup, or cake-decorating gel beneath his tongue, allow it to dissolve, and replenish the supply often. Since the victim will not be able to swallow, not much of the glucose will enter his stomach and then his bloodstream, but you will have done all you can. Transport him to professional medical assistance as quickly as possible.

# Diabetic Coma

The breathing of a victim of *diabetic coma* will often be rapid and consist of deep sighs; his skin will be warm and dry; and his breath will smell sweet or fruity. The victim may suffer a *convulsion* or *seizure* and/or lapse into unconsciousness. If either of those conditions is evident, open and maintain the victim's *airway,* or treat as detailed below under *Convulsions and Seizures.*

Most diabetics who are dependent on insulin carry injectable insulin with them. If the victim shows signs of diabetic coma and insulin is available, inject a dose into the muscle of the victim's arm or thigh. If insulin is not available, the victim should be transported to professional medical assistance. Since the serious effects of diabetic coma develop over a period of several hours, that transportation should be carried out as quickly as practical but does not need to be conducted as an emergency evacuation.

## CONVULSIONS AND SEIZURES

Prevent the victim from injuring himself but do not attempt to restrain him. Loosen his clothing. If his jaw is clenched, do not attempt to thrust an object between his teeth. If his mouth is open, insert a soft object such as a rolled handkerchief between his back teeth.

Most convulsions and seizures will last only a few moments, and your best course of action is to prevent the victim from injuring himself and observe him closely. Some victims will experience respiration difficulties immediately after the attack. If that occurs, maintain an open airway by placing the victim in a reclining position on his side or stomach. If he stops breathing, ventilate using a mouth-to-nose technique.

Once the convulsion or seizure has passed, the victim is likely to be exhausted and may be dazed or semiconscious. Allow him to rest quietly and do not attempt to give him any fluids until he is fully conscious.

If the victim has suffered convulsions or seizures in the past, the incident probably is not serious and requires no further intervention on your part. If the victim has never suffered a convulsion or seizure before, the incident may well be extremely serious. If the victim shows any of the other signs related to *stroke,* transport him to professional medical assistance as quickly as possible.

289

## STROKE

Stroke is the result of an insufficient supply of oxygenated blood to the brain. If the flow of oxygenated blood to the brain is interrupted for more than six minutes, irreversible damage can occur in that portion of the brain which has lost its supply of oxygen.

Stroke can be caused by a gradual narrowing of the arteries that supply blood to the brain, by the blockage of these arteries by a blood clot that forms elsewhere in the body such as in the heart, or by the rupture of an artery. The first two causes of stroke normally are associated with the elderly or those who suffer from heart disease. The rupture of an artery serving the brain, however, can be the result of an inherent weakness in the artery and can occur in young and otherwise healthy people.

The signs of stroke include partial or complete paralysis of the face muscles and/or the extremities on one side of the body (both sides of the body are rarely affected at the same time); varying levels of consciousness ranging from confusion or dizziness to a total loss of consciousness; difficulties with speech, vision, or swallowing; convulsions; and headache.

Stroke victims often suffer paralysis of the airway following the incident. If you suspect stroke, immediately check and if necessary open and maintain the victim's airway. A stroke victim is likely to be extremely frightened due to his inability to communicate. Calm and reassure him as much as possible. If he suffers paralysis, lay him with the paralyzed side down and pad his extremities carefully to avoid further injury.

There is nothing you can do aboard ship to relieve the symptoms of stroke or determine its likely consequences, which can range from mild and temporary disability to severe disability and death. Any victim who you suspect has suffered stroke should be transported to professional medical care as quickly as possible.

## EYE INJURIES

Small foreign bodies such as sand or grit lying in the lower half of the eye usually can be flushed away with clean water or a mild saline solution.

Foreign bodies that have adhered to the eyeball or are lodged under the upper eyelid usually must be removed manually. Have the victim look down and grasp the eyelashes of the injured eye with your thumb and index finger. Lay a matchstick or cotton-tipped applicator on top of the eyelid and fold the eyelid back over it. Carefully remove the object from the eyeball with a cotton-tipped applicator or a small piece of gauze folded into a point.

The victim of a blow to the eye from a blunt object may complain of difficulty in seeing or double vision. The eye may bleed inside the covering of the iris. Have the victim lie down and close his eye, then cover the injured eye with a sterile dressing loosely taped in place. Since both eyes move together, also loosely tape a dressing over the uninjured eye to prevent unnecessary movement. Transport the victim to professional medical assistance as rapidly as practical. The victim should remain lying down and stay as still as possible during transportation to avoid further potential injury.

If the eyeball has been penetrated by an object, make no attempt to remove it. Have the victim lie down. Do not apply any pressure to the eye, even if severe bleeding is present. If possible, place a paper cup or other protective covering over both the eye and the penetrating object and tape it in place. Loosely tape a dressing over the uninjured eye to prevent unnecessary movement. Have the victim lie as still as possible on his back and transport him to professional medical assistance as quickly as practical.

If the victim has suffered a chemical burn to his eyes, flush them with clean water continuously and thoroughly for ten to fifteen minutes. If only one eye is affected, turn his head so that the injured eye is lower than the uninjured eye to avoid flushing the caustic solution into the uninjured eye. If pain or instinctive reaction prohibits the victim from opening an injured eye wide enough to ensure thorough and complete flushing, place your thumb as close as possible beneath his lower eyelid and your index finger at the top of his upper eyelid and force the eyelids to remain open during the flushing process. Once you have thoroughly flushed out the injured eye, cover both eyes with a loosely taped dressing and transport the victim to professional medical assistance as quickly as practical.

# HEATSTROKE AND HEAT EXHAUSTION

Move the victim to the coolest possible area; use fans or air conditioning if available. Remove his clothing and immerse him in cold (not ice) water, cover him with towels soaked in cold water or sponge off his skin with cold water until his body temperature returns to normal. If the victim is conscious and not vomiting, administer liquids. Do not administer stimulants such as alcohol.

## HYPOTHERMIA AND FROSTBITE

### Hypothermia

Symptoms of hypothermia appear when the body's core temperature—normally 98.6 degrees Fahrenheit—falls below 95 degrees Fahrenheit. As the body's core temperature drops, hypothermia progresses through five general stages:

1. When core temperature falls to between 90 and 95 degrees, the victim is likely to shiver, stamp his feet, and jump up and down in an effort to create additional internal heat. When the core temperature drops below about 90 degrees, shivering stops.

2. With a core temperature from 90 degrees down to about 86 degrees, the victim will exhibit a loss of small muscle activity such as a lack of coordinated finger motion.

3. As core temperature drops below about 85 degrees, the hypothermia victim will become lethargic and sleepy and lose interest in battling his condition.

4. At a core temperature of around 80 degrees, the victim's pulse and respiration slow and become weaker. The victim may become irrational, then lapse into unconsciousness and finally into a coma.

5. When the core temperature reaches 78 degrees, death can occur. However, recent incidents and studies have shown that when core temperature is reduced rapidly (such as when individuals fall into icy water and become trapped), the body's metabolism can slow to remarkably low levels. Hypothermia victims have been revived after being deprived of oxygen for several hours without apparent damage to their brain, heart, or other vital organs. For that reason, rescuers attempting to revive a hypothermia victim should continue resuscitation efforts until the victim's body temperature has risen to near

normal levels and he or she still does not exhibit such vital signs as a heartbeat, a pulse, or breathing. Emergency medical technicians assume no hypothermia victim is dead until he or she is "warm dead."

Immediately remove a suspected victim of hypothermia from the cold environment.

If the victim is unconscious, check his or her respiration and pulse. If either is weak or absent, begin basic life support immediately by clearing an airway, administering mouth-to-mouth ventilation and, if necessary, chest compressions.

As soon as respiration and a pulse are restored, move the victim to a warm area, strip away any wet clothing, and wrap the victim completely in warm blankets. Hypothermia victims whose core temperature has fallen low enough to weaken their respiration or pulse or trigger irrational behavior or unconsciousness can experience severe cardiac arrhythmias as their core body temperature returns to normal, and they must be transported as rapidly as possible to professional medical assistance. If medical help is more than fifteen minutes away, attempt to arrange helicopter evacuation.

If a victim of mild hypothermia has not lost consciousness, has strong respiration and pulse, and is alert and well oriented, he is unlikely to require hospitalization. Make the victim rest, keep him warm and dry, and administer small sips of warm liquids until the victim's external body temperature returns to normal.

## Frostbite

Transport the victim to shelter. If possible, warm the affected area by immersing it in tepid water, then gradually adding warm water until the water temperature is between 102 and 105 degrees Fahrenheit. If warm water is not available, warm the affected area by wrapping it in clothing or blankets. Do not rub the affected area, do not apply excessive heat, and do not allow the victim to expose the affected area to excess heat. Discontinue warming efforts as soon as normal skin color returns to the affected area. If normal color does not return to the affected area but it continues to exhibit a whitish color, transport the victim to professional medical assistance as quickly as possible.

## SEASICKNESS

While seasickness itself is hardly a life-threatening emergency, extreme cases can lead to severe dehydration, which can have serious consequences.

The malady results from a disruption of the balance mechanism in the inner ear, which can be triggered by the motion of the vessel on the sea and/or by such visual signals as a tossing foredeck or rolling waves.

The best approach for individuals who are prone to seasickness is to prevent its onset. Many individuals find the most effective preventative is a patch affixed to the mastoid bone just behind the ear, which slow-releases a dose of 0.5 mg of scopolamine every twenty-four hours. These patches normally contain a total of 1.5 mg of the drug and are designed to be effective for seventy-two hours. If protection for longer periods is required, additional patches may be affixed over the mastoid bone on alternate sides every seventy-two hours. Others find they are best helped by oral motion-sickness compounds such as Dramamine or Bonine. Either type of preventative should be employed at least four hours prior to embarking on any trip to sea, and either can cause extreme drowsiness and a dry mouth. Still other people have reported success from wristbands that purport to work through exerting force on an acupressure point, but their comfort may be more psychological than physical as there is little scientific evidence to support the claim.

Once at sea, anyone who begins to feel queasy should refrain from eating heavy foods or drinking alcoholic beverages. Some people do, however, find that nibbling on a soda cracker and sipping on a carbonated beverage helps to settle their stomach.

Individuals who feel a bout of seasickness coming on should stay on deck rather than going below. Confinement in a closed space often makes the malady worse and can trigger vomiting, where fresh air often dissipates the malady's symptoms. It's best if such individuals station themselves at the vessel's most stable point, such as in the cockpit of a sportfisherman, rather than on its flying bridge. Focusing their eyes on the horizon rather than on the vessel or the sea tossing around them may also help restore a sense of equilibrium to the balance mechanism in their inner ear and cause the symptoms of seasickness to subside.

Individuals who experience severe seasickness to the point of actually vomiting often react in one of two ways: after the initial attack, some people "get their sea legs" and have no further problems; others find themselves completely unable to keep anything in their stomach and become caught up in a cycle of violent vomiting. If this goes on for more than about twelve hours, it can lead to serious consequences from dehydration. The most dependable treatment is simply to return the individual to shore. After a few hours on dry land, normally he or she will be able to take liquid nourishment and will recover without medical attention.

If returning to land is impossible (such as on a long open-water voyage) or does not relieve the symptoms, the most effective treatment is administration of Dramamine or Compazine suppositories. After the administration of two or three suppositories about four to six hours apart, most people will normally be able to take enough liquids to avoid dehydration until they can reach land. Once onshore, they should seek professional medical assistance.

## WHEN TO CALL FOR EMERGENCY EVACUATION

Evacuating a victim from your vessel to another vessel or a helicopter can be an extremely hazardous undertaking for the victim, for those aboard your own vessel, and possibly for the crew of the rescue unit to which the victim is to be transferred, especially if the weather is rough.

Your decision whether or not to attempt emergency evacuation should be guided by your answers to five critical questions:

- Does the victim require professional medical assistance you cannot provide aboard your vessel in order to survive?
- How quickly must he get to that professional medical care in order to live?
- How quickly can you transport him there aboard your own vessel?
- How quickly can he be transported there by another vessel or a helicopter?
- Is the difference between the time you can get him to professional medical care and the time he can be transported to that care by another vessel or a helicopter sufficient to justify exposing the victim, your crew, and the crew of the rescue vessel or aircraft to the potential hazards of emergency evacuation?

Your answers to the first two of those questions depend on the nature of the victim's emergency and your estimation of the seriousness of his condition. Emergencies that put life in critical danger and about which you can do virtually nothing without advanced medical training and life support equipment include: *heart attack; stroke;* severe *airway obstructions* you cannot relieve; serious *head injury;* severe *internal bleeding;* severe *external bleeding* you cannot control; significant *open chest or abdominal wounds;* significant *third-degree burns;* severe *poisoning.* Transporting victims of these medical emergencies to professional medical care as quickly as possible and by any means possible is absolutely critical if they are to survive.

Your answers to the last three questions depend on circumstances: How far are you away from professional medical care? What is your vessel's maximum speed and how long will it take you to transport the victim there? How soon can an emergency vessel or helicopter reach you? How severe is the weather and what hazards will it impose on the evacuation procedure?

## Conducting Emergency Evacuation

If your answers to the above questions convince you that emergency evacuation is necessary, contact the Coast Guard on VHF channel 16 or SSB frequency 2182 kHz to arrange for the dispatch of a rescue unit. Once you reach the Coast Guard, they usually will instruct you to shift to a working channel, which most likely will be VHF channel 22A or SSB channel 2670 kHz. Be prepared to tell them why emergency evacuation is necessary and give them detailed information about your vessel's position and wind and sea conditions. Once evacuation is agreed on, it's imperative that you or a crew member you assign the task monitor the working frequency until the evacuation is complete.

While the rescue unit is en route, prepare the victim for evacuation. Tag him with a brief but specific description of the injury or illness he has sustained or the symptoms he has exhibited, list any medications you have administered or procedures you have performed, and include any other information you are aware of that might be pertinent (i.e., the victim has previously suffered heart problems or epileptic attacks or is allergic to certain medications). If the victim is unconscious, include his or her name, age, next of kin, where next of kin can be reached by telephone, and the victim's blood type if you know it.

296

In cold weather, if the injuries permit, the victim should be dressed warmly, but avoid loose-fitting clothing or headgear that could become entangled in hoisting equipment. If the injuries permit, the victim should be fitted with a life jacket.

Clear an evacuation path aboard your vessel. To avoid exposing the victim to the weather, it's best if you can keep him or her inside the vessel until the rescue unit arrives, but clear a wide, unobstructed path between the holding area inside the vessel and the area on deck from which the victim will be offloaded. If a litter is required to transport the victim to the rescue unit, the Coast Guard will provide one. If the nature of the victim's illness or injuries will require you to bring the litter inside your vessel to load the victim, you will need to clear an unobstructed path that will admit a rigid litter approximately seven feet long by two-and-a-half feet wide.

You and all members of your crew should put on life jackets before the rescue unit arrives, even those who are assigned to stay inside the vessel as their presence might be requested on deck. Make certain your flare kit, spotlight, and any other signal devices you have on board are accessible and ready for service in the event they are required to pinpoint your location, but don't fire a flare unless requested to do so by the rescue unit or the coast station.

If the rescue unit the Coast Guard dispatches is to be a ship, break out your fenders and dock lines in preparation for rafting alongside it.

## Helicopter Evacuation

If the rescue unit the Coast Guard dispatches is a helicopter, it will be an H-3, which is designed to fly a maximum of 300 nautical miles seaward from the closest refueling point, loiter over a vessel for a maximum of 20 minutes, then return to land. Coast Guard rescue helicopters normally do not conduct rescue operations in conjunction with the U.S. Navy.

For helicopter evacuation, you will need to clear a hoist area aboard your vessel. On a large powerboat, the preferred hoist area normally will be its highest and aftermost deck, which in most cases will be the cabin top. If your dinghy is stowed on the cabin top, launch it if possible to get it out of the way and tow it astern on a long painter. Also lower and secure any bimini tops on the upper deck and any masts and/or antennas that will not be needed to communicate with the coast station or the helicopter.

If the evacuation must be conducted at night, arrange to light the hoist area and any obstructions with mast lights and/or hand-held flashlights. Hand-held flashlights must, however, always be focused on the hoist area or any obstructions and not pointed toward the helicopter, as they could temporarily blind the pilot.

Assign each member of the crew specific duties such as manning the helm and the radio, lighting the hoist area and any obstructions, receiving the litter on deck, getting the patient to the hoist area, and steadying the litter as it is hoisted into the helicopter. Once the helicopter arrives overhead, the noise from its rotors will be deafening and normal spoken communications will be impossible. Agree on a simple set of hand signals for such commands as "wait," "go back," "come on," and "okay." The accepted signal for the helicopter to lower the litter is to hold both arms horizontal with fists clenched and thumbs pointed downward. The accepted signal for the helicopter to hoist the litter is to hold both arms above the horizontal with fists clenched and thumbs pointed upward.

As the helicopter approaches your position, the pilot will normally contact you by radio and ask for particulars of wind and sea conditions and your vessel's hoist area.

Helicopter pilots normally fly from the starboard seat, the chopper's hoist is mounted on the starboard side, and due to the counterclockwise rotation of the helicopter's rotor it is most maneuverable if the wind strikes it from ahead or on the starboard forward quarter. For maximum visibility, therefore, the helicopter pilot normally will want to put the starboard forward quarter of his craft toward your vessel.

Once the helicopter arrives (see Fig. 11.10), reduce your vessel's speed to the minimum required to maintain steerage. If the pickup is to be made from your vessel's stern, put the wind 30 degrees on your port bow. If the pickup is to be made from your vessel's bow, put the wind 30 degrees on your starboard bow.

In many cases the helicopter's hoist man will first lower a trail line which will be attached to the bottom of the litter and will allow your crew to guide the litter to the hoist area. This line will be nonstatic and can be handled safely.

When the litter approaches your vessel, allow it to touch the deck and discharge any static electricity before handling it.

At no point in the evacuation should the helicopter be attached to your vessel by either the trail line or the hoist line. Make certain neither becomes entangled with any part of your vessel and warn your crew to stand clear of

298

*Fig.* 11.10: *In evacuating a victim by helicopter, guide the litter to your vessel's deck by using the trail line, but never tie it off and make sure it doesn't become entangled.*

both. In severe weather, the helicopter pilot may instruct you to detach the litter from the hoist cable in order to give him more maneuverability while you load the patient. In other cases, you may have to move the litter from the hoist area to the inside of your vessel to load the patient. The litter must never be moved from the hoist area without first detaching it from the hoist cable.

Put the victim in the litter, making sure his or her arms and legs are well inside. If the litter is provided with straps, use them to strap the victim in the litter securely. Normally it is not a good idea to cover the victim with a blanket as it could become entangled in the hoist mechanism.

Do not give the helicopter the hoist signal until you are certain the patient is well secured in the litter and all your crew are clear of the litter, the hoist cable, and the trail line. Once you are sure everything is ready,

299

signal the helicopter to hoist the stretcher with the "thumbs up" signal.

During hoisting, use the trail line to steady the litter until it is clear of the vessel. Hoisting the litter with the victim in it is potentially the most dangerous part of the evacuation process, particularly in heavy winds and/ or seas. Use all available crew to help steady the litter, but caution them to watch themselves as well. The last thing you need in this situation is to have one of your healthy crew members fall overboard.

During the hoisting operation, the pilot will attempt to hold the helicopter as steady as possible and allow the hoist man to bring the litter aboard with his electric winch. Once the litter is clear of your vessel, throw any remaining part of the trail line overboard to leeward, making certain it does not become entangled with any part of your vessel or any of your crew.

Note: Except where specifically noted, the recommendations in this chapter assume the victim is an adult or a well-developed child about eight years old. For infants and children less than about eight years old, the procedures are essentially the same, but the frequency at which procedures are executed and the force exerted by the rescuer may vary considerably. If you are likely to have infants or children under about eight aboard your vessel frequently, you should secure specialized training in dealing with any medical emergencies they might experience.

# CHAPTER 12

# LOSS OF POWER OR STEERING

• • •

If you have a mechanical problem with your vessel around home, it's a fairly simple matter to call a mechanic to come fix it. But once you launch into extended cruising, at some point you're almost certain to find yourself with a balky engine or transmission a long way from the nearest engine shop and will have to solve the problem yourself. To do that, you need to have at least a basic understanding of how a gasoline or diesel engine and its associated marine transmission and underwater gear work:

Reduced to its essentials, even the most elaborate gasoline (Fig. 12.1) or diesel (Fig. 12.2) marine engine is a fairly basic device which must have only three things in order to start and continue to operate: a source of motive

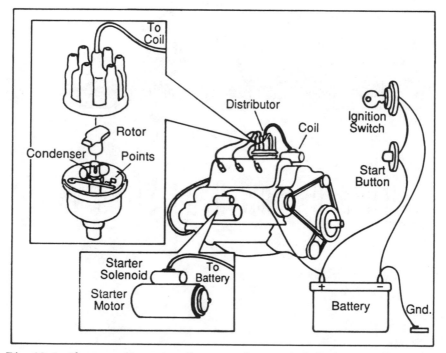

*Fig. 12.1: If your gasoline engine refuses to crank, a quick check of these vital elements of its starting circuit should identify the problem. (Reprinted from* Chapman's Nautical Guides: Emergencies at Sea, *Hearst Marine Books)*

302

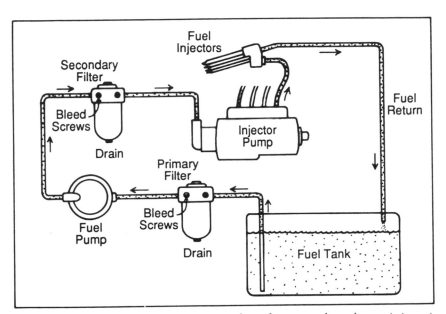

*Fig. 12.2: In troubleshooting a diesel engine that refuses to crank, make sure it is getting an adequate flow of fuel and that no air is trapped in its fuel supply system. (Reprinted from* Chapman's Nautical Guides: Emergencies at Sea, *Hearst Marine Books)*

power to get it started; a dependable source of clean, combustible fuel, and—in the case of a gasoline engine—electrical current to burn that fuel; and some means of dissipating the exhaust gases and excess heat it generates.

Both gasoline and diesel marine engines employ essentially the same starting system for initiating their operation, which includes the engine's battery, the ignition key or starter switch, a starter solenoid, and a starter motor. (The starter solenoid and starter motor normally will be the two cylindrical units bolted to the side of the engine. The starter solenoid will be the smaller of the two and will be connected directly to the battery by the battery's positive [red] cable. In some cases, the starter solenoid is an integral part of the starter motor.)

Both gasoline and diesel marine engines also employ essentially the same type of lubrication and cooling system for dissipating the exhaust gases and excess heat they generate. Therefore, the troubleshooting procedure for identifying and solving some problems is the same for both gasoline and diesel marine engines:

*Problem:* You turn the ignition key or depress the engine start button and nothing happens.

First, check the battery. If your vessel is equipped with a battery paralleling switch, make certain it is set to the battery of the engine you are trying to start. Also make certain the vessel's transmission is in neutral. Most modern marine engines have a neutral safety switch which prevents the engine from being started if the transmission is in gear. Make certain the ignition key is switched to the "on" position. If you have a voltmeter on board, check the voltage across the battery's positive and negative terminals. If you detect no—or almost no—voltage, the battery is dead and must be recharged from an external electrical source before it will develop sufficient voltage to start the engine.

If you don't have a voltmeter aboard, check the battery's acid level; if the battery's plates are exposed in one or more cells and the battery made no attempt to turn the engine's starter motor, it is probably fully discharged and probably will not generate enough voltage to start the engine without being recharged from an external electrical source.

On a vessel that has more than one battery, set the battery paralleling switch to "all" and attempt to start the engine with another of the ship's batteries. (If the engine starts, don't forget to reset the battery switch to the engine's battery in order to recharge it.) If the vessel is fitted with an

AC electrical generator, attempt to recharge the battery through the vessel's battery charger. If you have neither a charged battery nor an AC generator aboard and cannot start the engine by hand-cranking it, you have no chance of starting the engine. If you are inshore, you might try reaching safety by using your dinghy for auxiliary power as discussed below. If you are offshore, about your only alternative is to call for assistance.

On a 12-volt system, if your check of the battery's voltage with a voltmeter shows it is charged to at least 7 volts and the level of battery acid is close to the fill ring, make certain the cables connected to the battery's positive and negative terminals are tight and clean of corrosion. If not, clean and tighten them. Also make certain the cable connected to the battery's negative terminal is clean and tight where it is connected to ground. Make certain the cable connected to the battery's positive terminal is tight and free of corrosion where it is connected to the starter solenoid.

If you find no problem with the battery, its controls, or its cables, check the starter switch. First make certain the wires connecting it to the battery and to the starter solenoid are clean and tight. If the starter switch is connected to a separate key switch, also check the connections between them. If you have a voltmeter aboard, close the ignition switch (i.e. turn it to the "on" position) and check the voltage across its terminals. If you detect no voltage, the switch itself could be bad. Check it with the key in the "on" position by shorting across its terminals with a screwdriver. If the starter motor attempts to turn, the switch itself is malfunctioning and you will have to temporarily bypass it to start the engine. If nothing happens, the switch is probably all right and the problem is either in the battery, the starter solenoid, or the electrical connections in the engine's starting circuit.

Next, check the starter solenoid. The starter solenoid serves two important functions: it delivers electrical current to the starter motor, and it mechanically engages the starter motor and the engine until the engine starts, then disengages them.

If you have a voltmeter aboard, close the ignition switch and check the voltage between the battery side of the starter solenoid and ground. On a 12-volt system, the starter solenoid should be receiving a minimum of 7 volts of starting current from the battery. Check the voltage between the starter solenoid terminal serving the starter motor and ground. Also check the voltage between the starter motor terminal and ground. If you have lost voltage at any of those points, you will have isolated your problem and may be able to correct it by cleaning the appropriate terminal connections. If cleaning the terminals does no good, the electrical windings inside the starter solenoid are probably corroded and there is little you can do if you don't have a spare aboard. Call for assistance.

*Problem:* You turn the ignition key or depress the engine start button and hear a clicking sound.

The problem is either low voltage in the battery or a mechanical problem inside the starter solenoid.

First check the condition of the battery. If you have less than seven volts across the battery's terminals, the battery will have to be recharged before it will start the engine, or you will have to use another of the vessel's batteries. If you have at least seven volts across the battery terminals, check all the connections between the battery, the ignition switch, and the starter solenoid. Corrosion at any of those connections could reduce voltage to the point that the starter solenoid will not turn the starter motor, which in turn will not crank the engine.

There are two other possible problems. One is that rust or corrosion has frozen the starter solenoid's helical spring or plunger which engages the starter motor and the engine. Try rapping the starter solenoid sharply on its case two or three times to see if you can free the spring or the plunger. The other possible problem is that the starter motor is not firmly secured to the engine. It is that mechanical connection which provides the starter solenoid's ground. If the bolts securing the starter motor to the engine block are loose, clean off any corrosion and tighten them.

*Problem:* You turn the ignition key or depress the engine start button and the starter motor struggles but will not crank the engine.

Check the voltage across the battery terminals and at all connections. On a 12-volt system, if you have at least 7 volts at the starter motor terminal, either the starter is defective or one or more engine cylinders or its fuel line is locked with water, air, or gas vapor. If the blockage is in one or more engine cylinders, removing the spark plugs from a gasoline engine or the injectors from a diesel engine and trying to crank the engine will clear it. Clearing an air lock on a diesel engine is covered below.

*Problem:* You turn the ignition key or depress the engine start button and the engine starts but then stops as soon as you release pressure on the start button.

The ignition switch or start button is probably rigged with an auxiliary starting shunt whose ballast is defective. You will have to bypass the ignition switch to start the engine and keep it running.

*Problem:* You can start the engine and it will run for a few minutes but quickly overheats.

Shut the engine down immediately and troubleshoot its lubrication/cooling system. Inspect the engine's dipstick to make certain it has sufficient oil in the sump to keep it lubricated. If the oil in the engine sump is below the "full" mark on the dipstick, add oil but be careful not to overfill the engine. Also check the oil on the dipstick for the presence of water. If you detect water, you may have a hole in the engine's water jacket. If that is the case, you probably also will notice an abnormally high reading on the engine's oil pressure gauge. There is nothing you can do to keep an engine with a ruptured water jacket from overheating, and you will have to call for assistance.

Check the engine's freshwater cooling reservoir. This is just like checking the coolant in an automobile engine. Allow the engine to cool down before removing the reservoir's pressurized cap as it could release steam and/or scalding water. If the reservoir is low, fill it to within about two inches of the neck. If the reservoir was low simply because you forgot to refill it before you left the dock, topping it off will probably solve the overheating problem. If the engine runs for a few minutes but overheats again, either the engine's freshwater pump is malfunctioning or its raw water cooling system is not operating properly.

To check the freshwater pump, remove the plug on the side of its housing and make certain it is full of water. If it is not, fill it and replace the plug. If the engine continues to overheat, the pump's impeller may be defective. If you have a spare impeller on board, install it. If you do not have a spare impeller on board, you will probably have to call for assistance.

To check the vessel's raw-water cooling system, look at the engine's exhaust outlet at the vessel's transom. When the engine is running, it should be discharging a significant stream of water. If it is, the raw-water cooling system is functioning properly. If it isn't, the problem is most likely a clogged or malfunctioning through-hull fitting on the raw-water inlet or a failed impeller in the engine's raw water pump. To check the raw water pump, loosen the clamps on the raw water hose where it enters the engine's

307

raw-water pump. If water begins to seep out of the junction, you probably have adequate raw water reaching the pump but its impeller has failed. If you have a spare impeller on board, install it. If you do not have a spare impeller on board, you will not be able to repair the pump and must call for assistance.

If water does not seep from the junction, carefully loosen the hose from the inlet of the raw-water pump. If no water gushes from the hose, the problem is most likely a clogged or malfunctioning raw-water inlet. Reattach the raw-water inlet hose to the raw-water pump and tighten its clamps. Make certain the sea cock or gate valve serving the raw-water inlet is open. If it is open, the raw-water inlet is probably clogged and you will have to go beneath the vessel to remove the obstruction.

*Problem:* You turn the ignition key or depress the engine start button and the engine turns over but will not fire.

If a vessel's engine doesn't start after turning over for about thirty seconds, don't just keep cranking it as you will simply run down the battery. Find out why it isn't starting and try to eliminate or solve the problem.

Since the engine turns over, the problem is not in its electrical starting circuit but is in its ignition or fuel system. The procedure you must employ for identifying and attempting to solve the problem will differ significantly depending on whether you are dealing with an engine powered by gasoline or diesel fuel.

## Gasoline Engine

First, troubleshoot the ignition system. Remove a wire from one of the spark plugs. Hold it with some kind of insulating material with its end about a quarter of an inch from the engine block and try to start the engine.

If you do not see a spark when the engine turns over, the problem is electrical and probably is in either the coil, the condenser, or the distributor. The distributor will be a basically round housing which will have one wire leading into it and wires leading out of it to each spark plug. The wire leading into it will be connected to the coil. Remove the coil wire from the distributor cap, hold it with some kind of insulating material with its tip about a quarter of an inch from the engine block, and crank the engine.

If you see no spark, remove the distributor cap by releasing the spring clips at either side. This will reveal one or two sets of points and a small cylinder which is the condenser. Tap the ignition switch or start button two or three times, which will cause the distributor shaft to rotate which should cause the points to open and close. If the points do not open and close, they may be fused together. Separate and clean them with a knife edge or sand-paper and tap the ignition switch again to make sure they open and close properly. By tapping the ignition switch or start button, rotate the distrib-utor shaft until the points are closed. Turn on the ignition switch and open the points with a screwdriver. Each time you open them, you should see a spark jump between the end of the coil wire and the engine block.

If you do not see a spark at the end of the coil wire, either the coil or the condenser is defective. If you have a spare of the defective part aboard, install it. If you do not have a spare of the defective part aboard, you will not be able to start the engine and must call for assistance.

If you have a spark at the end of the coil wire but do not have a spark at the end of the spark plug wire, the problem lies in the distributor itself.

The inside of the distributor cap will be lined with one contact for each of the engine's cylinders. These contacts are energized in turn by a rotor, which receives current at its top from the coil wire and distributes it to each contact inside the distributor cap as it spins on the distributor rotor. Make certain the inside of the distributor cap is absolutely dry. If possible, spray it with a water inhibitor such as CRC. Scrape down the contacts inside the distributor cap until they are shiny. Also scrape down the top of the rotor where it comes in contact with the coil wire, and its flat surface which transmits electrical current to each of the contacts inside the distributor cap. Reas-semble the distributor cap, making certain all the wires leading into it are seated securely and that the other ends of the spark plug wires are securely seated to the ends of the spark plugs.

If the engine still will turn over but will not fire, the distributor cap is probably defective. If you have a spare distributor cap on board, install it. If you do not have a spare on board, you will not be able to start the engine and will have to call for assistance. (It's possible the problem is in the spark plugs, but it's unlikely since all the engine's spark plugs are not likely to go bad at once. If you have spark at the end of the spark plug wire held about a quarter of an inch from the engine block, you can test the plugs by removing them from the block, reattaching their wires, laying them where you can see the gap at their business end, and cranking the engine.)

If you have spark at the end of the spark plug wire or at the end of the spark plug itself, either the spark is not hot enough to ignite the fuel, or the problem lies in the fuel system itself.

If the spark is not hot enough, the problem is either that the engine's generator or alternator is not putting out sufficient voltage or you have significant resistance somewhere in the ignition circuit which is causing a voltage loss. Since you can't get the engine started, you can't check the output voltage of the generator or alternator. You can, however, check the belt driving the generator or alternator. Check its tension by pushing down on it halfway between the pulleys to which it is attached. If it is absolutely rigid, it could be freezing the alternator or generator rotor and will have to be loosened. If it deflects more than about half an inch, tighten it. To adjust tension on the belt, loosen the bolts in the generator or alternator mounting bracket, pry the generator or alternator away from the engine block to tighten the belt or push it toward the block to loosen the belt, then resecure the mounting bolts. Also recheck all terminals in the ignition system to be certain you have eliminated all possible resistance.

If you have spark at the spark plugs and the engine will turn over but not fire, the problem is probably in the vessel's fuel system.

Remove one of the engine's spark plugs. If its tip is wet, the engine's cylinders are flooded with gasoline. Wait about ten minutes to give the excess gasoline time to drain from the cylinders, then try to start the engine again.

If the engine still will not crank, you probably have an obstruction somewhere in the engine's fuel or air intake system.

Remove the air filter, which normally will sit on top of the carburetor, and try to start the engine. If the engine runs, a clogged air filter is your problem. If you have a spare filter aboard, install it. If you don't have a spare aboard, simply leave the air filter off the engine and replace it when you reach shore.

If replacing or removing the air filter does not solve your problem, visually check the carburetor fuel bowl. It should be full and the fuel clear.

If the bowl is empty, the carburetor is not getting fuel. Check to make certain you have fuel on board. If your vessel has a fuel manifold, make certain you are feeding the engine from a tank that contains at least sufficient fuel to reach the level of the fuel pickup pipe. If you are certain you have sufficient fuel in the tank serving the engine, your problem may be a clogged fuel filter. Replace it with a fresh filter or remove it altogether. If you still do not see fuel in the carburetor bowl, check for a clogged fuel line. Unscrew the fuel line between the fuel pump and the carburetor bowl and try to blow air through it. If you cannot easily blow air through it, clean the fuel line.

If you are certain you have fuel in the tank serving the engine but see no fuel in the carburetor bowl and cannot locate a plugged filter or fuel line, the problem is probably a defective fuel pump. If you have a spare fuel pump on board, install it. If you don't have a spare on board, you will have to call for assistance.

## Diesel Engine

A diesel engine does not require an electrical ignition system to ignite its fuel; instead, it ignites its fuel by the heat of compression. A diesel engine, therefore, has no distributor, coil, points, condensers, or spark plugs. If a diesel engine will turn over but will not crank, the problem is most likely to be in its fuel system, which consists of a primary filter/separator which removes large particles and water from the fuel, a fuel pump, a secondary filter which removes small particles from the fuel, and the injectors themselves which inject the fuel into the engine's cylinders. Most marine diesel engines utilize unit injectors which do the entire job of pressurizing the fuel. Some marine diesel engines, however, have a separate high-pressure pump which delivers fuel to the injectors at about 20,000 psi. A diesel engine does not burn all the fuel which is fed to its injectors. For that reason, in addition to its fuel supply line, it also has a fuel return line through which unburned fuel is returned to the tank. The fuel supply line is susceptible to air locks, which can prevent the engine from starting.

If the vessel is equipped with a manual shutdown system which stops the engine by shutting off its air supply, make certain its controls are set in the open position (i.e., the plungers are pushed all the way into their seats). Some marine engines are equipped with mechanical or hydraulic governors. If the engine is equipped with such a device, make certain the stop lever on the cover of a mechanical governor is in the "run" position; on a hydraulic governor, make certain the stop knob is pushed all the way in. If the engine is equipped with an air filter or breather, make certain it is not clogged.

Visually check the bowls housing the engine's primary and secondary fuel filters; both should be full of fuel and the fuel clear. If you see excess water in the bowl of the primary filter, drain it off. If the primary filter bowl is full but the secondary filter bowl is empty, your problem may be a

311

clogged primary filter; try replacing it. If both bowls are full, and the fuel in the primary filter bowl is clear but the fuel in the secondary filter bowl is dark, your problem may be a clogged secondary filter. Try replacing it. (Some secondary filters are not housed in a bowl but are simply a screen-type filter in the fuel line itself. To find out if fuel is flowing through an in-line filter, loosen the connection on its outlet side and attempt to crank the engine. If fuel flows from the fitting, the filter is probably clean. If fuel does not flow from the outlet fitting, retighten it, loosen the fitting on the filter's inlet side, and try to crank the engine. If fuel flows out of the fitting, the filter is clogged. Remove and clean it. If no fuel flows from the fitting, your problem is either a lack of fuel in the tank, a clogged primary fuel filter, or a malfunctioning fuel pump.)

If the bowl of the primary filter is empty, the engine has lost prime and you must reprime it. Make certain you have at least enough fuel in the tank serving the engine to reach the fuel pickup tube and that any valves in the fuel system serving the engine are in the open position. If necessary, shift the fuel manifold to serve the engine from a tank that contains sufficient fuel to reach its pickup tube. Some vessels are fitted with automatic fuel priming pumps, which are handy gadgets. If your engines aren't equipped with priming pumps, experiment to see if one of your tanks is installed high enough in the boat to be above the dry engine's fuel inlet. If it is, you may well find that when you set your fuel manifold to fuel the engine from that tank, gravity will force fuel through the primary filter to the fuel pump and you can crank the engine. As you reprime the engine, you will have to clear the air from the fuel system by opening the bleed screws on the primary and secondary filters and possibly the fuel pump, which is covered below.

If both the primary and secondary filter bowls are empty, your problem is probably a malfunctioning fuel pump. If you have a spare fuel pump on board, install it. If you do not have a spare fuel pump on board, you will probably have to call for assistance.

If both filter bowls are full and the fuel is clear, your problem is probably an air lock in the fuel supply line. The housings for both the primary and the secondary filters should have bleed screws. Remove the bleed screw on the primary filter housing and attempt to start the engine. If air rather than fuel flows out the bleed screw opening, let all the air escape before replacing the screw, then try to start the engine again. If that does not clear the lock, repeat the process with the bleed screw on the secondary filter housing. If you clear an air lock but it reoccurs, make certain all fittings along the fuel supply line are tight and check the seating of O-rings and check valves in both the primary and the secondary fuel filters.

If fuel flows from both bleed screw openings when you remove the bleed screw but the engine still will not start, remove the fuel line from one of the injectors and try to start the engine. If fuel does not flow from the fuel line, your problem is probably a malfunctioning injector pump. If you have a spare injector pump aboard, install it. If you don't have a spare injector pump on board, you will not be able to get the engine to run and will have to call for assistance.

*Problem:* The engine runs, but when you shift to forward gear, the vessel does not make headway.

Shut down the engine immediately and troubleshoot the vessel's transmission, shafts, and propellers to identify the problem and attempt to remedy.

In the engine room, check the coupling between the transmission and the propeller shaft. If it has come loose, tighten it. If it is broken and you have a spare coupling aboard, install it. If the coupling is broken and you don't have a spare coupling aboard, you will have to call for assistance.

If the coupling is not the problem and you can go over the side, check the vessel's underwater gear. If the prop is fouled, clear it. With the engine off but the transmission in gear, attempt to rotate the propeller. If the propeller rotates while the shaft does not, you have sheared off the key which joins the two together. Replacing the key involves removing and replacing the propeller, which will be virtually impossible at sea. You will have to call for assistance. If both the shaft and the propeller rotate while the transmission is in gear, your problem is probably that the transmission itself is not engaging. If neither the shaft nor the propeller turns, have a crew member shift the transmission to neutral and again try to rotate the propeller. If neither the propeller nor the shaft will turn, you probably have a frozen cutlass bearing. Replacing it at sea will be virtually impossible, and you will have to call for assistance.

If your troubleshooting to this point indicates your problem lies in the transmission, return to the engine room and have a crew member start the engine and shift to forward gear while you check to see if the shaft exiting from the transmission is turning. If it is not, have a crew member shift the transmission from neutral to forward several times. If this does not engage the transmission, check the linkage between the helm control and the trans-

313

mission itself. If it is mechanical, tighten it as necessary. If it is hydraulic, check the fluid level in the hydraulic pump and its fluid supply lines. Also check the level of fluid inside the transmission and top it off if it's low—but be sure not to overfill. If you find no problem with the transmission's linkage or its fluid level, your problem is inside the transmission itself. Some marine transmissions are equipped with "come home bolts" which, when engaged, lock the transmission to the engine's flywheel. If you have to engage these bolts, be aware that whenever the engine is operating, the transmission will be in gear. Once you near a dock, you will probably need to shut down your engine and get someone else to tow you to it or use your dinghy as auxiliary power to come alongside. If your transmission is the problem and it does not have "come home bolts," there is little you can do to repair it. You will have to call for assistance.

*Problem:* The engine runs and when you engage the gears the vessel will go forward or backward, but the vessel will not answer its helm.

First check to see if your rudder has been carried away or severely damaged. If your rudder is still attached and will pivot, troubleshoot the vessel's steering mechanism.

On vessels with hydraulic steering, make certain the hydraulic fluid reservoir is full. If it is not, you probably have a leak in a hose, a fitting, or an O-ring somewhere in the system and will have to locate and repair it before you top off the reservoir. Even after you have stopped the leak and refilled the reservoir, you still may not have full steering control because of air trapped in the hydraulic lines. The hydraulic system should have an air bleed valve in the fluid reservoir, the pump, or the lines. Locate it and bleed the air out of the system, then add enough fluid to the reservoir to replace the air you have expelled.

On vessels with mechanical steering, trace out the system to locate the problem, which most likely will be a broken cable, chain, clamp, or sprocket wheel. Once you identify the problem, replace the broken part if you have a spare on board or attempt to rig a temporary repair that will hold together long enough to get you to shore.

The loss of rudders on a twin-screw vessel can be temporarily offset by steering with the engines. But if the rudder of a single-engine vessel has been carried away entirely or its post so badly bent that it will not pivot, you probably will have to jury-rig a replacement. The easiest replacement to construct will be a sweep made from a hatch cover and a boat hook lashed to a vertical stanchion on the stern. A more difficult alternative is to rig a replacement out of lines and blocks.

*Problem:* You are fairly close in shore but your vessel's engine(s) will not run and all your efforts to repair it have failed.

If you have a dinghy with an outboard motor, you may be able to use it to reach safety. Rather than trying to tow your vessel with the dinghy, lash it alongside as shown in Fig. 12.3. If your vessel's steering system is operative, the operation can be conducted in greater safety by lashing the dinghy's engine down in its fore-and-aft position and steering with your main vessel's controls. If your main vessel's steering is not operative, you will have to steer with the dinghy engine. If the weather is unsettled, be sure you wear a life jacket.

If you are unable to restore sufficient propulsion to reach safety and cannot get to shore using your dinghy as emergency power, use your marine radios or audible or visual distress signals to summon assistance.

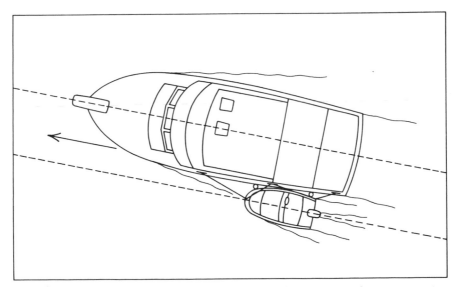

*Fig. 12.3:* A dinghy lashed alongside may provide "get-home" power and emergency steering for a disabled power cruiser.

You normally will be able to summon assistance from the Coast Guard or a commercial towing service by calling them on VHF channel 16 or SSB frequency 2182 kHz, then switching to a working channel. If you are unable to reach either the Coast Guard or a commercial towing service, broadcast a Pan Pan urgency signal on VHF channel 16 or SSB frequency 2182 kHz. If other boaters who might be able to render assistance are nearby, employ visual and audible distress signals to attract their assistance.

## TIPS ON TOWING AND BEING TOWED

Unless towing operations are conducted carefully and with proper procedures, they can be dangerous to both of the vessels involved and to their crews. Here's the right way to do it:

1.  If possible, use braided nylon for the towing line. For a given diameter, it is stronger than three-strand twist nylon line and has sufficient elasticity to absorb the shocks and strains of towing. When three-strand twist nylon breaks under a heavy load, it snaps back like a whip and can inflict serious injury on crew members aboard either vessel.

2.  Using a bridle aboard the towing vessel will distribute the strain and help the vessel being towed track in a straighter line. The bridle should not, however, be rigged to the towing vessel's stern as it will severely restrict the towing vessel's maneuverability. Instead, rig the ends of the bridle as far forward on the towing vessel as possible in order to leave the stern free to turn as needed. Wrap the line where it comes in contact with the towing vessel's house to keep it from marring the surface. Rig the bitter end of the towing line to both forward cleats on the vessel being towed and lead it as nearly as possible directly over the vessel's bow rather than off to either side.

3.  Post lookouts on both vessels to watch the tow line, but be certain they are positioned well clear of the line to avoid injury if it breaks and whips back. The lookout on the towing vessel should be especially alert to keep the line from fouling the towing vessel's propeller.

316

4. The vessel to be towed will track straighter if it is trimmed slightly by the stern (i.e., shift weight aft) to keep its bow light. The vessel being towed should keep an anchor ready for instant deployment in case the tow line breaks.

5. The towing vessel should take up slack on the tow line slowly and begin the tow with just enough power to overcome the two vessels' inertia. Once underway, it should maintain a moderate speed to keep the vessel being towed from yawing.

6. If any sea is running, adjust the length of the tow line to keep both vessels synchronized on the crests or in the troughs of successive waves. If the two vessels are not properly spaced, the towing vessel will run down the face of one wave while the vessel being towed is struggling up the back of the next wave, creating maximum resistance. Conversely, while the towing vessel is struggling up the back of one wave, the vessel being towed will run down the face of the wave behind, possibly resulting in a collision.

7. If the towing vessel's intention is to bring the vessel being towed to a dock, come to a gradual stop a good distance off and pull the vessel up to the towing vessel with the tow line. Never attempt to fend off either vessel with hands or feet, which could become trapped between the two hulls and broken or crushed. Lash the two vessels together so they will both respond to the towing vessel's steering. This will allow the towing vessel to bring the vessel being towed to the dock under control rather than out of control at the end of a long tow line.

8. If the towing operations must be conducted at night, the towing vessel should shine a searchlight on the vessel being towed to warn other vessels in the vicinity of the relationship between the two vessels.

9. If the towing operation must be conducted in fog, the towing vessel should sound one prolonged blast and two short blasts of her horn every two minutes. If the vessel being towed is manned, it should sound one prolonged blast and three short blasts on its horn immediately following the signal of the towing vessel.

# CHAPTER 13

# IF YOU GO AGROUND

•   •   •

Running aground can be a traumatic experience, particularly if the grounding is unexpected and your vessel has significant way on when it strikes the bottom. Regardless of the drama of the situation, you need to keep your wits about you. In some cases, doing the right thing quickly can free your vessel in moments; doing the wrong thing—or waiting too long to do the right thing—can leave your vessel exposed to serious damage and your crew exposed to possible injury. Panic reactions are likely only to get you in a worse predicament.

Any time your vessel goes aground, check first for crew injuries. When a sizeable vessel strikes the bottom at even three or four knots, your crew can suffer significant personal injuries as inertia slams them into bulkheads or tosses them from their bunks. Quickly assess any injuries to your crew to determine if they are serious enough to require you to immediately call for assistance.

Next, check for damage to your vessel's hull, steering, and propulsion system. In a hard grounding, rudders, struts, and drive shafts can be torn away, leaving gaping holes that can allow hundreds of gallons of water to gush into your hull in seconds. If your vessel has suffered any severe threat to the integrity of its hull and you require assistance, get off a distress or urgency call immediately as your batteries could quickly be shorted out by rising water and leave you with no means of radio communication. The correct procedure for transmitting either is covered fully in Chapter 10. If your hull's integrity has been breached in the grounding, you're probably better off allowing your vessel to remain grounded until you can make temporary repairs.

If no crew have been injured and your vessel does not appear to have been seriously damaged, quickly determine which way deep water lies. In warm tropical waters, go over the side to assess the situation firsthand. In cold or murky water, take soundings around your vessel with a boat hook or lead line to figure out which way you need to move your vessel to get back to water she can float in.

In tidal areas, the state of the tide at the time of a grounding is critical. If the tide is rising and your vessel is not actually banging on the bottom, you can afford to relax and let the tide come in and lift it free. Even on a rising tide, if wind and current are in the direction of the obstruction, you should immediately set an anchor toward deep water to keep your vessel from going harder aground. If the tide is falling, you must work quickly and purposefully if you are to free your vessel as the tide ebbs.

After the state of the tide, wind and current normally will be the two most critical elements in deciding whether you can free your vessel quickly or whether you will be left high and dry for hours. In either case, try to make the situation work for rather than against you. If wind and current are pushing your vessel toward deeper water, attempt to turn your stern toward the wind and current to give them additional area to work against.

If your vessel doesn't seem to be hard aground, your prop(s) and rudder(s) are clear of the bottom, and you are certain deeper water lies astern, try backing down with your engine(s). But don't try that maneuver more than a couple of times, and then only for about a minute each time. You could easily clog your engine's raw water intake with sand or mud and cause it to overheat, which is only going to compound your woes. Unless you're certain deep water lies ahead, it's not a good idea to try to go forward since that's probably what got you in trouble in the first place.

If you are not able to get your vessel off the bottom quickly and wind and/or current are setting you harder aground, the first thing you must do is set a kedge anchor toward deep water as quickly as possible (Fig. 13.1) and keep its rode taut so you don't drift up farther on whatever your vessel's keel is resting against. In order to get the kedge out far enough from your vessel and in the correct position to do some good, you normally will have to launch your dinghy. In warm waters and calm weather you can deploy the kedge more rapidly by resting it on a boat cushion or other floating platform and swimming it out to where you want to set it.

If you're going to try to refloat the vessel yourself, first lessen its draft

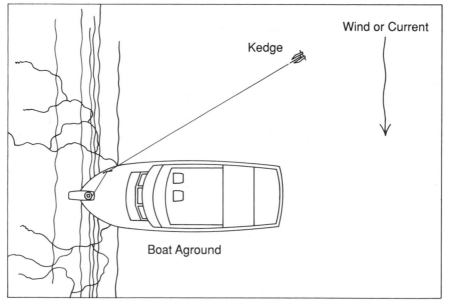

*Fig. 13.1:* *A kedge anchor set 45 degrees to wind and/or current with its rode led to your anchor windlass can help you pivot your bow off a grounding.*

any way you can. Shift as much weight as possible, including the crew, to the shallow water side, which may help force her toward deeper water. Before you try backing off whatever you've run up on, check your raw water strainers and, if they have gotten clogged, clean them out. Have a crew member maintain tension on the kedge with a half- or S-turn around a stern cleat while you back down slowly and steadily.

If going astern doesn't work, the next step is to try to pivot your vessel to get her bow pointed back toward deep water. If you have a dinghy with a sizeable engine, use it to try to pull her bow around. If your vessel is only lightly aground, you might try leading the rode of the kedge anchor forward and using your anchor windlass to crank her bow around. If your vessel is hard aground, however, most electric anchor windlasses won't stand up to the strain this maneuver will put on them.

If it becomes obvious you're not going to get your vessel off the bottom until the tide floods, about all you can do is protect her hull as best you can until the rising tide refloats her. Set out boat hooks, dinghy oars, or anything else you can lay your hands on against the sheer as braces (but pad them well). If she's about to lie on her chine or the turn of her bilge, pad it with any type of cushioning material you have on board.

## Extricating a Grounded Vessel with an Assisting Vessel

Here are some helpful tips for situations when a second vessel is involved in freeing a grounded vessel:

1. Before approaching a grounded vessel, the captain of the assisting vessel must make certain that he can provide assistance without allowing his own vessel to become grounded.

2. If yours is the vessel aground, to help avoid potential disputes over salvage rights it's best to pass your tow line to the assisting vessel rather than accepting a line from the vessel offering assistance (see Legal Aspects of Accepting and Providing Assistance, page 324). To avoid the possibility of the tow line fouling the prop of the assisting vessel, bend a floating messenger line such as polypropylene ski rope onto your tow line, weight its bitter end, and heave it

rather than the tow line. If the distance between your grounded vessel and the assisting vessel is too great to heave a messenger line, attach the tow line to your own vessel and ferry it over to the assisting vessel in your dinghy, allowing it to pay out as you go. If you have no dinghy, in warm waters you can swim the line over. Wear a life jacket, attach the tow line to your own vessel first, and support its coils on a float, allowing it to pay out as you go. If the assisting vessel lies downwind and downcurrent from you, attach a float to the tow line or a messenger line and allow it to float down to the vessel offering assistance.

3. If yours is the assisting vessel and you must pass your tow line to the grounded vessel, make certain you can approach the grounded vessel close enough to heave the tow line or a messenger line without endangering your own vessel. If yours is a single-screw vessel, it will be more maneuverable and its prop exposed to less danger if you approach the grounded vessel bow-on. If yours is a twin-screw vessel which you are adept at handling in reverse and the bottom poses no threat to your props, backing down on the grounded vessel will leave your bow pointed toward open water and put you in the proper position for making the tow.

   If you cannot approach the grounded vessel close enough to heave a messenger line, row or swim the line over as above or attach a float to its bitter end, launch it upwind and upcurrent of the grounded vessel, and allow it to float down to the vessel in distress.

4. Once a tow line has been passed, the captains of both the grounded vessel and the assisting vessel should see that it is attached to the strongest point of their respective vessels. On many modern boats that point of attachment should not be a deck cleat because they often are not strong enough to withstand the severe stresses involved in freeing a vessel that is hard aground. Normally it is best to pass a line entirely around the house, padding it heavily at the points of greatest stress.

5. The propellers of all boats produce far more power going ahead than they do in reverse, therefore the bow of the assisting vessel should be pointed toward open water. While it is attempting to pull the grounded vessel free, the maneuverability of the assisting vessel will

322

be severely restricted and provision must be made to keep the assisting vessel itself from being swept aground. If wind and current are striking the assisting vessel from other than abeam, the tow line should be rigged to the assisting vessel's stern and the pull made in a straight line. If wind and current are striking the assisting vessel on its beam, the tow line should be attached just aft of abeam on the upwind or upcurrent side to allow its bow to be headed into—or at least quarter to—wind and current.

In conditions of strong beam wind or current, the captain of the assisting vessel may need to set his own kedge 45 degrees to windward (see Fig. 13.2) and have a crew member maintain a strain on the anchor line to help keep his vessel's bow from falling off and possibly having his own vessel swept aground. The anchor winch, however, should be used only to help keep the bow of the assisting

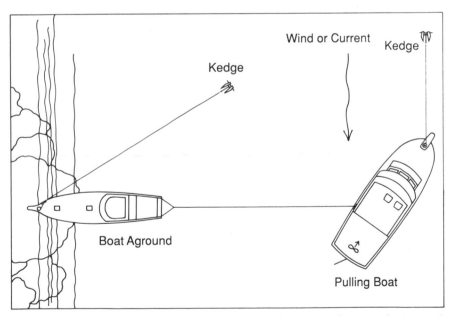

**Fig. 13.2:** *When attempting to extricate another vessel from a grounding, you should attach the tow line to your vessel just aft of amidships to allow your stern to maneuver.*

323

vessel into or quarter to wind and current. It should not be used to help exert pulling force itself as it normally will not be strong enough to stand the strain involved.

6. Before the attempt to free the grounded vessel begins, the captains of both the grounded vessel and the assisting vessel should have a clear channel for communicating with each other. That preferably will be over a working VHF radio channel such as 6 or 68. If one or both vessels does not have a working VHF radio aboard, they should agree on a set of hand signals with which they can communicate.

7. Before the towing operation commences, the crew of both vessels should stand well clear of the tow line. Under the pressure of towing, it can snap and lash back toward either vessel and cause severe injuries.

8. Before the attempt to free the grounded vessel begins, its captain should make certain he has a kedge out and a crew member taking up slack in its line to keep his vessel from being swept back aground once the vessel is freed. If his vessel is without power, it's also a good idea to have a crew member ready to set a second anchor if necessary once his vessel is freed.

9. During the towing maneuver itself, the captain of the assisting vessel should exert slow, steady pressure on the tow line and avoid sudden accelerations which can break the tow line or cause severe damage to one or both vessels.

## LEGAL ASPECTS OF ACCEPTING AND PROVIDING ASSISTANCE

In most cases where your vessel is aground, you can accept assistance from a fellow recreational boater without concern that he might lay claim to your vessel under maritime law pertaining to salvage rights. Maritime law on salvage rights is extremely ill defined and in most cases relates primarily to vessels that have been legally abandoned. In most cases, in order to claim salvage rights, the captain of a salvaging vessel must show that the vessel had been abandoned by its owner, who was making no attempt to salvage the vessel himself. The fact that you are aboard the vessel and making an attempt to extricate it from danger is what the lawyers call "proof on its face" that you had not abandoned your vessel, and therefore the laws on rights of salvage would not apply.

In the absence of a contract, you can also accept assistance from a fellow recreational boater without undue concern that he will attempt to charge you an exorbitant fee for his services. Unless he states a price for his services before the attempt to free your vessel commences and you agree in front of witnesses to pay his stated fee, any subsequent attempts he made to charge you would fall under the "just and reasonable" concept. If he took you to court, he might succeed in making you pay him something for his efforts, but his charges would have to be "just and reasonable" for the service he performed. You could find you are liable for any damages to his vessel that resulted from his attempt to assist you, but they would probably be covered by the liability clause of your boat owner's insurance. Even if he does state an unreasonable fee and you verbally agree in front of witnesses to pay it, most of the lawyers I've discussed the matter with say you could argue that the contract was made under duress, and a court would probably order you to pay only a fee that was "just and reasonable" for the service performed.

If you are dealing with a commercial towing service, however, the situation can be significantly different. Their representative, either the captain of the vessel they send to assist you or someone in their office you talk with over the radio, will clearly state a price and require that you agree to pay it before assistance commences. The price some of these services charge are outrageous, but if you agree to it, you probably will have no choice but to pay it.

The hull insurance of a good yacht policy normally covers the cost of towing and assistance if it is required to keep the yacht from suffering further damage.

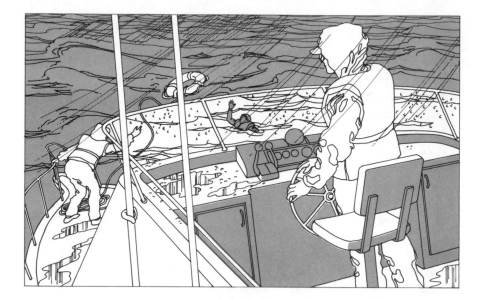

# CHAPTER 14

# CREW OVERBOARD

•  •  •

Crew-overboard emergencies are not nearly as common on powerboats as they are on sailboats, where crew members are often scrambling around the deck, but they do occur, most likely in bad weather.

Before you head out on a cruise, you should instruct your crew on their responsibilities should anyone fall overboard. Make sure they stay current on the procedure by conducting periodic crew-overboard drills.

You should also make certain your vessel is equipped to keep a crew-overboard situation from turning into a disaster. All the life jackets aboard your cruiser should be Type I and each should be fitted with at least reflective patches and a whistle. A number of experienced cruisers also add a personal rescue light and possibly a Class mini-B EPIRB to each of the life jackets aboard. You should also have one of the commercially available COB rigs mounted on your vessel's transom and have several Type IV throwable Personal Flotation Devices mounted at strategic points around your vessel fore and aft. Other valuable equipment in a crew-overboard situation includes a water-activated COB strobe light; at least one, preferably two, hand-held searchlights; and a good supply of white parachute flares and their associated launcher.

Your basic procedure in a crew-overboard situation should go like this:

Any person on board who sees someone go overboard should immediately and loudly shout, "CREW OVERBOARD!," continually keep his or her eyes on the COB, point emphatically toward the person in the water, and not assume, accept, nor be given any other duties. This reaction must be instantaneous. Once a crew member sees someone go into the water, he must keep his eyes constantly on the person overboard and not allow his gaze to be distracted for even an instant. Under the best of conditions, a human being in the sea can be difficult to spot. In heavy seas or conditions of poor visibility, spotting him or her can be virtually impossible. Once visual contact is lost, it can be extremely difficult if not impossible to reestablish. If you are at the helm and see someone fall overboard, make certain someone else on board has the person in the water in sight and order him or her to keep the person in sight before you return your attention to running the boat.

The crew member who is keeping his eye on the COB will provide your primary reference for returning to him. By emphatically pointing toward the COB with his arm fully extended, this "spotter" will give you vital information as to how to maneuver to return to the pickup point. Hopefully the spotter will be able to remain in your full view as he performs this vital task, but keeping the COB in sight is his first—indeed his only—responsibility. If necessary, another crew member must relay the spotter's directions to you.

If several people on board spot the COB, they likewise should keep their eyes fixed firmly on him and point emphatically in his direction until you order them to assist in handling the vessel or getting the person back on board. One crew member, however, must be clearly assigned as a spotter to keep the COB in sight and point to him and be given no other task.

Jettison your COB rig the moment you hear the CREW OVERBOARD! cry. If you don't have a COB rig aboard, throw a life jacket, life ring, or floating cushion overboard. Your purpose is not only to give the COB something to cling to, but to provide yourself a visual reference to return to his vicinity. If the person goes overboard at night, in rain or in fog, throw your COB light overboard as well. Unless the weather is calm, visibility is excellent, and you have the COB clearly in sight, it's also a good idea to have a crew member jettison anything that floats and is easily visible at about one minute intervals throughout the rescue process. If you encounter difficulty in immediately locating the COB, this trail of floating objects will give you information about wind and current conditions and will be invaluable in helping you determine how to conduct your search for him most effectively. It's a good idea, in fact, to keep a large magazine or catalog close to the helm for just this purpose and have a crew member tear out a page, ball it up, and throw it overboard at one-minute intervals.

Note your compass heading, the wind speed, the wind direction, and the time. If you lose sight of the COB and must conduct a search for him, you will find yourself calculating current vectors over time to estimate the direction in which the COB is likely to have drifted and the distance he or she is likely to have been carried. The base line of that search will be the reciprocal of the course you were running when you first realized he had gone over the side. There is no way you can establish that base line if you do not know your original course, so note it before you make your turn. The time the person went overboard is equally critical. In the tension of a search, time can become compressed and you could easily be mistaken as to how long the COB has been in the water and thus miscalculate his most likely position. If at all possible, write these factors down. If that is impractical, tell them to another crew member with orders to help you remember them in case any of them slip your own mind in the excitement.

Reduce throttle and reverse your course in as tight a turn as possible. If the wind is from other than dead astern, make your turn to leeward. The objective of this maneuver is to get your vessel turned around and headed back toward the COB as quickly as possible and, starting from a position as close as possible to the point at which the CREW OVERBOARD! alarm was sounded, to travel back toward him on as close as possible to a reciprocal of your original heading.

If you do not reduce speed before making your turn, it can describe an arc of up to several hundred yards, depending on how fast you are going, which will alter your starting point on the reciprocal by the diameter of the turn's arc.

As nearly as possible, you want to spin your vessel on its keel so you begin the reciprocal course as close as possible to the point at which you began to make the turn. If yours is a single-engine boat, reduce throttle, shift to neutral, shift briefly to reverse and give a brief burst of throttle to lose as much headway as possible, reduce throttle, shift back to forward gear, then make your turn tightly. In a twin-screw boat, do the same, but leave your windward engine in forward and put your leeward engine in reverse to pivot your vessel in the tightest possible turn.

The reason for turning to leeward if the wind is other than dead downwind is that from the moment the COB went over the side, he has been floating downwind. By turning your vessel to leeward, you increase your chances of putting yourself on a reciprocal that will intercept him. If you turn to windward, you are increasing your vessel's divergence from his likely course. Reaccelerate toward the person in the water, following directions of the crew member pointing toward him, and approach from downwind to within about ten feet. By approaching the COB from downwind you reduce the likelihood of your vessel being driven down on him by wind and current. You also increase your ability to maneuver with less danger of striking him with the vessel or its propeller(s). To further reduce the danger of injuring the COB with the vessel, approach only to within about ten feet rather than bringing the vessel right up to him or her.

As you approach the person in the water, shift your engine to neutral to reduce the danger of striking him or her with a rotating propeller, but leave it running in case you require it for additional maneuvering, and have a crew member on board throw a line to the person in the water. He or she should use a floating line if possible to reduce the danger of fouling the line in your vessel's prop just when it is most needed for maneuvering. Assuming the COB is conscious and able to function, throwing him a line to bring him to the vessel is safer than bringing the vessel right up to him or having another crew member enter the water.

In settled weather, bring the COB aboard over your vessel's transom (but only after double-checking to make certain your engine is in neutral). In unsettled weather, amidships will be the most stable part of the vessel and is therefore the safest place to hoist a COB aboard. If you attempt to bring the COB aboard at the stern in heavy weather, the stern could be lifted on a wave and the COB could be struck by it or trapped beneath it.

If the person in the water is injured or unconscious, you will need to approach to within about ten feet and send a crew member into the water to retrieve him. Entering the water to rescue an injured or unconscious person can be dangerous and arduous, and the assignment should be given to *your strongest crew member*. Allow no one to enter the water without being attached to the vessel by a safety line, as he could be swept away from the vessel by wind and current, which would merely compound your problems. The rescuer should remove his shoes and wear a life jacket for his own protection and to provide additional buoyancy during the recovery procedure.

If you require the assistance of other vessels in locating or recovering a COB, the proper signal to transmit is the Pan Pan urgency signal rather than the Mayday distress signal. The format for transmitting it will be found in Chapter 10. You may precede the Pan Pan urgency signal with the radiotelephone alarm signal only in a COB situation and only if you feel you cannot obtain the required assistance without it.

In crowded conditions, if you will be able to retrieve the COB yourself but may have to violate the normal rules of the road to do so, use the Pan Pan urgency signal to alert other vessels in your vicinity to your intentions and instruct them to stand clear.

The Pan Pan signal can be directed toward one or more specific vessels or to "all ships." Once the emergency has passed, you are not required to cancel a Pan Pan urgency signal addressed to one or more specific vessels. If you broadcast a Pan Pan urgency signal "to all ships," however, once the emergency is ended you must cancel it using the format in Chapter 10.

## Tips on Conducting a COB Search

If a member of your crew sees a fellow crew person go overboard during daylight hours and the visibility is good, recovering him or her using the above procedure is relatively simple.

But if no one sees the COB go over the side, or you lose sight of him, here are some tips for conducting a search which should improve your chances of a successful recovery (see Fig. 14.1):

1. As soon as the COB alarm is sounded, note the time and your present speed and heading, then stop your vessel.

2. If no one saw the COB go over the side, attempt to establish the amount of time that has elapsed since he was last seen on board.

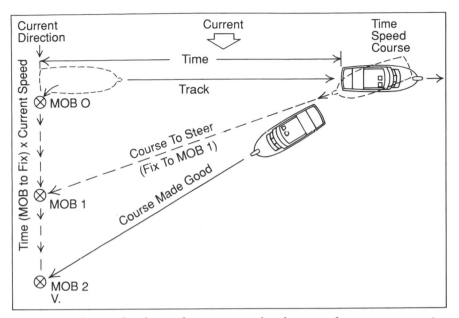

**Fig. 14.1:** *This search technique for a person overboard accounts for any current running and the direction and distance the victim is likely to have drifted since he or she was last sighted.*

3. Plot your vessel's present position on your chart and label it as FIX. If your vessel's track is not already charted, plot it as a reciprocal of your present heading. (To compute a reciprocal course from a present course of greater than 180 degrees, subtract 180 degrees. If your present course is less than 180 degrees, add 180 degrees.)

4. From the time elapsed since the last sighting of the COB and your vessel's speed during that time, plot the most remote point along your vessel's track at which the COB is likely to have gone over the side. Label that point as COB 0.

5. A person in the water presents so little surface to the wind that wind speed and direction can be virtually discounted as factors in determining the COB's likely speed and direction of drift. Because two thirds to three fourths of the COB's bulk is in the water, he will be affected far more by current. Determine the speed of any

331

current that is running and establish the direction in which it is setting. You should always be aware of the speed and direction of set of any current that is affecting your vessel. If you are not already aware of those factors when the CREW OVERBOARD! alarm is sounded and cannot determine them from your navigational instruments such as a Loran unit, here's how to quickly get a basic estimate: Lay your vessel directly head-to-wind and reduce power to the minimum required to maintain steerage. Note the position of your watch's second hand and, at your mark, have a crew member at the point of your bow toss overboard a half-full gallon milk jug or other similar container which can be sealed. Note the number of seconds ($T$) it takes the jug to float from bow to stern. Divide your vessel's LOA by $T$ and multiply the result by .6, which will give you the current's approximate speed in knots.

To determine the approximate direction of the current's set, observe the angle at which the jug floats away from your vessel with a hand-bearing compass. If the jug drifts dead downwind, you can use the wind's angle as the current's direction of set. If the angle of the jug's drift differs significantly from the angle of the wind, you know that a strong current is running whose direction of set is not coincident with the wind angle. In that case, disregard wind angle and use the current's direction of set in your calculations.

Plot the direction of set as a line through the point you have labeled COB 0 and note its estimated speed.

6. Based on the elapsed time since the COB was last seen and the speed of the current, plot the COB's estimated present position along the line of the current's set and label it COB 1.

7. Plot a course from FIX to COB 1 as the course you will steer with lookouts posted at your vessel's highest point. Measure the distance from FIX to COB 1 and calculate the time it will take you to get there based on your vessel's speed alone. Remember that during this run, your vessel will be affected by the same current set and drift which is affecting the COB. Factor the current's effects into your vessel's speed and heading and label the resulting position as V 1.

8. If your reaction was instantaneous and your figures are precisely correct, V 1 and COB 2 will coincide. Regardless of the point along

your vessel's track where the COB actually went over the side, theoretically he will have drifted right onto your course. Since it is unlikely your reaction was instantaneous or that your figures were exactly precise, he could be to either side of your course, but at least you will have determined a line of position along which to conduct your search.

9.  Once you have worked out the COB's estimated present position and the direction and speed he is likely to drift, use the Pan Pan urgency signal to enlist the aid of any other vessels that might be in that vicinity or along his line of drift.

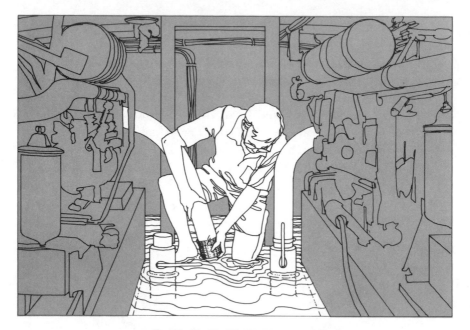

## CHAPTER 15

# SEVERE HULL DAMAGE

• • •

A significant quantity of water coming into your vessel's hull can quickly become a dangerous, even life-threatening emergency. At the first sign that there has been a serious breach of your hull's integrity, do whatever you must to quickly identify where the water is coming in and the nature of the leak with which you are dealing. Speed here is of the essence. If a dangerous amount of water is gushing into your vessel from an inaccessible location beneath a berth or below the galley sole, for instance, don't be delicate about stripping away whatever is blocking your view of the problem. You can repair a few hundred dollars of damage much more cheaply than you can replace your entire boat, and you can't replace human lives at all.

Other than hull damage resulting from a collision, the most common sources of significant leaks are the failure of through-hull fittings, hoses, underwater exhausts, rudder posts, and stuffing boxes. Check those locations first.

If your vessel has suffered hull damage as the result of a collision, be alert to the possibility that the collision might also have damaged the vessel's electrical system. Water is an excellent, potentially deadly, conductor of electricity. If a live electrical wire has been knocked loose and is discharging current into bilge water, anyone stepping or reaching into the bilge water could receive a serious, possibly fatal, shock. If any electrical wires have been pulled loose and come into contact with bilge water or you notice any electrical sparking, shut down the main breakers in your vessel's AC and DC electrical panels before exposing yourself to the water in the bilge.

The action you take to try to stem the flood of water coming into your vessel will depend on the nature of the leak itself:

If the problem is a ruptured raw-water intake hose, simply closing the sea cock or gate valve that serves it should solve the immediate problem. If the hose is one that delivers cooling water to your main engine(s) or your generator(s), shut the engine or generator down until you effect repairs to avoid the danger of burning it out.

Stuffing boxes are designed to weep a minimal amount of water as a lubricant and to ensure that they are not too tight, but vibration can cause the packing nuts to work loose and allow a significant amount of water to enter the hull in a short time. Make certain you always have on board a pair of large pliers, a wrench, or a special packing nut tool big enough to retighten the nuts if they work loose underway.

All through-hull fittings serving raw water intakes should be fitted with a sea cock or gate valve, but if you come across one that isn't, you can at least slow the flood of incoming water by wrapping the hose with waterproof tape and/or rags. Every vessel's engine room should be equipped with several rolls of a product called Syntho-Glass resin-impregnated tape. The resin sets up within thirty minutes of being saturated with water and forms a strong, temporary repair. Since it is heat-resistant to 1,100 degrees Fahrenheit, it can even be used on exhaust systems and mufflers. It can be wrapped around a broken hose or balled up and used to plug small openings such as a failed through-hull fitting.

Every through-hull fitting should have a conical wood plug of appropriate diameter attached to it with a piece of light line. If a through-hull fails and its sea cock or gate valve cannot be closed, simply ram the plug home to stem the flow of water. Shaft glands should also be fitted with wooden plugs. In 1989 a sailing vessel went down off Bermuda because its prop became entangled in a fishing net and the entire shaft was literally wrenched out of the boat. One life was lost in the incident. Plugs should also be fitted to any rudder post glands that open into the hull.

If the problem is a breach in the hull itself as a result of a collision, stuff the opening from inside the hull with any soft materials you can lay your hands on such as berth cushions, pillows, or blankets (but never life jackets, you might need them). As quickly as possible, reinforce these soft materials with something flat and solid such as a hatch cover or dinette table top and wedge it into place with whatever bracing material you have at hand such as a dinette table support, a boat hook, or dinghy oars. You can also reduce the flow of water by covering the hole on the outside of the hull with a collision mat or awning material held in place by ropes. Water pressure outside the hull will help hold it in position. If you are going to try to reach shore with such a rig in place, make certain its top edge is well above your vessel's waterline.

As soon as you have the source of the incoming water under a reasonable degree of control, make sure your vessel's automatic electric bilge pumps are working properly by placing your hand near their water inlets to check for suction. If you don't feel water being sucked into a pump, make certain its inlet is not clogged with debris, that its float valve is not stuck in the "off" position, and that it is receiving proper electrical power.

The best electric bilge pump—or even two or three of them—probably can't handle a serious breach of hull integrity. The electric bilge pumps typically found on vessels under 50 feet are rated at about 1,500 to 2,000 gallons per hour, which translates to only 25 to 33 gallons per minute. Those on vessels over 50 feet may go up to about 3,500 gallons per hour, but that works out to less than 60 gallons per minute. A four-inch hole in your hull well below the waterline could easily admit as much as 200 gallons per minute.

You can supplement your vessel's electric bilge pumps with manual bilge pumps, the largest of which can move up to a gallon a stroke. The problem, of course, is that you have to have the crew to man them, and operating them is strenuous work. Most people will not be able to operate a good-sized manual bilge pump at 30 to 40 strokes per minute for more than about

10 minutes, so you'll have to set up a rotating schedule.

In a serious emergency, you can remove a significant quantity of water from your vessel by using your main engine and/or the engine powering your electrical generator as an emergency bilge pump. The raw water pump on a typical six-cylinder diesel engine, for instance, has a flow rate of about 75 gallons per minute and one on a 12-cylinder engine pumps up to 140 gallons per minute. Here's the procedure: If the engine is running, turn it off. Close the sea cock or gate valve of the through-hull fitting serving the engine's raw water intake, disconnect the hose clamps, remove the hose from the through-hull, cover its end with some kind of screening to keep out debris (if nothing else, cut the screen out of a portlight), lay the end of the inlet hose in the bilge, and restart the engine. The end of the inlet hose must be completely covered by bilge water to ensure that the engine gets an adequate supply of cooling water. You should also post a crew member at the end of the inlet hose to make certain it does not become clogged and to alert you when the engine pumps out enough water to the point that it is no longer receiving an adequate supply of cooling water.

The instant you doubt your ability to control the flow of water coming into your vessel's hull or at least pump the water overboard faster than it is coming in, broadcast a Pan Pan urgency message over VHF channel 16 or SSB frequency 2182 kHz using the format in Chapter 10, and do not omit any items. If you reach the Coast Guard and are within range of one of their helicopters or C–130s, they may be able to air-drop an emergency, gasoline-powered bilge pump to you. The instructions for operating it will be on the canister. Don't put off making at least an alerting call as your batteries could quickly be shorted out by the incoming water.

The moment you become convinced you are not going to be able to keep your vessel from foundering, broadcast a Mayday distress message using the format in Chapter 10. If you don't get a satisfactory reply to your Mayday, set off visual and possibly audible distress signals. Even if you cannot see any other vessels in your immediate vicinity, fire a red parachute or meteor flare. It might be spotted by a vessel out of sight over the horizon which will come to investigate. If other vessels are nearby, sound repeated short blasts on your horn, raise and lower your fully extended arms, display your orange distress flag with square and circle, and/or fire an orange smoke flare.

These steps, of course, assume you are far from shore when your hull's integrity is seriously breached. If you are inshore and can reach shoal water, simply run your vessel aground. You may do some damage to your hull and possibly your underwater gear, but at least you will keep her from going under. If all else fails, launch your life raft and go through your abandon-ship drill, which is covered in Chapter 17. If your vessel doesn't sink completely but is simply awash, stay near it if at all possible as you will have a better chance of being spotted by rescuers.

## CHAPTER 16

# FIGHTING FIRES AFLOAT

• • •

The potentially disastrous effects of a fire at sea and what you should—and should not—do if one erupts are best illustrated by the experience of a friend of mine, Sumner Pingree, when a turbocharger caught fire in the engine room of his immaculate sportfisherman *Roulette* off the coast of Puerto Rico.

"We were running with the engine room door open to get more air to the engines," Sumner told me later. "The mate was in the cockpit when he spotted the fire and slammed the engine room door shut. By the time my son Richard was halfway up the flying bridge ladder to tell me about the fire, smoke was everywhere. We had already lost power on the starboard engine and the generator. I yanked the port engine back to idle and immediately got off a Mayday call to the Coast Guard. I said I was not declaring an emergency at that moment but had a fire on board and asked them to stand by. We opened the engine room door to see what was going on. Our Halon system had already gone off and extinguished the fires. As best we could tell, the high-pressure fuel line on the starboard engine had ruptured and saturated the insulating blanket around the turbocharger, and it had been ignited by the hot exhaust gases which power the turbocharger.

"Since the fire was out, we thought we were okay. But while we were trying to figure out exactly what had happened, the fire reignited with a whoosh. I raced back up to the bridge to call the Coast Guard again, but the fire had already burned through the battery cables and the radio was dead. Within two or three minutes the entire cockpit and main salon were engulfed in flames. Flames were all around me. I yelled to everybody to abandon ship. We launched the life raft and leaped into the sea. Ten minutes after we first realized we had a fire aboard, we were swimming. I was amazed how quickly she burned."

In the situation they faced aboard *Roulette,* Sumner and his crew did some things that were very right and a couple of things that proved to be disastrous. We'll examine their actions in detail and see which was which.

## Tips on Fire Defense

Your first line of defense against a fire on board is preventing it from occurring in the first place, and doing that involves a lot of plain common sense. Make certain, for instance, that all your vessel's electrical wiring is properly installed and protected by appropriately sized fuses on all circuits, then check periodically for corrosion and chafe. Regularly check your vessel's fuel fill system to make certain all its connections are tight, and always ground the fuel fill nozzle to your fuel fill deck plate before you pump fuel aboard. Also keep a close eye on the fuel and lubrication lines on your engine(s) and generator(s) and replace them at the first sign of fraying or leaking. Never store flammable materials near a heat source or allow oily rags to accumulate in an enclosed space. And be extremely careful with open flames such as those around a shipboard barbecue grill.

Your second line of defense against the potentially disastrous effects of a fire on board is to protect your engine spaces with an automatic engine room fire-extinguishing system and mount appropriately sized portable fire

340

extinguishers of the proper class in strategic areas throughout your vessel: just outside the engine space door or hatch; on the flying bridge; in the pilothouse, salon, and belowdecks accommodations; and in the galley. The law doesn't require you to carry a portable fire extinguisher in your dinghy, but it's a wise precaution.

If you take those precautions and still have the misfortune of a fire aboard your vessel, here are some suggestions for handling it:

## ENGINE ROOM FIRE

### Shut Down Engines/Generators

When Sumner pulled his port engine back to idle rather than shutting it down altogether, what he didn't realize was that it was sucking the fire suppressant chemical out of his engine room, and at the same time sucking fresh oxygen into the engine room to refuel the fire.

If fire erupts in your vessel's engine room, the first thing you should do is shut down all engines and generators that share the engine space involved with the fire. This will also help close off any supplies of fuel or lubricating oils that might be fueling the flames.

### Close Engine Room Doors/Hatches

A fire cannot continue to burn without oxygen. Shutting any open engine room doors or hatches will help starve the fire of oxygen and snuff it out.

### Activate Automatic Fire-Extinguishing System

If your vessel's engine room fire-extinguishing system has not discharged automatically, activate it manually. Automatic engine-room fire extinguishers are normally quite dependable and discharge as soon as a fire raises the temperature in the engine room to their activation point. But like anything else mechanical, particularly in the corrosive marine environment, they can malfunction, in which case you will have to activate your vessel's system manually. Your vessel should have manual activation levers at both its flying bridge and pilothouse steering stations, in the salon, and in its belowdecks accommodations.

## Transmit a Mayday or Pan Pan Call

The best thing Sumner Pingree did in the fire aboard *Roulette* was to immediately transmit a Mayday distress call. As his experience proved, had he waited to make his call until after he assessed the damage the fire had caused, it would have been too late.

Any time you have fire break out in the engine room, go ahead and transmit at least a Pan Pan urgency call and message to alert potential rescuers that you may need their help. If the situation seems serious, you are fully justified in transmitting the Mayday distress call and message. Use the format detailed in Chapter 10 and do not omit any items. If, by the time you get in contact with someone, you are not certain you will require assistance, have them stand by while you assess the situation. If, while you are doing that, your radio is disabled, at least someone will be alerted to your problem and your position.

## Prepare to Launch Life Raft

The minute you realize you have an engine room fire aboard your vessel, take the precautions of ordering a crew member to stand by the life raft and prepare to launch it, and order your crew into their life jackets. If you are able to quickly bring the fire under control, you can order a stand-down and have lost nothing. If the fire gets out of hand and you must abandon ship, you will at least be that much further along in your preparations.

## Allow Engine Space to Cool and Ventilate

When you've got smoke boiling out of your engine room and your automatic fire-extinguishing system has discharged, there naturally is a great temptation to yank the engine room door or hatch open immediately to see what's going on. But don't do it! Wait at least fifteen minutes to be certain the engine and any flammable material in the engine room have cooled below the reflash point.

If your engine space is protected by a $CO_2$ fire-extinguishing system, once you are certain the fire is out and any metals and flammable liquids in it have cooled below the flash point, open the engine space and allow it to ventilate fifteen minutes before you enter it. In concentrations sufficient to choke off a fire, $CO_2$ is deadly. If you must enter an engine space where a $CO_2$ system has discharged before it has had time to ventilate (to rescue a person trapped in the space when the system discharged, for example), cover your mouth with a piece of fabric as a filter, hold your breath, and do not crouch down any lower than is absolutely necessary. $CO_2$ is heavier than air and will tend to sink toward the vessel's bilges.

Halon is also heavier than air and will sink into the vessel's bilges, but it is safe to breathe in the 5 to 7 percent concentrations normally used in automatic engine room fire-extinguishing systems.

## Open Doors/Hatches Carefully

Before opening any door or hatch that may have fire behind it, feel its exterior first. If it's too hot for you to hold your hand against, the fire is probably still burning. Even if the door or hatch is cool enough for you to hold your hand against it, have a portable fire extinguisher ready for action and open the door cautiously. The door or hatch may be heavily insulated. Even if it is relatively cool, fire could be raging on the other side of it, or you could experience a reflash.

If your vessel is not equipped with an automatic fire-extinguishing system and you plan to try to put the fire out with a portable extinguisher, open the door cautiously, stay as low as possible since heat and flames tend to rise, and keep the door between yourself and the possible fire.

## Direct Extinguisher Stream at Base of Flames

A stream of a portable fire extinguisher directed at the flames of a fire does little good. You must get the stream at the base of the fire to rob it of heat and oxygen at its source. Hold the stream as steady as possible. Once you get the stream focused on the base of the fire, keep it there until you are sure the fire is out. Do not use short bursts of fire suppressant as that can give the fire time to reignite between bursts.

## GALLEY FIRE

Galley fires are most likely to be fueled by flammable liquids such as grease, propane, or alcohol, or by combustible solid materials such as paper, wood, or fabric. A good type A/B extinguisher will be effective against both types.

If no fire extinguisher is available, use "at hand" materials such as baking soda or a water-soaked towel. Water will put out an alcohol fire but may spread the flames. Baking soda is a good dry chemical suppressant as it robs the fire of oxygen. Rather than just dumping baking soda on the fire right out of the box, dump some in your hand, then broadcast it at the base of the flames. Do not use water on grease fires. The grease will float on top of the water and can carry flames to other parts of the vessel such as wood cabinets and drapes.

Make certain any fuel supplying the fire is turned off at the source. Most galleys that use propane for cooking are equipped with an electronic control that allows you to turn off the propane at the tank. (The propane tank itself should be housed in its own, well-ventilated compartment on the vessel's exterior.) Unburned propane is heavier than air and will sink to the vessel's lowest point, where it could explode. If you extinguish a propane fire, be certain the propane is turned off at the tank so unburned propane does not build up.

## ELECTRICAL FIRE

A primary concern in fighting an electrical fire is that you use a suppressant that is not a conductor of electricity. Type C fire extinguishers use chemicals that are not electrical conductors. The suppressant used in foam-type extinguishers will corrode electronics; the suppressant used in $CO_2$ and Halon extinguishers will not.

If possible, restrict an electrical fire's access to oxygen. In most electrical fires, the initial combustible material is the insulation around the wiring itself. Fires in electrical wiring insulation cannot be sustained without a great deal of oxygen. In many cases, simply encasing circuit panels in a heavy metal box and closing up the box if a fire breaks out will be sufficient to extinguish it.

Never use water to extinguish an electrical fire. Water is an excellent conductor of electricity. If you throw water on an electrical fire and are standing in water yourself, the electrical power could be conducted through the water and electrocute you.

## ACCOMMODATIONS FIRE

Fires in a vessel's accommodations will most often be fueled by such combustible material as wood, paper, or fabric. You should have a type A extinguisher mounted in your accommodations where you and your crew can get to it easily, even in the dark. If no type A fire extinguisher is available, flood the base of the fire with water, which is an effective suppressant for type A fires.

If possible, restrict the fire's access to oxygen. Type A fires cannot continue to burn without a generous supply of oxygen. Robbing a fire of oxygen simply by closing a door or hatch often can help rob it of oxygen and snuff it out.

## FIRE ON DECK

A common source of deck fires aboard yachts is the gasoline used to fuel the dinghy's outboard motor. Although Coast Guard regulations do not require that a fire extinguisher be carried in most dinghies, you should keep a type B extinguisher aboard and make certain it is handy any time you are handling gasoline.

If an on-deck fire is fueled by such combustible materials as wood, paper, or fabric, extinguish it with a type A extinguisher or water. Water is an excellent suppressant for extinguishing type A fires. You should always keep handy on deck a stout bucket with a rope tied to its handle that is long enough to allow you to scoop up water from over your vessel's side-rails.

If possible, jettison the burning material overboard. The closest water to extinguish a deck fire normally will be the water in which your vessel is floating. If possible, use a dinghy oar, whisker pole, or other long object to push the burning material over the side.

# CHAPTER 17

# ABANDON-SHIP PROCEDURES

• • •

Abandoning ship is a procedure filled with potential hazards and should be undertaken only if your vessel is fully involved with a fire or is in imminent danger of sinking. In many cases, even vessels that have been seriously holed will remain afloat for hours or even days due to their natural buoyancy or to air trapped inside their hulls or superstructure.

At the first inkling that a fire or a breach of your hull's integrity may become serious enough to require you to abandon ship, mentally run through the steps the procedure requires and alert your crew that you are considering this extreme course of action. But don't give the actual abandon-ship order until you are certain there is no way you can contain the fire or the hull damage to allow you and your crew to remain on board until help arrives. (The recommended procedures for fighting a fire on board are covered fully in Chapter 16. Recommended procedures for dealing with severe hull damage will be found in Chapter 15.)

## Dress Warmly

If the situation aboard your vessel is serious enough for you to consider abandoning ship, you and your crew may already be dressed in warm clothes and wearing life jackets. But if a serious emergency arises suddenly (a fire or severe hull damage resulting from striking a submerged object in the middle of the night), as soon as you even wonder if you might have to abandon ship, put on warm clothes and your own life jacket and order your crew to do likewise. If you have to order your crew into the raft, they could very well wind up in the water, and warm clothing and a life jacket could prove to be, literally, the margin between life and death.

Exposure to hypothermia (extreme loss of body heat) is one of the greatest dangers you and your crew will face in the abandon-ship situation. Long pants, long-sleeved shirts, jackets, and sweaters can help preserve valuable body heat, even if they are soaked.

## Put on Life Jackets

In offshore situations, all the life jackets aboard your vessel should be Type I and at a minimum should be fitted with reflective patches and a whistle. It's even better to also equip each of them with a strobe-type personal rescue light and mini-B or Class S Emergency Position Indicating Radio Beacon (EPIRB).

Immersion suits are cumbersome and expensive, but they are absolute necessities aboard any vessel that ventures into waters 60 degrees or colder. Without an immersion suit, survival times in waters of that temperature can be less than an hour. In an immersion suit, you are likely to survive up to eight times longer than you would without one.

## Prepare to Launch Life Raft

Instruct a trained crew member to stand by the life raft and prepare to launch it. As a part of the routine safety training aboard your vessel, you should have thoroughly familiarized at least one crew member with your life raft and its proper deployment. That crew member should, for instance, know to make certain the raft is tethered to the main vessel before it is launched. Ideally, you will stow your life raft on deck in its own canister, and it will be equipped with a $CO_2$ automatic inflation device. If you carry your life raft belowdecks and/or it must be manually inflated, the crew member should know where it is located and how to inflate it quickly.

## Transmit a Mayday Distress Call and Message

While your crew is preparing to launch the life raft, transmit the Mayday distress call and message the moment the situation aboard your vessel becomes serious enough for you to decide to abandon it. If you delay transmitting the distress call and message, rising water or fire could disable the batteries that power your radio in a matter of minutes. The circumstances under which you should transmit both the Pan Pan urgency call and message and the Mayday distress call and message and the correct procedure for doing so are covered fully in Chapter 10.

## Gather Abandon-Ship Bag and Other Emergency Supplies

If your boating takes you off the beaten path, you should have assembled an abandon-ship bag that you can grab quickly on your way to the life raft. A list of suggested contents is given in Figure 17.1. The abandon-ship bag should be fitted with flotation and a 50-foot floating lanyard, which you hopefully will have time to attach to your life raft before you depart your vessel. Its most important contents will be at least a half-gallon of fresh water per person or a hand-operated reverse-osmosis watermaker or solar still.

One item you should be certain gets into the life raft is your vessel's EPIRB. Other items that normally will not be part of your abandon-ship bag but that you should try to grab if you have time include your hand-held VHF radio (preferably in a waterproof container), any special medications or eyeglasses you require, your passport, and a few dollars in American currency. It's a good idea, in fact, for each member of the crew to keep special medications, eyeglasses, their passport, and a few greenbacks close by their bunk in a waterproof container which they can grab quickly on their way out.

# SUGGESTED CONTENTS FOR ABANDON SHIP BAG

### Signaling Equipment

1 Class B mini-EPIRB (if no Class S EPIRB packed in life raft canister)

3 SOLAS-type red parachute flares

3 SOLAS-type white parachute flares

3 SOLAS-type red hand-held flares

3 SOLAS-type orange smoke canisters

12 cylume chemical light sticks

1 waterproof flashlight with spare batteries

1 waterproof compass

1 signaling mirror

### Fishing Equipment

1 filet knife in scabbard

1 spool thirty-pound test fishing line

20 feet wire leader

3 medium fishing spoons

1 sixteen-inch spear gun

1 wire saw

2 propane cigarette lighters

### Provisions

1 hand-operated watermaker or solar still

1 one-gallon folding plastic jug

2 packages high energy freeze-dried food per person

### Clothing/Personal

1 long-sleeve shirt per person

1 sun visor or billed cap per person

1 pair sunglasses per person

1 thermal blanket per person

2 rolls toilet paper in self-sealing plastic bag

### Medical Supplies

1 vial seasickness pills

2 tubes sunburn cream

1 jar petroleum jelly

1 tube antiseptic ointment

1 vial Demerol pain pills

*Fig. 17.1: A well-stocked abandon-ship bag supplies the essentials that add up to survival.*

If you have time, also grab any additional flares or other signaling devices, water, provisions, and clothing you can get to quickly.

## Launch Life Raft

Make certain the life raft is tethered to your vessel and launch it. Ideally, your life raft will already be tethered to your vessel in its canister. If it's not and you fail to tether it, there is a good chance it can be swept away by the sea.

In calm seas, launch the life raft at your vessel's stern, where the freeboard is likely to be lowest and loading and boarding the raft will be easiest.

In heavy seas, launch the life raft to leeward amidships, which will position it opposite the most stable part of the vessel, make it easier to board, and provide a bit of protection from the weather in the lee of the vessel's doghouse or superstructure. Another reason for launching the raft to leeward is that the inflation lanyard on most $CO_2$-equipped life rafts is 25 to 40 feet long and must be pulled out entirely before the life raft will inflate. Launching the life raft to leeward will carry it away from your vessel and speed the inflation process. A life raft launched to windward is likely to be blown up onto the vessel, making boarding it difficult. As heavy seas lift the stern of your vessel, a life raft launched to windward can become trapped under it and could be punctured by the rudder or propeller. In a heavy sea, launching a life raft to windward does create the possibility that the vessel could be driven down on it. To avoid that, do not pull the life raft's tether line up tightly to your vessel, but leave two to three feet of slack in it.

Once you launch the raft, one crew member should steady it while a second crew member boards. If you have time, the crew member in the life raft should release the heaving line attached to the side of the raft and throw it back to a crew member on deck. The tether line should then be slackened and the life raft lashed alongside the vessel by its tether and heaving line attached to your vessel at angles of approximately 45 degrees, which will make the life raft more stable and easier to board and load. Again, leave enough slack in the lines to allow the life raft to ride two to three feet to leeward of your vessel's hull.

## Load the Life Raft

Load your crew and emergency supplies into the life raft and have them fend it off from your vessel while you load your emergency gear to avoid snagging the life raft on anything that might puncture it. If at all possible, the crew should step or jump directly from your vessel into the life raft rather than jumping into the water and then trying to crawl up into it. If you can accomplish this maneuver, you lessen the danger of crew members being swept away from the raft. In cold waters, you also reduce the danger of their suffering the effects of hypothermia.

## Activate EPIRB

A Class A EPIRB and a Type 406 Category 1 EPIRB are automatically activated by immersion in water. A Class S EPIRB packed inside a life raft is automatically activated when the life raft inflates. Class B, mini-B, and C EPIRBs and Type 406 Category 2 EPIRBs must be manually activated. Make certain your EPIRB is securely attached to your life raft and activate it as soon as you enter the raft.

## Fire a Flare

It makes sense to fire a red meteor or parachute flare as soon as you depart your vessel. In heavily traveled areas, there is a reasonable possibility it will be sighted by a nearby vessel. Even in remote areas, there is always the possibility it will be spotted by a vessel out of your line of sight over the horizon or obscured by darkness or weather, and that such a vessel will come into your vicinity to investigate its source. Do not fire any other flares until rescuers are in sight or hearing.

## If Possible, Stay Near Main Vessel

Keep the life raft tethered to your vessel as long as possible. Obviously if your vessel is afire or about to sink, you will have to cut the lines tethering the life raft to it. But if your vessel is merely awash, keep the life raft tethered to it as long as possible. (In heavy seas, free the heaving line and pay out the full length of the life raft's tether to keep the raft away from your main vessel and avoid its being trapped beneath it or punctured by any protrusions.) You may be able to go back aboard for other supplies or provisions you failed to get into the life raft when you abandoned ship, and even an awash vessel provides a larger target for potential rescuers to spot than a lone life raft.

351

## TIPS ON LIFE RAFT SURVIVAL

If you should ever have the misfortune to find yourself adrift at sea in a life raft for an extended period of time, here are the tough realities of some of the problems you would face and several hints which might ensure your chances of surviving the ordeal.

1. No matter how tantalizingly close land may seem, *never* leave the life raft and attempt to swim for shore.

    Distances over water are deceptive and your goal almost inevitably will be much farther away than you think it is. You may well be in a severely weakened state physically—and perhaps mentally—and find you are unable to swim even a short distance which you could handle easily under more normal circumstances. You also expose yourself to the dangers of hypothermia and attack by sharks.

2. Assume rescue, if it comes at all, will arrive later rather than sooner.

    Don't delude yourself into thinking that just because you activated an EPIRB, help is on the way. Class C EPIRBs are intended only for inland or inshore use. They broadcast distress signals only on 156.75 MHz (VHF channel 15) and 156.8 MHz (VHF channel 16) which cannot be picked up by the COSPAS/SARSAT satellites or by overflying aircraft but only by VHF radios. Their maximum range is advertised as 20 miles, but with their antenna so close to the water, it is doubtful their signals will reach that far under any but ideal conditions.

    Class A, B, mini-B, and S EPIRBs broadcast distress signals on 121.5 MHz and 243.0 MHz. Their 121.5 MHz signals are monitored by overflying commercial aircraft and may be received by the COSPAS/SARSAT satellites. Their 243.0 MHz signal can be received by only a few of the COSPAS/SARSAT satellites and certain military aircraft. There are several limitations on the operations of these EPIRBs of which you should be aware. Their 121.5 MHz signal, for example, is subject to interference, may not be compatible with the COSPAS/SARSAT satellites, and sources other than EPIRBs transmit on that frequency which can make discrimination

352

of an actual distress signal difficult. In order for the COSPAS/ SARSAT satellites to pick up a signal from one of these EPIRBs and relay it to a ground receiving station, the satellite must be in view of the EPIRB and the receiving station simultaneously. Even if you must abandon ship in an area not covered by the satellites, however, the Coast Guard recommends you activate your Class A, B, mini-B, or S EPIRB as soon as you leave your vessel in the hope that its signal might be picked up by overflying commercial or military aircraft.

Both categories 1 and 2 of Type 406 EPIRBs broadcast distress signals on 406 MHz and 121.5 MHz. The 406 MHz component of signals broadcast by the Type 406 EPIRBs can be received and stored by the COSPAS/SARSAT satellites, then relayed when the satellite comes in view of a ground receiving station. Thus, the coverage of Type 406 EPIRBs is worldwide. The 121.5 MHz component of Type 406 EPIRB signals is also monitored by commercial aircraft and can be used by rescuers as a homing signal.

Even if your Class A, B, mini-B, or S EPIRB signal reaches the Coast Guard, there are several reasons they are not likely to launch a full air-sea rescue search for you immediately. One is that over 90 percent of the distress signals the Coast Guard receives from both marine EPIRBs and their close cousins, the Emergency Location Transmitters carried aboard aircraft, turn out to be false alarms due to the unit being activated accidentally. (Of the 7,700 alerts the Coast Guard receives over 121.5 MHz in a typical quarter, it ultimately determines the source of only about 220—less than 3 percent. In those cases in which it is able to identify the source of the alert, only about 14 turn out to be genuine distress situations.) Another is that the Coast Guard's expanded responsibilities for illegal drug interdiction have strained its resources and it may not have men or equipment available to deploy immediately. A third reason is that the Coast Guard is under tremendous pressures to hold down its expenses (it now costs some $7,000 per hour to operate a C-130 air-sea rescue aircraft). For those reasons, the Coast Guard has an extensive—and time-consuming—list of procedures it goes through to try to confirm that a signal from a Class A, B, mini-B, or S EPIRB represents a genuine emergency. Even if the Coast Guard receives a 121.5 MHz distress alert that was relayed from a satellite, in the absence of other corroborating evidence of an actual distress such as receipt of a distress call over VHF or SSB radio or receipt of the EPIRB signal by an overflying aircraft, it will normally wait for verification by a second satellite pass before it launches a search, and that can take up to two hours. For these reasons, the average time between the receipt of a distress signal from one of these EPIRBs and the commencement of full-scale air-sea rescue effort is twenty-six hours!

Once a full air-sea search is initiated, the rescuers still have to find you. If your Class A, B, mini-B, or S EPIRB's signal is picked up by a satellite, it provides a fix that is accurate only within 10 to 20 nautical miles. If its signal is picked up by a lone aircraft flying overhead at 35,000 feet—a typical altitude for over-water flights—that single fix narrows the area potential rescuers must search only down to some 600 square miles, which is still a lot of ocean.

You can considerably improve your chances of rescue by using one of the new Type 406 EPIRBs. The Coast Guard responds much more rapidly to distress alerts received from this type EPIRB because the 406 MHz component of its signal transmits a 121-bit serial number which is distinctive to a particular unit. For Type 406 EPIRBs registered in the U.S., the Coast Guard can use that serial number to access a computer at Suitland, Maryland, operated by NOAA, which stores information about the vessel carrying that EPIRB. With that information, they can check with the vessel's owner or his representative to confirm that the vessel is in fact in the vicinity from which the signal was received.

A Type 406 signal received by a COSPAS/SARSAT satellite significantly narrows the search area as it provides a fix accurate to within 1.5 to 3 nautical miles.

3. Ration your water and provisions on the basis of an extended stay at sea.

Those who have spent long periods adrift at sea on a life raft say that for the first few days it's fairly easy to ration food and water. After about a week, however, it's easy to convince yourself you might as well go ahead and eat and drink everything you have on board because if you save it, you won't live long enough to benefit from it.

As we said above, fresh water will be your most precious commodity. Half a cup of fresh water or other liquid per person each twenty-four hours is about the minimum required to sustain life over an extended period. On that basis, a half-gallon of water per person would be sufficient only for a little over two weeks, after which a hand-held reverse-osmosis watermaker or solar still becomes indispensable.

*Never* drink unpurified seawater. The salt it contains leads only to faster dehydration and eventual death.

4.  Depression will be your most deadly enemy.

No matter how long your ordeal lasts, you must keep up your spirits at all cost. Think of home, family, and friends. If you are religious, think of your God. When hopelessness tries to close in, exert all your strength to shove it out of you mind.

One of the earliest signs of depression will be a disinterest in food. If you encounter that in any of your crew, you must force them to eat. Failure to do so will only hasten their spiral into death.

5.  In cold water, hypothermia will be your second most dangerous enemy.

In a survival situation in cold waters, do everything you can to conserve body heat. Remain as much as possible in a fetal position and use available clothing to cover your head and your crotch area, which are the two greatest areas for loss of body heat.

6.  In tropical waters, your second worst enemy will be sharks.

Bill and Simone Butler survived sixty-six days in a life raft after their sailboat was rammed by whales and sank 1,200 miles off the coast of Central America. "We were attacked by thirty to forty sharks a day," Bill told me after they were rescued. "They didn't attack the raft with their teeth but butted it with their heads. They came at us day and night so that it was almost impossible for us to get any rest, and each one would ram us ten to fifteen times. They would slam into us at bullet-speed, then flip over on their backs and spray the raft with urine. They could spray urine eight, ten, fifteen feet into the air. To finish off the attack, they'd give the raft a great slap with their tails."

7.  Fish and turtles are your most likely source of life-sustaining protein.

In the open ocean, sea creatures tend to congregate in the shadow of any bit of flotsam they happen across—such as your life raft. Bill and Simone Butler survived their ordeal largely because of the four to five hundred pounds of fish—mostly triggerfish—Bill was able to catch. In one instance, Bill was able to catch a small turtle and wrestle it into the raft. In another, a marauding undersea predator drove a school of flying fish to the surface near his raft and he was able to catch four of them by hand.

The fishing supplies you include in your abandon-ship bag, including artificial and preserved baits, can well provide the critical margin between life and death.

8.  Sea birds can be your second most valuable resource.

Sea birds frequently alight on life rafts and can be caught if you move quickly. Their flesh provides both edible protein and a valuable source of bait to catch other sea creatures.

## TIPS ON AIR-SEA RESCUE

### Rescue by Commercial Vessels and Aircraft

Within twelve hours after Bill and Simone Butler's boat sank out from under them, a commercial vessel came within a quarter of a mile of their life raft but never spotted them. Commercial vessels are required to keep a lookout posted at all times but are notorious for failing to do so.

If you are adrift in a raft and spot a vessel or low-flying aircraft in your vicinity during the day or hear its engines at night, fire off a red meteor or parachute flare. If it's during the day, wave your arms at your sides, preferably holding some bright article of clothing in each hand. If the sun is shining, use a signal mirror. In the case of an aircraft that's not actually searching for you, you'll probably get only one brief chance to attract the attention of its crew. In the case of a vessel, if you managed to get your VHF radio aboard the raft, transmit a Mayday call over channel 16. (Do not point the radio's antenna at the ship but hold it straight up; radio waves radiate from an antenna in concentric circles.) If you spot a ship and signal to it but after about fifteen minutes it does not alter course in your direction, fire one more flare, transmit one more Mayday if possible and continue to wave or flash your signal mirror. If you get no response after that, it's likely they have no lookout or radio watch posted and further effort on your part is probably useless. In either case, don't make the mistake of draining your hand-held VHF radio's battery or firing all your flares in a single encounter. You may need both desperately if you happen upon another low-flying aircraft or a commercial vessel that is maintaining a lookout.

## Rescue by U.S. Coast Guard Ships and Aircraft

The Coast Guard conducts air-sea search and rescue efforts with cutters or smaller vessels; fixed-wing aircraft such as the C-130; and helicopters. The H-3 helicopters it uses are designed to fly a maximum of 300 miles from shore, loiter for a maximum of 20 minutes to effect a pickup, then return to shore.

As soon as you see a Coast Guard vessel, fixed-wing aircraft or helicopters or hear its engines, fire off a red or white meteor or parachute flare if you have one. In the case of an aircraft, aim the meteor in front of it; they are virtually blind to the rear. As a second choice, in daylight fire a hand-held red flare or orange smoke canister, use a signal mirror if the sun is shining and wave your arms at your sides; at night fire a hand-held flare or activate your personal rescue or man overboard light. If you managed to get a hand-held VHF radio aboard your raft, turn it on and broadcast a Mayday distress message on channel 16, remembering to hold it straight up.

If the Coast Guard spots you, what happens from that point on will depend primarily on the type of search and rescue craft that has located you and the state of the weather at the time.

If you are located by a Coast Guard ship and the sea is calm, it will probably just come alongside your life raft and take you aboard. If a heavy sea is running, the cutter is more likely to launch a rescue team in one of its small boats (probably a rigid-bottom inflatable) to come get you.

If you are located by a helicopter and it approaches you, stay as nearly as possible in the center of your life raft and hang on to it tightly, as the helicopter rotors' strong downdraft can flip it over. If the weather conditions are at all manageable, the helicopter's crew probably will lower a rescue sling, basket, net, or seat. If you are not able to communicate with them via a hand-held VHF radio, use hand signals: arms horizontal and thumbs down to tell them to lower the conveyance; arms raised vertically and thumbs pointed up to tell them to hoist it. If those aboard the life raft are able to get into or onto the conveyance that is offered, do so one at a time. If anyone on board the raft is not physically able to manage the transfer, one of the

357

helicopter crew will likely enter the water to assist you. If anyone on the raft is seriously injured, the crew will probably lower a rescue litter to hoist that person aboard.

If you are located by a C-130, it will circle you and wiggle its wings to let you know you have been spotted. If you do not have an operable hand-held VHF radio aboard, it will probably drop you a package containing one along with other survival supplies. If that becomes necessary, the aircraft normally will approach your raft from downwind at an altitude of about 300 feet, drop the package about 100 feet from you, then continue to pay out a 200- to 300-foot lanyard attached to the package, which they will attempt to drop right on top of or to windward of you so that it will drift down across your raft. A C-130 cannot effect a pickup at sea but will radio your position to the nearest Coast Guard ship or helicopter in your vicinity. It can stay aloft for up to fourteen hours and normally will circle your position as long as its fuel supply will allow it to. As its fuel begins to run low, it may be replaced on station by a second aircraft. If it must leave you, don't panic. It has relayed your position to a helicopter or ship which can pick you up. Help is definitely on the way, but it may take it a while to arrive. If you are out of range of a helicopter and have to wait for a ship to pick you up, it will be steaming toward you at only about 10 knots, so be patient and hang on.

PART FOUR

· · ·

KEEPING
THINGS
HUMMING

· · ·

## CHAPTER 18

# LIFE ABOARD

•   •   •

You'll quickly develop your own routine for living aboard that best suits your personality and life-style, but the cruising life does present both unusual challenges and opportunities, so here are a few suggestions.

## LOCAL PROVISIONING

I've mentioned elsewhere that if you'll be cruising outside the U.S. you should take as many provisions with you as possible. You'll be surprised at the number of familiar products you'll run into in foreign countries, but

361

they're likely to be considerably more expensive than they are at home. One exception is alcoholic beverages, which often are cheaper offshore because of American taxation policies.

Canned hams and dairy products from the Scandinavian countries and New Zealand are widely available, safe to eat, and last for months on board without refrigeration. Local bread is almost always safe, even if the girl behind the counter does handle it barehanded. Eggs normally are okay, but to stave off the possibility of salmonella poisoning, always cook eggs thoroughly.

In less developed nations, stay away from the local water. It can contain bugs that don't bother the locals because their systems are used to them but can wreak havoc on the internal workings of visitors. If you must drink local water, boil it first. Better still, drink bottled water. In tropical areas especially, be wary of local meats. Many tropical countries don't have the sanitary food handling practices we enforce in this country and often lack adequate refrigeration, so you run a fair risk of ingesting unusual bacteria that can make you ill. Also be cautious about local vegetables. Foods that you peel such as fresh fruit or squash or things you shell like beans and peas are usually okay, but be careful with leafy green vegetables. If you buy vegetables like lettuce in a local market, be sure to wash them thoroughly, preferably in a mixture of a teaspoon of bleach to a gallon of water.

## PERSONAL SAFETY AND COMFORT

If you'll be cruising in tropical areas, don't forget that the sun's rays can burn you quickly, and excessive exposure to their ultraviolet rays contains the danger of skin cancer which can be deadly. Be sure you carry along plenty of lotion with a high sunblock rating (15 to 25 is not excessive), use it often, and reapply it each time you come out of the water. Be sure you have a wide-brimmed hat and wear it when you are outside for any length of time. When wading in the water, especially around reefs, wear cheap plastic sandals or an old pair of tennis shoes to protect yourself against dangers like sea urchin spines.

## HARVESTING THE SEA

Unless you're an experienced fisherman or diver, you shouldn't depend on seafood as a major part of your on-board provisions. But the seas through which we cruise are alive with all manner of tasty critters, and with a bit of planning, practice, and effort you can supplement the fare you bring from home with some succulent morsels (Fig. 18.1).

You can put seafood on the grill or in the oven or frying pan four ways: by trolling, by casting, by bottom fishing, and by skin or scuba diving. In some areas you can simply take a stroll along the beach at low tide and rake clams from the sand or pluck oysters from rocks.

## Trolling

Trolling is the easiest way for cruising yachtsmen to catch fish. The typical 6- to 8-knot cruising speed of a displacement-hull powerboat is ideal for trolling; if you operate a planing-hull vessel, you'll have to pull back to about that speed to get any results. Along the Atlantic coast from Florida to New England, trolling can produce bull dolphin, Spanish or king mackerel, bluefish, wahoo, and yellowfin or bluefin tuna, all of which are delicious eating. Off the California coast you can catch albacore tuna, which is mouthwatering baked, broiled, grilled, or smoked. Farther north you'll find salmon.

For saltwater trolling, I'd suggest a pair of stout rods about five feet long. You don't need expensive rods made of graphite or boron; inexpensive rods of fiberglass will do the job just as well. The main area to check in a rod is the guides, which should be of stainless steel and firmly bonded in place. Rods with roller guides are nice but are significantly more expensive.

Select trolling reels rated to handle 30-pound test line. The basic difference among trolling reels is the type of "drag" they employ. That's the internal mechanism that allows you to put varying degrees of pressure on the fish both when he strikes and when you are getting him to the boat. The old standby is the "star drag," which is identified by a star-shaped wheel at the base of the crank. Personally I find the star drag clumsy and difficult to work with. I prefer the lever-action type which adjusts by sliding a thumb-nut forward or backward.

**Fig. 18.1:** *A little effort with a rod and reel can often yield tasty results, such as this bottom-dwelling snapper caught by jigging.*

For general offshore meat fishing I'd suggest you use 30-pound test monofilament line. Attach a stainless steel snap swivel that opens like a safety pin to the end of the line with a fisherman's knot. The swivel part will keep your line from twisting and the snap part will keep you from having to tie a fresh knot each time you want to change lures or switch over to a jig for bottom fishing. If you want to get fancy, ask a friendly fishing mate to show you how to tie 15 feet of double line into the end of your rig with a Bimini twist and attach the snap swivel with a knot called a cat's paw.

To avoid having to mess with bait, either live or dead, choose a good selection of artificial lures such as silver spoons, bucktails, and skirted lures in a variety of colors ranging in size from about two to four inches long. Attach a five-foot section of leader material to each lure. Monofilament leader of about 50-pound test is easy to handle and adequate for dolphin and mackerel, but you'll need stainless steel wire leader to handle toothy critters like bluefish and wahoo. Tie a one-inch loop in the end of the leader which will attach to your line swivel. For making connections in leader material, pick up an inexpensive crimping set. Store each lure with its leader in a Ziploc bag to keep the leader from tangling.

Miscellaneous items you'll need include a selection of one- to two-ounce lead weights, a file to sharpen the hooks on your lures, a pair of fishing pliers with a line cutter on the side, a couple of pair of cotton work gloves, and a small tackle box to put your loose gear in. Also pick up a fighting belt which straps around your waist and provides a socket in which you can seat the rod butt while you are bringing a fish to your boat. Choose the type with a woven fabric belt and a Velcro fastener. The type with leather belts will bleed onto your clothing when they get wet. If your vessel's cockpit is not equipped with rod holders, pick up a couple of the type that you can attach with a screw clamp at a 45-degree angle to the cockpit coaming or a life-line stanchion. You'll also need a short billy club and a gaff about four feet long. For fish under about five or six pounds, you'll find a landing net is easier to use than a gaff. Buy one with a four-foot handle and a basket about 18 inches across.

Trolling while cruising works best with one person minding the helm and a second person in the cockpit tending to the fishing lines, preferably with an intercom system set to the listen position so the fisherman can let the helmsman know when he or she gets a strike and needs help getting a fish in the boat.

Once you are at sea and have your boat set up on course, dig your trolling gear out of the locker, trail a pair of lures off your stern—one about 20 feet off your transom, another about 50 feet back—and set the drag on your reels to the "strike" position. You'll probably need about an ounce of weight on each lure to get it to run about two to four feet under the surface of the ocean. For salmon, you'll need a planer (which you can find at a tackle shop) to get your lure to run about 15 to 20 feet down.

If you come up on a weed line, have the helmsperson run parallel to it as close as possible without getting the weeds caught up in your lures. Bait fish often hang out in the shade of weed lines to feed on the organisms it houses, and they attract the meat fish you are after. As you troll, experiment with different types and colors of lures, and vary the depth at which you troll until you get a strike.

You'll know a fish has struck your lure when the rod tip bends sharply downward and line starts stripping off the reel. The most common reason people lose fish is because they panic when the fish strikes. Let the fish continue to take line. Yell to the helmsman that you have a strike, at which point he or she should pull the throttles slowly back to idle. Calmly remove the rod from its holder, seat its butt in the fighting belt's socket if you're using one, and brace yourself in the cockpit squarely facing the direction in which the fish is running. When you're ready, lower your rod until it is about parallel to the water. In one smooth movement, flip the drag forward into the full position and sharply pull the rod back until it is vertical—and hold it there. You may not feel anything for a second or two while the fish pulls all the slack out of the line. Then you'll feel a sharp pull as all the slack is taken up and the hook is set in the fish's mouth. If the fish doesn't pull too hard, he's fairly small. Leave your reel's drag in the full position and simply crank him up to the boat.

If a fish pulls really hard once the hook is set, quickly ease back your drag to about the halfway position. Don't panic if he's still stripping line off the reel. Let him take line until he tires. Once he quits taking line, begin to slowly crank him toward the boat, adjusting your drag as necessary to allow you to gain line, but never tighten it so snugly that he can't strip off line if he makes another run.

If only two of you are aboard, once you are sure you have the fish well hooked, let the helmsperson know. He or she should take a quick look around to make sure no other boats are in the vicinity, slip the gears to neutral, then come back to the cockpit, slip on a pair of gloves, and stand by to help you boat the fish if necessary.

In fighting any fish, never let your rod dip below about 45 degrees to the horizontal. You need its springing action to keep pressure on the fish and keep a big fish from breaking the line. If you drop the rod tip to the horizontal and release that tension, the fish often will throw the lure, or a big fish will get a direct pull on the line and break it.

Be especially alert as you get the fish up to within about ten feet of your boat's transom. Often when a fish gets close enough to see the stern of your boat, he will exert a renewed determination to escape. If that happens, you may have to ease your drag a bit and allow him to run until he calms down and tires further, then you can bring him the rest of the way to the boat. Remember to keep your rod tip well elevated to maintain pressure on the fish.

If he's less than about two feet long, the person mating for you should be able to scoop him up in the net and bring him aboard. If he's not a variety you want to keep, leave him in the net to help control him, back the hook out of his mouth, and ease him back into the water. If the fish you've brought to the boat is longer than about two feet, check to make certain it's a variety you want to keep. If not, first try dipping your rod tip toward the water. In some cases, as soon as you release tension on the line, the fish will throw the hook and swim away. If that doesn't release him, try to use your rod to lift him vertically out of the water and right up against the transom. The mate (assuming he or she is right-handed) may then be able to slip his or her right hand down the leader to the hook and work it free. If that doesn't work, have the mate try to hook the gaff under the fish's gill without seriously injuring it, bring it aboard, then remove the hook and lift the fish back over the side.

If you've caught a sizeable fish you want to keep, the mate should try to gaff him perpendicular to his side just below his dorsal fin and lift him over the transom in one smooth movement. If you've caught a sizeable fish such as a wahoo—which has a truly vicious set of teeth—or a bull dolphin which can thrash around a cockpit wildly, give him a sharp whack on top of his head right above his eyes with the billy club to quieten him down before you attempt to remove the lure.

## Casting

For cast fishing after saltwater species, I'd suggest a couple of six-foot spinning rods and reels sized to handle 15- to 20-pound test monofilament line and a good selection of artificial lures such as plugs, spinners, silver spoons, and bucktails about one to three inches in length. Tie one eye of a small swivel to the end of the line, tie a five-foot length of monofilament leader to the other eye of the swivel, then attach a snap swivel to the end of the leader to accept the eye on your lures.

In some areas it's possible to catch fish right off the bow or stern of your anchored boat. For best results, take your dink out in the early morning and late afternoon and cast along the shore of bays and marshes in 10 to 12 feet of water, especially off points or marshy areas with lots of grass, which is where fish such as sea trout tend to bed. You can also use this rig to cast for bull dolphin around any sizeable debris you run across at sea. They love to hang out in the shade of a floating plank or crate.

Bull dolphin normally travel in sizeable schools. If you catch one, you often can catch several more with a technique called "bailing." It works this way: when you get one bull dolphin solidly hooked, don't boat him immediately. Instead, bring him up to within a few feet of your boat's stern and allow him to swim around. The theory is that a hooked bull dolphin emits some sort of distress cry which attracts other bull dolphin in the school. Cast a second lure about 20 to 30 feet beyond the hooked dolphin and retrieve it with fairly rapid jerks. Chances are good you'll hook a second dolphin. Boat the first dolphin, leave the second dolphin in the water, and repeat the process of casting beyond him and retrieving in sharp jerks. It's not unusual when using this technique to boat 10 or 20 dolphin in as many minutes. Keep the rotation process up until you get no strikes on five or six casts, which probably means that the school has moved on.

## Jigging

Jigging is a type of fishing for species which normally are found at or near the bottom of a body of water near a protective hole or rocky outcropping. As a rod and reel for saltwater jigging after snapper and grouper, use the same gear you buy for trolling; for jigging after salmon in northern water, use your spinning outfits.

The jigs you'll need vary from area to area. It's best to buy the type of jig that fishermen have found works best in a particular area, and that are already made up by a local tackle shop. They'll normally have two to three single or treble hooks dangling by short stainless steel leaders off a center leader which has a one- to two-ounce weight at the bottom and a loop at the top which attaches to the snap shackle already on your line. For snapper and grouper, you'll normally need to bait the hooks with grass shrimp or small pieces of cut bait. Salmon jigs normally use small silver discs called "flashers."

Snapper and grouper hang out in deep holes in reefs. Check with local fishermen in each cruising area for the location of their favorite snapper and grouper holes. If they're not willing to share that information with you, try jigging as you drift over a reef until you start getting some strikes or your depth-sounder indicates the presence of a deep hole in the reef.

To work a jig, drop it straight down until its weight hits the bottom, crank in about two feet of line, then work the rod tip up and down in an arc of about 12 to 18 inches. If snapper or grouper are in the vicinity, they'll normally start hitting within about ten minutes. If you don't start getting strikes in one location within about 15 minutes, move on down the reef and try again.

## Skin and Scuba Diving

If you are adept at skin or scuba diving, you have an even better chance of putting seafood on the grill or in the pot, but make sure you know what laws govern spearfishing and lobster or crayfish gathering in each area you visit (Fig. 18.2). Some countries allow spearfishing if you are skin diving but not with scuba gear. Some countries allow spearfishing with devices called Hawaiian slings but not with spearfishing guns. Many nations that have lobster or crayfish (lobsters have claws; crayfish don't) in their waters allow you to catch them by hand but do not allow you to take them with spearfishing equipment, set aside certain seasons when it is illegal to gather them, and specify a minimum tail length or carapace width. If you get caught violating these laws, the penalties can be severe.

If you go spearfishing, never tie a fish you have just speared to your body while you look for another likely target. The bleeding fish trailing along behind you is an open invitation to sharks. Once you spear a fish, get him out of the water and ashore or into your boat or dinghy as quickly as possible.

**Fig. 18.2:** *Skin or scuba diving can put succulent lobster or crayfish on your table, but be sure you know and observe the laws governing their capture.*

You'll seldom find either lobster or crayfish in open water during daylight. Look for them around rocky outcroppings or under any sort of debris on the ocean bottom. The best time to go after lobster and crayfish is at night when they come out to feed. Lobsters and crayfish are virtually blind and you can get quite close to them before they detect your presence. But when you attempt to grab or net one, remember that his instinctive avenue of escape will be to retreat from any perceived threat. He normally will go backward, so if possible get a hand or net behind him. In tropical areas, you might want to pick up a "tickle stick," a fiberglass rod about five feet long and a half-inch or so in diameter with a slight curve in one end. A crayfish hiding in the rocks is likely to dart back into his hole the instant he senses your presence. Often you can ease the tickle stick right up under him, gently stroke him on his tail, and since the perceived threat seems to be behind him, he'll come straight toward you into your net.

## Gathering Clams and Oysters

If you take an observant walk at low tide along a tropical beach or an outcropping of rocks in the northern latitudes, you can often gather enough clams or oysters for a meal or at least some tasty appetizers. Clams burrow about two to three inches into sand at low tide and betray their location by spitting little bubbles out of their holes. All you have to do is dig down with a shovel or rake to bring them to the surface. Oysters cling to rocks in colonies and you can often simply pluck them off.

Opening clams and oysters involves a bit of an art. If you plan to gather either of these critters, pick yourself up a short, thick-bladed oyster knife for opening them; a long thin blade used for that purpose will almost inevitably snap. To avoid jabbing yourself, which is painful and creates the possibility of a nasty infection, wear a thick glove or cradle the clam or oyster in a thick pad. Insert your oyster knife just to one side of the animal's hinge and twist sharply.

## GUESTS ABOARD

Consider this scenario:

You've invited friends to fly in to meet you on a Caribbean island on a Friday afternoon and cruise with you for a week. You arrive at the agreed-on harbor at the appointed time, but your guests don't show on schedule. You place half a dozen expensive High Seas radiotelephone calls trying to locate them with no success. They finally show up Saturday evening and explain that they had to postpone their departure because their dog was ill. They'd have called to inform you of the delay but didn't know how to reach you.

They each lug aboard your vessel two huge, hardside suitcases which you have no place to store. The wife is wearing high heels that gouge your topsides, and the husband is puffing a big black cigar. Over the next seven days he smells up your entire vessel, scatters ashes all over the flying bridge, and burns a hole in the salon settee. You need to get underway first thing Sunday morning to keep to the schedule you've laid out, but the husband has failed to bring his allergy medication. The only pharmacy on the island is not open on Sundays, so you must delay your departure until Monday. You finally get underway and have barely cleared the breakwater before the wife gets seasick. You give her a scopolamine patch, but it's too late for it to do much good so she spends the entire day moaning and groaning in the salon. In midafternoon she does manage to struggle down to the guest head and promptly clogs the toilet up with a tampon. You spend the morning of the following day unclogging the toilet, then the afternoon searching for Perrier water, which the wife insists is the only liquid she ever drinks. The husband ignores your warnings about the tropical sun and by Wednesday is so badly sunburned you must divert to the nearest island that has a doctor. While you're taking the husband to the doctor, the wife goes reef walking in her bare feet and steps on a sea urchin. She spends the next two days with her foot propped up while your wife brings her Perrier water. The husband is unhappy because he always has lamb chops on Thursday evening and can't believe you don't have any on board. On Friday he starts complaining about an aching tooth. "I'm not surprised," he announces. "It's been twinging on and off for a month or so." You offer penicillin to fight the infection but he's allergic to it.

You preserve your sanity with the thought that in twenty-four more hours you can deliver your guests to the airport and get them off your boat. A storm front delays your arrival at the island from which they are to depart and they miss their flight. You grimace and try to book them on the next day's flight. "I'm sorry, sir," the ticket agent informs you, "we don't have any flights leaving the island until Wednesday."

It doesn't have to be this way. If you will be having family and friends aboard as guests—particularly if they are not experienced boaters—it's a good idea to prepare a standard letter you can send them well in advance of their planned visit to get a few basics out of the way. Some of the areas you might want to cover include:

1. A suggestion that they tend to any potential medical problems in advance of their departure and instructions that they bring with them any special medications and/or food and drink they require. If they are prone to seasickness, suggest they obtain a supply of scopolamine patches and apply the first one six hours before your planned sailing.

2. Information regarding passports and any visas, immunizations, or health certificates they will be required to have and specific instructions on your meeting date, time, and place.

3. Instructions on how to reach you by VHF or High Seas marine operator. Include the telephone number they should call to reach an appropriate marine operator, the name of your vessel, its radio call sign, and your approximate location in the two weeks or so prior to their arrival. If you will be meeting in the boondocks, it's a good idea to schedule a contact three or four days prior to their departure to confirm that everyone is still on schedule.

4. A list of the clothing they should bring appropriate to the climate of the area you will be cruising. This is a good place to ask them to wear only boating shoes aboard to protect both themselves from a fall and your topsides from scarring. If you'll be cruising in the tropics, make sure the list includes a broad-brimmed hat and at least one pair of long pants to avoid sunburn, a light jacket or sweater for cool nights, and a pair of old sneakers or plastic sandals for reef walking. Also let them know what kind of clothes they should bring for evenings ashore.

   If storage space in their stateroom will be limited, caution them not to bring more clothing than they really need and suggest they bring soft-sided luggage that can be rolled up and stuffed in a drawer or locker.

Once your guests arrive on board, it's a good idea to have a typewritten sheet or two for them to read covering the essentials of life on board. Many experienced cruisers I have visited with put this information in the guest stateroom and ask their guests on arrival to read it at their first opportunity. If your vessel is not equipped with a watermaker, for instance, instruct them to take "Navy showers" (i.e., wet themselves down, turn off the water, lather up, then rinse) to conserve your water supply. This is also the place to tell them that aside from toilet paper, they should put nothing in your marine head that they haven't eaten first.

Include in the sheet any ways of doing things aboard your vessel which you, as its captain, feel are appropriate. If you prefer your guests not try to handle lines or anchoring or take the dinghy out alone, for instance, or prefer that they restrict smoking to the cockpit or aft deck, this sheet is the place to mention it.

You don't want to alarm anyone, but your sheet should include instructions on what your guests are to do in the unlikely event of an abandon-ship situation. Also suggest that at night they keep their passport, eyeglasses, any special medications, and a bit of cash in a sealable plastic bag by their bunk which they can grab quickly should you have to leave the vessel hurriedly.

## CHAPTER 19

# MAINTAINING THE ESSENTIALS

• • •

During a cruise you probably won't be able to maintain your vessel as immaculately as if she were tied to your home dock, but if you don't keep up with essential maintenance on a consistent basis, the penalty is likely to be at least a significant loss in your vessel's value, which could cost you hundreds or thousands of dollars to restore. Even worse, lack of essential maintenance could result in the failure of a critical part or system just when you need it most. On the plus side, a consistent program of maintenance will help protect your investment in your boat and alert you to potential problems so you can correct them before they cause a serious difficulty.

Begin your maintenance program before you ever depart on a cruise.

Start by assembling a complete collection of owner's manuals for every basic system and important piece of equipment on your vessel, and organize them alphabetically or in some other logical grouping in a set of loose-leaf notebooks. Extract from them the manufacturer's maintenance recommendations and compile that information into a maintenance calendar for your particular boat that tells you what maintenance tasks you need to perform daily, weekly, monthly, semiannually, annually, or after a certain number of operating hours. Most manufacturers' literature will also include a list of spare parts, supplies, and tools you'll need to perform recommended maintenance; make sure you get all of them aboard. It's a good idea to develop an inventory system that tells you where spare parts and supplies are stowed aboard your vessel and helps you keep track of their use so you can replace depleted supplies at the earliest opportunity. Also make a list of manufacturers' hotline telephone numbers you can call to ask questions or order parts if the need arises. For offshore cruisers, some manufacturers will list a single-sideband radio channel they monitor.

If you need a vital part in a remote location and cannot contact the manufacturer or supplier direct, try calling Cruise Net via a land line or High Seas marine operator at (212) 741-1439. This company specializes in locating yacht parts and shipping them worldwide, and has connections with several large boat yards that can even fabricate parts that are no longer available. If you have a really difficult problem or installation, they can even send you a mechanic. Of course they will charge you for any services they perform.

## ENGINE MAINTENANCE

Your most critical maintenance tasks will be to keep your main engine(s) and the engine that powers your AC electrical generator humming smoothly.

If you are not intimately familiar with the care and feeding of a diesel engine, I strongly recommend that you attend one of the owner maintenance courses offered by diesel engine distributors. You can find out where and when these courses are held by contacting the distributors in your area of the make of engines aboard your vessel or contacting the manufacturer's home office. Owner maintenance courses are normally held over about two days, during which you learn the basics of a diesel engine's four flow systems—fuel, oil, coolant, and air—and the specifics of how those systems are handled in your vessel's particular make of engine. If at all possible, attend a course that covers the make of engine with which your vessel is equipped because there are significant differences between the flow systems of two-cycle diesels manufactured by companies like Detroit Diesel and four-cycle diesels made by companies like Caterpillar and Cummins. It's also best to attend a course that is tailored to the specific concerns of the owners of marine diesels rather than engines used in trucks or industrial equipment, even it if involves a bit of travel and some additional expense on your part. The best of these courses will not only cover the theory of diesel engine operation but will give you some hands-on instruction in such matters as timing, disabling, and changing an injector. If you can't find such a course in your area, you can get at least a general overview of diesel engine maintenance by monitoring a diesel engine mechanic's course at a local community college. If attending any kind of diesel engine course is out of the question, at least get a good diesel mechanic to walk you through a diesel's basic operation and show you how to change fuel and oil filters, replace a water pump impeller, prime a dry engine, and clear an air lock.

## FUEL FLOW MAINTENANCE

Maintaining a dependable flow of clean fuel to the engines on board your vessel begins with the fuel itself and the tanks in which it is stored.

The diesel fuel you take on board your vessel is likely to be full of all manner of contaminants, such as rust from storage tanks, sludge, and plain old dirt. But the most troublesome contaminants are algae, fungi, and other microorganisms that live off nutrients in the fuel itself. If their growth is not prevented or checked, they can congregate together in large strings, clumps, or mats of black, brown, or green "slime" which can clog your primary and secondary fuel filters and damage metal fuel tanks and rubber gaskets. At best, this buildup will require you to change your fuel filters much more frequently than if you were working with clean fuel; at worst it can actually shut off your engine's fuel supply which—under Murphy's Law—invariably will happen when you are trying to navigate a twisting, poorly marked channel at night in the midst of a raging storm.

There is not much you can do to improve the quality of the fuel you buy. You can, however, maintain good fuel-handling procedures and treat your fuel with biocides to inhibit microorganism growth. If your vessel has

377

dark globules in its fuel filters or its engine room has a faint odor of rotten eggs, it probably has slime buildup in its tanks. You can also check for the presence of microorganisms in diesel fuel with test kits available from your fuel dealer. Two of the best of those are the SaniCheck kit from Fuel Quality Services, Inc., P.O. Box 317, Buford, GA 30518, or the Microb Monitor Test Kit produced by Boron Oil Co., 1876 Guildhall Building, Cleveland, OH 44115.

If your vessel shows signs of significant microbial buildup, you would be wise to clean its tanks thoroughly before embarking on an extended voyage. The best way to do that is to drain and properly dispose of all the fuel on board and have the tanks thoroughly cleaned with pressurized steam. If your vessel's tanks don't have clean-out ports or are otherwise inaccessible, fill them with fresh fuel. (If necessary, drain off enough fuel to allow you to add at least one third of their capacity in fresh fuel to allow proper mixing and dilution of the biocide you are going to add.)

As the fuel is flowing in, add to it a biocide in the proportions directed by its manufacturer. In the case of Biobor JF from U.S. Borax, for example, the concentration should be 270 parts per million (2.8 fluid ounces per 100 gallons of each tank's capacity). Another good biocide is Kathon FP 1.5 from Rohm and Haas, but note that its recommended concentrations are half those of Biobor JF. Do not exceed the biocide manufacturer's recommended concentrations. Allow the biocide to work at least twenty-four hours, preferably forty-eight hours, before operating your vessel. As you burn the fuel, the biocide will circulate through your vessel's entire fuel system to clean it. As you burn this load of treated fuel, the microorganisms destroyed by the biocide will migrate to your fuel filters. If you suspect you have a severe case of microbial buildup, this could shut down your fuel system entirely. Restrict your first several hours of operation to fair weather and areas where you can deal with a shutdown, if it occurs, until you can clear it. Carry at least a case of fresh primary filter elements and half a case of secondary filter elements on board, check your fuel filters at least every half-hour, and change them if they begin to clog.

Even with clean tanks, your battle against microorganisms isn't over. They can still get into your tanks in fuel you take on and even condense into your fuel from the air that flows into your tanks through their vents.

Though these bedeviling little critters subsist on nutrients in the fuel itself, they cannot exist without water. Therefore, your first line of defense is keeping water out of your fuel. Since diesel fuel is the lighter of the two fluids, most of the water it contains or that evaporates out of the air in the tank and mixes with it will eventually settle to the bottom of the tanks of a vessel at rest. Of course you will prevent the water in your fuel from reaching your engine by trapping most of it in the fuel/water separators on your engine(s), but that doesn't do anything to prevent water getting into your tanks in the first place. One way to do that would be to install fuel/water filters in your fuel inlet hoses to separate as much water (and other contaminants) as possible out of the fuel before it ever gets into your tanks. I know few cruisers who do that, but it's an idea that could pay big dividends—particularly for the long-distance cruiser who must take on fuel in remote ports that contains God-only-knows what. Some cruisers add isopropyl alcohol to their fuel as a water precipitant. This is not a good idea, particularly in vessels with fiberglass fuel tanks built prior to about 1980, as it can deteriorate the resins used up until then. Isopropyl alcohol in concentrations of 1 pint per 124 gallons of fuel is appropriate only to prevent diesel fuel from freezing during the winter in northern climates.

Your second line of defense is to keep your fuel treated with a biocide to inhibit the growth of any bugs that get into it. For this, you can use a lower level of concentration than is needed for a cleanup. In the case of Biobor JF, this maintenance level would be 135 ppm or 1.4 fluid ounces per 100 gallons of fuel. If you operate your boat only about twenty-five hours a month, you should add biocide at a maintenance level to every load of fuel you take on. If you run your engine(s) more than about twenty-five hours a month and thus consume fuel rapidly, you need to add biocide at a maintenance level to only about every third or fourth load of fuel you take aboard.

A biocide is about the only additive you should put in your fuel on a regular basis. In particular, stay away from any additives that contain heavy concentrations of isopropyl alcohol or metallic substances such as barium. If you are getting heavy carbon buildup on your diesel engine's injectors which causes it to run rough or emit heavy smoke, the first step is to have a good mechanic check their fuel flow adjustment. If that doesn't solve the problem, ask him about using a detergent dispersant, which eases the surface tension of the molecules in fuel and helps prevent particulate matter from conglomerating. Some cruisers favor STP's Concentrated Injector Cleaner for this purpose, but I would not add it to my fuel without the advice of a diesel mechanic I trusted.

Follow your engine manufacturer's recommendations regarding fuel filters exactly. Most diesel engine makers specify a 30-micron element for the

379

primary filter and a 10- to 12-micron element for the secondary filter. Some skippers try to use a 2-micron element in the secondary filter on the theory that because it is finer it will trap more contaminants, but unless your engine manufacturer specifies such an element, don't use it. A 2-micron element is so fine that the fuel pump has to work harder to force fuel through it. The reduced fuel flow can prevent adequate fuel reaching the injectors and curtail the engine's performance. Change your fuel filters religiously according to the manufacturer's suggested schedule. Under normal operation, that will be at least every 300 operating hours.

Another good idea is to install mechanical fuel pressure gauges on the outlet side of each engine's secondary fuel filter. If the fuel is flowing properly, these gauges should show about 60 to 70 psi when the engine is running at 1,800 rpm. A drop in their normal readings will alert you that either your primary or secondary fuel filters—or both—are clogging up and need to be changed. Without these pressure gauges, you won't know that clogged filters have shut off the fuel supply to the engine until it stops. If the needle on a fuel pressure gauge flutters, it is indicating that air is leaking into the fuel system.

If a diesel engine begins to run rough, suddenly sounds louder, begins to misfire, or will not produce as many no-load rpm at full throttle it as it did formerly, the problem may be air leaking into its fuel system. You can check for air in a diesel engine's fuel system by performing a "spillback test": Loosen the fuel return line where it enters the tank; put the end of the line in the bottom of a gallon bucket and run the engine at about 1,200 rpm. If the fuel is cloudy or air bubbles to the surface, you have an air leak, and the air is probably getting into the system somewhere between the fuel tank and the fuel pump. (If a leak is after the fuel pump in the fuel flow system, it will not suck air into the system but will spray fuel out of the engine's fuel line or one of its fittings.) If the fuel in the primary filter bowl is cloudy, the air leak is between the tank and the primary filter. If you cannot find any leaks between the fuel tank and the fuel pump but the engine is still running rough, disconnect the fuel line on the inlet side of the fuel pump, connect a flexible hose to it, and run the other end of the hose to a fuel tank. If the engine continues to run rough, your problem may well be a leak in the fuel pump itself.

Another cause for a diesel engine running rough is a clogged, blown, or mistimed injector. To check the injectors, remove the engine's valve cover and run the engine in neutral at around 1,200 rpm. Use a screwdriver to disable each injector in turn by holding down its follower. If an injector is functioning properly, you should notice a significant decrease in rpm as you temporarily disable it. If you notice no difference in rpm, the injector is not functioning properly.

To retime an injector, make certain both exhaust valves are open and the injector is all the way up, then loosen the rocker arm linkage and insert the injector timing tool between the rocker arm linkage and the injector follower. Adjust the rocker arm linkage so that the timing tool just clears the top of the injector follower.

If a diesel engine suddenly begins to emit heavy black smoke, the problem may be a "blown" injector, which most often results from a minuscule amount of water in the fuel getting into the sac at the tip of the injector below the needle valve. The heat of compression inside the cylinder (which normally reaches about 1,000 degrees Fahrenheit) boils the water which loosens carbon inside the tip. That loosened carbon plugs up most or all of the tiny holes in the injector tip which measure only five to ten thousandths of an inch in diameter. On the next compression stroke, the pressure inside the injector tip goes from its normal 20,000 psi of pressure to over 50,000 psi, which literally blows off the tip of the injector. The tip itself will be blown out through the exhaust. The heavy black smoke is the result of unatomized fuel being sprayed into the cylinder. The only remedy for a blown injector is to replace it with a spare or disable it. Before changing or disabling an injector, be certain to close the valves in both the fuel supply and return lines. If you don't have a spare injector aboard, disable a blown injector by diverting fuel from it: remove the spring screw, disengage the rack, then install your shortest fuel jumper from the blown injector's fuel inlet to its fuel return as a fuel bypass.

Any time you work on your engine's injector, you should retighten all critical bolts with a torque wrench to the manufacturer's recommendations listed in your owner's manual. If the owner's manual doesn't list the torque, use 90 foot-pounds of pressure on the rocker arm bracket bolts; 25 foot-pounds on the injector hold-down bolts; and 12 to 14 pounds on the fuel jumper line nuts. Be sure you don't overtighten the fuel jumper line nuts, as you could crack the line's flaring and create a leak. To check for leaks after retightening a fuel jumper line nut, replace the valve cover, run the engine a few minutes, shut the engine down, then remove the valve cover. You should see a small pool of lubricating oil around the joint where the fuel jumper line joins its nut. If you do not see a puddle of oil there, the fuel jumper is leaking and must be replaced. Also check for any clean streaks on the cylinder head, which indicate fuel leakage. If fuel leaks around the cylinder head are not corrected, the fuel could catch fire. At the least, it will go directly into the lubricating oil sump and be recirculated back through the engine, which could destroy it.

## Oil Flow Maintenance

The primary mission of a diesel engine's oil flow system is to lubricate all its moving parts to prevent metal-to-metal contact and thus excessive wear. The key to doing that is maintaining the oil's pressure at normal operating speeds at the manufacturer's recommended levels, which usually will be between 50 and 70 psi. If an engine's oil pressure does not rise to at least 50 psi within about 10 seconds of starting it, or at the engine's normal operating speed its oil pressure drops below 50 psi or rises above 70 psi, shut the engine down immediately, determine the cause of the incorrect pressure, and correct it before restarting the engine. Operating a diesel engine with inadequate oil pressure can destroy it in a matter of minutes. Low oil pressure can result from an inadequate supply of oil in the crankcase sump; a leak in the oil supply line; or a malfunctioning oil pump. Excessively high oil pressure can result from coolant or fuel getting into the oil flow system.

The oil flow system's secondary mission is to help extract excess heat generated by the engine's operation. Some high-horsepower marine diesels generate so much excess heat they use oil coolers to help extract it. Check your engine manufacturer's specification for oil temperature in normal operation, which usually will be around 200 to 235 degrees or about 20 degrees higher than the engine's coolant temperature. If an engine's oil temperature falls below that figure or rises above it, shut the engine down immediately, locate the problem, and correct it before restarting the engine.

Diesel engines are designed to consume a little oil during normal operation, with a quart every 10 to 12 operating hours a typical rate. You should check your engine's oil at the end of every day's run. After shutting down an engine that has been run long enough to get up to its normal operating temperature, wait at least 15 minutes before checking its oil level to give all the oil time to drain down into the sump and show up on the dipstick. If you will be running for more than 12 hours, shut the engine down at the end of that period and check its oil level. Keep the level of oil in the sump within no more than a sixteenth of an inch of the "Full" or

"F" mark on the dipstick, and be sure you never overfill the sump. Be especially cautious if an engine appears to suddenly quit using oil or appears to have more oil in the sump after a period of operation than it did at the start. Either could be an indication that fuel or coolant is leaking into the lubricating oil system, and the results could be disastrous.

Be sure you use lubricating oil that meets the engine manufacturer's specifications. For normal operation, that will be straight (not multigrade), heavy-duty oil with an SAE viscosity grade of 40 and an API classification of CD I or CD II. Its total base number, or TBN (which measures the oil's ability to neutralize acids), should be between 7 and 10, and its sulfated ash content should be below 1.0 percent. Be sure you use a detergent oil. (Each time a diesel cylinder fires, some of the exhaust gas blows by the piston's compression rings and gets into the crankcase where it mixes with the engine's lubricating oil. Detergent oil helps keep those contaminants in suspension in the oil until it is removed at the next oil change.)

For extended operations in areas such as South and Central America and Mexico, where diesel fuel normally contains higher levels of sulfur (above 0.5 percent) than is found in fuel available in the U.S., you should use an oil with a total base number higher than 10, even though it contains more than 1.0 percent sulfated ash. You will also need to decrease the interval between oil changes, which is discussed below.

As long as an oil meets the engine manufacturer's specifications, brand name means nothing and you can safely use the brand on which you can get the best price. Never use oil additives.

Be sure you use only oil filters that meet the engine manufacturer's specifications. In most cases those specifications will call for a 12-micron element. Change oil filters every time you change the oil. If you don't and an oil filter becomes clogged, you won't know it as the oil will simply bypass the clogged filter and recirculate potentially damaging contaminants through the engine. (Marine diesel engines are designed to have lubricating oil bypass the oil filter when the engine is started cold so it will be heated to operating temperature more rapidly.)

Also make sure you understand and rigorously follow the engine manufacturer's recommendations on oil change intervals. For normal cruising, most marine diesel engine manufacturers recommend changing lubricating oil after every 150 hours of operation. If you do extensive cruising in the waters of South or Central America or Mexico where diesel fuel contains high levels of sulfur, once you begin burning diesel taken aboard in those areas you should use a lubricating oil with a TBN above 10 to help neutralize the acids that high-sulfur fuel contains and shorten the interval between oil changes to get that sulfur out of your engine. If you don't, it will eat up the cylinder liners and cause damage that will be extremely expensive to repair. To be on the safe side, I recommend that if you use an oil with a TBN of 20 to 30 you reduce your oil-changing interval to 100 hours. If you are using an oil with a TBN of 10 to 19, change oil every 50 hours. An even more scientific answer to the problem would be to send a sample of your engine oil into a laboratory for analysis after about every 500 hours of operating in those areas and follow the recommendations on oil-change intervals contained with the lab's test report.

## Coolant Flow Maintenance

The whole purpose of the cooling system on a marine diesel engine is to get rid of the excess heat the engine's operation generates. Most marine diesel cooling systems consist of two parts: a sealed fresh water system which circulates coolant through the engine to absorb excess heat, then through one side of a heat exchanger where the heat is dissipated; and a raw water system which picks up sea water, circulates it through the other side of the heat exchanger to extract the heat from the fresh water, then dumps the water with its captured heat overboard. A few marine diesels don't have a raw water system but circulate fresh water through a keel cooler to dissipate its captured heat directly into the sea. If a marine diesel's cooling system is working properly, the temperature of its coolant will remain between roughly 170 and 190 degrees Fahrenheit.

You should check the level of coolant in your engine's reservoir after every run and keep it about two inches below the fill cap to allow for expansion. If possible, use distilled water or the purified water from a reverse-osmosis water maker. Nondistilled or nonpurified water contains large amounts of minerals. When it is heated, those minerals precipitate out of the water and adhere as a whitish scale to the hottest part of the engine, which normally will be the cylinder head (also called the fire deck). As that scale builds up, it acts as a very effective insulator, which can destroy your cooling system's efficiency. One sixteenth of an inch of scale, in fact, equals the insulation of about four inches of cast iron and can reduce heat transfer by up to 40 percent. If your cooling system cannot efficiently dissipate the excess heat your engine generates, the metal overheats and raises the temperature of your lubricating oil. As the temperature of the lubricating oil exceeds about 250 degrees, it breaks down. The result is metal-to-metal wear, which further increases the temperature inside the engine until the engine fails, most often with a cracked cylinder head. If you encounter an engine with heavy scale buildup, the best product I have found for cleaning it out is the 2015 Twin Pac Cooling System Cleaner and Conditioner produced by Nalco Chemical Company.

If you operate your vessel in freezing temperatures, you should of course use the recommended concentration of antifreeze. Be sure you use only a low-phosphate, low-silicate permanent type antifreeze such as that produced by Nalco. If your cruising is only in tropical areas where freezing is not a danger, I don't recommend using antifreeze at all as it is less efficient in dissipating heat than water alone.

Another problem with cooling water is the rust it can cause, and you must add a good rust inhibitor to your coolant and keep it up to the correct concentration. Don't count on antifreeze alone to protect your engine against rust. Even the best antifreeze contains only minute amounts of rust inhibitor and you need additional additives. Use a nonchromate inhibitor such as Nalco Chemical's Nalcool 3000. Properly inhibited coolant can also help protect an engine against cavitation pitting and keep the coolant's pH level between 7.5 and 11, which is where it needs to be to avoid lead phosphate corrosion (also called "solder bloom"). You can buy a test kit from Nalco which will tell you when the concentration of inhibitor in your cooling system is at its correct level. If you find you must add water to your cooling system frequently, be aware that in the process you are also diluting your rust inhibitor. If that's the case, you should test your coolant every month or so and, if necessary, bring the concentration of inhibitor back up to the recommended level. Don't use chromate inhibitors. Chromate is highly destructive to some engine seals, and doesn't get along with the ethylene glycol in antifreeze. The two in combination will turn your coolant into a dark green gel or slime which will plug up your coolant system, fry your engine, and destroy it. If you encounter an engine whose coolant has been turned to gel, the best product for cleaning up its coolant system is Nalco's Nalprep 2001.

The flow of coolant through your engine and its heat exchanger is controlled by a thermostat, which normally is located in a housing on the top of the engine at its front end and reads the coolant's temperature through a sensor mounted in or near the heat exchanger. (Engines whose cylinders

385

are in-line normally have one thermostat and one sensor; V-block engines normally have a separate thermostat and a sensor on each bank of cylinders.) When you start a cold engine, the thermostat normally remains closed to circulate the water only through the engine without going through the heat exchanger to bring the engine up to its operating temperature more quickly. When the engine gets up to operating temperature, the thermostat opens to circulate water through the heat exchanger. If a thermostat fails, it normally will do so in the open position. The first sign of thermostat failure in the open position will be that the engine is slow to reach its operating temperature. If a thermostat fails in the closed position, you'll know soon enough as the engine will quickly overheat because its coolant is not being circulated through the heat exchanger. You should, of course, include several thermostats and thermostat sensors, along with their associated seals and gaskets, in your spare parts inventory and replace a failed thermostat or sensor immediately.

One other problem you may experience with a coolant thermostat is the buildup of scale on its sensor or the thermostat itself, which, due to the scale's insulating qualities, will result in false readings. If you notice your temperature gauge reading lower than normal, check the sensor and the thermostat. If either exhibits a white scale, it's a sign of problems in the coolant itself. Scraping the scale off will provide only a temporary fix as the scale is likely to reform quickly. The best way to solve the problem is to clean the engine up with Nalco's 2015 Twin Pac product, then flush the system and refill it with water and Nalcool 3000 in the recommended concentration.

Most diesel engines have pumps on both their fresh water and raw water cooling systems. Keep an eye on the housings of both pumps for any signs of leaking, which indicates the seal is deteriorating and should be replaced. Any time you have your boat hauled out of the water, be sure to close the sea cocks on your raw-water inlets in the hull to keep from draining the raw water pump and having to reprime it. Put your engine's ignition keys over the seacock to make certain you don't return the boat to the water and start the engines without reopening the sea cocks.

## Air Flow Maintenance

A proper amount of air flowing into a diesel engine where it is mixed with fuel is essential to the engine's proper operation. Once the air/fuel mixture is burned by the engine's heat of compression, the air must be properly exhausted from the engine to help carry away excess heat and contaminants.

The key to maintaining a proper flow of air into the engine is to keep its air filters (sometimes called air silencers) clean. Some marine diesel manufacturers install replaceable paper filters on their engines' air inlets. Others use permanent type air filters which must be cleaned periodically. Check your owner's manual to determine the type of air filters with which your engine is equipped and follow the manufacturer's recommendations for replacement or cleaning.

The first sign of an engine getting an insufficient supply of air will be black smoke from its exhaust, which is the result of incomplete fuel combustion due to a lack of air in the air/fuel mixture.

Some marine diesel engines require so much air for proper combustion that they are equipped with turbochargers, which force additional air into the combustion process. A turbocharger is powered by the engine's exhaust gases flowing over its turbine wheel, which turns at up to 100,000 rpm and spins its compressor wheel at the same speed. The shaft connecting the turbine wheel and the compressor wheel lies in an aluminum or bronze bushing, which reaches temperatures of up to 900 degrees Fahrenheit and must be continuously lubricated by an external oil line running from the engine's cylinder block to the top of the turbocharger housing. Turbocharger maintenance therefore begins with keeping the engine's lubricating oil clean by changing the oil and oil filters and replacing or cleaning the engine's air filters at appropriate intervals.

You can extend the life of turbochargers by starting and stopping your engine correctly. If a turbocharged engine has not been run for more than about two months, before cranking it, remove the oil supply line from the top of the turbocharger housing, pour about a pint of clean engine oil into the housing, and rotate the compressor wheel by hand to lubricate the shaft. Add enough oil to fill the housing, then replace the oil supply line securely. After starting a turbocharged engine, allow it to idle for two to three minutes before applying a load to ensure that the turbocharger shaft is properly lubricated. Never shut down a turbocharger engine that has reached normal operating temperatures without running it at idle speed for three to five minutes, which gives the turbocharger time to cool. If you shut it down without allowing proper cooling, the 900-degree heat inside the turbocharger can cook the lubricating oil around its shaft and lead to shaft failure.

With the engine turned off, you should also periodically remove the air inlet housing and check the turbocharger's compressor wheel and its housing for excessive dust or dirt buildup. If they are dirty, clean them and replace or clean the air filter. Also make sure the compressor wheel is not making contact with its housing and its shaft turns easily but does not have any play in it. If the shaft does have play in it, the bearings may soon fail. If the bearing fails while the turbocharger is operating, you will hear a high whining noise and may notice excessive vibration. Rebuilding a failed turbocharger is not a job most cruising boat owners will be equipped or knowledgeable enough to undertake. Unless you have a spare turbocharger aboard and can install it, do not operate the engine until you can get it to a qualified diesel mechanic who has the parts and know-how to rebuild the turbocharger.

## MARINE TRANSMISSION MAINTENANCE

Your marine transmissions are likely to be the least troublesome equipment on your vessel. About all you should have to do to maintain them properly is to make sure their fluid level is correct every time you prepare to start your engines and replace the fluid (and filters if your transmissions are equipped with them) according to the manufacturer's recommendations.

## UNDERWATER GEAR MAINTENANCE

You should have your vessel hauled, thoroughly scrub its bottom, and check all underwater fittings at least once a year. When operating in tropical waters, a haulout and bottom cleaning every six months is advisable. You'll usually need to repaint the bottom about every two years in northern climates and annually in tropical waters.

While your vessel is out of the water, check all its through-hull fittings, impellers, and underwater gear carefully and clean, repair, or replace any items that are clogged, cracked, or loose. Check your rudder zincs frequently and replace any that show excessive deterioration. Pay special attention to your props. Even a small ding can reduce their efficiency, cause you to burn added fuel, and induce vibration, which can create its own nightmares.

Between haulouts, go over the side at least once a month with a mask and snorkel and check for algae buildup, which can dramatically slow your speed and increase your fuel consumption. As soon as a thin coat of algae builds up on your hull, scrub it clean or the buildup will accelerate rapidly.

## HULL AND TOPSIDE MAINTENANCE

Thoroughly scrub your topsides down with a mild detergent after every offshore run to remove salt, rinse the detergent off thoroughly and chamois all exposed surfaces dry. Pay special attention to completely drying stainless steel posts and railings to prevent rust and varnished surfaces to prevent spotting. You'll find that if you go over the fiberglass portions of your topsides about every three months with a good fiberglass polish, dirt and grime will be less likely to adhere to them.

You probably won't have the time or inclination on an extended cruise to keep any wood trim on your vessel in top shape, but do practice at least preventive maintenance. At the first sign of clouding or pitting in varnished surfaces, sand the area smooth, apply a thin, even coat of varnish, allow the area to dry thoroughly, sand lightly, and apply a second coat of varnish. If you allow clouded or pitted varnish to go very long without treatment, you will have to strip the entire part down to bare wood and start building up your varnish protection from scratch. In the tropics, oiled exposed wood should be reoiled about every six weeks. If it goes unprotected for longer than that, it is likely to dry out and crack.

## ELECTRICAL SYSTEM MAINTENANCE

The primary enemies of your vessel's electrical system will be chafing of its wiring and moisture, which leads to corrosion around its terminals. As Murphy's Law dictates, a short or corrosion will wipe out a vital instrument just when you can least afford to do without it. It's a good idea to go through your vessel about once a month checking those sections of your vessel's wiring which normally are inaccessible for signs of chafing. If you notice chafe wearing through an electrical wire, wrap the wire immediately with electrical tape and secure or pad it so it will not be chafed again. If you notice corrosion building up on your electrical system's terminals, shut down the circuit, clean the corrosion off with a stiff brush or scrape the terminal down to bare metal, then spray the terminals with a good moisture inhibitor such as CRC. If corrosion builds up on your battery terminals, scrape them and the battery connectors down to bare metal, reinstall the connectors securely, then smear them liberally with petroleum jelly to help seal out moisture.

## ELECTRONICS MAINTENANCE

The main thing you can do to protect your vessel's marine electronics is to keep moisture out of them. About once a month, check the terminals and connectors on the back or underside of your communications and navigation units for signs of corrosion. If you spot any, clean it up and spray the area with a good moisture inhibitor.

# PART FIVE

· · ·

# IN FOREIGN WATERS

· · ·

# INTERNATIONAL BUOYAGE, LIGHTING, AND CHART SYSTEMS

• • •

Once you have become familiar with the buoyage, aids to navigation lighting, and chart systems used in U.S. waters, you will have little difficulty translating that knowledge to the waters of other nations—provided you recognize a few basic facts and understand a couple of fundamental differences.

## Buoyage Systems

In Chapter 2 we explained the basic buoyage system now in use in U.S. territorial waters—the International Association of Lighthouse Authorities' System B—Combined Cardinal and Lateral System (red to starboard)—and pointed out that that same system is in effect in North and South America, the Bahamas, Korea, and Japan. Navigation using the buoyage systems of Canada, Mexico, and along the northern coast of South America, therefore, is little different technically from navigating in U.S. waters.

Nations on the continents of Europe, Africa, Asia (excluding Korea and Japan), and Australia employ the IALA System A—Combined Cardinal and Lateral System (red to port)—in which red marks are to port when entering a channel from seaward.

Having made that basic distinction, however, I must note that some confusion can arise in the Caribbean, where areas that physically are in IALA Region B and therefore might be expected to use the System B of buoyage do not, due principally to their political status. The Windward Islands of Guadeloupe and Martinique, for instance, are departments of the government of France and employ the IALA System A buoyage used by their motherland. The islands of Aruba, Bonaire, and Curaçao off the northern coast of Venezuela are dependencies of the Netherlands, and also employ System A buoyage.

One other fact that should be noted is that among the favored cruising grounds of American yachtsmen, Canada has developed a buoyage system whose completeness, accuracy, and maintenance equals that in the U.S. The Bahamas, Mexico, South America, and many of the islands of the Caribbean, however, have not had the resources to develop and maintain so extensive a system. In many of those areas—particularly outside major commercial roadsteads—aids to navigation are inaccurate or nonexistent and the cruising yachtsman is very much on his own. In those areas, proper navigation by alert coastal piloting and all the electronic means at the helmsperson's disposal is an absolute must.

## Aids to Navigation Lighting Systems

One major advantage of the IALA Systems A and B to the cruising yachtsman is that light patterns and their meanings are now essentially standard throughout the world—with the important difference that in System A red is to port entering from seaward and in System B red is to starboard entering from seaward.

In the varied cruising grounds the world has to offer, there may be some minor differences in buoy shapes, but the meaning of their lights—where they exist—is the same.

## Charting Systems

Between the U.S. Defense Mapping Agency, the British Admiralty, the Canadian Hydrographic Service, and the French government's maritime mapping agencies, there are few areas of the world that are not charted with reasonably up-to-date accuracy. Furthermore, in the past fifty years the symbols used in nautical charts have become highly standardized, with the English language as their basis. Virtually any of the international charts available through the sources listed in the Appendix will utilize symbols that are readily recognizable to a knowledgeable American cruiser.

Most charts published by foreign nations do present depth and height in meters rather than the feet-and-fathoms system employed on most charts produced in the U.S. Most foreign charts, however, include an easy-to-use scale for converting meters to both feet and fathoms. Should you encounter a foreign chart that utilizes kilometers, convert distances to nautical miles by multiplying kilometers by .54.

# CHAPTER 21

# KEEPING LEGAL

• • •

In most cases, the legal aspects of cruising the waters of foreign nations involve little more than a bit of bureaucratic red tape and the payment of a few dollars' worth of fees. You can, however, save yourself a good deal of grief and money if you know what to expect and make proper preparations. Here's what to look for:

## Leaving U.S. Waters

Prior to departing on a voyage outside U.S. waters, you should, of course, make certain your ship's papers (documentation papers issued by the federal government or registration papers issued by the state in which the vessel is principally used) are up-to-date. Also be sure you have proof of insurance covering the waters you intend to cruise and know how to contact your insurer quickly in case you have a problem. Each person on board should also have a U.S. passport that will remain valid for the duration of their voyage and it should contain any visas that are required in advance. Each person aboard should also have a current International Certificate of Vaccination, which records any immunizations required by the countries you will be visiting. If you plan to do any driving in other countries, you should also have a valid International Driver's Permit, which can be obtained through the American Automobile Association. You should also have a good supply of crew lists, which give the name, age, nationality, and home address of all on board, or a typewriter and plenty of carbon paper to make them up en route.

If you have on board expensive new items manufactured abroad such as still and video cameras or portable electronics, you might want to register them with the U.S. Customs Service before you leave to avoid any possibility of being charged import duty on them when you return to the U.S.

Most private yachts don't do it, but you can have your vessel inspected by the U.S. Public Health Service and receive a Bill of Health, which can make the entering process to other countries somewhat easier.

Some countries prohibit certain items (particularly firearms, which we'll discuss in detail in a moment) and/or limit the amount of certain merchandise (such as cigarettes and alcoholic beverages) you may bring into their nations. Some countries ignore their own regulations, while others levy stiff import duties on quantities you declare in excess of their limits and impose stiff civil or criminal penalties for failure to declare excess merchandise or prohibited items. Prior to leaving the U.S., you should determine any prohibitions or limits imposed by the countries you plan to visit by contacting their embassy or consulate in this country, or talking to other cruisers who have visited those countries recently, and decide before you cast off what you are going to declare. If you plan not to declare anything, make provisions for keeping it well out of sight.

If practical, it's also a good idea to have the equivalent of a hundred dollars or so in small denominations of the currency of the countries you will be visiting, which usually can be obtained at larger banks.

Prior to departure and at points along your route, you should check the internal political situation in the countries you plan to visit as well as their political relations with other nations that might be included in your itinerary. You could encounter situations in which a country is in political turmoil or refuses to grant entry to vessels that have previously entered the waters of a nation with which it is having problems. The best sources of information on potential difficulties are the U.S. State Department, its embassies in foreign countries, and other cruisers who have recently visited the areas you plan to cruise.

Private yachts documented or registered in the name of a United States citizen and not engaged in commerce are not required to "clear" (i.e., secure permission to sail) before departing U.S. waters for a foreign port.

## ENTERING FOREIGN COUNTRIES

When you enter the waters of a foreign country for the first time, make certain your initial landfall is a legal point of entry. In many countries, the smaller fishing villages closest to the border don't have customs or immigration offices. If you go ashore looking for one, technically you have entered the country illegally and might have some rather complicated explaining to do when you finally locate a customs official farther down the coast. Your best source of information on where to clear is a good cruising guide or other cruising folks who have been there before you.

Prior to entering a port of entry you should hoist your plain yellow quarantine flag prominently and as high as practical on a flag halyard or radio antenna on the starboard side of your vessel. In the international flag system, this is the Q-flag which signals you are formally requesting pratique (i.e., permission to enter from that nation's health service).

Try to time your arrival so you enter a legal port between 9:00 A.M. and about 3:00 P.M. Monday through Friday, except on religious or political holidays or the president's birthday, or during the siesta hours of noon to 2:00 P.M. The point is that if you try to clear on weekends or after normal business hours, you may well be hit with fairly stiff overtime charges. "Normal business hours," of course, are whatever the guy with the badge on his chest and the gun on his hip jolly well says they are.

Anchor up in the harbor or tie to the dock and just relax for an hour or so. Chances are the dockmaster, the harbormaster, or a helpful fellow yachtsman will come along to tell you what to do next. If no one turns up in a reasonable length of time, you as the captain and owner should go ashore alone, taking along the ship's papers, the crew's passports and health certificates, at least three copies of your crew list—preferably typed—and some local currency. If the country you are entering requires you to present clearance documents from your previous port of call (which are discussed below), be sure to take them along as well.

Entering a foreign port normally involves dealing with at least four agencies: a customs service, which checks for any prohibited or limited items and collects any applicable duties; an immigration service, which is concerned with the legal status of individuals on your vessel; a health service, which is concerned with the presence of any infectious diseases among those on board; and, in some countries, an agricultural service, which inspects the vessel for any prohibited plants or animals. Some countries also require clearance by some type of federal or state militia and possibly a maritime authority of the port you have entered.

In most countries, customs and immigration are handled by a single agency, and you may find one official will handle work for all four groups. In some countries, however, you may have to deal with four or more separate individuals in as many offices.

The entry process normally must be completed each time you enter the waters of one country from the waters of another country. In one special exception, U.S. yachtsmen who wish to cruise in Canada can obtain at their initial port of call a permit that allows free and repeated entry into Canadian waters from May 1 to October 1. Once this cruising permit is secured, the yacht to which it is granted may cruise throughout Canadian waters, but reports of arrival must be made at any Canadian port visited where a customs officer is located, and the permit must be surrendered on the yacht's final departure from Canadian waters at the end of the season.

If the entry process is conducted in the customs office ashore, chances are it will be crisp, efficient, and over quickly. You normally will be issued some type of document that permits your vessel to cruise the waters of the foreign nation for a specified period of time. If you plan to visit other ports in that country, be sure to ask whether you are required to present your cruising permit or whatever the document is called each time you go ashore and, if so, to whom. Also ask if you are required to formally clear before you depart that nation's waters. Once the formalities are completed, haul down your quarantine flag and hoist in its place the courtesy flag of the nation you are visiting. If your vessel does not have a flag halyard, the courtesy flag should be flown from your bow staff.

If the customs officer comes aboard your boat, tell your crew to make themselves scarce belowdecks until the bogeyman is gone, then spread out your documents on the salon table. Be polite and friendly, but not overly so, and try to keep things on a businesslike basis and get the procedure over with quickly. If the official seems inclined to chat, offer him a seat. If he seems impressed by your boat say something like, "Yes, she is nice," but don't offer a tour unless one is requested. That's an open invitation for him to start opening drawers and poking into lockers.

To this point, keep the booze out of sight. If the official seems in no hurry to get down to business, then offer him some "refreshment," not "a drink." If he accepts, rattle off your list of options from soft drinks to beer and whiskey and let him make the choice. If he has a couple of shifty-eyed corporals with him, don't offer them anything without clearing it with the *comandante,* then provide soft drinks rather than beer or liquor.

As early as possible, nudge your papers forward a bit and hope he will take the hint and get on with the business at hand. If he ignores the move, be on your guard. It's a sad fact of the cruising life, particularly in poorer third world nations, that customs and immigration officials are paid less than a living wage with the expectation that they will make up any shortfall by hitting up visitors for either cash or a "gift" of goods that are hard to come by in their own country. Yachtsmen are often favorite targets for these rip-off artists, so you need to know the ropes. Chances are the official will eventually take a cursory glance at your papers and start talking about "problems," most likely that you are trying to enter after normal business hours—even though it's eleven o'clock on an otherwise unremarkable Thursday morning. Try to get the difficulty stated clearly. If there is a real problem, try to get it cleared up quickly. If he continues to be vague, he's probably just looking for his *mordita,* or *baksheesh,* or whatever they call it where you happen to be, so give a deep but silent sigh and say something like, "If there is anything I can do to get this problem straightened out. . . . " That gives him the opening he's looking for to hit you up for a few bucks without directly asking you for a payoff. The average hit will run around five to twenty-five dollars, disguised as a "fee" of some sort. As soon as you fork over the dough, all "problems" will magically disappear. But don't expect a receipt.

Once your papers are stamped, he may continue the chat and admire the quality of your scotch, which is your cue to offer him another drink. If he persists in hanging about after that, offer him the rest of the bottle and try to work him toward the door. Some experienced cruising people carry along a case of rot-gut for just such occasions and keep the good stuff hidden.

After he's gone, relax, get the good stuff out of the bottom galley drawer, forget the rip-off, and enjoy your visit.

## DECLARING FIREARMS

If you carry firearms on board your vessel for self-defense you are faced with the question of what you should do about declaring them when you enter other countries. The first step I would suggest you take toward answering that question is to determine the current attitude of the authorities in each country you plan to visit regarding weapons, and what they are likely to do if they find their laws regarding declaring them have been violated. The best source of up-to-date information on that topic will come from other cruisers who have visited those countries recently.

In most of the countries you will visit, if you declare weapons the customs official will simply take note of their presence and tell you not to carry them on deck or ashore. In a few countries—the Netherlands Antilles islands of Aruba, Bonaire, and Curaçao being a prime example—the customs officials will impound your weapons during your visit and hand them back to you—along with your dock lines—when you depart.

In most cases I would declare them, especially in Venezuela and Guadeloupe. In those countries, detailed searches are common, and if you are found to be carrying undeclared weapons you will be arrested and your entire vessel confiscated. You may carry rifles and shotguns into Canada if you declare they are to be used for hunting. If you declare a handgun, Canadian authorities will either seal it in a pouch which must be presented—unopened—when you exit the country, or they will impound it and tell you that you can pick it up on your way back across their border.

In entering a few countries, I would not declare any weapons on board my vessel but bury them deep—really deep. In countries like Mexico and Jamaica, any weapons you declare will be confiscated and you will not get them back. You may also be arrested and your entire vessel can be confiscated. If you are carrying weapons aboard your vessel and decide not to declare them, remember also to keep their ammunition and any descriptive literature or cleaning apparatus well out of sight.

401

## IF YOU ARE BOARDED

The escalating war on drugs by the governments of the United States and a number of other countries makes it increasingly likely that if you cruise extensively, sooner or later you will be boarded at sea and your vessel subjected to a detailed search. As the master of a vessel flying the American flag, in fact, the authority most likely to board you is the U.S. Coast Guard. On land, as American citizens we have all manner of Fourth Amendment rights against unreasonable search and seizure. In most cases, law enforcement personnel must have "probable cause" to suspect we are breaking the law before they stop and search us. It would not be unreasonable to think we carry those same rights when we go to sea. Not so. When it comes to our legal rights in a boarding situation, the blunt truth is we don't have any. Under 14 U.S. Code 89, the Coast Guard has the right to stop and search any U.S.-flag vessel anywhere (even outside U.S. territorial waters) and at any time, whether or not they have a reason to believe any U.S. law is being violated. The same goes for U.S. Customs if the vessel (whether of U.S. or foreign registry) is within our nation's twelve-mile custom zone.

If you are shown a blue light by either of these agencies, you must stop. You cannot refuse to allow their personnel to board your vessel, nor can you stop them from searching every nook and cranny of your vessel (including ripping out bulkheads and the like, though they are liable for repairing any damages they inflict), or even searching your person and that of everyone else aboard.

As the master of your vessel, you can be held responsible for any illegal substances found on your vessel, whether or not you are aware they are on board. If illegal drugs are found on your vessel, no matter how minuscule the amount, you and everyone on board can be arrested on the spot and handcuffed. The Coast Guard or Customs Service boarding party can assume control of your vessel and take it into the nearest U.S. port, where it can be seized under an administrative procedure that does not involve any court review. If you can prove in court you didn't know the drugs were aboard, you may get your boat back, but it may involve court action and the payment of heavy legal costs and impoundment fees, and your vessel may suffer extensive damage for which you are unlikely to be reimbursed. In view of the risks, you need to be extremely careful about what you allow guests or crew to bring on board your vessel, particularly if you are reentering the U.S. from another country.

So much for being boarded by U.S. authorities. What if you are stopped by authorities of another country?

On *Summer Wind*'s voyage to Alaska, Frank and Lee Glindmeier were making a night run about 20 miles off the coast of Nicaragua when a blip appeared on their radar and started to close on them like a bullet. The vessel refused to answer Frank's call on VHF, and he had to change course twice to avoid a collision. It turned out to be a Nicaraguan gunboat with a 50-mm machine gun on its bow. Frank finally was able to shout across the water enough broken Spanish to explain they were peaceful American yachtsmen. The gunboat backed off but escorted them until ten o'clock the next morning when they reached the border.

Since hearing Frank's rather harrowing tale, I've done a good bit of thinking of how I would handle such a situation. You will have your own ideas, but these are mine:

Most nations of the world claim a territorial limit of three miles off their shores and a customs zone of 12 miles. Other nations claim up to a 200-mile territorial limit. The military forces of governments that are threatened by armed insurrection frequently patrol 100 miles or more off their shores and stop any vessel they encounter. If my cruise plan called for me to run off the coast of a nation I knew was in political turmoil, I would inform the U.S. Coast Guard of my schedule and set a deadline by which, if I didn't contact them with an "all-clear," they would come looking for me. I would make my run at night, stay as far offshore as possible, and know at all times exactly how far I was off the coast in case the matter came into dispute later. I'd also make the run without lights and remove my radar reflector.

If in the course of the run I was approached by another vessel, I would carefully note my position and contact the Coast Guard or anyone else I could reach to tell them what was going on. If I thought the approaching vessel was official, I would turn on my running lights and shine a light on my American ensign. I would not, however, shine a spotlight directly on the approaching vessel as that could draw fire. I would maintain speed and course until ordered to stop or until the approaching vessel blocked my path. I would try to contact the vessel on the radio. If that failed and they hailed me over a loudspeaker, I would appear on deck but show no firearms.

If ordered I would stop, but I would make every effort to argue them out of boarding my vessel. If they insisted on boarding, I would have little choice but to allow it but would be coolly indignant while arguing my right to cruise in international waters without interference. I'd drag out my U.S. passport and my vessel's documentation papers. If asked if I was armed, I'd declare any weapons on board. Hopefully, once they'd checked me out and found I wasn't trying to smuggle M16s to the guerrillas, they'd let me go on my way. If they insisted I put into the nearest port, I'd go into my indignant act again. If they continued to insist, I'd try to argue them out of placing any of their personnel on my boat, arguing that in light of their superior speed and firepower, I had little choice but to follow them.

If all argument failed, I would do as ordered but only under the severest protest, liberally invoking the name of my brother the senator, my uncle the president, and any other fiction I could dream up on the spot. I'd also keep trying to contact the Coast Guard until ordered away from my radio at the point of a .45.

If I was forced into port, either under tow or under my own power, the minute I touched land I'd raise hell to see the nearest U.S. consul, rousting him out of bed if necessary. If that was refused, I'd demand to see the superior of the individual I was dealing with and start my indignation routine all over again.

As a last resort, I'd steal a spoon and try to dig my way out of jail.

If I was convinced the vessel approaching mine was unofficial and might really be carrying sea pirates, I'd handle the situation entirely differently. I would not turn on my running lights. I'd try to reach the Coast Guard and, failing that, broadcast a Mayday. I'd try to determine the approaching vessel's size, speed, manpower, and firepower. If it tried to impede my progress and I couldn't outrun it, I'd take every evasive action possible, up to and including ramming it, but in no case would I stop or peacefully submit to its crew boarding my vessel. Instead, I'd make as much of a show of force of my own as possible, letting the intruders see all men on board, hopefully armed, but keeping the women out of sight. If it looked like there was no way to avoid a fight, I wouldn't start shooting until they did. But after the first shot was fired, even though I'm not Catholic, I'd cross myself, say three Hail Marys, and throw everything at them but the kitchen sink. I never met any real sea pirates face to face, but I like to think they basically are cowards who, if opposed strongly, would break off the engagement and go looking for easier prey.

## LIGHTING REGULATIONS

If your vessel is registered or documented in the United States and its lights comply with the U.S. Inland Rules appropriate to its type and size, you may legally operate in international waters.

Though as a skipper of a U.S.-registered or -documented vessel you are not required to comply with differing international requirements regarding the positioning of your vessel's navigation lighting, you are required to comply with the International Regulations regarding their use any time you are in waters they cover. The only significant difference you'll encounter there is that the International Regulations make no provisions for the "special anchorage areas" found in the U.S. Inland Rules, in which anchor lights are not required for vessels less than 65.6 feet in length. The only exception regarding anchor lights contained in the International Regulations is for vessels less than 23 feet (7 meters) in length anchored in areas free of waterborne traffic.

The International Regulations include the exemption for vessels under 23 feet anchored in areas free of waterborne traffic found in the U.S. Inland Rules, but do not recognize the "special anchorage areas" the Inland Rules allow.

## MARINE RADIOTELEPHONE AND AMATEUR RADIO OPERATIONS

In order to transmit legally over your vessel's VHF (including hand-held units) and single-sideband marine radios while in foreign waters, you must have a valid Ship Station License and a Restricted Radiotelephone Operator Permit, both of which are issued by the U.S. Federal Communications Commission. Your U.S. license and permit will be honored by all but a tiny handful of foreign nations, and you are not required to have any specific license or permit from the host country.

Except for those channels used for Public Correspondence, the VHF channels used most frequently in U.S. waters are simplex (i.e., they transmit and receive on the same frequency). With the exception of channel 15, the international distress, safety, and calling channel, the VHF channels used most frequently in countries outside the U.S. are semiduplex (i.e., they transmit on one frequency and receive on a different frequency). Modern synthesized VHF marine radios are programmed for both U.S. and international channels and automatically set the appropriate transmit-and-receive frequency or pair of frequencies when a channel is dialed in to the unit. Figure 21.1 lists the international channels normally built into modern VHF marine radios along with their transmit and receive frequencies and their assigned use. As quickly becomes obvious from that list, the most important VHF channels for cruisers in foreign waters are likely to be channel 22 for communicating with other nations' equivalent of the U.S. Coast Guard, and channel 78 for communicating with other noncommercial vessels.

In single-sideband operation, the transmit and receive frequencies of channels in the high-frequency 4-MHz to 24-MHz bands are the same worldwide. The transmit and receive frequencies of channels in the medium-frequency 2–3-MHz band vary from country to country and must be manually programmed into a single-sideband radio's memory.

In order to legally transmit over the amateur radio frequencies from your vessel while it is in the territorial waters of foreign nations with which the United States has third-party traffic agreements, you must have an appropriate class station/operator license which is issued by the FCC and a Reciprocal Operator's Permit issued by the nation from whose waters you wish to transmit. You should apply for a Reciprocal Operator's Permit from each nation you plan to visit well in advance of departing the U.S., as processing your application can take up to six months.

## CLEARING FOREIGN COUNTRIES

Some countries require you to clear with their customs officials prior to departing their waters, which basically ensures that you have paid all fees due and their police aren't looking for you. If required, the clearing process usually involves nothing more than returning any cruising permits you received for cancellation. In a few cases, you may be required again to produce all the documents you presented in the initial entering process. Some nations require payment of a departure tax before you are granted clearance to sail.

If clearance is required, be sure to respect its provisions and keep any clearance documents you are issued as a part of your ship's papers. The next country on your itinerary may require you to produce a clearance document from your last port of call before they will grant entry to their nation.

## RETURNING TO U.S. WATERS

The procedures for a private vessel reentering the territorial waters of the United States after landing in a foreign country are substantially the same as those detailed above for entering a foreign port. On your return to the U.S., be sure your initial port of call is a legal port of entry. Hoist your quarantine flag, go ashore alone with your ship's papers, crew passports, crew list, and some U.S. currency to contact the nearest office of Customs and Immigration and request entry.

# CHAPTER 22

# CASH AND CORRESPONDENCE

• • •

In addition to the normal preparations regarding finances and correspondence you'd make for an extended cruise in U.S. waters (such as arranging for income to be deposited directly to your bank account, prepaying all the bills you can, and setting up a draft or arranging with a relative or friend to pay those you can't settle before you go), there are a few other things regarding these matters you might want to do before departing for foreign waters.

## Carrying Cash

You'll find it advisable to carry more ready cash on an international voyage than you'd require for a journey in domestic waters. You can't very well give a customs official who wants his *mordita* a check, and you might need fuel, provisions, or repair services in some out-of-the-way place where cash is the only acceptable means of exchange. I suggest you keep a cushion of at least $2,000 to $2,500 available at all times in case you encounter a major expense that can be handled only with cash on the barrel head, but I wouldn't carry more than about $5,000 in cash aboard at any one time. If your vessel is robbed or sinks, most marine insurance policies won't cover the loss of cash.

Carry most of your cruising cash in U.S. dollars (preferably in bills no larger than a twenty, as in many foreign countries breaking larger denominations can be a problem). For the rest of your cash, go to a large national or regional bank and get at least $100 or so in the currencies of each of the countries you plan to visit to pay customs and duty fees, which you may have to do before you can go ashore to make a currency exchange. Break your cash up into several packages, stash them in various locations around your boat, and make yourself a cue card to help you remember where you hid them.

## Traveler's Checks

Carry the bulk of your cruising funds in traveler's checks. If the U.S. dollar is rising against the currencies of the countries you plan to visit, get your traveler's checks in U.S. funds. If it's falling against those currencies, get traveler's checks in those currencies. Most large national and regional banks can provide traveler's checks in British pounds, French francs, Spanish pesos, or the other currencies that might be most useful in the particular areas you plan to cruise. Be sure to keep the receipts for any traveler's checks you buy in a safe location separate from the checks themselves. As with cash, never keep all your traveler's checks in one package but break them up into several parcels so that if thieves hit your boat, they hopefully will miss some of the funds you've squirreled away.

## Credit Cards

Carry a wide variety of credit cards and use them whenever possible to pay major expenses such as fuel and marina bills, repair services, and shoreside expenses. But make sure you have someone at home who can get the bill and pay it monthly to avoid racking up interest charges, which can run as high as 22 percent per year. In my travels to some thirty-five countries around the world, I have found Mastercard, Visa, Diner's Club, and Carte Blanche the most widely accepted. As in the U.S., American Express is also widely recognized, but many smaller merchants refuse to honor it because of its higher discount rate.

Many credit card issuers allow you to get cash advances against your card at their offices abroad, but I'd suggest you do that only in a real emergency. The interest rates on cash advances run from 18 to 20 percent per annum, and the clock starts running the minute the cash is in your hand. Cash advances are not granted the interest grace period accorded to merchandise or service purchases.

If you pay a bill rendered in a foreign country with a credit card, then pay the credit card charge in U.S. dollars, the rate of exchange will be the one in effect the day the charge clears your account. I've done this a number of times and never felt I was treated unfairly on the exchange rate.

## Replenishing the Kitty

The best arrangement for periodically replenishing your cruising funds during an extended international voyage is to maintain an account in a large international bank that has branches in the countries you plan to visit. With today's sophisticated banking computers, often you can get cash within hours, even though you are thousands of miles from home, and pay little for the service.

In areas where these banks do not have offices of their own, they usually maintain correspondent relationships with local banks. Get a list of your bank's correspondents and try to work through one of them when you need a fresh infusion of funds. You will get quicker service than you will at a noncorrespondent bank and probably save money in the bargain. With this kind of a setup, your home bank can send you money by wire transfer to its correspondent bank in about two days, and the transaction usually will cost you only about ten dollars.

In my experience, the two U.S. banks with the most foreign branches are Chase Manhattan and City National Bank of New York. Another international bank with widespread offices is Barclay's Bank of Britain.

Some cruisers carry a letter of credit from their home bank and draw against it at a local bank when they need money. Others carry their home bank's cashier's checks. I've tried both arrangements and found neither satisfactory. The local bank normally will want to process the transaction and collect the funds from your stateside bank before they release money to you. The process can take a week to ten days—even more in especially remote areas—and processing fees can run the equivalent of $25 U.S. or more, plus the costs of telegrams or telex messages.

## Converting Dollars

Once you are in a foreign country, generally you will find that banks are the best place to convert U.S. dollars to the local currency or cash traveler's checks. In many countries abroad, banks have limited hours of operation and catching them when they are open can call for a bit of extra planning, but their exchange rate usually will be better than currency exchange houses, which are open longer hours. Even when changing money at a bank, shop for the lowest rates as even they can vary a percentage point or two. In some cases you will find bank branches at railway stations and airports have longer operating hours than the main office or branches in town.

## FORWARDING MAIL

The best way to get mail in foreign countries is to have the person or agency forwarding it for you send it to guests who are planning to meet you along your route three or four days prior to their departure. Having guests hand-carry mail to you is the surest way to make certain it will arrive.

If your schedule of guests is not going to be frequent enough to make that a viable forwarding system, give the person handling mail forwarding for you the addresses of marinas, yacht clubs, and resorts you plan to visit along the way and your approximate arrival dates at each. Have them gather together only the important items from a month or so worth of mail, put it in a sturdy envelope, and mail it to your destination marked with your name, the name of your vessel, and "Hold for Arrival." Caution them, however, to allow as much as two weeks for surface mail to arrive at its destination and not to include checks, cash, or other items of value. If you have an American Express card, its offices will hold mail for you, and you may be able to set up the service through your bank's offshore branches or their correspondent institutions.

If you prefer not to ask a relative or friend to handle mail forwarding for you, there are a number of companies that will do it for you—for a fee of course. Cruise Net, (212) 741-1439, which specializes in working with yachtsmen, has a subsidiary which will handle both mail forwarding and bill paying for you. They also work with a travel agency that arranges travel to remote locations for some of America's largest engineering, construction, and oil firms and operates a message center. This combination of abilities might make them useful for coordinating travel arrangements and communicating with those who plan to join you in the boondocks.

## Importing Parts

If you must have parts shipped in to you in a foreign country, be aware that when you go to pick them up, the post office or shipping agent who received them will probably require a customs clearance before they can be released to you. Most likely you will have to take a copy of the bill of lading which describes the items to the host country's customs service for clearance. You will probably also be hit with heavy import duties, which in some cases will equal or exceed the value of the parts themselves.

I once had an interesting experience in that regard: Just before leaving for Mexico where I was to meet a friend and cruise the Baja aboard his yacht, the friend called and said he had burned out a large electrical panel on his boat. Could I pick up a replacement and bring it with me? I obtained the item required, which was about four feet square and, with a full complement of circuit breakers, weighed about thirty pounds, and cost close to a thousand dollars. When the pilot of the aircraft I had chartered to take me to my destination loaded the panel, he cautioned me that Mexican customs would probably try to collect a stiff import duty on it. The Mexican customs official at Mexicali was indeed most curious as to what it was. I explained that I was a professional photographer and took a small strobe light which was all of six inches long out of my camera case. The electrical panel, I explained, was necessary to control the vast amounts of electricity the strobe unit consumed. The official nodded knowingly and passed me through without a problem.

You'll be much better off to carry everything you think you'll possibly need with you. If you find you've forgotten something you can't do without, try to buy it locally.

# EPILOG: THE WONDERS AWAIT

• • •

Whether your dream cruise is a placid run of a few months down the ICW or an around-the-world jaunt that will take years to accomplish, the wonders of the world await you.

They may show themselves in the quiet ripples of sunset across a Georgia salt marsh, in the cry of a loon in the North Channel, in a sun-drenched morning washing over a crescent beach in the Virgins, in the splendid isolation of a snug anchorage in the Inland Passage, in puffy clouds drifting across the twin peaks of Bora Bora.

It doesn't really matter how the wonders come to you, or where, for come they will. And they will be bounteous reward for the efforts you've expended to find them.

And there will be wonders of a different sort.

There will be a day in your cruising adventures when the customs man has abused you, the sea has battered you, that monster of an engine down below has developed a halting malaise you cannot cure, the generator has died, the charts were wrong, and none of the lights were where they were supposed to be. But somehow you will work your way to an anchorage, take three tries to get your hook set in a bottom with the consistency of oatmeal, and there will be a nagging surge running from a direction you cannot quite divine.

But after a cold supper, after your crew and guests are bedded down, after you have made your rounds and know all is secure, you will sit exhausted for a moment on the flybridge or in the cockpit, and then the realization will come to you: "I did it! I took what the world and the sea had to throw against me, and I brought my ship and all aboard her to safe harbor." A faint smile will make its way across your lips, and you will feel a warm glow of pride from somewhere deep inside.

And on that night, you will sleep the sleep of angels.

# APPENDIX: THE SHIP'S LIBRARY: RECOMMENDED PUBLICATIONS

• • •

Depending on the area you plan to cruise, here are some of the basic documents you ought to consider including in your ship's library:

I. Charts and publications from the National Oceanic and Atmospheric Administration (NOAA)
   A. Nautical Charts
      The free *NOAA Chart Catalogs 1–4* list all the charts published by NOAA's National Ocean Service (NOS). The scale to which charts are drawn (e.g., 1:50,000, in which one inch on the chart equals 50,000 inches on the earth) is important. The smaller the second number, the larger the scale of the chart and the greater the detail it shows. (A chart with a scale of 1:12,500 will show much more detail than a chart drawn to a scale of 1:50,000.) In general, the larger the scale of a chart the better. The primary NOAA charts you'll be interested in are:
      1. Conventional nautical charts, which come in four varieties:
         a. Harbor charts, which are drawn to a scale of 1:50,000 or larger and provide the detail you'll need for navigating in harbors and small waterways. I recommend you purchase charts for any major harbors your itinerary calls for you to pass through. The smaller-scale charts you'll

415

need for cruising major stretches will show major harbors, but not in the detail you'll need to navigate through them safely.

b. Coast charts, which are to scales from 1:50,001 to 1:150,000 and are designed for navigation inside offshore reefs and in large harbors and some inland waterways. These are the basic charts you'll need for cruising large bodies of water like Long Island and Puget Sound.

c. General charts, which are to scales from 1:150,001 to 1:600,000 and are intended for offshore navigation but provide sufficient detail for fixing your position through visual contact with aids to navigation or by depth soundings. These are the charts you'll need if your cruising plans call for you to do considerable offshore running along the U.S. coast and enter and leave ports along the way frequently.

d. Sailing charts, which are to scales of 1:600,001 and smaller and are used as plotting charts for offshore navigation beyond the areas where visual position fixes are possible. These charts are of interest primarily to offshore cruisers and don't show sufficient detail to be of value in inland cruising.

2. Small Craft Charts, which are drawn to scales from 1:10,000 to 1:80,000 and published in folded formats which make them ideal for use on smaller vessels. These are the route charts you'll need for cruising the Intracoastal Waterway and the book-format charts you'll want for cruising the Great Lakes, but in many cases you may want to supplement them with larger-scale charts of major harbors and large open bodies of water.

3. Marine facility charts, which are conventional charts overprinted with locations of marine facilities and other information of interest to recreational boat owners. These charts are nice but duplicate much of the information you'll find in cruising guides.

4. Marine Weather Services charts, published by NOAA's National Weather Service (NWS), are a series of fifteen charts which show radio stations and broadcasting areas for all

U.S. coastal waters and Puerto Rico. The primary benefit of these charts is to give you the location of visual storm warnings and the frequencies and weather broadcast schedules of FM commercial radio stations in particular areas. If you are within the broadcast area of an NWS VHF-FM radio station, your VHF radio will pick up its signals automatically on its WX1–WX4 channels, so it's not really necessary for you to know the frequency. (You can also buy bound groupings of reproductions of NOAA charts covering specific geographic areas, the pros and cons of which are discussed below under Chart Kits.)

B.  Chart No. 1

*Chart No. 1,* published jointly by the National Oceanic and Atmospheric Administration (NOAA) and the Defense Mapping Agency (DMA), is really not a chart at all but a 100-page book that fully explains all the symbols and abbreviations used on the nautical charts produced in the United States. It is required reading for any cruiser. Spending a couple of hours browsing through its storehouse of information and keeping it aboard for frequent reference will give you a far better understanding of the information your charts provide and make them far more valuable.

C.  Coast Pilots

The nine volumes of NOAA's *U.S. Coast Pilot* offer a far greather wealth of information about America's coastal waters and the Great Lakes than can ever be crammed onto charts. You should definitely have aboard the volume or volumes that cover the areas you plan to cruise. The areas covered by the various volumes are as follows:

Volumes 1–5:  Atlantic Coast
  Volume 1:  Eastport to Cape Cod
  Volume 2:  Cape Cod to Sandy Hook
  Volume 3:  Sandy Hook to Cape Henry
  Volume 4:  Cape Henry to Key West
  Volume 5:  Gulf of Mexico, Puerto Rico, and U.S. Virgin Islands
  Volume 6:  Great Lakes and Connecting Waterways
Volumes 7–9:  Pacific Coast

Volume 7: California, Oregon, Washington, and Hawaii

Volume 8: Alaska—Dixon Entrance to Cape Spencer

Volume 9: Alaska—Cape Spencer to Beaufort Sea

D. *Tide Tables*

The annual editions of the *Tide Tables* allow you to predict high and low tides at any point along the U.S. coast from the tip of Maine all the way to the Aleutians and provide useful information on sunrise and sunset, moonrise and moonset, the phases of the moon, and reduction of local mean time to standard zone time.

Four volumes are available covering: east coast of North and South America (including Greenland); west coast of North and South America (including Alaska and Hawaiian Islands); Europe and west coast of Africa (including Mediterranean Sea); and central and western Pacific Ocean and Indian Ocean.

E. *Tidal Current Tables*

The annual editions of the *Tidal Current Tables* list the predicted time of daily maximum and minimum tidal currents and slack water, current velocities and the directions of ebb and flow at 54 reference stations and more than 2,400 subordinate stations. Separate volumes cover the Atlantic coast of North America and the Pacific coast of North America and Asia. They are invaluable in planning voyages through passages of high current flow.

(NOAA also publishes annual *Tidal Current Charts* which depict the hourly velocity and direction of tidal ebb and flow at 11 selected major U.S. harbors, and *Tidal Current Diagrams* covering Long Island and Block Island sounds and Boston Harbor. The information is of interest to commercial fishermen and the masters of large commercial vessels, but is not really required aboard recreational vessels.)

NOAA charts and publications are available from a network of authorized sales agents whose addresses are listed in *Chart Catalogs 1–4* or by mail from: NOAA Distribution Branch (N/CG33), National Ocean Service, Riverdale, MD 20737. If you charge to Visa or MasterCard, you can order NOS publications by phone: (301) 436-6990.

II. Publications of the U.S. Coast Guard

    A. *Navigation Rules, International-Inland*

        This publication gives the Rules of the Road for operating in both inland and international waters and delineates where each applies. A copy of the *Navigation Rules* is required to be aboard all self-propelled vessels greater than 39.4 feet (12 meters) in length.

    B. *Light Lists*

        The *Light Lists* give far more detailed descriptions of aids to navigation than can be printed on nautical charts. In a confusing situation, they can provide valuable information in helping to identify a specific aid. They are available in seven volumes:

> Vol. I: Atlantic Coast (St. Croix River, Maine, to Toms River, New Jersey)
>
> Vol. II: Atlantic Coast (Tom's River, New Jersey, to Little River, South Carolina)
>
> Vol. III: Atlantic and Gulf Coasts (Little River, South Carolina, to Ecofina River, Florida; Puerto Rico and U.S. Virgin Islands)
>
> Vol. IV: Gulf Coast (Ecofina River, Florida, to Rio Grande, Texas)
>
> Vol. V: Mississippi River System
>
> Vol. VI: Pacific Coast and Pacific Islands
>
> Vol. VII: Great Lakes

        Coast Guard publications are available from the U.S. Superintendent of Documents, U.S. Government Printing Office, Washington, DC 20402. If you charge to Visa or Mastercard, you can order by phone: (202) 783-3238.

III. Worldwide Marine Weather Broadcasts

In addition to its Marine Weather Services Charts available through NOAA's Distribution Branch, the National Weather Service also publishes *Selected Worldwide Marine Weather Broadcasts,* which provides valuable and complete lists of the sources of weather information in the U.S. and abroad. It is available from the U.S. Superintendent of Documents, U.S. Government Printing Office, Washington, DC 20402. If you charge to Visa or Mastercard, you can order by phone: (202) 783-3238.

IV. Publications of the U.S. Corps of Engineers

A. Charts and Maps of the Lower Mississippi River

Available from the Corps' Vicksburg District, P.O. Box 60, Vicksburg, MS 39180.

B. Charts of the Upper Mississippi River and Illinois Waterway

Available from the Corps' Rock Island District, P.O. Box 2004, Rock Island, IL 61204

C. Charts of the Missouri River

Available from the Corps' Omaha District, 6014 U.S. Post Office and Courthouse, Omaha, NE 68102

D. Charts of the Ohio River

Available from the Corps' Ohio River Division, P.O. Box 1159, Cincinnati, OH 45201

E. Charts of the Black Warrior, Alabama, Tombigee, Apalachicola, and Pearl Rivers

Available from the Corps' Mobile District, P.O. Box 2288, Mobile, AL 36628

V. Publications of the Tennessee Valley Authority (TVA)

A. Charts of the Tennessee TVA Reservoirs and the Tennessee River and Its Tributaries

Available from the Tennessee Valley Authority, Maps and Engineering Section, 416 Union Avenue, Knoxville, TN 37902

VI. Publications of the Department of Defense

A. Charts of Foreign Waters

These charts cover virtually all the waters outside those of the United States and are available from the Defense Mapping

Agency, Combat Support Center, Attention PMS Washington, DC 20315-0010.

VII. Publications of the Canadian Hydrographic Service

A. Charts of Canadian Coastal Waters and the Great Lakes

Available from the Canadian Hydrographic Service, Department of Fisheries and Oceans, Institute of Ocean Sciences, P.O. Box 8080, 1675 Russell Road, Ottawa, Ontario, KIG 3H6.

In addition to these official publications, a wide range of chart kits and cruising guides available at retail outlets, through marine book clubs and catalogs, or direct from the publisher provide valuable information of which anyone cruising the areas they cover should take advantage:

A. Chartbooks and Chart Kits

These are bound groupings of color reproductions of NOAA charts covering specific geographic areas and often contain supplemental information. They typically contain 80 to 100 or more charts and retail for about $60 to $100. Since conventional and small-craft NOAA charts are now priced at $13.25 each, there is no question that buying chartbooks and chart kits is cheaper than buying a full set of charts for each area you cruise. But in some cases the size reduction of the NOAA charts required to fit a chartbook or chart kit's format may make some important details unreadable.

Among the better chartbooks and chart kits are the ones produced by the Better Boating Association, which are sold through marine catalogs and book clubs, and the Richardson's Chartbooks, which are available through marine book clubs or direct from Richardson's Marine Publishing, P.O. Box 23, Streamwood, IL 60103.

B. Cruising Guides

These are general guides that offer a great deal of useful information on popular cruising areas. Among the best of them are the four volumes of the *Waterway Guides* (Waterway Guide, Inc., 93 Main Street, Annapolis, MD 21401, (301) 268-9546) covering the Atlantic and Gulf Intracoastal Waterways; the *Yachtsman's Guides* (Tropic Isle Publishers, Inc., P.O. Box 611141, North Miami, FL 33161), which cover the Bahamas, the Virgin Islands, and Puerto Rico; and the *Street's Guides to the Eastern Caribbean.*

# Index

• • •

423

## B

Binoculars
   *See* Instruments (piloting)
Boarding (law enforcement), 402
Bridge
   clearance, 30, 71
   opening signals, 70
   restricted hours, 30, 71
   tender, 30, 71
Buoys
   *See* Navigation (aids to)

## C

Cash
   carrying, 408
   converting, 411
   replenishing, 410
Chartbooks, 421
Chart kits, 421
*Chart No. 1*, 417
Charts (nautical), 144, 395, 415
Coast Pilots, 31, 417
COLREGS
   defined, 52
   demarcation line, 52
Compass (hand-bearing)
   *See* Instruments (piloting)
Coolant flow maintenance, 384
Course
   intended, 154
   plotting, 33, 149
Credit cards, 409
Crossing (course)
   *See* U.S. Inland Navigation
      Rules
Cruise (shakedown), 24
Cruising guides
   *See* Guides (cruising)
Current diagram
   *See* Piloting (coastal)

## D

Dead reckoning
   *See* Piloting (coastal)
Depth-sounder, 174
Distance vs. daylight, 29
Diving (skin and scuba), 277, 369
Docking
   alongside pier, 96
   bow line, 103
   dock lines, 97, 98, 110
   entering slip, 114
   fenderboards, 114
   fenders, 97, 114
   spring lines, 104
   tying up, 107
   walking, 98
Dock line
   *See* Line (dock)
Dock masters, 95

## E

Electrical system maintenance,
   389
Electronic navigation
   *See* Navigation (electronic)
Electronics maintenance, 390
Emergency (medical)
   airway obstruction, 260
   anaphylaxis, 273, 286
   bleeding, 270
   breathing, 262
   burns (chemical), 280
   burns (heat), 279
   chest pain, 275
   circulation, 266
   coma (diabetic), 286, 289
   communications, 254
   convulsions, 289
   dislocations, 275
   drowning, 276
   evacuation, 295